Pied Piper

The Many Lives of

Noah Greenberg

Noah Greenberg

PIED PIPER

THE MANY LIVES OF

NOAH GREENBERG

James Gollin

LIVES IN MUSIC SERIES No. 4

PENDRAGON PRESS
HILLSDALE, NY

Other titles in the series LIVES IN MUSIC:

No.1   *Hugues Cuenod: With an Agile Voice*
Conversations with François Hudry

No.2   *Nicolae Bretan: His Life—His Music*
by Hartmut Gagelmann

No.3   *Entrancing Muse: A Documented Biography of
Francis Poulenc* by Carl B. Schmidt

Library of Congress Cataloging-in-Publication Data

Gollin, James.
    Pied Piper: the many lives of Noah Greenberg/by James Gollin.
        p.cm.--(Lives in music; no. 4)
    includes bibliographical references (p.), discography (p.) and index.
    ISBN 1-57647-041-5
    1. Greenberg, Noah. 2. Conductors (Music)--New York (State)--
New York--Biography. 3. Early music specialists--New York (State)--
New York--Biography. 4. New York Pro Musica. I. Title. II. Lives in
music series: no.4.

ML422.G73.G65 2001
780'.92--do2 1
[B]   00-068826

TABLE OF CONTENTS

*I*LLUSTRATIONS

*I*NTRODUCTION

To his family, to his host of friends and colleagues, and even to his ill-wishers, Noah Greenberg was "larger than life." To Noah's biographer, this oft-repeated phrase came to mean all sorts of different things. It certainly meant something on the literal level. Noah was a big man physically. His presence in a room was dominating. His manner was ebullient. His appetites were lusty. His opinions were clear-cut and strongly held. His impact on others was such that thirty-five years after his death, people's memories of Noah and his doings are as fresh as if they had seen him yesterday.

In Noah's case, "larger than life" also meant that no one style or way of life was enough to contain or explain the man. There was Noah the Greenwich Village bohemian and Noah the dweller on comfortable West End Avenue—"downtown Noah" and "uptown Noah." There was Noah in the jeans and black turtleneck of the merchant mariner and Noah in the Ivy League tailoring of J. Press. There was Noah who talked the salty language of the Bronx streets and Noah who took tea with the Robert Woods Blisses and the Mrs. W. Murray Cranes. Above all else, there was Noah the Trotskyist and labor organizer and Noah the musician-entrepreneur-promoter, the cofounder of and driving force behind the brilliant New York Pro Musica.

As far back as 1953, I was a devotee of the group of young singers and instrumentalists that called itself—in those early days — the New York Pro Musica Antiqua. Sometimes alone, sometimes with a young woman for companion (when I could afford a second ticket), I attended their concerts at the 92nd Street YM-YWHA. They seemed to me to have little in common with other recitals and orchestral concerts. Those musical events were solemn, edifying occasions. Middle-aged people in formalwear would perform on a stage a million miles from where I was seated. It was all very serious, very uplifting. Laughter was not encouraged.

Pro Musica concerts at the "Y" were different. There the musicians, all ten of them, were young and serious in performance, but never stiff or solemn. Some of the songs they sang were funny. Even in grave liturgical works, they seemed to be enjoying themselves.

Who was the man who, hands held high, directed this ensemble with such panache? What sort of musician, what sort of person, was he? To answer these question, I found myself exploring not one but the several worlds in which Noah Greenberg lived at ease.

If he wishes, Richard French, musicologist, professor, quondam music publisher, can justly claim to be this book's "onlie Begetter." Dick French calmly asked, "Why not?" when I blurted out, at a lunch in New Haven with a mutual friend, that I would love to write Noah Greenberg's biography. Dick, as president of Pro Musica from 1960 through its disbanding in 1974, had turned over the organization's archives to the Music Library at Lincoln Center. Dick made access to the archives easy for me. He also put me in touch with Noah's daughters, Anne Greenberg Donovan and Jane Greenberg Cameron.

Young when Noah died (Anne was eleven, Jane, six), Anne and Jane shared with me their own memories of their father and the much sharper images of Noah—sometimes etched in acid—passed on to them by their mother. They have also allowed me to draw on family memorabilia, including photographs, letters, diaries, and personal papers. Most important, Anne and Jane have urged me to write truth, not hagiography. Both have expressed the feeling that if I wrote a truthful book, it would in some measure "give them back their father." If *Pied Piper* does this and nothing more, in my mind it will be a ringing success.

As my initial research led me onward, I made the delightful discovery that everyone I was contacting was eager to see this book written and the record of Noah's life (or lives) and accomplishments set forth. The names of those I did contact and the particulars of the help many of them were kind enough to render are found in the acknowledgements that follow the final chapter.

One person not mentioned in the acknowledgements has played a huge part in this work. It was Jane Gollin who joined me at those long-ago Pro Musica concerts at the "Y." It is she who continues after the forty-three years (thus far) of our marriage to bring both love and judgment to bear on everything I write.

James Gollin
New York City

CHAPTER ONE

⊖HE TRUMPET AND THE LIONS

(JANUARY 1958)

⊖he yard-long straight trumpet, crafted in Siena in 1406, did exactly what a silver trumpet should do. Such trumpets are heard in fairy tales and romances, signalling the entries of princes and bishops into the turreted and bannered cities of a child's dreams. This one, ringing brilliantly on a clear winter afternoon, heralded to an expectant gathering in a vaulted stone hall that just such a stirring event was about to begin. But first — silence. Within seconds, a figure in monkish garb took his place behind a lectern and spoke: "Welcome, good people, watch and listen." And to the whine of a three-string medieval fiddle and the tinging of bells and tambourines, there entered a procession of performers, cloaked and bejeweled in colors as brilliant as the trumpet blast had been: reds, greens, white, and glittering gold. At the head of the hall, the personages in the procession paused before ranging themselves in splendor on each side of a magnificent raised throne. Again there was a hush. Only when a king, crowned and sceptered in gold, strode forth in state to take his place did the performers bow low and give voice: *"Rex, in aeternum vive!"* In nine episodes full of formal movement and gesture, sometimes declaiming or singing to the accompaniment of instruments, sometimes silent, the performers brought before the rapt audience an ancient story of royal arrogance, prophetic courage, and divine retribution, all foreshadowing a miracle, the birth of a Savior of mankind.

Years later, people who were present would recall, with total clarity and a kind of awed yearning, the things they had heard and seen. For some, what lingered in memory was a piece of irony: a song in sycophantic praise of a doomed king, *"Jubilemus Regi nostro, magno et potenti . . ."* issuing in pristine purity from the throats of boy cho-

1

risters. Others remembered a catch in the throat when a second
king, torn between love of a loyal counsellor and the demand of his
own laws, consented against his will to a terrible punishment. For
many, the most gripping and dazzling moment came at the end,
when an angel in gold and white suddenly appeared to bring the
message from on high that *"Natus est Christus, Dominator orbis / in
Bethlehem Judae . . ."*

As the last echo of the recessional *Te Deum laudamus* died away
and the players and singers vanished, the hush that fell over the hall
lasted and lasted. Afterward, people stood blinking in the late afternoon sun and trying to orient themselves to everday reality. Many
said that they felt strangely calm and at peace, at one with the simple
folk for whom this same play had been played so many centuries
ago.

The harpsichordist Albert Fuller was in the audience that day.
Fuller is a man not easily impressed, but all he could do when asked
about his reaction was to breathe, "What a trip!"[1]

The day was Thursday, January 2, 1958. The place was The Cloisters, the four-acre assemblage of early medieval architecture and
medieval art in Fort Tryon Park at the northern end of Manhattan.
An audience of three hundred had braved chilly weather and a bit-
ing northwesterly wind off the Hudson to climb the cobbled walk-
way to the entrance and file into the Romanesque Hall. The event
was the first presentation in perhaps seven hundred years of *The
Play of Daniel*, a twelfth-century musical dramatization of the Biblical tale of Daniel and Belshazzar, rooted in medieval Christmas liturgy and originally performed by *"la jeunesse de Beauvais,"* the youth
of a small cathedral town about thirty miles north of Paris. The
performers at The Cloisters were the singers and instrumentalists of
the New York Pro Musica Antiqua. They themselves were mostly
young, and Pro Musica itself was not yet five years old.

The ecstatic reviews in the newspapers paid due homage to various luminaries associated with the production. Lincoln Kirstein,
known since his Harvard undergraduate days for his support of
ventures in literature and the performing arts, had put up the money
for *Daniel*. Kirstein's ruling passion was ballet.[2] His interest in the

[1]Albert Fuller, May 19, 1998.

[2]Lincoln Kirstein (1907-1995) is best known as cofounder, with George Balanchine,
of the School of American Ballet (1934) and of the New York City Ballet (1948). But
by his own account, Kirstein variously wanted to be a first-rate painter, poet,literary
editor and dancer. Thus, at Harvard in 1926, Kirstein, with Varian Fry as partner,
founded the literary magazine *Hound & Horn*; and in 1928, with Edward Warburg,

liturgical drama of the Middle Ages was marginal, but he adored color and light and "Biblical scenes, the 'quest for the Holy Grail,' stereoscopic incidents of proud pageantry,"[3] as he loved high art. *Daniel*, with its kings and princes of Babylon, its satraps and angels and lions, was spectacle and art together. So Kirstein had agreed to finance the production. Assuming the title of producer, he had immersed himself, as he loved to do, in the details of staging, directing and costuming.[4]

When it was decided that some literary device was needed to introduce the drama and link its separate scenes more closely, no less a personage than the poet W. H. Auden had agreed to create one. "Probably around the summer of 1957," according to Edward Mendelson, Auden's biographer and literary executor, "Auden wrote a verse narrative to be spoken between episodes . . ."[5] Auden's Christian faith, hard-won in an era of unbelief, made the *Daniel* narrative a labor of love. To capture a medieval religious mood without lapsing into preciosity, Auden made deft use of the alliterative verse patterns of Early English (Anglo-Saxon) poems like *Beowulf* and *The Seafarer*, in which the initial sounds of key words in the first half of each line are echoed in the second half: e.g., "Doom is dark and deeper than any sea-dingle"; "Welcome, good people / Watch and listen." The result is a retelling of the Daniel story in a style as austere as the drama itself.

Meyer Schapiro of Columbia University, one of the most distinguished of American art historians, lent his immense knowledge of medieval art to the production. But there always was, in the words of one of his students, "a certain remorselessness in [Schapiro's] brilliance."[6] He was thus exceedingly displeased when his prescribed model of *Daniel's* angels — authentically medieval — was set aside in favor of a figure that might have been (and probably was) taken from a Botticelli painting done three hundred years later.[7]

Agnes Mongan, and John Walker III, started the Harvard Society for Contemporary Art. The money to help further Kirstein's ambitions came from the Filene's department store fortune.

[3] Lincoln Kirstein, *Mosaic: Memoirs*, p. 160.

[4] Nikos Psacharopoulos, who taught directing at the Yale School of Drama and was resident director of the Williamstown (Massachusetts) Theater Foundation, was the actual director of *The Play of Daniel*. Robert Fletcher was the costume and set designer.

[5] Edward Mendelson [ed.], *The Complete Works of W. H. Auden: Libretti, 1937-1973*, pp. 751-752.

[6] Anatole Broyard, *Kafka Was the Rage*, p. 58.

[7] Joel Newman, April 16, 1997; September 9. 1998.

Since its formation in late 1952, the New York Pro Musica Antiqua had acquired a devoted following, mostly in New York City but also on the touring circuit and in the Berkshire hills of southwestern Massachusetts, where the ensemble had spent several summers relaxing, concertizing, and rehearsing new repertory. None of its six regular singers and five instrumentalists, talented as they all were, was a "name" performer, not even the most extraordinary of them, a twenty-nine-year-old Juilliard voice graduate from Akron, Ohio named Russell Oberlin. What made Oberlin extraordinary was, first of all, his vocal range, which extended from mid-tenor all the way up to alto, and, secondly, the exceptional sweetness and power of the voice itself. In sum, Oberlin's was that rarest of all male voices, a true countertenor. Hearing it as the voice of the Herald Angel in *The Play of Daniel*, who at the end of the drama appears to announce from on high the birth of Christ, was an electrifying experience. But countertenors are not tenors, and *Daniel* is not *Pagliacci* or *Il Trovatore*. It would be several more years before Oberlin would attain something approaching fame.

*   *   *

Nobody in the enthralled audience at that first performance would have turned away from the staging and the bejeweled costumes, or stopped listening to the music, to focus on a tall man in street clothes standing at the back of the hall. But someone was indeed there: a bulky, bespectacled figure, fidgeting slightly, resisting the urge to light a forbidden cigarette or go get himself a Scotch on the rocks, yet intently following every detail of the performance. On the face of it, the thirty-eight-year-old Noah Greenberg seemed the least likely person in the world to be the moving spirit behind a medieval sacred opera and musical director of the production. Noah Greenberg never attended a music school or conservatory, never received any formal training in music history, took almost no music lessons, and never spent the days, months, and years of practice needed to become proficient on a musical instrument. Yet in fact it was Noah Greenberg's musical imagination, drive, persuasiveness, and buoyant self-confidence that had turned a few pages of medieval music in a 19th-century scholarly anthology into this wonderwork of contemporary art.

From boyhood on, Noah had walked the world with a bearish swagger, letting all and sundry know that here was someone possessed of immoderate appetites and boundless, infectious energy and charm. The terms his family, friends and colleagues used, and still use, to describe the man underscore thrice over this aspect of his character: "a vast bear"; "larger than life"; "a locomotive"; "a man who knew no limits"; "he never took 'no' for an answer." In every conversation about Noah Greenberg, the descriptive adjective that recurs most often is "enthusiastic."

One friend from Noah's adolescence, Robert Levenstein, a gifted pianist and, incidentally, a New York State junior chess champion, said of Noah:

> I had known precocious youngsters before, but never had I known any with such singleminded purpose and unbounded ambition to succeed in a chosen profession. It was as if music was his whole life.[8]

For despite the lack of formal training, and amid a youth and young manhood crammed with utterly different activities and driven by powerful extra-musical concerns, Noah's hobby, obsession, and guiding star was music.

Before Noah Greenberg, a huge repertoire, indeed more than half of the entirety of Western music, was known only to scholars and was dry, dusty, and abstract even to them: the music of the Middle Ages, the Renaissance, and the Baroque. It became Noah's mission to discover, explore and interpret this music and bring it to life. To be sure, there were performers of early music before Noah Greenberg. Some, like the harpsichordists Wanda Landowska and Ralph Kirkpatrick, were brilliant virtuosos. But they confined themselves to the solo Baroque repertory. Their harpsichords were modern versions, ill-sounding, badly designed, cranky and almost impossible to take on tour.[9] The eccentricities of their stage behavior— Kirkpatrick's long, long meditative pauses, Landowska's onstage slither and absurd theatrics over the placement of her red plush cushion, which had to be exactly so before she would seat herself at her instrument—smacked of the excesses of nineteenth-century musical showmanship. And although both performers struggled against the hushed, almost worshipful performance tradition they inherited, as if one had to approach Bach and Handel and Scarlatti on

---

[8] Robert Levenstein, letter, April 20, 1997.

[9] Toward the end of his career, Kirkpatrick acquired and concertized on a fine modern instrument built by William Dowd. His recordings, however, were made on an inadequate German instrument. Landowska, although she had built up a small collection of early instruments, performed and recorded only on her elaborate Pleyel, a harpsichord that looked like a concert grand piano but emitted only a relatively feeble sound.

one's knees,[10] they defined and presented themselves as temperamental autocrats who sought disciples as much as listeners, an attitude that affected their playing in public and narrowed its appeal.

In contrast, polite bloodlessness was the hallmark and curse of the first of the twentieth-century ensembles that essayed early Renaissance motets, late Renaissance madrigals, or Baroque instrumental and choral works. In fairness, this subdued style was itself partly an effort to apply the lessons of scholarship, partly an attempt to adapt powerful modern instruments and contemporary vocal practice to the demands of earlier music, and partly a reaction against nineteenth-century sentimentality and grandiloquence. Still, if a thunderous two-thousand-voice *Messiah* woefully overinflated Handel's music, a timid, bleating "cathedral sound" version was hardly an improvement.

In his brief life—he died at age forty-seven, in 1966—Noah Greenberg's greatest service to music was to bring to life a wonderful repertory. But scarcely less important was his impassioned determination to have early music performed as it should be performed. That is, with due care for its sonorities and due respect for historical accuracy, but also—and above all—with expressive richness and fullness.

Noah's native ground, the world in which he grew up and to which he always belonged, was the New York political and cultural milieu of the 1930s, 1940s and 1950s. This small, uneasy realm has been much examined, largely by the several dozen New York liberal intellectuals, most of them Jewish, most of them formidably verbal, who were, at least in their own minds, its ruling figures. During the years in question, and in particular the Eisenhower and McCarthy years, their writings were stylish mixtures of somber political argument, scornful analysis of American materialism and middlebrow culture, and shrewd, often brilliant, criticism of literature, theater and the fine arts. Afterward, in their memoirs, these same men and women took the measure of their little kingdom, from the East Bronx and City College to the Upper West Side and Greenwich Village, not neglecting its summertime extensions in Wellfleet and Westport and on Martha's Vineyard. In scores of books and articles, they reported, seldom with objectivity, on its folkways. They gleefully carved up

---

[10] Kirkpatrick in particular strove to break away from the reverential. Hornist Willie Ruff speaks of him as listening to and learning from such masters of jazz piano as Art Tatum, Fats Waller, and Willie "The Lion" Smith. Willie Ruff, "A Musician's Legacy," *Yale Alumni Magazine*, April, 1995, pp. 20-23.

and served up their own lives along with those of their fellow intellectuals, friend and foe alike. "When Philip Rahv or Delmore Schwartz finished tearing apart a friend," wrote a friend of both, "little remained but a pile of bones."[11] Some of them sauced their often bitter reminiscences with hard-core who-got-staggering-drunk and who-fucked-whom-on-whose-kitchen-table gossip.

Taken at face value, their versions of the New York cultural world —often fascinating reading—make it out to have been a combination of *shtetl*, senior common room, gin-sodden wife-swapping weekend, and shark tank.

Noah Greenberg knew many of these people. At various times of his life, he passed out socialist literature with Irving Howe, ate lunch on Fourteenth Street with Manny Geltman, and swam in the chilly Atlantic with Nancy and Dwight Macdonald; he drank and socialized with "the other Greenbergs"—Clement, Martin and Sol —at Daniel Bell's parties on Riverside Drive; read *Partisan Review* and *Commentary* and *Politics* and *Dissent*.

Yet Noah was not really of one blood with these New York literary intellectuals; not another snorting, trampling member of what one of them[12] called with a characteristic sneer, "the herd of independent minds." He was, for one thing, younger than many of them. For another, he had never gone to college (and would always envy those who had). For yet another, he was usually too busy. During the 1940s, Noah was either holding down factory jobs or else away at sea for weeks on end, and only intermittently at home on Fourteenth Street. During the 1950s and 1960s, as New York intellectuals were twitching their mantles and making their hungry way to fresh woods and pastures new, Noah Greenberg, his *métier* clear at last, was dealing with the thousand and one details of creating and leading a small successful musical organization.

The question of *métier* is all-important. For the literary crowd, literature was what mattered most, with politics a close second — and on many an occasion the order was reversed. In many respects, the Fifties in America were, in Lillian Hellman's contemptuous phrase, "scoundrel time." This was the era when Soviet Communism was casting a dark shadow over the world; when a coterie of media tycoons, exiled nationalists, and ditsy U. S. lawmakers could half-convince the country that traitors in the State Department had,

---

[11] Irving Howe, *A Margin of Hope,* p. 143.

[12] Harold Rosenberg, *The Tradition of the New,* p. 207. (The phrase is the title of Part Four of the book.)

among other villainies, "lost China;" when our best response to Communist aggression was no longer the Marshall Plan but the witch hunt, the blacklist, and the tipsy ravings of the Senator from Wisconsin.

And yet . . . as Noah's Workers Party comrade Irving Howe was to observe, "here in New York we had that outburst of modernist art called 'action painting,' perhaps the richest creative impulse of our moment."[13] Jackson Pollock, Willem de Kooning, Franz Kline, Arshile Gorky, Ad Reinhardt, Robert Motherwell, Mark Rothko, Grace Hartigan, Helen Frankenthaler, Jane Freilicher, Nell Blaine — these and dozens of others nearly as gifted were bringing new vitality to American painting through their obsession with the purest, most basic elements of painting: color, form, size and scale, and gestural manipulation of the paint itself.

And yet . . . in the 1950s, John Berryman, Robert Lowell and Elizabeth Bishop, none of them New Yorkers, were the mad, sad sachems of the tribe of American poets. W. H. Auden and, on occasion, Dylan Thomas could be seen and heard and known in the city. But also, a gaggle of younger poets was drifting into and out of — mostly into — New York, where its members mingled happily with the painters. Its chiefs were Gregory Corso and Allen Ginsberg representing the Beats and Frank O'Hara, James Merrill, John Ashbery and Kenneth Koch representing themselves. Its watering-holes were the San Remo on MacDougal Street and the White Horse Tavern, a few blocks west on Greenwich Street. In the mid-Fifties, the poets revived an old tradition (or lifted it from the program of the 92nd Street YM-YWHA) and began reading their work aloud at Village hangouts like Figaro's and the Café Wha.[14]

There was also, of course, a New York music scene—or, rather, numerous New York music scenes. Lincoln Center was hardly more than a gleam in the eye of John D. Rockefeller III and his allies,[15] but the traditional forms of classical orchestral music and grand opera were richly served up at Carnegie Hall, Town Hall, and the "Met" on 39th Street; and the business side of classical music was centered on 57th Street, where impresarios like Sol Hurok and the artists' rep-

[13] Howe, *op. cit.*, p. 197.

[14] One of the liveliest accounts of the goings-on among the poets is that of the painter Larry Rivers, in his "unauthorized autobiography," *What Did I Do?*

[15] Groundbreaking for the $175 million Lincoln Center complex did not take place until 1959. Philharmonic Hall, the first of the Lincoln Center theaters to be completed, opened in April 1964.

resentatives, dominated by CAMI, Columbia Artists' Management, had their offices. In adddition to this "uptown" scene, the province of the city's and the country's musical Establishment, there were other, smaller "downtown" classical music universes. One centered on the cluster of American composers whose members had studied with, or at least known, the celebrated Nadia Boulanger. This "Boulangerie" was an establishment in its own right. Indeed, it had been one since the spring of 1928, when Aaron Copland and Roger Sessions jolted the public with the first of their three Copland-Sessions Concerts of contemporary American music. Among its other composer-members were Roy Harris, Paul Bowles, Marion Bauer, Carlos Chavez, Elliott Carter, and Walter Piston. The group had its own organization, the League of Composers, run by the formidable Claire R. Reis; and through the mid-1940s, its own publication, *Modern Music,* with Minna Lederman as editor. Copland and Virgil Thomson, both still going strong in the 1950s, shared the headmastership.

Arnold Schoenberg had been living in Los Angeles since 1934, and since the end of the Second World War his twelve-tone approach to composition had been undercutting traditional methods. Schoenberg's chief American disciple, Milton Babbitt, was at Princeton. But a center of atonal and other new musical forms was the New School for Social Research on West 12th Street, where Henry Cowell had been director of music (and chief advocate of American avant-garde music) since 1928. A few blocks away, Cowell's pupil John Cage was incorporating chance sounds and electronic signals into the works he was creating for the dance company of Merce Cunningham.

Finally, there was the "midtown" scene of Broadway musical comedy and—overshadowing all else in terms of both output and financial muscle—of popular music in all its protean forms. Over this, the sheet-music publishers still held great power, but the record companies were king.

Perhaps not enough time has gone by to allow us to use the term "renaissance" to label what was taking place in the arts in New York. Perhaps it's more prudent to note simply that a great deal that we now treasure was going on in the cold-water flats, commercial lofts, and scruffy storefronts of Lower Manhattan. One of the great chroniclers of the period, Theodore H. White, summed up matters admirably in his autobiography:

There had long been a broader cultural underbase in New York

City than in any other city of the Western world; London, in some years, might have better theater; Paris, better painting; Vienna, at one time, might have offered better music. But New York in the fifties reached an art level that it has never since, even in peril, let drop; whether in music, or in painting, or in architecture, or in dance, or in theater, New York was beginning to offer either the finest or the equivalent of the finest in the civilized world.[16]

It is with New York's painters and poets and dancers and composers, its creators, rather than with its *literateurs,* that we should associate Noah Greenberg and the New York Pro Musica. Like the painters and poets and composers, his *métier* was that of maker. Like them, he had a huge appetite for the new. And the old music to which his appetite led him *was* new: new to our time and our sensiblity.

When all is said, the reason for reading the story of this man's life and career, as for writing it, is best expressed by one of Noah Greenberg's oldest friends. Jesse Simons knew Noah as a young fellow-radical in New York, as a wartime worker on the West Coast, as a struggling would-be musician in postwar New York, and then at last during his years of success. "I knew dozens of the people who were around in those days," Simons says. "Politicals, labor people, intellectuals. We were all going to make the world a better place. But the only one who really left the world a better place than he found it was Noah, with his music."[17]

---

[16]Theodore H. White, *In Search of History,* p.370.
[17]Jesse Simons, April 17, 1997.

CHAPTER TWO

ᏢRINCELING IN THE BRONX

(1919-1932)

$\mathcal{T}$he Bronx. Immigrants began it. Immigrants built it. It became—it remains—a harbor for successive waves of newcomers to the land. In 1639, a Swedish sea-captain, Jonas Bronck, produced the first ripple. Near where East 138th Street now intersects the Grand Concourse, Bronck and a small team of indentured immigrants from Sweden, Holland, and Germany cleared the trees, built themselves houses and barns, and began growing corn and tobacco. When Bronck died in 1642, his settlement died with him, but the small river east of his land, flowing south into Westchester Creek and the East River estuary, was still called Bronck's River. The borough would be named after the river, not the man.

In 1841, a branch of the New York Central Railroad crossed the Harlem River from Manhattan and began pushing northeastward, linking the numerous small villages of the area: Melrose, Morrisania, Claremont, Tremont, Fordham, Bedford Park, Norwood, Williamsbridge, Woodlawn, Wakefield. Many of the Italian masons and Irish trackworkers who built the line lived along it. They and the thousands of exiled Germans who settled there in the wake of the Revolution of 1848 formed the next wave of immigrants—a pond-sized wave compared with what was to follow.

The year 1883 saw the extension of the Third Avenue Elevated Railway across the river to 132nd Street, and the beginning of a population tsunami. In 1904, the Interborough Rapid Transit Company opened the first Manhattan-Bronx subway. From that point, urban development probably went further and faster in the Bronx than in any other city in the country. Farmland—through the 1920s, Bronx truck farms supplied vegetables to the city—gave way to street upon street of dun-colored five- and six-story apartment buildings. The Grand Concourse and Boulevard, started in 1890, was modeled on the Champs Elysées and intended as a great avenue affording Manhattanites access to the green reaches of Bronx Park and Van Cortlandt Park. But it turned into a choice middle-class residential strip, the prestige address for Bronx dwellers. Until 1925, its broad central roadway was a turf track for horses and carriages, but starting in 1902 its side roadways were paved. They had to be, to allow easy access to the scores of new apartment buildings that now lined it on either hand.

The market for this housing was enormous: the hundreds of thousands of immigrants were crowded into the slum districts of Manhattan. The Irish came from Hell's Kitchen (the West Forties) to Norwood and Fordham; the Italians from Little Italy (the West Thirties and Greenwich Village) to Belmont and Tremont ("Beautiful Hill" and "Three Hills" in Italian: reminders that the West Bronx in particular is not flat). The Slavs came from the Upper East Side to Mott Haven and Morris Port. The Jews fled the hellish Old Law tenements of the Lower East Side and settled in neighborhoods all over the Bronx. In 1870, the population of the future borough (most of it still part of Westchester County) was lower than 100,000. By 1910, it was 1.4 million. It would stay at that level for another 40 years.

Jewish writers have supplied dozens of descriptions of how it was to live in the Jewish neighborhoods of the Bronx of those times. Irving Howe, in his autobiographical *A Margin of Hope*, sets the stage in bleak enough language:

> The East Bronx . . . formed a thick tangle of streets crammed with Jewish immigrants from Eastern Europe, almost all of them poor. We lived in narrow five-story tenements, wall flush against wall, and with slate-colored stoops rising sharply in front. There never was enough space. The buildings, clenched into rows, looked down upon us like sentinels, and the apartments in the buildings were packed with relatives and children, many of them fugitives from unpaid rent. These tenements had first gone up during the early years of the century, and if not quite so grimy as those of the Lower East Side in Manhattan or the Brownsville section of Brooklyn, they were bad enough.[1]

*   *   *

In 1918, people were dying of hunger in Warsaw. The First World

---

[1]Irving Howe, *op. cit.*, p. 2. For readers curious about Bronx geography, the East Bronx was everything east of Jerome Avenue, the West Bronx was the relatively narrow strip lying between Jerome Avenue and the Harlem River.

War was drawing to a close, but the greatest battles of the Eastern Front—Tannenberg, Lûdz, Gorlice—had been fought on Polish soil, and as historian Norman Davies writes, "the cost in lives and livelihoods was incalculable."[2] Two years earlier, Germany and Austria, with the war in their favor, had carved up Poland between them. And in March, 1918, the newly-minted Bolshevik government of Russia had signed the Treaty of Brest-Litovsk, taking Russia out of the war and in effect ceding Poland to Germany. But on Armistice Day, November 11, 1918, the defeated German Army marched out of Warsaw, ending the military rule which had begun in August, 1915. Chaos followed. "The collapse of law and order in November 1918 produced a rash of anti-Jewish outrages in country areas and in towns such as Lwûw and Pinsk. . . . Hostility toward the Jews was inadvertently heightened by American and British Jewish pressure groups at the Paris peace talks of 1918."[3] It was a terrible time to be a young Jewish couple in Warsaw. For Lillie and Harry Greenberg, the decision to emigrate was not a hard one. Carrying out the decision was another matter.

Even after the Armistice was signed, Poland and the rest of Eastern Europe was a place of horror, its fall crops unharvested, its transportation and communications disrupted, its villages and towns unruly, its populations literally starving, and the Spanish influenza epidemic reaching its height.

Eighty years after the fact, family members are unable to say how the young Greenbergs contrived to make their way from Warsaw to a seaport; whether they traveled alone or with others (one version of events has it that Lillie made the trip unaccompanied, with Harry either preceding or following her); on what vessel they managed to gain passage across the Atlantic. "Young Greenbergs" is no exaggeration: Lillie was eighteen, her husband only seventeen or perhaps even sixteen.[4] Lillie, moreover, was at least four months pregnant. One can only imagine what the journey was like—or where the money came from to pay for it—and respect the courage and tenacity of the pair.

---

[2] In his *Heart of Europe* (p. 113), Davies cites "calculations based on the territory of the inter-war [Polish] Republic, [which] reveal that a population of 30.9 million in 1914 had fallen by 4.6 million by 1919—a decrease of 14.9 per cent."

[3] Adam Zamoyski, *The Polish Way: a Thousand-Year History of the Poles and Their Culture*, p. 345.

[4] Rema Sessler, March 1, 1997. Rema Sessler, née Davidson, is Noah Greenberg's first cousin, the daughter of Lillie Greenberg's sister Dora and Morris Davidson, Noah's "Uncle Moniek."

Lillie and Harry Greenberg with baby Noah, 1919 (Courtesy Greenberg family)

Family was awaiting them in New York. Lillie Greenberg's maiden name was Sogenstein, and the Sogensteins were a numerous and outgoing clan. Lillie was the youngest of three sisters, and the elder two, Dora and Bronka, may not yet have arrived. But Aunt Annie, Lillie's mother's sister, was living in the Bronx, at 1436 Crotona Park East, a fine address, at the corner of 170th Street. Annie, married to a Cooper Union engineering graduate who worked for one of New York's subway companies (then privately-owned), took Lillie in, eventually found the Greenbergs an apartment in the same building, and may have helped Lillie look for work. None of this could have been easy. The wartime rush of business in New York was winding down. The flush times of the Twenties were several years away, and in any event neither Lillie nor Harry spoke English. Their everyday language was Yiddish. In due course they would enroll in night school like tens of thousands of other immigrants to learn the language of the new country.

On April 9, 1919, Lillie gave birth to the Greenbergs' first and only child. Labor and childbirth too could not have been easy. Lillie's health was never robust. In the phrases of the day, "she was delicate. She had a weak heart." Her family would always treat her with special consideration as one who was not strong. Noah, however, was a robust and healthy infant, weighing seven-plus pounds at birth and destined to grow into a tall (six-foot-two-inch) and brawny adult. An only son and for many years an only grandson, Noah occupied the stereotypical princely place at the center of his family.

As a toddler, Noah would in all likelihood have been left in the care of his grandparents and great-aunt Annie, because both Lillie and Harry held full-time jobs. Harry, a leatherworker, found employment with the Coward Shoe Company. Lillie had studied millinery in Warsaw and became a milliner in New York, making and trimming women's hats for firms in what was then one of the major trades in the city's garment industry. Both joined trade unions. Harry belonged to the Boot and Shoe Workers Union. Lillie was a member of the Millinery & Ladies Straw Hat Workers, which despite its genteel name was one of the most ambitious and militant of garment-industry unions. Its membership, small in the 1920s, shot upward during the Depression following passage in 1934 of the Wagner Act, which required employers to allow union organizing during work hours.[5]

According to Noah's cousin Rema, Lillie and Harry Greenberg were loyal union members but not labor activists. Nor were they active politically, although they were socialists as a matter of course. Of the politics of the Jewish Bronx in the 1920s and 30s, Irving Howe says:

> Socialism, for many immigrant Jews, was not merely politics or an idea, it was an encompassing culture, a style of perceiving and judging through which to structure their lives. So diffused had the socialist idea become in the immigrant world since the days of [Eugene V.] Debs and [Morris] Hillquit that . . . almost everyone seemed to be a Socialist of one sort or another. This was not really true, it was a mistake easy to make.[6]

Socialism certainly was the ruling credo of the Sogenstein-Greenberg family circle. For most members, socialism meant "Left Socialism." "Left Socialists," although they might deplore Stalin's takeover of the Soviet Communist Party following Lenin's death in 1921, and even follow Leon Trotsky out of the Party, still believed in the Russian Revolution. That is, they still believed that the Soviet

---

[5] In 1929, the Millinery & Ladies' Straw Hat Workers Union had 3,987 members. By the end of 1934, membership had risen to 12,647.

[6] Howe, *op cit.,* p. 9.

Union was a true workers' state. Following the Russian model, they believed that revolution—and only revolution—would allow workers elsewhere in the world to gain power and achieve a just society.

Lillie and Harry Greenberg were far from being Left Socialists. On the contrary, Lillie's brother-in-law (and Noah's uncle) Morris Davidson, his memory perfectly clear at ninety-five, said of them, "they were sonofabitch right-wingers." To be sure, they were "right-wingers" only in a very special sense of the term. His daughter Rema hastened to explain: "He means that they were socialists, but they were very, very anti-Communist."[7]

At least as important as politics in the Greenberg household were issues of language and culture. Lillie Greenberg in particular was a "Yiddishist." This term, let it be understood, means much more than "Yiddish-speaking": Yiddish was of course the everyday language of virtually all Eastern European Jews. A Yiddishist, apart from speaking and reading Yiddish in full awareness of its infinite subtleties, ironies, and substrata of meaning, was someone devoted—passionately devoted—to both the spoken tradition and the burgeoning (if short-lived) literary culture of the "mama loshen," the mother tongue. This was the culture of Sholem Aleichem and, in twentieth-century "Amerike," of Chaim Grade, Eliezer Greenberg, Isaac Bashevis Singer and a handful of others now scarcely remembered. It is a pungent blend of the humanism of the German Enlightenment, the fervent joyousness of the Hasidic mystics and the ineffable corner-of-the-eye and side-of-the-mouth humor of ghetto and *stetl*. To a Yiddishist, being a Jew had far less to do with Jewish religious observance than with a deep love of the linguistic birthright and the determination never to forget, much less deny, one's roots. Just as German Jews, assimilationists long before reaching America, looked down on Yiddish as the superstition-ridden *argot* of the lower classes, so were Yiddishists, secularist or religious, contemptuous of German Jews for their nervous rejection of the very essence of Jewishness.

So strong was *Yiddishkeit* in the Greenberg household that for years small Noah spoke only Yiddish. Lillie's sister Dora would protest: "I know it's very important to keep Yiddish alive, but you're not being fair, the other kids are making fun of him." Still, not until Noah was four and a half and nearly ready for school did his parents relent and allow him to speak English.

[7] Rema Sessler, March 1, 1997.

The devotion to Yiddish was no evidence of narrowness. On the contrary, Noah's cousin Rema remembers his mother as a highly educated woman.

> My Aunt Lillie actually did go to college, to *gymnasium* [an upper school combining the last two grades of high school and the first two of college] in Warsaw. And what I remember very much about her is that this woman read Montaigne's *Essays* over and over, and I also remember that she was reading Sarah Orne Jewett, *The Country of the Pointed Firs.*[8]

Jewett's wonderful story of Dunnet, Maine is quintessential New England storytelling. (Willa Cather thought it equal to *The Scarlet Letter* and *Huckleberry Finn.*) What was its special appeal for a young Polish-Jewish mother struggling to make ends meet in the teeming Bronx? Did Jewett's evocation of "the rocky shore and dark woods, and the few houses which seemed to be securely wedged and tree-nailed in among the ledges" of Penobscot Bay bring back memories of Poland's Baltic coast or its upland lakes and forests? Or did Lillie enjoy the story purely for its own sake? Rema cannot say.

The Greenbergs and their relatives certainly had a fondness for nature. Like thousands of others, they sought a way to escape the steamy city during the summers. The Maine seacoast was a million miles away, but Westchester County was not. Indeed, a rich mixture of motives led New York Jewish families to this particular stretch of country.

> During [the 1920s], leaders of Jewish workers' organizations anticipated decline as a consequence of the end of the mass migration from Eastern Europe. To reinforce leftist ideologies—in some cases, Yiddish culture as well—they encouraged the formation of adult camps under organizational sponsorship. . . .
>
> At the same time, several groups of left-leaning Jews and a small cadre of non-Jewish Anarchists founded summer camps and colonies in northwestern Westchester County. Undeveloped sites adjacent to the Bronx presented an important advantage over areas more distant from New York City. Traveling from the city to the Poconos, Catskills, or Berkshires required three or four hours; it took less than half as long to reach Peekskill and its environs, where most of the settlements were located.[9]

In the 1940s, both the Davidsons and the Greenbergs could afford

---

[8] Rema Sessler, March 1, 1997.

[9] Bella Round Shargel, "Leftist Summer Colonies of Northern Westchester County, New York," in *American Jewish History*, IX, Summer 1994, p.338.

to acquire land and build or buy bungalows in one of these left-leaning encampments, Shrub Oak Park. But in the 1920s, the two families rented land, first from a farmer named Voitch in Ardsley and later in the Cortlandt area further to the north, where they pitched tents and camped out. The primary purpose, at least in the beginning, was simply to get away from the Bronx and make contact with nature. In Cortlandt, just below Peekskill on the west side of the county, the campground was an enormous field framed by tall trees. "The story goes that there was a stream and a waterfall [in Cortlandt] and Noah would go in there on a hot day and come out and say "S'iz a machiah!" (Yiddish for "It's a pleasure!"), and so they named it Camp Machiah."[10] Noah would revisit Camp Machiah in-season and out for years. Summertimes that combined recreation and relaxation in idyllic surroundings with family life and pleasurable work were hugely important to Noah throughout his entire life.

Lillie and Harry Greenberg later settled into an apartment at 105 Hawkstone Street, a two-block-long street running west from the Grand Concourse to Walton Avenue in the High Bridge district, today a couple of blocks south of what is now the Cross-Bronx Expressway. But during the years of Noah's boyhood and adolescence, the Greenbergs, having left Aunt Annie's building, lived several blocks to the north and west, at 1744 Clay Avenue. Clay Avenue runs northward from 165th Street in the Melrose district, forms the eastern border of Claremont Park and dead-ends at 176th Street in Tremont. No. 1744 is very near its northern end.

No family records of Noah's early schooling have survived, but the move from Crotona Park East to 1744 Clay Avenue meant that Noah would probably have been enrolled in P. S. 58, at Washington Avenue and 176th Street. A walk of a few blocks, with bustling Webster Avenue the only wide street to cross, covered the distance between home and school.

In a certain sense, Noah was lucky in the timing of his school years. In the decade 1921-1930, the population of the Bronx rose by nearly 75 per cent. The New York City Board of Education, striving desperately to keep abreast of the floodtide of school-age children, built and staffed dozens of new elementary schools and, anticipating the bulge in teenage pupils, began construction of 31 new high schools. Schools, if not education itself, became a main concern of the city's Establishment. Children in schools were not children run-

[10] Rema Sessler, March 1, 1997.

ning wild in the streets, and schools were places to inculcate "American values" like industriousness and obedience to authority, along with the three "R"'s, in the city's unruly immigrant hordes. Educational standards, like construction standards, were thus fairly high —far higher than they had been before the citywide "Board of Ed" was formed in 1898. The schools were crowded and perennially understaffed, but in the years before the Depression they did their job of mass education remarkably well.

One telling image of Noah Greenberg as an elementary schoolboy has survived the depredations of time. The vacant lot behind the Greenbergs' apartment building on Clay Avenue was the ballfield on which the neighborhood teams did battle. Some adult with a Kodak rounded up the members of one team and snapped them in classic team-photograph pose. Noah's friend Rubin Baratz is in the picture along with a dozen other Bronx urchins, bats and gloves prominent. Noah is on the right, in a dark v-neck pullover a couple of sizes too big for him. He is larger than the other boys, but, as Baratz notes, clearly younger. As a look at the picture will reveal (see below), they are ten-and eleven-year-olds; Noah is more like nine; the baby fat has not yet melted off him. Noah is holding out to the camera what might be a catcher's mitt but is probably a first-

Noah, 2nd row, r. ". . .somebody who will never let himself be left out. . ."
(Courtesy Clara Meyerson Hancox)

baseman's mitt. The lad seated directly in front of Noah, with his own big mitt and a mask perched on his leg besides, is clearly the team's official catcher. Most striking is the expression on Noah's face. He is squinting into the camera and smiling a smile that at first glance looks unfocused and babyish—not at all like the looks, cocky or sulky, on the other boys' faces. Yet in Noah's smile as in his pose, kneeling while the other boys in his row are seated, is the determination of somebody who will never let himself be left out or overlooked, even if he's not fully part of whatever it is that's going on.

As a grown man, Noah told a story on himself that more than bears out this aspect of his character. It happened during one of the summers at the Greenbergs' Camp Machiah. By his own account, Noah was twelve or thirteen and one of the ringleaders of the gang of kids whose parents were tentdwelling vacationers in Cortlandt. On one of their forays through the woods and fields, the youngsters came upon a patch of poison ivy. "Betcha you won't lie down and roll around in *that*," was the dare. Noah told his daughter Anne: "I said, 'Betcha I will,' and I did. I had to go to the hospital. I knew at the time it was the stupidest thing I could ever do, but I couldn't not do it." Acting the leader and accepting the risks that go with leadership were traits that followed Noah out of childhood into adolescence and beyond.

CHAPTER THREE

Music, Politics, Romance

(1933-1936)

$\mathcal{T}$he distance between 1744 Clay Avenue and Boynton Avenue at 172nd Street is about a mile and a quarter, not much of a walk for a healthy fourteen-year-old. On Boynton, barely east of the narrow trickle in a scrap of park that calls itself the Bronx River, is the main entrance of James Monroe High School. A sprawl of apartments and one- and two-family homes had transformed the flat East Bronx from farmscape to cityscape in a generation. Intended to accomodate the swelling student population of Tremont, East Tremont, West Farms, and Soundview, James Monroe High was one of the largest of the 31 high schools built during the Twenties. An imposing structure, it occupies a full city block, half of an undivided two-block tract, its athletic fields taking up the other half. The need for the school was great. According to Board of Education Records,[1] construction began in the spring or early summer of 1924, and interior finish was near completion in January 1926, but the first freshman class started school on September 14, 1925, the smell of mortar, concrete and varnish strong in its nostrils. By 1927, with only three of its four grade levels filled, it had 6,069 students "on register."[2]

James Monroe was thus a relatively young institution when Noah Greenberg, at age 14, enrolled as a freshman in September 1933. But

---

[1] Sadly, a fire at James Monroe High School in the mid-1980s destroyed most of the school's early records. I have drawn on what information is available in the Archives of the Board of Educationm, City of New York, now in the Special Collections Division, Teachers College Library, Teachers College, Columbia University.

[2] Because of absences and truancies, the number of a school's students "on register" is rarely if ever the number actually in school on a given day. But even by New York City standards, James Monroe was a very large high school.

by then the school was bursting at its seams. One reason was the Depression, which had brought school construction to a halt. Another was that with jobs almost nonexistent—and with adults competing bitterly for the few that did open up—fewer students were giving up school for work at the legal leaving age of 14. Still another, hard to believe today, was that for thousands of youngsters, being in school meant being given a meal, perhaps the only one that day. It is salutary to be reminded that during the Depression, New York's schoolteachers had their pay cut by 10 per cent, yet "many were purchasing food, preparing school lunches, providing clothing, and even sending food home to the families of their pupils." So widespread was the practice, indeed, that in 1931 the Superintendent of Schools and the President of the Board of Education formed the Winter School Relief Committee to pool volunteer efforts.[3]

At all events, in Noah Greenberg's freshman year James Monroe had on register well over 9,000 students. That year, one classroom in P.S. 102, a nearby grade school, was taken away from its students and assigned to James Monroe as an annex. In 1934, four other classrooms in neighboring elementary schools became Monroe annexes.

Still, despite overcrowding so serious that many students had to be placed on "special schedule" (arriving at school before 8:30 in the morning or staying in class after 3:30 or both), James Monroe afforded its students a remarkable education. Kate Simon, whose graphic portrayals of her Bronx girlhood and adolescence are at least as absorbing as her travel writings, loved the school's "unusually permissive curriculum."

> First of all, no math was demanded, none at all, the school's most bountiful gesture for one blinded by the simplest combination of numbers. Instead, a music course, where I first heard [Schubert's Eighth Symphony, "The Unfinished"] in its truncated entirety, and a lovely piece of weaving that was a Brahms quartet. An essay on the differences among the Beethoven symphonies earned me a startling compliment from the teacher, a swift little woman who swooped close to the phonograph like a plump hawk when a particular phrase or combination of instruments possesed her and, impelled by her passion, possessed us.[4]

A school in which a ninth-grader could be encouraged to write an essay on the Beethoven symphonies was clearly a splendid school for a Noah Greenberg.

[3] *The First Fifty Years, 1898-1948: Golden Jubilee Report of the Superintendent of Schools, Board of Education, City of New York*, p. 115.

[4] Kate Simon, *A Wider World: Portraits in an Adolescence*, p. 8.

The Jewish Bronx—it hardly needs saying—was steeped, was virtually marinated, in music. Families so poor that a pair of new shoes was a luxury would scrape together money for a battered upright piano (for girls) or cheap violin (for boys) and lessons from a neighborhood teacher; or for a wind-up phonograph and a few thick albums of 78rpm shellac discs. Families too poor even for these things would come together on weekend evenings and sing the folksongs and operetta songs of the Old Country and the workers' songs of the new. Men and women who worked sewing, cutting or pressing machines by day were connoisseurs of music by night. All kinds of music mattered. The virtues and weaknesses of the great cantors who drew crowds to their synagogues were as hotly argued as those of Caruso and Chaliapin and Kreisler and that new German at the New York Philharmonic, Walter Damrosch.

Music was adored in the Greenberg-Sogenstein-Davidson family circle. "We all sang," Rema Davidson Sessler remembered. "My mother, my aunts, everybody." She herself played (and still plays) the piano, as did Sibyl, her older sister. Their much younger brother Michael gave up the piano for the cello, and before setting aside the cello for a career in computers was a cellist with the New Orleans Philharmonic under Werner Torkanowsky. The Greenbergs were no less devoted to music. According to Noah Greenberg's daughters, their grandfather Harry had a good tenor voice and liked to use it. But more than this, Rema Sessler recalled,

> Harry was a very, very intelligent and actually intellectual man who brought chamber music to my family. My people loved opera, symphony, but I can remember Uncle Harry bringing a quartet, or a Haydn trio, and he would say to my parents, 'You have to listen to this.'[5]

As for Noah, it must be remembered that he was an only child and by all accounts an unusually precocious and determined one. How or why it happened, no one in the family can recall, but someone—perhaps his mother or father, but equally possibly Noah himself—must have decided that he had exceptional musical talent, because in 1933, the same year he entered high school, he began to study composition with Arnold Zemachson.

Zemachson himself is an interesting figure. Born in 1892 near Vilna, then in Russia, he was the son of Simon Zemachson, one of

---

[5] Rema Sessler, March 1, 1997.

the great composers of 19th-century Jewish liturgical music. The young Zemachson came to this country in 1910 and began composing seriously in 1915. By 1926, he had completed a respectable body of work, and he was putting the finishing touches on a big orchestral *Chorale and Fugue* in D minor dedicated to Leopold Stokowski.[6] The Philadelphia Orchestra under Stokowski gave the work its debut performance in November 1931, and over the next five years it was played and generously received in Cleveland, Chicago, Los Angeles, Cincinnati, Detroit, and New York.

So when he agreed to take on Noah as a pupil, Zemachson had already gained a measure of renown and was looked upon as a highly promising young (he was 41) composer.

According to Noah's own account, he worked with Arnold Zemachson through 1935. Curiously, few of Noah's musical friends from this period remember Zemachson or can find traces of his influence in his youthful pupil's musical development. Yet there may well be such traces. On one side of his head, Zemachson was a contrapuntalist, fascinated by fugue and by such supposedly archaic forms as the motet and the concerto grosso. On the other side, he was a Russian, in love with rich melody and lush orchestration. "In a sense," wrote a reviewer of *Chorale and Fugue*,

> [Zemachson] has devised a means of unifying the humanistic Bach with the mechanistic today. . . He has invented a theme of Oriental beauty. He has developed it in fugal form; but no matter how much one admires his craftsmanship in the development, one is enthralled by his Judaistic tone colorings.[7]

Presumably Noah absorbed from Zemachson some theory and harmony and the rudiments of thematic construction and orchestration, all of which would one day stand him in good stead in the preparation and scoring so vital to effective performances of early music. But he would also have soaked up the drama that could be gained by combining rigorous musical structure with novel and expressive sonorities.

In those pre-computer days, writing down music—especially orchestral music, with its multiple staffs, clefs, rhythms, and sets of notes—was both arduous and exacting. Under Zemachson, Noah

---

[6] The score of the Chorale and Fugue calls for three flutes, two oboes, English horn, two clarinets, two bassoons, contrabassoon, four horns, three trumpets, three trombones, bass tuba, tympani, triangle, tambourine, bass drum, small drum, cymbals, two harps, organ, and strings. So the adjective "big" seems handsomely justified.

[7] Harry R. Burke, in the *St. Louis Daily Globe-Democrat*, Saturday, January 18, 1935.

may also have acquired the exceptional skill in music notation and copying which led to his first professional employment in music years later.

Just as no one remembers how Noah and Zemachson met, so no one remembers how or why they parted.[8] But not long after matriculating at James Monroe High, Noah made the acquaintance of yet another older musician, one whose tutelage, taste and influence was certainly to shape his entire future career.

Harold Brown was born in New York in 1909. He studied violin in childhood and adolescence and made ambitious plans for a musical career as composer, choral conductor and instrumentalist. Noah's friend Jesse Simons, who knew Brown well during the 1940s, remembers hearing that these plans were temporarily thwarted by Brown's parents, Sam and Rose, who were insistent that their slender, darkly handsome son become a doctor; and that Brown's frustration over this family conflict contributed to a growing bitter streak (acknowledged by many others who knew him) in Brown's makeup. Be this as it may, Harold Brown graduated from Columbia in 1929, only months before the stock market crash, and during the Depression and afterward continued to study and compose music, supporting himself and his first wife, Lucy, an aspiring concert pianist, as a substitute teacher in the city high schools. It was probably in 1935 that Brown, then on the faculty at James Monroe, met Noah Greenberg. Noah at 16 was an ebullient young man, full of wit, quick with words, hungry for experience, and blessed with a gift for making others, including people much older than he, follow his lead. "When he walked into a room, even as a kid," one of his friends says of him, "his presence was electrifying." Harold Brown was of a very different stripe. Introverted, intense and argumentative, he held very strong views on music and on everything else, most especially on politics.

Harold's politics were intertwined with his music. In November 1934, New York's Mayor LaGuardia had reluctantly instituted a 2 per cent city sales tax. The city's liberals rose in protest. Norman Thomas denounced the tax as a "disaster" that "taxed the poor to support the poorer. Harold Brown set to a sour little tune in three flats, meant to be sung as a round, the words of a leftist rhymester who signed himself Dan Shays:

---

[8] The reason may have been lack of money on Noah's part, or Zemachson's own commitments

O LaGuardia, O don't you play with me

For you're out to gyp the people

With a sales tax on your knee.

This, along with four other "Workers' Rounds in the Form of Dedi-cations," was published by the Pierre Degeyter Music Club. Named after the composer of the *Internationale*, the Degeyter Club was an offshoot of the Communist-backed International Music Bureau. Harold signed the single sheet of music "H. Brown," and identified himself as a member of the Composers' Collective of the Degeyter Club. This in itself is revealing.

> Although the Collective was under the auspices of the Degeyter Club, the members wanted more independence and a wider mem-bership than the Party-controlled Degeyter Club would allow. . . . There was never a complete break from the parent organization, but friction and disagreements increased during the years of the Collective's existence, from 1931 to 1936.[9]

Harold Brown, of course, was no more radical than many another gifted young New Yorker. Only 26 himself and highly intelligent, he had a lot to give as a teacher of music. He also had a young man's craving to be liked and admired by those he taught. And he both admired and envied Noah's easy friendliness. So Harold Brown, convinced of Noah's talent—a boy who at 16 had been *composing* for three years!—and further warmed by his charm and willingness to learn, promptly took him in hand.

The first thing he did was to discourage his protegé's desire to study piano intensively. Noah was too old, Harold assured him, which meant that his fingers could never acquire the needed agility and flexibility. Furthermore, his hands were too large. (They were indeed large, as contemporary photographs indicate. Whether or not they were "too large" is another question.) Besides, if Noah wanted to play a musical instrument, Harold had just the right one. The James Monroe Student Orchestra, of which Brown was faculty advisor, needed a string bassist—someone tall enough to wrestle

---

[9] Aaron Copland and Vivian Perlis, *Copland: 1900 through 1942*, pp. 222-223. Jacob Schaefer, Leon Charles and Henry Cowell founded the Composers' Collective, and Marc Blitzstein was its secretary. Its primary purpose was to produce songs of left-wing propaganda, but a nod was given to "instrumental music . . . now threatened by the collapse of bourgeois culture." Membership stamped the individual mem-ber as a Communist. Henry Leland Clark, who joined in 1934, told Perlis that "[i]t was dangerous to belong to the Collective, and even more dangerous later on to have been connected with it."

with the bass viol, someone with a left hand big enough to press down hard on the strings and at the same time span the wide distances between notes on the fingerboard. In April of 1934, the James Monroe G. O., its student organization, had come up with "$165 to erect a wire mesh cage on the stage . . . for the purpose of storing musical instruments," including the school's own bass viol. The opportunity was there, the instrument was there—free of charge— and if Noah worked at it, an opening in the All-City High Schools Youth Orchestra might be within reach. Anyway, being an instrumentalist was only a means to a much broader end. The important thing was to become a musician in the full sense, Harold Brown's sense, of the word.

Noah did take up the string bass. He seems to have mastered it well enough to play in the student orchestra. At least, his senior-year listing in *The Monrovian*, the James Monroe High yearbook, mentions "orchestra" as his one extracurricular activity. And much of what he did outside of school also involved music: concertgoing, studying scores borrowed from the New York Public Library, listening to recordings. (Noah's family was one of the few that owned a good phonograph.) Much of what he did, but not all. Matching Noah Greenberg the budding musician stride for stride through adolescence was a *doppelganger*, Noah Greenberg the budding political.

Jesse Simons ascribes to Harold Brown a "critical role"in interesting Noah in socialism and Trotskyism, and he is probably right. But independent of Harold, and indeed well before he and Harold had met, Noah had carried his zest for music, politics, and sociability into the midst of a crowd of Bronx school-age radicals. Noah's friend Israel Kugler, a member of the same crowd, described it this way:

> Noah Greenberg was part of a group of teenagers drawn from the Amalgamated Houses, Sholem Aleichem Houses in the West Bronx; the houses on Allerton Avenue and Adee Avenue in the East Bronx. The political spectrum of this group which went out on outings and house socials was mostly communist with myself and Noah generally left socialist.[10]

"Izzie's absolutely right," Clara Hancox, who in those days was Clara Meyerson, said in an interview.[11] "There were eight or nine

---

[10] Israel Kugler, letter to Mark Davenport [n.d., but probably June or July, 1993]. Musicologist Mark Davenport is the son of the late LaNoue Davenport, an instru mentalist (recorders, sackbut, viols) long associated with the New York Pro Musica.
[11] Clara Hancox, May 12, 1997.

girls and nine or ten boys, and we hung out together at my apartment at the Politzian Houses at 808 Adee Avenue, but some of us
lived in the 'Commie Coops.'" Hancox, like Kugler, was referring
to the Bronx apartment buildings that various labor, political and
cultural organizations, following a tradition begun long before in
Europe, either purchased or built and turned into cooperative housing for their members. For example, the Amalgamated Houses at
Sedgwick Avenue and Mosholu Parkway, which opened in 1927,
were sponsored by Sidney Hillman's Amalgamated Clothing Workers Union. The "Commie Coops" were buildings at Bronx Park East
and Allerton Avenue collectively owned by Communist Party members until their sale in 1946.

Among the girls Clara Hancox named were the two Braslaw sisters, Nora and Anita, Faye Kalisher, Fagie [Florence] Aranow and
Helena Moore. As for the boys, "there was Noah, and Milton Zaslow
—his party name was Mike Bartel—Willie Leader, Henry Goldstein
and the two Izzies, Israel Kugler and his cousin Israel Horowitz,
and Rubin Baratz," Noah's boyhood friend who later became Clara
Hancox's first husband.[12]

"Izzie Kugler's partly right about the politics," Hancox added.
"Izzie himself stood out among our friends because he definitely
was a socialist and the rest of us were not. In fact, I called him Izzie-
the-socialist."

Clara Hancox herself was far more than merely one of the crowd.
"We were each other's first," she said, meaning no more than that
she was Noah's first girlfriend, Noah her first boyfriend.

"Where did I meet him? I met him in the house, in the apartment,
of one of the other people in our gang." The year was 1934. Noah
was 15, Clara was 16 and a junior at Evander Childs High School.

> I was a Zionist, a Labor Zionist. We were very politically con-
> scious, and he was . . . I don't know what his politics were when I
> met him. We immediately started going together. He taught me
> music." Clara's father was an amateur musician and a cantor. "And
> so when I met Noah, I was well brought up by my father in music.
> But not in Noah's music. Noah wanted Brahms. He 'inducted' me
> into César Frank's Symphony in D Minor, with its heavy orches-
> tration. Early music came much much later."

From the start, the pair breathed in with the soot of the streets the
radical politics that was the Depression birthright of Jewish kids in
New York.

---

[12]Clara Hancox and Rubin Baratz, May 19, 1997.

Noah and Clara Meyerson, 1934. "We were each other's first"
(Courtesy Clara Myerson Hancox)

Those were wild times, and I suppose in a way that I should be glad that I lived through all that, that Noah, that we all lived through that . . . the period of *intense* awareness and sensitivity with what's going on in the world and the sense that we were all in a sense responsible and Noah was very strongly like that. He was *never* a Zionist." Clara remembers "walking down the street in the neighborhood where I lived, because he used to visit there all the time, and arguing about this like learned grownup people."

He joined the most radical of the period's student political organizations, the American Student Union, dominated on most campuses by Stalinists rather than socialists. His inscription in his friend Lou Becker's yearbook read, "Long live the American Student Union!"[13] But the important thing for Noah at 15 and 16 was "class equality, all classes should be equal"—for a sensitive teenager, a perfect, if perfectly self-contradictory, political philosophy.[14]

The mid-1930s *were* wild times. Student demonstrations were commonplace. Irving Howe remembered one at De Witt Clinton High, led by a shaky coalition of communist and socialist student groups, "with several of us getting up on chairs [in the cafeteria] to shout rhythmically 'lower lunchroom prices.'[15] The demonstrators'

---

[13] Avel Austin and Lou Becker, December 1, 1997.
[14] Clara Hancox, May 12, 1997.
[15] Howe, *op. cit.*, p. 28.

ardor cooled to zero when the school principal, with a faint smile, told the demonstrators that the lunchroom was already operating at a loss, and if they wanted to take it over he would try to arrange it.

Sometimes, however, matters turned more serious. Near the end of March 1935, a coalition of parents' groups on the left of the political spectrum proposed to the New York City Board of Education that students be given time off between 11 a.m. and noon on April 12 for a demonstration "as a means of expressing publicly their belief in peace and international good will."[16] This was to be a high school version of the annual Student Strike Against War at City College. Predictably, the school authorities took a dim view of the idea. Noah's principal, Henry E. Hein, a redoubtable personality who headed James Monroe High School from its opening in 1925 through the 1940s, joined his four fellow members of a Student Activities Committee in pointing out the "numerous grave dangers that might result." On March 28, the Superintendent of Schools of the City of New York rejected any proposal whereby

> the pupils would be permitted to leave school . . . congregate in crowds around the school building, listen to addresses by persons not connected with the school system, and then return . . .

This would compromise "the safety of pupils while in the street." It would also raise "the possibility that [pupils] might be misled by speakers or agitators" and the likelihood of injury or property damage. Most dreadful of all, "we think that such a demonstration implants wrong ideas in the minds of pupils in respect to their relationship to the properly constituted lawful authorities."

"Hatred of militarism," wrote Irving Howe, "was a feeling shared by many students, including some who didn't think of themselves as radical."[17] A great many disregarded the ban and did cut classes to demonstrate in favor of "peace and international good will," and against Hitler's program of German rearmament, Mussolini's buildup of forces in Eritrea and, all causes ultimately being local, the establishment of ROTC units on high school campuses. No record of Noah's participation exists, but while he would argue politics with passion, he was almost certainly too young and too preoccupied with school, music and friends to put his ideals to the test.

When a similar demonstration was proposed in 1936, the Board of Superintendents went further, warning

---

[16] This account is largely drawn from the Minutes of the Board of Superintendents, Board of Education, City of New York for years 1935 and 1936.

[17] Howe, *Margin of Hope*, p. 29.

that pupils who deliberately disobey the orders of the educational authorities cannot expect to receive honors or to be admitted to the Arista or other honor societies. . . . Certainly, pupils who disobeyed instructions last year and disobey them again this year, after fair warning, cannot expect honors if the principal considers that the repeated offenses counterbalance their good academic work.

For parents and students to whom good school grades and honors programs were precious passports out of the slums, this was no idle threat. (It was somewhat weakened by the concession that violations of the ban would be dealt with on a case-by-case basis.) Again, although Noah's friends at De Witt Clinton High and City College were active demonstrators, Noah probably did not take part.

Clara Hancox laughed out loud at the suggestion that hers and Noah's romantic friendship consisted of debates on Marxian dialectic on the one hand and discussions of music on the other. "Noah was playful, just as I was. He loved language. He loved making up nicknames for people. Mine was 'Havoc,' because I was always jumping up and down and turning things upside down and laughing louder and singing louder than anybody else." She added: "Noah and I had things to say to each other. And so we wrote to each other." They wrote to one another for years after 1936, when they were no longer a couple and after Clara had gone off to put herself through the University of Iowa. "And our letters were very affectionate and full of fun and private jokes. Especially private jokes. And they were very funny and the kind of private jokes, the kind of doubletalk, that only Noah and I could do with each other." What the jokes were about, she would not say. But there was great affection also. When Clara turned 21 in 1939, Noah sent her a book of El Greco's paintings and drawings—she still owns it—inscribed simply "to Havoc, because she's 21."

Overlapping with the one set of Noah's friends, the radicals, was a smaller second set, the musicians. In this second group was the pianist Robert Levenstein and classical music devotees Barry Brook, Israel Horowitz, Noah himself and, when his time and duties allowed, Harold Brown. All became professionally involved in music.[18] The members of both circles knew one another—indeed, in

---

[18] Robert Levenstein, Barry Brook and Harold Brown all became music educators. Levenstein, like Brown, taught music in the city high schools. Brook took degrees at City College of New York and Columbia, taught for many years at Queens College, received his doctorate in musicology from the Sorbonne (Paris) in 1959 and gained international distinction as a musicologist. Israel Horowitz became (*cont.*)

time Helena Moore would become Robert Levenstein's wife — and Clara, as Noah's girlfriend and musical initiate, moved freely in both. But as both Barry Brook and Robert Levenstein testify, Noah seldom mixed politics with music. "We met in October, 1934." Levenstein recalls,

> He was then 15, in his last year [sic] of high school and I was 20, in my last year of City College, so there was always that age difference. We met at the close of a piano recital by James Friskin of the Juilliard School faculty, who played the entire Book II of Bach's Well-Tempered Clavichord. We shared each other's reactions to his playing and I compared his detached and didactic style to that of Harold Samuel, who in my estimation was the greatest Bach performer in the world, because of his lively approach to the music. . . . We then discussed symphonic music, orchestras and conductors and as I recall were always in complete agreement. Noah's idol was Brahms.

Elsewhere in the same letter, Levenstein commented: "It was as if music was [Noah's] whole life (aside from his political beliefs, which we never discussed.)"[19]

Kate Simon remembered what poor Bronx kids did in the 1930s (and later) to hear live music. Of one of her beaux,

> [i]t was Joe who managed to get to the Lewisohn Stadium early enough to buy the twenty-five-cent concert seats, and it was Joe who knew friendly Carnegie Hall ushers who let us climb, for fifty cents, often for nothing, to seats in the top balconies.[20]

Noah and his musical friends employed the same simple strategems. At Carnegie Hall, according to Barry Brook, "one person would approach an usher who would let him in for maybe a quarter. Then that person would gather ticket stubs off the floor of the balcony and at intermission go out and pass them out and let the rest of us in." On Saturdays, Brook said, "Noah and Bob Levenstein and I would go down to the 58th Street Public Library, which is where they had the records in those days, and we'd get there early and reserve a listening booth and stay there all day listening to records."[21] Levenstein recalls one Lewisohn Stadium con-

---

Artist & Repertory Director of Decca Classical Records, in which post he arranged Pro Musica's Decca contracts and supervised the recordings.

[19] Robert Levenstein, letter to the author, April 20, 1997. In October, 1934, however, Noah Greenberg was in his third year of high school, not his last year.

[20] Simon, op. cit., p. 27.

[21] Barry Brook, December 21, 1996.[22]Levenstein, letter, April 20, 1997.

cert after which "Noah was not shy of approaching José Iturbi to show him a favorite score he had borrowed from the music library.[22]

"Picking up ticket stubs? That's what we did on my 16th birthday," Clara Hancox says. "Noah took me, we had fifty-cent SRO tickets to Carnegie Hall, the Bach B Minor Mass, and we sat on the floor. At intermission, he went down and picked up stubs from people who had orchestra seats and we heard the rest of the B Minor in all that red velvet. And we had dinner afterward. At Nedicks." Nedicks, for readers unversed in New York City folkways, was a chain of eateries (no plates, just waxed paper, and no stools) that makes today's Burger Kings and Kentucky Fried Chickens seem like the Oak Room at the Plaza. But for fifteen cents at Nedicks you could get a hot dog with sauerkraut and mustard and an orange drink as pale as a winter sunrise. And Noah was not above distracting the counterman's attention—"Hey, there's no mustard in this jar!"—to make him forget to collect the fifteen cents.

It was in 1935 or 1936 that Noah entered a citywide classical music contest sponsored by R. H. Macy & Co. Contestants had to identify some classical recordings played on loudspeakers in the vast Macy's Herald Square store, by composer, orchestra, conductor and soloist. Noah came, listened, filled out two entry blanks—one for himself, one for Clara—and won both first and second prizes. The prizes added up to an armload of record albums, many of them Noah's favorite Brahms symphonies. "He gave them to me," Clara recalls, "and after sixty-something years I still have them."[23]

In time, as Israel Kugler noted, "[t]he political ferment pressed many young socialists like Noah and myself further to the left and we became part of the Trotskyist movement."[24] For an entire decade, Noah would indeed base his actions on his answers to the biggest social questions. But his first act as a 17-year-old high school graduate displayed no such broad-based ambitiousness.

In the spring of 1936, Harold Brown's marriage was breaking up, and Harold found himself with time on his hands and room to spare in his Manhattan apartment. "When you finish school," he said to Noah, "come share the place with me." Sometime after graduation, Noah left Clay Street and the Bronx. Well supplied by his mother with linens and dishes, he moved in with Harold Brown.[25]

[22]Levenstein, letter, April 20, 1997.
[23]Rubin Baratz, June 11, 1997; Clara Hancox, September 6, 1997.
[24]Israel Kugler, letter to Mark Davenport.
[25]Edith Schor, March 7, 1997.

Noah Greenberg, teenage philosopher
(Courtesy Greenberg family)

CHAPTER FOUR

JOINING THE MOVEMENT

(1937-1939)

They made an odd pair, Noah the big, cheerful, outgoing 17-year-old and Harold, the brooding old-young man ten years his senior. But in fact the arrangement between them was not so unusual. In Depression-era New York, a roof over one's head was a blessing to be treasured. Virtually the only way a high school graduate could afford to move out of a parental home as often as not crowded with grandparents, aunts, uncles and siblings was to find someone older willing to share an apartment. Conversely, a young person lucky enough to be "living out" in a place of one's own — even in one room plus bathroom and kitchen privileges in somebody else's apartment — was an object of envy. "Sometimes we were in luck," wrote Irving Howe of the Saturday nights of his radical youth, "a comrade had access to an apartment, that precious rarity in New York, and we hurried over for the pleasures of retreat and privacy."[1]

On this first occasion, the arrangement seems to have lasted for over a year. By the spring or early summer of 1938, Noah was again living in the Bronx. But he and Harold would join forces again in 1939, and the apartment-sharing went on well into the war years.

Evictions were common during the Depression, but Manhattan landlords, hard-pressed themselves, were also granting new tenants concessions of up to several months' rent. The net effect was that New Yorkers, especially the younger and poorer, tended to change residences fairly often. As a substitute high school teacher, Harold Brown earned something like thirty dollars a week. In 1936, this amount was more than enough for two people to live on, but the

[1] Howe, *op. cit.*, p. 43.

work and the pay were intermittent, which may have been why Harold and Noah had to leave Harold's apartment on West 70th Street. (One friend[2] distinctly remembers that they were "kicked out," but whether for nonpayment of rent, making too much noise, or some other reason is uncertain.) Later, the two would live on Riverside Drive and still later at 210 West 19th Street before taking up residence under very different circumstances on East 13th and 14th Streets.

No one, not even close friends of both men, recalls the specifics, but it seems likely that Noah, in exchange for room, board and the opportunity to study intensively with Harold, would, like a European apprentice, take on essential household chores—always within the parameters of what a couple of young bachelors with much else on their minds would consider "essential." It may also be that we can date from this period one of Noah's lifelong passions, cookery.

What else Noah was doing to keep body and soul together is not known. Several years later, according to Jesse Simons, Noah was working on a P.W.A. (Public Works Adminstration) youth project on Staten Island. If he had found similar work earlier, he might have been bringing in thirty cents an hour, $14.40 for a forty-eight-hour week, to be pooled with Harold's thirty dollars. Noah was industrious, and he probably held some sort of job, but what it was and what it earned him is a mystery.

Far more important, of course, is what went on between Noah and Harold in music.

Although Arnold Zemachson played a part in the process, Harold Brown is widely and rightly credited for kindling Noah Greenberg's interest in early music. Noah himself was always quick to acknowledge the indebtedness. But this awakening came about in the context of a much broader exposure to the older man's musical tastes, practices, and philosophy. For Harold was a musical polymath. An accomplished string player (a violist with the Baltimore Symphony Orchestra during the 1940s and later with the New York City Ballet Orchestra), he knew at first hand the endless hours of practice and physical effort required to gain even passable skill as a performer. This knowledge strongly shaped his own views—and Noah's views—of both the price and the value of virtuosity. More important, Harold Brown was a near-contemporary with a promising future as a composer. In 1930, at age 21, he had been Columbia University's Mosenthal Fellow in Music Composition. In 1931, he

[2] Edith Schor, March 7, 1997.

was in Paris, attending Nadia Boulanger's famed *Ecole normale de musique* classes in musical analysis. Among his American classmates were two future notables, film composer Bernard Hermann and composer-critic Elie Siegmeister. In Brown's resumé, his chamber music is undated, but by 1936, when Noah moved in, he was at work on his Symphony No. 1 and on a suite for string orchestra.

Noah, who had already tried his young hand at composition, was now introduced at a far more professional level to the practical/ political side of the composer's trade. That is, having given birth to musical ideas and found the right vocal or instrumental form in which to express them, the composer must get them down on paper and then must somehow, in the midst of bad times—and for most serious American composers, the bad times are never-ending —persuade an orchestra, an opera company or some other musical entity to pay him for the right to perform them.

For Harold, this was never easy. There would be some early successes. In 1941, for example, Howard Hanson had his Eastman School of Music Symphony read through and record the Introduction and Allegro of the Symphony No. 1. But the recording was never released. As time wore on, Harold would find it harder and harder to attract the attention of the musical establishment. But at the outset of Noah's apprenticeship, neither Noah nor Harold himself was unduly concerned about future success or failure. What mattered was music itself.

Perhaps the most important factor of all in Noah's musical education is that Harold Brown, beyond being both performer and composer, was a thinker. Prowling far and wide through music history in search of a philosophy of music, Harold found what he sought. Its principles were simple, and in Harold's strange mind they took on the quality of dogma. Thus, beauty and meaning in music are functions of musical structure. In both composition and performance, structure itself must always be evident and is perhaps best discovered in vocal music. Energy and forward movement are vital. Accenting weak beats and upbeats and phrasing across the bar line are the ways to impart energy to music. Instrumental technique should aim at fluidity and plasticity of execution. But most conservatory teaching, which values virtuosity above all else, is suspect. Success especially is suspect. The "star system" that showered the most publicity and the most lucrative engagements on virtuosi who had worked up flashy performances of a few warhorses was deeply corrupting, a betrayal of what music should be.

"Harold was an educated musician," said one friend of Noah's who knew Harold well, "but he was also a self-educated one who held strong opinions about everything.

> Harold had all sorts of views on Mozart, his deficiencies. The trouble with Mozart was that he could never have an orgasm! What he meant was really that [Mozart] didn't follow through, and he used as an example the G-minor Quintet, with its tragic beginning and then its last movement was very cheery. This is just an example of how opinionated [Harold was].[3]

Behind this absurdity lay Harold's conviction, far from absurd, that virtuosity and fecundity in composition do often go hand in hand with blandness, academicism and fear of giving offense. (Significantly, Harold himself found composition slow and difficult.) Then, too, in large-scale Romantic works, structural weaknesses are very often covered up by ornate orchestration, a process that violates the very nature of music. (So much for Noah's beloved Brahms, so much for Tchaikowsky, whom Brown would later nickname "Lowsky," and Rimsky-Korsakoff.) As for opera, nothing later than Mozart—or perhaps Gluck—is admissible.

Harold's less-is-more esthetic, and his music as well, owe a good deal to the composers Nadia Boulanger admired, in particular Fauré, and to Auric and Poulenc of *les Six*. But it is informed as well by the barebones thinking of modernists in other fields. ("Poetry," said Ezra Pound, another hater of Romanticism, "should be at least as well-written [meaning as undecorated] as prose." And of course in architecture there was Le Corbusier's "A house is a machine for living in" and in painting the seeming simplifications of Stuart Davis and Piet Mondrian.) Especially in its more disdainful judgments, the Brown esthetic also owes far too much to the arrogance and iconoclasm of youth and to Harold's chronic dissatisfaction with life. Its saving grace is that in the search for examples to lend substance to his philosophy, Harold went back in time to music that nobody else was thinking about. Back beyond Bach and Handel to sung polyphony in which structure is indeed all-important. To monophonic chant, in the sonorities of which classical conventions of rhythm and tempo are dissolved. To music for instruments like the lute, the viols and the recorders that only a few eccentrics in England and Germany could build and play (or try to play).

For Harold as for Noah, it was a learning process. Night after night and on weekends, Noah listened as Harold, cigarette in hand,

[3] Rickie Flanders, March 15, 1997.

expounded on the virtues of Tallis and Buxtehude. Together, they pored over editions of Heinrich Schütz and Melchior Frank and a dozen other early Baroque composers "liberated" by Noah from the 58th Street Music Library. They puzzled out Gregorian neumes and tried to imagine what the masses of Isaac, Ockeghem, Josquin, and Orlando Lasso would sound like if singers could be found to sing them. They would have to be good singers, Harold felt — not necessarily great voices or even professionals, but musically literate people who could follow a part, keep time, listen and heed the director.

By the fall of 1937, most of Noah's musical companions other than Harold had scattered. Barry Brook was in his sophomore year at City College. Bob Levenstein had just taken a temporary job and had also signed up for a Master's degree in music education. "As I recall, [Noah] was disappointed because I would be working at a job unrelated to music. (Heresy!)"[4] Clara Meyerson and Rubin Baratz had left New York for Iowa City, the University of Iowa, and marriage to each other. Nevertheless, Harold and Noah may already have been recruiting new blood for the first of several informal singing groups the two would assemble over the next twelve years.

One of their early recruits was an acquaintance of Harold's and later of Noah's, a young pianist named Lucy Cogan.

> My sister had gotten to know [Harold] through a friend at Michigan. Harold came to a party that my sister gave, a small party, and Harold came and that's how I met him. Later, Harold came to our house and I had a copy of the Beethoven Violin Concerto . . . [an] orchestral reduction for the piano. And Harold played the violin and I played the piano. I was sixteen or seventeen. Sixteen.[5]

In the spring or early summer of 1938, Noah struck up a conversation with a fellow-passenger on the Bronx-bound Broadway subway. "I was living on Pelham Parkway," Edward Riesenfeld recalled, "and I think Noah was living around Allerton Avenue, the next stop."

> We got to talking and it turned out that we had a good deal in common, Schubert *lieder*. . . . I had just graduated from City College, and I was studying voice with a private teacher and was interested in Schubert and English folksongs, and naturally so was Noah. So we became friendly.[6]

---

[4] Levenstein, letter.
[5] Lucy Dames, March 17, 1997; September 17, 1997.
[6] Edward Riesenfeld, September 17, 1997.

Lucy Cogan remembers with amusement her first encounter with Noah. Noah had come calling with Harold on her older sister, Claudia.

> He brought Eddie [Riesenfeld] along for my sister's younger sister [that is, for Lucy herself]. And Eddie had a book of Gerard Manley Hopkins which he read to me all evening long. But then Eddie was a singer—he had a lovely voice, but unfortunately he didn't have a good sense of rhythm—but we both belonged to the chorus that Noah and Harold ran.[7]

Harold, as noted, believed deeply, and taught Noah, that there was much to learn from going back to the very roots of Western music. The two of them must have persuaded Eddie Riesenfeld, because in the fall of 1938 all three took the course in Gregorian chant offered by Mother Margaret Stevens, R.S.C.M., at the Pius X School of Liturgical Music of the Convent of the Sacred Heart on Convent Avenue near City College.[8]

There may well have been informal evenings of singing and musical talk throughout 1938 and 1939. But the "chorus" of which Lucy Cogan spoke began meeting only in 1940. And before its first meeting, momentous events had taken place in Noah's life.

*   *   *

Ten years earlier, in the fall of 1928, a New Yorker named Max Shachtman was reaching a fateful decision. At 24, Shachtman had been in the underground Communist movement since his student days at De Witt Clinton High School in the Bronx and a national leader of the U. S. Communist Party, which had been legalized in 1922, for three years.[9] In his hands now was a copy of a document so explosive that James P. Cannon, Shachtman's close colleague, had had to smuggle it out of the Soviet Union. The document was Leon Trotsky's *A Criticism of the Draft Program of the Comintern*. Circulated at the Sixth Congress of the Communist International, it bluntly asserted that the Stalinization of the Russian Communist Party was crippling Communism everywhere. At issue was whether absolutism or some looser form of leadership (under Trotsky's aegis) would best further world revolution. Cannon, Shachtman, and a third col-

---

[7] Lucy Dames, March 17, 1997; September 17, 1997.

[8] Edward Riesenfeld, September 17, 1997; Jesse Simons, "Noah Greenberg Recalled," unpublished memoir derived from Mark Davenport interview.

[9] This account of the beginnings of Shachtmanite socialism is largely drawn from Albert Glotzer and Marguerite Glotzer, "Max Shachtman—A Political-Biographical Essay," in *Bulletin of the Tamiment Institute/Ben Josephson Library*, 50: April 1983, pp. 3-8.

league, Martin Abern, were convinced that Trotsky was right. But Stalin controlled the Comintern apparatus. He moved swiftly to expel Trotsky from the party and send him into exile. By Thanksgiving Day of 1928, the three Americans had been dismissed from the Central Committee of the U. S. party and expelled from the party itself, along with dozens of other active members.[10]

A few months later, Abern, Cannon, Shachtman and other expellees started the Communist League of America and with it the American Trotskyist movement. For the next ten years, Max Shachtman was one of the leading Trotskyists in this country, sounding a steady and courageous alarm in the teeth of many of his erstwhile colleagues against the evils of Stalin and Stalinism.[11]

The conventional portrait of the professional revolutionary is that of the zealot—dedicated, cold, humorless—like Gletkin in Koestler's *Darkness at Noon*. Max Shachtman was the living denial of the stereotype. He was cultivated, a bibliomane like Trotsky himself, witty, lightning-fast on his feet and devastating in debate.

Irving Howe, for many years one of "Max's boys," said of Shachtman that "[h]is was a face you'd expect to find in a bazaar or a diamond center: swarthy, expressive, shrewd."[12]

Albert Glotzer, a lifelong socialist and a historian of the movement, was another Shachtman intimate.

> [His] friends remember him as a colorful, energetic gregarious man, always ready to enjoy an off-color joke or to prolong a one-liner to the breaking point while savoring the drama of his Yiddish accent.[13]

Above all, Max Shachtman loved kids. He had begun his Communist career as editor of a paper called *The Young Worker*. He knew how to talk to youngsters—with wit and humor, skipping the revolutionary sloganeering—how to listen and how to harness youthful energy and idealism. Young himself when Trotskyism got its start, he wanted the Trotskyist movement in America to be a youth movement. As the "low dishonest decade" of the 1930s neared its end, he turned Trotskyism almost into a Children's Crusade. And what children! Among those who became followers of Max Shachtman in 1938 and 1939 and, under his tutelage, members of the Socialist

---

[10] *Ibid.*, p. 3.
[11] *Ibid.*, p. 5.
[12] Howe, *op. cit.*, p. 40.
[13] Glotzer, *op. cit.*, p. 7.

Workers Party, were the novelists Harvey Swados and James T. Farrell, the critics Irving Howe and Dwight Macdonald (an old man of 30), the writer, editor and future deep-dyed conservative Irving Kristol, the historian and future deep-dyed conservative Gertrude Himmelfarb (Kristol's future wife), a budding social scientist named Daniel Bell—and the 19-year-old Noah Greenberg and a round half-dozen of his friends: Lucy Cogan, Eddie Riesenfeld, Harold Brown, Israel Kugler, Israel Horowitz, Milton Zaslow and, back from the midwest, Clara and Rubin Baratz. Ideologically, it was not a big step. In practical terms, it was the difference between high-school speechifying and the gritty work of taking a special brand of radical politics into the streets of New York.

Nobody quite remembers when and how Noah joined the Socialist Workers Party. He might have signed up at Doremus Hall on the City College campus, on the memorable night in 1937 when Max Shachtman faced off against the Stalinist Morris Schappes. The two were debating the Moscow trials,[14] and in Israel Kugler's phrase, Shachtman "wiped the floor with him, and what a victory that was for democratic socialism."[15] Equally, it might have happened in 1938 at a "mass meeting" ("A hundred and fifty people," scoffs one SWP veteran, looking back more than half a century, "that's what we called a 'mass meeting.'") where Max Shachtman beguiled the crowd with his mixture of crazily comic stories and hard-hitting anti-Stalinist rhetoric. Whenever it happened, one lover of language and art and ideas fell instantly under the spell of another. "Noah loved Max because he was so funny and so quick," Jesse Simons said, "and Max loved Noah, this big, smiling, friendly kid. Whenever he saw him, he'd come up and pinch his cheek. And tease him about his music."

If several of Noah's old friends preceded him or gravitated with him into the Socialist Workers Party, the SWP in turn brought him new friends. Many of these were true "politicals," young men and women who had made up their minds to work full-time for "the movement," the generic term for the oncoming socialist revolution. In a kind of ritual of baptism (and to protect themselves against reprisals from employers and the authorities), these professionals of-

[14] The infamous "show trials," characterized by extorted confessions and fabricated evidence, set up by Stalin and Beria to purge the Party of Old Bolshevik rivals like Bukharin, Radek, Kaminev and Zinovieff. "On February 5,1988, the Soviet foreign ministry announced that the evidence in the 1938 trials had been 'gathered illegally' and 'the facts had been falsified.'" David Remnick, *Lenin's Tomb*, New York, p. 68.

[15] Israel Kugler, remarks, in "The Legacy of the Workers Party, 1940-1949," p. 19.

ten operated under "party names." Thus, Shachtman himself was "Trent." Herman Benson was known in the SWP and afterward as "Ben Hall." Albert Glotzer was "Gates." The brilliant Ernest Rice McKinney was "Courtney." Emanuel Geltman was "Manny Garrett." Among Noah's high school friends, Iz Kugler became "Charlie Stewart" and Milton Zaslow turned himself into "Mike Bartel." There would come a time when Noah too would choose to employ a party name.

Shachtman's followers were by no means enlistees in an all-male battalion. "Our socialist girls were vivid, bright, sometimes beautiful," Irving Howe recalled.[16] In turn, the girls liked Howe, although not without a touch of mockery. "He was always sitting there twisting a lock of his hair in his fingers," one of them said. "Then he acquired a girlfriend, and he'd come to meetings and sit there and twist a lock of *her* hair."[17] Of the women in the movement, Howe found most admirable

> a group of students who were seriously interested in politics and culture, intent upon battling for place and definition, and trying also to be sexually attractive in the styles mandated, more or less, by American society.[18]

Lucy Cogan and Clara Baratz certainly fell into this category. So also did several other young — extremely young — women. One was Blanche Weiss. Blanche, 16 in 1938, was so dedicated a radical that at age eight she had interrupted the speaker at a street-corner meeting with a pointing finger and a shrill cry of "That's a lie!" Some listeners, amused, called out "Let the kid talk!" and Blanche did. She "spewed out a whole string of the ideas I'd heard from my father," a Communist deeply learned in the lore of the worldwide socialist movement.[19] After digesting a huge pile of leftist tracts, including Lenin's "What Is To Be Done?," Blanche at 14 had applied for membership in the Tremont Avenue branch of the Young Communist League. But when she came to realize that most other YCL members were ignoramuses and that Party functionaries from "downtown" had no interest in allowing free discussion of anything, she resigned in disgust. The Trotskyists, Blanche thought, might be a little less rigid. But Max Shachtman himself had to swear to her, when she stormed up to the podium at her first Socialist Workers

[16] Howe, *op. cit.*, p. 26.
[17] Rickie Flanders, March 15, 1997.
[18] Howe, *op. cit.*, p. 44.
[19] Blanche Weiss Saia, January 28, 1999.

Party meeting, that the young dissenters seated next to her would be allowed to speak.

Aside from radical politics, the only other thing Blanche loved was music. The upright piano her mother bought her cost sixty dollars, "more than a month's pay." Her first lessons came from Ray Lev at the Third Street Music Settlement, where the charge per lesson was fifty cents. Blanche studied later at Cristadora House on Eighth Street. She and her friends saved their nickels and dimes for months to buy a good phonograph, "with cactus needles," and then scrimped to buy records for the weekly musical sessions she held at her mother's Bronx apartment.

At a SWP gathering, Blanche and Noah discovered their common passion for early music. "Noah would say, 'You like Palestrina? Well, I do too. You like so-and-so? Well, I do too.' It was as if we were competing against each other to be the only ones." Soon Noah was showing up at Blanche's musical evenings.

> One night he appeared with a pile of musical parts and began passing them out. My friends were saying, 'I don't read music,' I can't sight-sing,' and Noah said, 'Sure you can, it's easy," and he just pushed everybody into the music.[20]

Noah was friends with two other young women in the movement well worthy of Irving Howe's admiration. One was a slim, articulate and stunningly attractive brunette, a friend of Howe's, named Rochelle Kimmel but always called Rickie. The other was a tall, blue-eyed blonde, as attractive but with a quieter, more languid manner, Edith Schor. In 1938, both were only 15, but both were deeply committed to the movement. "Irving Kristol [at that time a Yipsel[21]] used to carry my books home from school," Rickie recalled with some amusement. "It was in Brooklyn. I went to Erasmus [Hall High School], he was in college. I was the youngest. In those days I was the baby of the bunch."[22]

Edith Schor lived in the Washington Heights section of Manhattan. Her political formation began early and rather casually. Like Clara Meyerson, she started off as a Labor Zionist. But "I was sitting in school one day, tenth grade, and I saw that the girl next to

---

[20] *Ibid.*

[21] A Yipsel, or YIPSL, was a member of the Young Peoples' Independent Socialist League. Kristol was recruited as a YIPSL by Irving Howe.

[22] Rickie Flanders, March 15, 1997. For that matter, Kristol's future wife, Gertrude Himmelfarb, was recruited by another youthful Workers Party member, Phyllis Jacobson.

me was writing a letter, and she was writing to 'Dear Comrade.' I said, '"Dear Comrade." Are you a socialist?' She said she was, and I said, 'Well, I'm a socialist too!'"

For socialists as for everyone else, the world truly was a darkening place as 1938 gave way to 1939. On September 29, Britain's Prime Minister Neville Chamberlain, meeting in Munich with Adolf Hitler, had conceded Germany's right to dismember Czechoslovakia and proclaimed that he had thus attained "peace with honor." In October, Hitler's armies had marched into the Sudetenland. On November 11—Armistice Day, in one of the grimmer ironies of history—word began to trickle out of Germany of the ghastly assault the night before on German Jews and their property, the assault known as *Kristallnacht*, the Night of Broken Glass. But so strong was the antipathy to war that the rest of the world looked on appalled and did nothing. For socialists in this country, indeed, there was nothing to do except try to alleviate the plight of those fleeing Europe. Rickie Kimmel, looking back over her shoulder at those times, put the position succinctly and eloquently:

> We accepted Trotsky's analysis of [a Second World War as] 'the death agony of capitalism.' We accepted the notion — when we called ourselves 'third campers' we certainly weren't in favor of the victory of Hitler. We wanted his defeat. We wanted the defeat of both imperialist camps at the hands of the working class. That in short was our position. And that is what I think we thought was going to happen in the course of the war.[23]

As war neared, the duty of the young Trotskyist was—simply— to preach socialism to all who would listen. Jesse Simons, whose party name was "Buddy," makes quite clear what this entailed:

> A common misunderstanding is that participation in a revolutionary political party is exciting, if not exhilarating. This is far from the truth. For those like Noah who did not work full time for the movement, most of what we did was mundane, repetitious and often boring. We gave out leaflets, spoke on street corners, attended or led classes on socialist theory, saw "contacts" (interested people) in the evening in an effort to recruit them, attended meetings at least once a week, and read lengthy mimeoed papers on internal disputes. Many of us contributed about 20% of our weekly wages.[24]

Still, the members of the Shachtman youth movement had energy left over for play. Irving Howe describes midnight walks filled with

---

[23] Rickie [Kimmel] Flanders, remarks, in "The Legacy of the Workers Party," p. 7.
[24] Jesse Simons, *op. cit.*, p. 9.

dispute and laughter following SWP branch meetings in the Bronx.[25] Whenever they could afford it, Noah and a gang of his friends from the movement would troop uptown from a SWP meeting to the fleabag movie houses on Times Square where foreign films were played. Noah loved foreign movies. In fact, he loved all movies, especially those with lots of slapstick action. Marx Brothers comedies were among his favorites.

There was also, as always in Noah's life, time and energy for music. And love.

Sometime during 1939, Noah moved back into an apartment with Harold Brown. In January, Harold had conducted a performance of his "Two Experiments for Flute Clarinet & Bassoon." Later that year, the year of war, he began work on "Choral Setting No. 1 for Women's Voices," a setting of Gerard Manley Hopkins's griefstricken "No Worst, No Worst, There is None." Eddie Riesenfeld, a Hopkins devotee, may have led him to the text. And Eddie, Lucy Cogan, Rickie Kimmel, Henry Goldstein, Rubin and Clara Baratz, Phyllis and Julius Jacobson, Blanche Weiss and others began to meet informally at the apartment—Edith Schor remembers it as being on Riverside Drive— to sing. Their musical material included Gregorian chants, Elizabethan madrigals and rounds, and by a happy coincidence a wealth of such music had just come to hand. With money from the W.P.A. Federal Music Project, the young composer-arranger Lehman Engel had put together an 18-voice mixed chorus, the Madrigal Singers. To supply this group with music for its concerts, Engel compiled a four-volume anthology, *Three Centuries of Choral Music: Renaissance to Baroque*. It was published in 1939, and Harold and Noah made good use of it in their get-togethers, following Engel's exhortation in his introduction to Volume I, *French-Netherland Music*. "Here," Engel said, "are four meager volumes with selections from the thousands of impractical, inaccessible tomes. Use them!"[26]

It was not music, however, that first brought Noah and Edith Schor together. Rather, it was politics.

[25] Howe, *op. cit.*, p. 48.

[26] Lehman Engel [ed.], *Three Centuries of Choral Music: Renaissance to Baroque*, "Preface to the Series," [in Vol. 1 (French-Netherland Music)], p. 3. The succeeding volumes cover Italian, German, and English music.

CHAPTER FIVE

MARRIAGE AND WORLD WAR

(1940-1942)

*I*n mid-March, 1939, Adolf Hitler sent his armies unopposed into Czechoslovakia and turned his attention to Poland. It became clear that the only hope for European peace was an alliance between Britain and France in the west and the Soviet Union in the east. The British and French tried halfheartedly over the summer to pursue such an alliance in Moscow. But on August 22 came the electrifying news that Hitler and Stalin, Nazi Germany and Communist Russia, had signed a nonaggression treaty. On September 1, Hitler invaded Poland and Europe was at war.

The Hitler-Stalin pact split the Socialist Workers Party wide open. For the Shachtmanites, the pact was vindication, confirmation of their long-held views of Stalin as a monster of deceit and treachery. Some members, anti-Stalinist but believers in Soviet Communism, held that Stalin's act was wise, that it would keep the Soviet Union out of a war in which the imperialist powers would destroy one another. Others saw in the agreement a ruse designed to buy time for the Soviet Union to re-arm.

The Soviet military thrust into Poland on September 19, and the takeover of Latvia, Lithuania and Estonia, further fanned the flames of dispute. In October, the Soviet Union opened "consultations" with Finland. The Soviets urgently wanted the Russo-Finnish frontier, 24 miles east of Leningrad, moved back to about 50 miles east. The Finns refused, and on December 1, the Soviet army attacked "a neighbor so infinitesimally small," in President Roosevelt's words, "that it could do no possible harm to the Soviet Union."[1] Again,

---

[1] Franklin D. Roosevelt, comments to the American Youth Congress, February, 1940; quoted in Charles E. Bohlen, *Witness to History*, p. 95.

Stalinists and Russophile socialists put forward a reason: the Soviets were merely seeking to defend themselves. If Germany signed a treaty with Finland, the existing border was an ideal launching-pad for an attack on Russia. Besides, the peaceloving Soviets had offered land and friendship in exchange for the border relocation. Invasion was only a last resort.

Max Shachtman's youngsters found themselves at odds with their closest friends over the pact and its consequences. Said Rubin Baratz: "I can remember an argument we had with Miltie [Milton Zaslow] on the Grand Concourse, with Noah and Miltie and I, in which Noah and I began arguing with Miltie that Stalin shouldn't have done it and Miltie was arguing that he should have done it."[2]

Behind the debates loomed an ominous question. Did these happenings mean that Soviet Russia, the motherland of the proletarian revolution, had now degenerated into nothing more than another imperialist state? This became known as "the Russian Question." At length, Leon Trotsky, in Mexico City, issued a statement of his views. Soviet behavior in Poland, the Baltic countries and Finland was deplorable and probably unjustified. But socialists had an obligation to defend the Soviet Union. Although "degenerated," it was still a true workers' state.

The doctrinal hairsplitting that followed need not concern us here. What does matter is that early in 1940 Max Shachtman broke with Trotsky over Soviet militarism and the Russian Question and marched his supporters out of the Socialist Workers Party and into the cold. What could socialism achieve without its strong all-enduring mother? "In our rickety little boat," Irving Howe wrote, "we had launched ourselves onto the dangerous waters of the problematic."[3]

By Howe's count, the members of Shachtman's splinter group, which dubbed itself the Workers' Party, "no doubt because we had so few workers among us," numbered "perhaps a thousand."[4] By 1943, Albert Glotzer estimated, membership was down to "three to four hundred people."[5] It was indeed a rickety little boat. But throughout the brief life of the Workers' Party,[6] two of its most ardent members were Edith Schor and Noah Greenberg.

[2] Clara Hancox and Rubin Baratz, May 19, 1997
[3] Howe, *Maargin of Hope*, p.80.
[4] *Loc. cit.*
[5] Albert Glotzer, *op. cit.*, p. 11.
[6] The Workers Party was formally organized in 1940. It was disbanded in 1948.

"I was a Trotskyist because my sister was a Trotskyist," Edith said at first of her 16-year-old self, adding later, "I joined because I was born to it. We were all born to it. It was our church and we didn't question it. I worked for it. I passed out leaflets. I went to meetings." Comrade Edith Schor stood five feet ten and a half inches in her stocking feet. She hated her tall self. "Who would dance with me? When I was fourteen, fifteen, I would cry myself to sleep every night." Then, at one of the mass meetings, Noah appeared. "He came over and started talking and grabbed hold. He was huge. I had to look up at him." She tilted her head back and smiled, a beautiful woman of 74 remembering an awkward, unconfident, and ravishingly beautiful girl of 16. "And I was overwhelmed. *Somebody wanted me!*"

Pairing up with Noah Greenberg had its dangers. "He had no limits. His mother lost a second child . . . so no more children, and she lived for Noah, and so [did] his father. And it's not so much that nothing was denied him, it's that he never knew any limits. Literally, he didn't know there should *be* limits." He told her stories of his "checkered past." "By the time he was 13 he was drunk in the park and one of the neighbors saw him and brought him home. He was having an affair with his girlfriend when he was 13."

But Noah's exuberance and love of music more than made up for his shortcomings. "I had just fallen in love with music. The *New York Post* used to give away free classical records, and I remember my first love was Mozart's 40th, and I used to go around singing Brahms's First. And then I met Noah Greenberg."

By the end of 1939, Edith and Noah were attending SWP meetings and socials together and Edith was a regular with other members of the movement at the weekly meetings of Noah's and Harold Brown's singing group. Early in 1940, against a backdrop of war and in the midst of the formation of Max Shachtman's new Workers Party, 17-year-old Edith Schor and 21-year-old Noah Greenberg decided to get married. Edith's family was far from approving. Noah's behavior in the role of fiancé left a good deal to be desired. One evening,

> we came back to my parents' house [for dinner] and went to the local bar and [Noah] practically passed out. And I took him up and he fell asleep on the sofa in my parents' living room, and the only reason [my mother and father] didn't slit my throat was that the wedding day was set."

Edith herself suffered last-minute qualms. "Even at 17, I suddenly realized that I shouldn't. . . . If only my mother had stuck to her guns."

Nevertheless, on June 21, 1940 (the same day that Hitler dictated the terms of armistice to the defeated French at Compiègne), the ceremony took place. The young couple went off to the apartment at 210 West 19th Street that Noah was sharing with Harold Brown. "It had a doorman," Edith said. "I was so impressed."[7]

Before long, the doorman was a thing of the past.

Harold had gone for the summer, to study with Aaron Copland at Tanglewood, and the newlyweds had the apartment to themselves. But they quickly realized that even on Edith's salary they couldn't pay their half of the sixty- dollar monthly rent and still eat, so they invited another couple, the Diamonds, to take over Harold's bed in the living room as paying guests. Nobody, least of all Harold, quite understood who was supposed to pay what and sleep where, and in any case the young Greenbergs wanted a place of their own. In August, they moved to an apartment on East 13th Street between Second and Third Avenues. It was small, but in a good location. Workers Party headquarters, "a ratty little red-brick building," was only a few blocks away.[8] Many friends from the movement lived nearby. Noah's and Harold's choral sessions continued at the new location and another newly-married Workers Party couple moved right across the street.

Jesse "Buddy" Simons was born in New Haven in 1918. "While I was in high school I became a Trotskyist in 1930.[9] Between 1930 and 1938, I helped organize the unemployed in New Haven, lived in Canada and operated a linotype machine to print a revolutionary newspaper."[10] In 1938, thoroughly seasoned in radical politics, Jesse came to New York, found work on various WPA construction projects and joined the Shachtmanite wing of the Socialist Workers Party. One of the people he met was Rickie Kimmel. "She was irresistible," Jesse said simply. "We got married."

Jesse and Noah met on the day Rickie and Jesse moved into their apartment. "We couldn't open a window and Rickie telephoned

[7] Edith Schor, March 7, 1997.

[8] Howe, *op. cit.,* p. 42.

[9] This would have made Jesse Simons a revolutionary in seventh grade, at age 12! But Jesse reproaches himself for some vagueness about dates in both interviews and his written recollections. In the latter, for example, he gives both 1938 and 1940 as the date when he first met Noah.

[10] Simons, *op. cit.,* p. 1, p. 2.

Noah. He came over and, to my embarrassment, effortlessly pulled the window down." The two young couples began spending time together.

> On alternate Saturdays, we had dinner at each other's house. Because Noah had a great collection of classical records, other friends would come over after dinner, or sometimes *for* dinner. We didn't have big rooms or big tables, we could only serve four or six. After dinner Noah would play records of classical music for us, and simultaneously would informally teach us about music.[11]

These Saturday night get-togethers were not at all like the regular meetings of Noah's and Harold's choral group. According to Jesse and others, Harold Brown rarely made an appearance. Saturdays, at least in the early hours, were given over to instrumental music, with Noah's tastes and ideas preeminent.

> Noah was a man of enormous enthusiasm. He was not a great public speaker, but in small groups he was absolutely mesmerizing. He occupied the whole room, not only because he was big and heavy, but his personality was . . . most ebullient, the most ebullient person, perhaps, I've ever known. Especially when he spoke of things he was enthusiastic about: drinking, eating, sex, music.[12]

Jesse particularly remembered Noah's dramatic demonstrations of the big differences between performances of the Beethoven piano concertos. Noah would first put a Walter Gieseking record on the phonograph. He would let his audience, curled up on the floor with drinks and cigarettes, hear a few measures before he lifted the tonearm and switched to another record and another. Then came Artur Schnabel's turn. This, Noah would exclaim, this is how it should be played.

"Those evenings were the beginning of my involvement with classical music," Jesse said. "This was one of the things which Noah gave me for which I am extremely grateful." Al Glotzer echoed the thought. "I didn't know much about Bach and Vivaldi. Well, [Noah] started to talk to us about Bach and Vivaldi and he played it and he converted a lot of us." And Rickie Flanders (Rickie Simons in those days): "We were all turned on by Noah's enthusiasm for music. . . . It was wonderful to sing Morley and learn *Alle Schweige* and those other things."

---

[11] *Ibid.,* p. 5.
[12] *Loc. cit.*

Edith Schor with friend Julius Goldstein at Rubin Baratz's apartment.
(Courtesy Rubin Baratz)

"We sang revolutionary songs long before Noah," Rickie added. They sang them around summer campfires. They sang them at movement gatherings. "[There would be meetings] with Shachtman talking and later in the evening we sang." But also, on some of those Saturday nights at Noah's, when the hour grew late and the lights were dim, she and Jessie and Lucy Cogan and Eddie Riesenfeld and sometimes Albert Glotzer and Manny Geltman and Clara and Rubin Baratz and Edith and Noah would begin to sing the songs of radicalism. "Spanish, Yiddish, German, Irish and Italian—everybody seemed to know them," Jesse said, "and I came to learn them."

But the time came swiftly for the singers to do more than sing.

"You know," said Al Glotzer, "in the 30s nobody could get a job. The war breaks out and America becomes 'the arsenal of democracy'—jobs everywhere. Our committee took up this question [of work]. We deliberately, consciously told our [young] people, 'Go into the factories and get into the unions.'" The unspoken last half of this commandment was, 'form colonies of Workers Party organizers and get control of the locals into your socialist hands.' In this, the Shachtmanites were following the lead of their brilliant labor theorist, Ernest Rice McKinney. McKinney, a black graduate of Oberlin, had joined the Army right out of college. He subsequently went from the Army into the Communist Party, from the Party into Reinhold Niebuhr's and A. J. Muste's pacifist Fellowship of Reconciliation and thence into Trotskyism and the Workers Party. McKinney, who had a hardheaded sense of proletarian reality, pointed out that even in the booming defense economy, any halfway decent factory job required training. So a group of Noah's friends and fellow WP members decided to teach themselves the elements of metalworking. "The big teacher," Al Glotzer said, "was Herman Benson."

Herman Benson is a respected, even revered, figure in New York City labor circles. For the past 50 years, he has matter-of-factly devoted himself to the fight for social justice and reform in the labor movement and beyond it. The organization Benson founded, led until 1996, and still serves is called the Association for Union Democracy, a highfalutin' name for a handful of determined men and women and a couple of battered computers. Its shabby offices are one flight up in a former mortuary on State Street in Brooklyn. It's the kind of neighborhood, hard-hit but recovering, where you ring and wait and somebody comes downstairs to look you over through a peephole before letting you in. Benson and his AUD stand up for

"the democratic rights of union members" (minorities, women workers, and unskilled workers in particular) against bureaucratic and
not infrequently autocratic union leadership. AUD fights equally
hard against anti-labor behavior on the part of government. But in
1941, Herman Benson was not the Elder Statesman of labor that he
is today. He was a quondam City College student, expelled in 1933,
he says cheerfully, for activism. (It's hard to imagine what Benson
could have done—did he bomb one of the alcoves in the cafeteria?
—to provoke City College, that seething arena of activism, to expel
him.) Benson was also a convinced member of the Workers Party
and a friend and comrade of Noah Greenberg.

> I first got to know Noah somewhere around 1939, and the reason
> I remember is that he was among the first of the comrades to get
> their own apartment. We were still sort of detached kids, young
> men and women, without any real place of our own, we sort of
> tended to come to his place to get together.[13]

"War was coming," Herman Benson went on. "There was a tremendous shortage of skilled help in the United States, we had come
through the Depression, they didn't train any toolmakers, they were
desperate for skilled workers.

> They set up these training courses, 30 days, I took one of them and
> got basic training in just one machine, and with 30 days's experi-
> ence you were way ahead of the vast multitude of everybody else.[14]

The idea, he said, was to get into a shop. "When there were these
big lineups outside of a factory, I mean I had 30 days' experience
and could bullshit my way in."[15] Once he was in, he could work
himself into the union and to start talking socialism to his shopmates.
But the notion of a training course stuck in Herman's mind.

> This was my idea, we got people to agree to take a course. They all
> chipped in their money in advance, we bought a lathe. Let's see,
> our office was at 114 West 14th . . . we must have gotten together
> five hundred dollars and we were able to buy a first-class lathe,
> which was an industrial type lathe. And we stored it at 114 West
> 14th, and when we went actually to take the machine out, some-
> body had stolen it. So we had to collect more money, we got a
> couple of hundred dollars, we bought an Atlas, which was a Sears-
> Roebuck lathe. It wasn't an industrial lathe but you'd learn the
> principles and we set that up in a basement on Second Avenue.

[13] Herman Benson, March 27, 1997.
[14] *Ibid.*
[15] *Ibid.*

When I say a basement, you know we opened the sidewalk thing and went downstairs.[16]

Installation consisted of plugging the lathe's power cord into the only electric socket.

In this underground academy, Herman Benson himself was the chief instructor. Julius Jacobson and Israel Kugler had also had some factory experience. (Kugler was an apprentice machinist at the Brooklyn Navy Yard.) They were the unpaid adjunct shop teachers. Their pupils included, among many others, Noah, Jesse, Avel Austin and Eddie Riesenfeld.

"We had a big heavy book," Jesse Simons recalled:

Machine Shop Practice. From the book we taught ourselves how to run the lathe. I think the lathe cost us a couple of hundred bucks. It wasn't a very big one, maybe 16 inches to 48 inches in length, at the most. . . .[17]

Noah and his fellow-novices learned how to set up the cutting tools to cut, shape, mill and knurl metalstock, and how to sharpen the tools themselves on a grinding wheel. They learned how to read inside and outside precision micrometers for gauging measurements as fine as one one-thousandth of an inch. "Nothing daunted us," Jesse added, "because we believed we could do anything, including changing the world."

Jesse thinks he remembers something else, although none of his contemporaries could confirm the recollection. "If my memory serves me right, we bought a small hand press and printed up false letterheads and then typed up references which we then used to get jobs." But Israel Kugler did observe that the youngsters would use the training to get themselves jobs, learn a bit more, get fired (sometimes for lack of skill, sometimes for preaching socialism too overtly), come back to Second Avenue, learn a little more still, and repeat the process.

In time, according to Herman Benson, Noah became one of the instructors.

This was in his proletarian, down-to-earth, earthy period. . . . And he used to come down [to the basement shop], he'd have his work shirt, he hadn't changed [from his regular job], soaked with perspiration, he'd be a real proletarian.[18]

[16] *Ibid.*
[17] *Op. cit.*, p. 8.
[18] Herman Benson, March 27, 1997.

"Noah," Israel Kugler wrote, "had a flair for whatever he took up. He was an excellent lathe hand/machinist."[19] Good enough to land a job in October 1940 as an engine lathe machinist for the McKiernan-Terry Corporation, manufacturing engineers, in Harrison, a grimy industrial town on the east bank of the Passaic River in New Jersey. He stayed with McKiernan-Terry through March, 1941, and according to personnel director C. M. Gunther, "while in our employ, his services, character and dependability were satisfactory."[20]

After a few interim months at E. W. Bliss Co. in Brooklyn ("his record, while with us, was very satisfactory"), Noah went to work at the end of August (1941) for the Ford Instrument Company, a division of Sperry Gyroscope, across the East River in Long Island City. Ford Instrument made, installed and serviced gunfire control equipment for the Navy. Noah's job description makes clear how skilled he had become:

> His duties consisted of performing operations, such as boring, turning, facing, threading, knurling and taper cutting on precision parts.
> . . He was required to set up his own machine from manufacturing blueprints, working to machining tolerances of .0002", using precision measuring instruments, such as the micrometer, vernier depth gage, height gage, and vernier calipers, as well as all other machinists' hand tools required for the particular job.[21]

To hold his Ford Instrument job, Noah had to catch a subway or perhaps the Third Avenue "El," cross the Queensboro Bridge at 59th Street, get himself to the Ford plant entrance at Rawson Street and Nelson Avenue, and clock in. Then he would work a full shift: probably the four-to-eight, but possibly the graveyard shift (eight p.m. to four the next morning), because Herman Benson, who worked nights, recalls seeing Noah at the Workers Party shop in the mornings, when he himself came in. That Noah could take on lathe instruction in addition to his defense-plant workload speaks volumes for his stamina, energy, and devotion to the Shachtmanite cause. Nor was this all. As so many others have already testified, Noah somehow also carved out time for music. "In that period [while] he was teaching people how to run the lathe," Herman said, "we would get together [to sing] and at that point he was going in

---

[19] Israel Kugler, letter to Mark Davenport, n.d.

[20] C. M. Gunther, letter, "To Whom It May Concern," January 25, 1945.

[21] H. B. Cress, Jr., Acting Industrial Relations Director, Ford Instrument Company, Inc., letter to U. S. Maritime Service, January 17, 1945.

for folksongs." Not the tender, lyrical ballads of Britain that Noah and Eddie Riesenfeld had studied, but rather "earthy stuff, that's right, music of the people. It was [his] big folksong and labor song period." For example? Suddenly Herman in his office began singing quietly, to the tune of *The Irish Washerwoman:*

> McGinty is dead and McCarthy don't know it,
>
> McCarthy is dead and McGinty don't know it.
>
> The both of them dead in the very same bed,
>
> And the one doesn't know that the other is dead.

"Noah," he said, "would sing that one at the top of his lungs."

Noah remained at Ford Instrument until September 22, 1942. He was there, that is, through the Japanese attack on Pearl Harbor, the U. S. entry into the war and the series of early Axis victories. When Noah left, the tide was only beginning to turn. In May and June, the U. S. Navy had checked the Japanese fleet in the Battle of the Coral Sea and had dealt it a heavy blow at Midway. But in September, the battle inside Stalingrad was raging and the U.S. Marines were struggling to hold Guadalcanal. Only in early November would General Montgomery recapture El Alamein, American and British forces land in North Africa and the Red Army crush the German 6th Army at Stalingrad. By then, Noah Greenberg, for the moment jobless, was busy making new plans.

"The dream of 'colonizing,'" wrote Irving Howe, "is as old as the radical movement itself, entailing a history of sacrifice, delusion, and frustration." But in the short run, the Workers Party, despite its tiny size and limited resources, was remarkably good at putting forth colonies.

> Dozens of our people settled in Detroit and Buffalo, where they found jobs in auto plants now shifting to defense production. Others went into defense plants in their own cities: New York, Philadelphia, Los Angeles.[22]

In Los Angeles, the weather was balmy, war plants were gobbling up tens of thousands of workers and handing out deferments to those in line to be drafted. Wages were frozen while stockholder profits were not, and the work force was thus ripe for socialist indoctrination. Among those who in 1941 and 1942 answered the call to colonize California were Lucy Cogan and Eddie Riesenfeld (they had recently wed) and Rickie and Jesse Simons. Early in December,

---

[22] Howe, *op. cit.,* p. 81.

Lucy and Eddie and their friends and party comrades Ann and Jack Levine were en route to California by car. They heard the news of Pearl Harbor in Abiline, Kansas, and drove straight through to Los Angeles without stopping, eager to begin earning a living and winning converts. Rickie and Jesse gave up their apartment, crammed their entire earthly possessions into three suitcases, and crammed themselves into the Upper West Side flat Herman and Hildreth Benson were already sharing with Avel Austin. "God knows how we managed," Jesse says in retrospect, but he and Rickie were determined to save enough rent money to pay for their train fare to California.

Early in 1942, even Harold Brown became a colonizer of sorts, leaving New York for Philadelphia and war work as a welder at Todd Shipyard. But Harold brought with him his expensive record-player and custom speakers and his collection of records and moved into an apartment in a brownstone at 22nd and Pine Streets owned by Jeanette and Alfred Seyden, Polish emigrés. The Seydens themselves were musicians: Jeanette, a singer, Alfred, a violinist. Their house was a block or two from the Curtis Institute of Music, and several Curtis Institute students were among their tenants. Before long, Harold was expounding on music to members of the corps of brilliant youngsters at Curtis that year, including the cellist Robert Lamarchina, the composer Ned Rorem, a 16-year-old pianist named Eugene Istomin, the somewhat older pianist Byron Hardin, and Leonard Bernstein, a grand old man of 24.

That year, Lenny Bernstein was seeing a great deal of Shirley Gabis, a very pretty, very talented girl just one year out of high school. Shirley had studied piano with no notion of becoming a professional musician, but she had "this great passion for music," as she put it, "and Harold was very struck by that. He said he would give me lessons even though he wasn't a pianist." He did give her lessons, throughout the summer of 1942.

> He was bringing this [message] to all the young musicians about Schnabel, he talked about Casals, about rhythm ... he opened me up as a musician, because he talked to me about musical ideas that I'd never heard anything about, he talked about an upbeat and a downbeat and it was a whole musical revelation.[23]

[23] Shirley Perle (Shirley Gabis), October 22, 1997. Her playing improved so markedly as a result of Harold's tutoring that Eugene Istomin, when he next heard her, insisted on teaching her himself and, in her terms, "sort of steamrollered me into Curtis." Later, as Shirley Rhoads, she went on to pursue a successful musical career.

Shirley thought that Harold, however musical, was personally "very dour." Also, "he was very intense, which was sort of interesting, but he was focused on some inner thing that was eating at him."[24] A 33-year-old's "inner thing" was not something Shirley at 17 wanted to explore. Nevertheless, the ripples from Harold's encounters with Shirley and with the "kids from Curtis" would still be spreading years later.

In mid-July 1942, Herman Benson left for Detroit. The Navy snapped up "Izzie-the-socialist" Kugler. "The government probably decided I was a dangerous radical," Kugler quipped, "so they drafted me." Avel Austin too joined the Navy. Noah was restless. More than one of his friends has suggested that his and Edith's marriage was already a troubled one. At the end of June, Herman and Noah spent a long weekend, or perhaps a whole week, in Pensylvania with two young women not their wives, Pearl Weinstein and Fanny Seidman. "There was no sexual element involved," Herman said of the situation, but it clearly did not bespeak marital concord. Edith herself did not recall the episode, but she was unhappy about Noah's behavior. "One day he suddenly said to me: 'I've never been anywhere.' What do you mean? 'I've never seen the rest of the country.' I knew then that he was getting ready to go to L.A." Why L. A.? Rickie and Jesse were out there, along with many other friends of both Greenbergs. And there was plenty of work to be had there.

One day—Edith remembers it as being a week or so after Thanksgiving—Noah packed his bags and headed westward. He promised to write. On January 2, 1943, Noah started work as a "shop mechanic on lathe work" for the Los Angeles Shipbuilding and Drydock Corporation in San Pedro, a town at the southern edge of Los Angeles west of Long Beach on San Pedro Bay. It would be nearly five months before Edith rejoined her husband in California.

---

[24] Shirley Perle, October 22, 1997.

CHAPTER SIX

𝒥HE BIGGEST LATHE IN SAN PEDRO

(1943-1944)

𝒥n 1943, San Pedro was a seven-day-a-week, 24-hour-a-day war machine, soaking up labor like some vast insatiable sponge. Over the previous 30 years, engineers had built enormous rock breakwaters to complete the transformation of a desolate area of salt creeks and tidal flats, discovered in 1542 by Juan Rodriguez Cabrillo, into the busiest harbor on the West Coast. San Pedro, built on the rise of land that protected the western edge of the harbor, had become a small, bustling port town with a population of perhaps 20,000, fiercely proud of its separateness despite its 1911 "affiliation" with Los Angeles. But the advent of war worked a further transformation upon it. As Hitler's U-boats began inflicting serious wounds on U.S. merchant shipping and as the Navy began to grow after Pearl Harbor, shipbuilding, not shipping, became San Pedro's major industry. To the south of the Southern Pacific drawbridge at the mouth of the harbor's West Basin, the fences and gates of shipyards cut off the waterfront from Regan Street and Harbor Boulevard. Other yards, including Henry Kaiser's huge California Shipbuilding Corporation ("Calship"), were situated on Terminal Island, on the east side of the main (north-south) channel. The industrial buildup was more than matched by the human buildup. Between 1941 and 1944, the winds of war swirled and whirled and blew some 90,000 workers into San Pedro's shipyards. The workers came from all over the country, lured by the high pay ($.95 an hour for common laborers $1.20 for master mechanics, a 48-hour week and time and a half for overtime).

San Pedro's population of shipbuilders was only a small fraction of the one and a half million shipbuilding workers nationwide,[1] but

---

[1] Selden Menefee, *Assignment: U.S.A.*, p. 197.

with their families they numbered more than enough to overwhelm the city's resources, especially its prewar housing supply.

In this respect, Noah and later Edith Greenberg were among the lucky. Noah, as a married man, found an apartment in Channel Heights. By agreeing to house Lucy Cogan (no longer married to Eddie Riesenfeld) as well, he secured a two-bedroom unit.

Most of the defense housing projects in San Pedro—at least three others had been authorized—were bleak barracklike structures with paper-thin walls and few if any amenities.[2] But Channel Heights was different. In 1941, the Federal government's National Housing Authority had acquired a 160-acre tract on the hillside overlooking the town and the main ship channel. It then signed up the Vienna-born modernist Richard Neutra to design the San Pedro project. The result was housing that to this day is beguilingly attractive.

> The plaster [interior] walls were painted in warm terra cotta and the long patios and outside stairways were of redwood that had been stained a deep, rich brown. Though the 600-unit development had been fitted into the great rolling site with a minimum of violence to the original topography, the landscaping had not yet fully taken. . . .[3]

Edith's and Noah's apartment, like all others, had its own kitchen and bathroom, a tiny balcony and slider windows that flooded the unit with light. When she left New York in May, Edith shipped Lucy's piano and Noah's records to San Pedro, where they were housed in the second bedroom.

Neutra's enthusiasm for Latin America had led him to bestow names like "Patzcuaro" and "Guanajuato" on the project's courts. Channel Heights dwellers, most of them defense workers, found these names weird and unpronounceable. "Patzcuardo" thus quickly became "Paddy's Square," and "Tobago Court" was instantly "Tobacco Road."[4] Castro Court, where the Greenbergs settled at number 1441, was straightforward enough not to need amendment.

From Channel Heights, Noah could walk but usually drove downhill through the streets of the town to Harbor Avenue and the big shipyards, a couple of miles away.

The Los Angeles Shipbuilding and Drydock Corporation, where Noah started working in January, 1943, was "L. A. Ship" to its em-

[2] Cabell Phillips, *The 1940s: Decade of Triumph and Trouble,* p. 181.
[3] Henry Kraus, *In the City Was a Garden,* pp. 15-16.
[4] *Ibid.,* p. 74.

Noah at Channel Heights,
worker housing designed
by Richard Neutra.
(*Courtesy Lucille Dames*)

ployees. Even before the war, it was the largest private ship-repair company between San Francisco and the Panama Canal, and thus a vital defense asset. In 1943, the Navy Department asked the Todd Shipyards Corporation to take over L. A. Ship and manage it for the government, and until 1994, when Todd Shipyards went out of business, the yard remained part of the Todd empire. L. A. Ship both built and repaired Navy vessels. Construction centered on smaller ship types, those of 10,000 tons or less. But repair was still its main business: millions of tons of ships passed through its repair wharves and ways.

L. A. Ship in wartime was a hive, its 90-acre yard and 71 buildings dominated by the huge cranes that rose, in one vewer's delightful mixed simile, "like mammoth beasts with elongated necks scanning a prehistoric world."[5] A dozen or more ships awaiting repair and several others at various stages of completion would be

[5] *Ibid.*, p. 15.

moored at its Works Division wharves or nested in its two drydocks. The yard also housed shops for such specialties as boilermaking, sheet metal work, and engine repair. Hardhatted workers, many of them women, were everywhere.

When Noah arrived, Jesse Simons was already at work there as a coppersmith, fitting and soldering plumbing and water lines aboard ship. According to Jesse, "Noah's shipyard job was in the machine shop operating the biggest lathe in the plant, making sections of propeller shafts." Because a ship's engine is amidships, while the propeller is at the stern, a propeller shaft is typically half as long as the ship itself. "[Noah's] lathe had to have a bed big enough and long enough to hold the [several] sections."

The rough casting would come from the forge to be hoisted into place on the lathe. There it was held horizontally between centers and further supported by rests.

> Noah's job was to [keep] an eye on the lathe, making sure that the coolant played on the cutting tool and the metal, and occasionally changing the tool. . . . So here's Noah who loves Gregorian chants and rounds, Beethoven and Schubert, a man who for most of his life studied music . . . running this enormous lathe.[6]

You have to bring the scene to life in your mind to appreciate it: the cavernous, clangorous machine shop with its grimy blacked-out skylights and its scarred concrete floor; the glare of artificial light from a thousand unshaded bulbs; the overhead hoists; the squealing laden hand trucks; the rows of drill presses, stamping machines, milling machines, grinders and turret lathes; the crowds of helmeted workers coming and going; the constant noise and movement. And there in the middle of it all, seated at his ease in a chair beside the biggest machine in the shop—Jesse makes a special point of the chair—is overgrown, smiling Noah Greenberg, who has somehow wormed his way into the best job in the house. A gregarious 24-year-old with a wisecrack for every occasion who seems to be friends with everybody, male and female, young and old.

The Workers Party contingent that set out in innocence to "colonize" San Pedro war industry was marching unwittingly into dangerous territory. Indeed, Jesse, Rickie, Lucy, Ann and Jack Levine, Frances and Vaughan O'Brian, Hal Draper, and Noah himself were the heirs to a long history of radicalism and anti-labor violence. As far back as 1909, the "Wobblies," the I.W.W. or Industrial Workers of the World, were organizing workers on the San Pedro breakwater

[6] Jesse Simons, *op. cit.,* pp. 10-11.

construction project. In 1923, the Marine Transport Workers Industrial Union No. 510, a Wobbly local, called a general strike in San Pedro. It met with little success, but it prompted a fearsome reprisal. A vigilante gang of townspeople raided an I.W.W. meeting, beating and burning those present. The vigilantes grabbed seven Wobbly organizers, tarred and feathered them and ran them out of town, threatening them with death if they returned.

No tarring-and-feathering or other dire fate befell Noah and his comrades, but they did have to be careful. Defense plants were unionized, and union activism was permissible on the shop floor and in the yard. *Leftist* activism, however, was a different matter. Thus, the main North American Aviation plant in Los Angeles, where Rickie Simons and Lucy Cogan began their California careers in April, 1942, had been the scene of a spectacular strike a year earlier, on June 4, 1941. The workers had gone off the job in defiance of President Roosevelt's demand that strikes be outlawed. The strike was led by a neighbor of Edie's and Noah's in Channel Heights. Henry Kraus and his wife Dorothy, who ran the UAW local at North American together, were Communists.[7] The UAW national leadership denounced the strike and the Krauses, but North American's workers, who had legitimate wage demands, stayed off the job. FDR wasted no time. He called in the Army to take over the plant and told local draft boards to cancel the deferment of any man who failed to report for work. The strike was over.

With labor scarce, aviation plants, North American included, were hiring women. But decent war jobs required training, so Rickie and Lucy signed up for a machine-shop course for women. With Eddie gone, Lucy needed transportation.

> Rickie had a Model A, and that's how we used to get to Long Beach from San Pedro. The first morning, this [course] was given by an old machinist, in kind of an old factory building where they had all the old machines, one next to the other, very unfamiliar to us, it had a sort of surreal atmosphere to it. He spent the whole morning showing us what can happen to you. Your hair can be caught, your fingers can be chopped off. Then there was the lunch break, and after [that] he said, 'Okay, girls, set up your machines,' and we didn't have the least idea what he was talking about . . .[8]

[7] As of the day of the strike, the Communist party line was to endorse the Hitler-Stalin non-aggression pact, preach isolationism and favor strikes as keeping this country militarily weak and therefore neutral. Eighteen days later, on June 22, Hitler invaded Soviet Russia and U. S. Communist leaders, to the cynical delight of the Trotskyists, did a perfect flip-flop on the question of the American war effort.

[8] Lucy Dames, March 17, 1997.

Lucy remembers trying to turn out a plumb bob on a lathe. (A plumb bob is the conical steel weight masons dangle on a string line to determine perpendicularity.) Hers started off too large but grew smaller and smaller as she shaved it down to give it the right shape, until finally it almost vanished. Still, "about two or three days later I got a job [at North American] running a lathe, facing gears." Rickie became a riveter, attaching "one piece of metal to another piece of metal. It was part of a plane, but I never knew which part."

North American Aviation in 1942 was plainly no place in which to proselytize for socialism. Lucy and Rickie did their jobs and, after hours, drove back to San Pedro to pass out *Labor Action* at the shipyard gates, where they could operate without being recognized. (Or so they told themselves. But two beautiful young socialists peddling newspapers to streams of workers in a sensitive defense industry are hardly likely to escape the attention of the higher-ups, and these two did not.) They stuck it out at North American for the better part of a year before deciding to seek work in San Pedro, where the shipyards had begun to open their gates to women.

In the spring of 1943, Edith Greenberg arrived in San Pedro, moved in with Noah and teamed up with Lucy and Rickie to look for work. The job hunt was soon over. All three young women were taken on at L. A. Ship and all three were hired as welder trainees. Edith soon became handy with an acetylene torch, but Rickie developed pleurisy and had to seek less strenuous work. On occasion, Edith kept watch while the other two took an unofficial break. It developed that somebody in the yard office had been keeping an eye on Rickie and her friends. "We were all put on the same job by some unknown, at the time unknown, benign character in management who, it turned out, figured us all out . . . he was very sympathetic. He knew us because we distributed *Labor Action* at the plant gate." The "benign character's" sympathy was not political in nature: apparently he simply enjoyed pretty girls. He arranged for the three to be trained in "layout" by one William Putz. They learned to read blueprints and mark on a ship's hull and bulkheads the openings to be cut for portholes and vents.

One reason for making the move to L. A. Ship was that the work at North American was boring and repetitive. "In the aircraft factory it's a very confined space," Rickie explained, "and you have your little job, and you're right here, doing your little job. And not only that, it's over and over again like an assembly line."[9] In con-

---

[9] Rickie Flanders, October 22, 1997.

trast, the shipyards were vast open spaces and the work was more varied and involved moving around. But a bigger reason was that Lucy, Rickie and Edie wanted to join forces with their comrades and, good Shachtmanites that they were, begin the task of infiltrating Local 9 of the International Union of Marine Shipbuilding Workers of America, CIO.

A number of issues, external and internal, afforded the Workers Party crew more than enough excuse for action.

> The [external] issues were price-fixing. Supposedly prices were fixed, but they were not, they were going up. The issue was wage freeze. The issue was the effort by some of the leadership of the CIO to get people to give up overtime pay. . . . The issue was the no-strike pledge. . . .The main fight in Local 9 was for democracy —for a democratic union.[10]

The opening move was an aggressive attack on Local 9 officials for failure to protect workers' rights under the Labor Agreement between the union and the shipbuilding companies, including L. A. Ship and Western Pipe. In this, the WP members were remarkably successful. Even before Noah had arrived, Jesse, Hal Draper, and others had wrested the leadership of Local 9 from its officers and had compelled the national General Examining Board to suspend the local's independence and appoint an administrator. The WP forces, only five or six strong but brimful of adrenalin, had "engaged in a battle with [the administrator] regarding the same matters."

Local 9 had controlled the hiring of San Pedro shipyard workers through its own independent hiring hall. But the local had just "surrendered" control of its hall to L. A. Ship "without a fight." The implication was that good hardworking union men would no longer have any say over who their shopmates would be.

The Workers Party position was that a "Stalinist gang of Moscow patriots was trying to take over Local 9." Lionel Stander, a Hollywood bit-part actor turned shipyard "burner" (a burner used an acetylene torch to cut the openings in hulls and bulkheads) was reported to be involved in this plot.

The next bone of contention had to do with shop steward elections. If each of the three shifts in each department elected its own shop steward, the tiny but determined WP contingent had a chance of acquiring real power in the local. But if the administrator ap-

---

[10] Rickie Flanders, *op. cit.*, p. 7. The account of efforts to take over Local 9 is drawn largely from articles in the WP weekly *Labor Action,* many of them written by Rickie herself.

pointed shop stewards—he evidently had every right to do so—he could put in his own allies, who would of course be "Stalinist stooges." When the elections were postponed, the WP line was that this was beginning of a "big sellout" to the Stalinists.

In April 1943, a few months after Noah arrived at L. A. Ship, the company asked the union to allow a 10-hour day for certain workers. This meant an awkward shift rearrangement and a sharp cutback in overtime pay. The union maintained that "the Navy wanted it to keep up badly-needed production." This development was made to order for Noah and his friends, and it seems that Noah played a key role in agitating for its rejection. In fact,

> Noah was able to do more than any of us because he was just sitting at the lathe conversing while awaiting completion of a cut. On the other hand, we had to do our work. For instance, I was a coppersmith, and, as such, I couldn't sit down any time at work. [But] Noah became a center of all the news and gossip in the yard.[11]

Nevertheless, in mid-April Local 9's rank and file agreed to a 10-hour day. It took effect only in certain critical departments and only for repair work, but it was less than a victory for the WP faction.

In theory, the American labor movement's patriotic no-strike pledge counted for little in the Workers Party. As Rickie Simons put it later, "The notion that the working class under any circumstances should bear the burden of a war whether it is a good war or a bad war is wrong."[12]

During the summer of 1943, Noah accordingly led a strike of the graveyard shift in the machine shop, to protest work hours, poor working conditions and other grievances. This was a one-day strike, more symbolic than actually intended to halt production. "By doing [such things]," Jesse pointed out, "we hoped to demonstrate our ability to lead and improve conditions, thus enabling us to educate and eventually recruit members." But the Shachtmanites knew well that a real strike effort would weaken their influence. John L. Lewis, who had led the United Mine Workers out on strike, was the most hated man in America, and the San Pedro WP had no desire to follow his lead.

Besides, there was great work to be done outside the yard. When San Pedro's grocers raised prices illegally and the government took no action, the Workers Party stepped in. Frances O'Brien, who had

[11] Simons, *op. cit.*, p. 12.
[12] Rickie Flanders, *op. cit.*, p. 9.

been active among San Pedro's oil workers, led a series of boycotts against targeted markets. When the white-supremacist Gerald L. K. Smith came to the area to speak, the WP led a "massive mobilization" against the man and his message. Said Rickie:

> We did a lot of community activity. We did a lot of work against Jim Crow. We came out against the gathering of the Japanese. I remember I arrived in San Pedro from New York the day that they were rounding up the Japanese, going in their cars with whatever possessions they could load, into internment camps. And we spoke up against that. We carried out a struggle in as many ways as we could.[13]

The combination of regular shift work, after-hours union politicking, and community organizing left very little time for relaxation. "I have fond memories," Rickie said, "of going from a hot shipyard where all I could think of toward the end of the day was going to the beach and going into that freezing cold water." The beach was Cabrillo Beach, several miles west of L. A. Ship beyond Fort MacArthur and the Navy athletic fields, and still a favored recreation spot. There were occasional parties, and according to Edith, Noah did make friends with one music-loving couple in the community who owned a piano and a record-player.

On September 18, 1943, Noah left L. A. Ship. His role as strike leader may have had something to do with his departure. It was, after all, an "illegal" strike, one contrary to the no-strike pledge and therefore quite possibly ground for dismissal. And "troublemakers" did get fired. In 1944, Rickie, Lucy and Edith were summarily let go at L. A. Ship, despite their "benign" friend in management, because they were "too friendly" with some of the black workers in the yard. There was no blacklist and they had no trouble landing other jobs. They simply moved a few blocks westward to Western Pipe & Steel Company, a shipyard about a mile east of L. A. Ship that was building destroyer escorts and icebreakers for the Navy. In Noah's case, none of his WP comrades recall that he was fired, and the letter of reference he took with him called him "a conscientious and energetic workman" and recommended him to "anyone in need of a [marine machinist]."[14] Five days later, he was at work at West Coast Shipbuilding and Drydock Company, a small yard at Berth 55 in the East Channel.

---

[13] *Ibid.*, p. 11.

[14] Letter, W. H. LeRoy, Assistant Machinery Superintendent, Los Angeles Shipbuilding and Drydock Corporation-"To Whom It May Concern," September 18, 1943.

Edith's recollection may hold the answer to Noah's job change. She pointed out that as a skilled worker in an essential industry, Noah had been given a draft deferment. But by the fall of 1943, with most materiel shortages overcome and the armed services in pressing need of men, "nobody was being kept out of the draft!" not even married men who could run big lathes. In 1942, Irving Howe had gone from being editor of *Worker Action* to Private First Class Howe, U. S. Army. As noted, Izzie Kugler and Avel Austin had joined the Navy. Jesse Simons was drafted in 1943 and sent into the Army Air Corps. Edith says that Noah's draft board withdrew his deferment but offered him one option. Because there was a serious manpower shortage in the Merchant Marine, the board would allow Noah to enlist in this service in lieu of being drafted into the Army. Merchant mariners drew better pay than soldiers, didn't have to wear uniforms, and rarely had to shoot at anyone or be shot at. And life at sea, though still dangerous, had grown considerably less dangerous than it had been during the first 18 months of war.[15] Once Noah made up his mind, it was simply a matter of waiting to be notified; and so his job at West Coast Ship may have been a fill-in one until his number came up. A letter from Harold Brown to Noah dated January 2, 1944, asking among other things about the "Army situation" bears out this likely explanation.

Noah left West Coast Ship on January 24, 1944. By the end of March, his mailing address was Section 144, U. S. Merchant Sailors' Training Station, Avalon, California. Unlike millions of other service trainees, Noah was not cut off from friends and family. "On a clear day," Rickie Simons said wryly of wartime San Pedro, "you could see Catalina Island. Of course, with the fog and smog, there never was a clear day." But Avalon was on Catalina Island. On weekend leaves, he could be home in Channel Heights.

---

[15] In March 1943, a secret inter-Allied conference in Washington had finally developed a winning strategy, a combination of close naval cooperation and the deployment of long-range antisubmarine aircraft, in the Battle of the Atlantic. The result was spectacular. In April, Allied shipping losses to German Admiral Carl Doenitz's U-boats were 245,000 tons; in June, 18,000. It was a grave defeat for Hitler's Germany.

CHAPTER SEVEN

ƏNIWETOK TO MURMANSK

(1944-1945)

"*M*essmen are waiters, scullions, dishwashers. They want to be promoted to cooks."[1] Sweating it out, literally and figuratively, as waiter, scullion, and dishwasher and yearning to be promoted to cook sum up in a nutshell Noah's first three months of active service in the Merchant Marine. Before this, however, Apprentice Seaman Greenberg, Noah, ID Cert. #548379, had to learn how to be a seaman. During his initial three months of training at Avalon, Noah wore a neat blue uniform with red insignia and a blue knit watch cap. Meals, living quarters and medical and dental care were courtesy of the U. S. Government, and he was paid $50 a month.

Messmen hardly needed training to scrub pots and work the "clipper." (The clipper was a big mechanical dishwasher, operated by heaving a lever back and forth to slosh a rack of dishes through soapy hot water. The electric dishwashers in some of the newer ships' galleys were the pride of their chief stewards.) Messmen were taught how to wait on table and the rudiments of safe food handling. But for the most part, basic training focused on "boat work." With hundreds of other recruits, Noah spent hours diving into the ocean from a tall tower and climbing over rails and swarming down landing nets into the water. The child who loved the freezing waterfall at Camp Machiah was floating in the freezing Pacific and learning, in the words of maritime service chronicler Robert Carse, "to swim under water, take pieces of [his] clothing and from them make buoys that will hold [him] up quite a while if properly used....[L]ater on outside, there will be need for such things."[2]

[1] John Scott Douglas and Albert Salz, *He's in the Merchant Marine Now*, p. 136.
[2] Robert Carse, *Lifeline: The Ships and Men of Our Merchant Marine at War*, p. 100.

In January and again in mid-March, Harold Brown had written to Noah at Channel Heights. One subject was Harold's odd love life. "Am in the throes of another dame—only it's just beginning. . . She's just the right age for me—16." He also indulged in churlish musical comment.

> The reading sessions of the philharmonic [sic] all fizzled. I just spoke to Lenny Bernstein, and he says there probably wont be any, but will try to show [my] score to Rodzinski anyway. . . that bastard Gene [Eugene Istomin] is pounding the piano all day long, so I can't do any work.

There were also anxious queries about Noah's plans. "Your last letters didnt say much about yourself, and everyone is wondering about Umbo [a misprint for "Jumbo," as Noah's New York friends sometimes called him] and when is he coming east etc."[3] Not until late April did Harold seem to know that Noah had shipped out as a merchant mariner. On April 24, he wrote that "amazing insomnia, which might seem to give me lots of time to write . . . just fucks me up." He added, "The account of your life is not too pleasant. Hope things let up a bit after a while."[4] By then, Noah was two-thirds of the way through his basic training, and a month later, he was at sea.

Noah shipped out for the first time on May 24, 1944, from San Francisco. His ship, the "Cape Alava," was not a Liberty ship, but a so-called "C" ship, prettier and much faster than the famed Liberties, on several of which Noah would serve later. Built in Seattle in 1941, the "Cape Alava" was 469 feet long, 63 feet broad in the beam and, fully laden, could carry about 10,000 tons of cargo. She normally shipped a crew of 10 licensed officers, 5 cadets, and 26 seamen, plus a Navy guncrew. She was owned by the United States Maritime Commission—which by 1944 controlled ail U.S. merchant shipping—and managed by American Mail Line. Her destination was almost certainly the South Pacific. In mid-February, Army and Marine combat units had recaptured Eniwetok in the Marshall Islands. The strategically-placed coral atoll became a key staging-point for further operations against Japan. The Diesel-powered "Cape Alava," with an average speed of 15+ knots and a 15,000-

---

[3] Harold Brown, letters to Noah Greenberg, January 2, 1944, March 18, 1944. Eugene Istomin, 19 years old, was preparing for his solo debut concert in New York on April 22, at which he played (in addition to Beethoven's "Waldstein" Sonata, the Chopin E-major Scherzo and the Schubert E-flat Impromptu) Harold's own Four Preludes. For several months, Harold had been living in a room in Istomin's parents' apartment at 225 West 71 Street.

[4] Harold Brown, letter to Noah Greenberg, April 24, 1944.

mile cruising range, would have been an ideal vessel to move vital supplies across the enormous Pacific distances.

A story that soon became part of the Greenberg legend probably had its origins on this first voyage. Noah's Workers Party comrade Avel Austin had joined the Navy in 1943, had been assigned to the U.S. Naval Construction Battalions, the "C.B."s or SeaBees, and in the spring of 1944 was stationed on Eniwetok. One broiling day, Avel was aboard a docked ship overseeing the unloading of cargo and was amazed to hear the crew lustily singing *Bandillera Rossa,* "Red Flag," a famous Italian revolutionary song. He asked a crew member where they'd learned the song and, in Jesse Simons's account of the event, "was told that the ship's cook had taught them, that the cook knew all these crazy radical songs." The cook, of course, turned out to be Noah Greenberg—actually only a messman—and he and Avel "had a joyful reunion in the middle of the war, in the middle of the Pacific Ocean."[5]

Noah was discharged from the "Cape Alava" on August 22, 1944, after not quite three months, most of it at sea. The place of discharge was San Francisco. The N.M.U. and the seven other strong seamen's unions had imposed wartime rules of employment on their own members: after a 15-day voyage, no time ashore was allowed; after a 30-day trip, seven days; after a 60-day trip, 14 days; and after any longer voyage, 21 days, the maximum amount of shore leave. Noah next shipped out, however, on October 27, some 67 days after he signed off the "Cape Alava." His double excuse for the delay was more than acceptable to the dispatchers at N.M.U. hiring halls. He and Edith had decided to go home. If Noah was going to be away at sea much of the time, and if shipyard work was winding down, as it clearly was, neither of them saw much reason to stay in San Pedro. Noah thus needed some extra time to pack up, make the move back to New York and find a place to live. And he needed even more time to enroll in a second Merchant Marine school for unlicensed personnel. This one was at Sheepshead Bay, Long Island, and Noah wanted to go there to be certified as a cook. Not as a third cook, as a second cook. Third cooks prepare and serve vegetables, but second cooks bake bread, muffins, rolls and pies.

In 1944, Max Shachtman's close associate Al Glotzer was living in New York at 215 Second Avenue, a building owned by I.B. Hammer and his wife, the couple who ran Hammer's Dairy Restaurant nearby on East 14th Street. "Noah moved into the building in an apartment

---

[5] Jesse Simons, *op. cit.,* p. 14.

that was rented by another comrade . . . he and Edie lived there." It was a short-term arrangement, but as Glotzer recalls, it had its flavorful aspect.

> [Noah] was a seaman, and then he was learning to bake. He wanted to be a baker, right? And he was learning to bake, going to school. And one day he comes running up the steps and I knew it was Noah because he was ponderous. And he says, 'I just made a pie, Al, and I want you to taste my pie.' And he runs downstairs. I hear the door open, then the door closes, then I hear boom boom boom [as Noah starts up the stairs] and then I hear a terrific noise, I open the door and he's down lying on the floor with his pie spread all over the place.[6]

This disaster notwithstanding, Noah won his certification. When he shipped out in late October 1944 aboard the SS "William C. Endicott," it was as "Cook & Baker."

This trip, a winter voyage on the "Atlantic run" that lasted well over two months, may have taken Noah to Italy and certainly did take him to England. The capture of Sicily in mid-August 1943 had given the Allies control of the Mediterranean, and by the end of June 1944 ships could safely sail up the Adriatic as far north as Pescara, with supplies for the Allied armies attacking the elaborate German defense system known as the Gothic Line. In addition, vessels on the Atlantic run were laden with materiel to be landed in England in support of Operation Overlord, the invasion of France, which had started on June 6. The length of the voyage—Noah signed off the "Endicott" on January 8, 1945—would indicate that the vessel touched at more than one port.

The "William C. Endicott" was a Liberty ship, built at a Kaiser shipyard in Richmond, California, near San Francisco, in 1942. Robert Carse wrote of the typical Liberty:

> she has two decks, three masts, five cargo holds, a single propeller, a steam reciprocating engine. . . Her average speed is about eleven knots [and] her normal crew complement is forty-four men.[7]

Noah shared a cabin with the first and third cooks on the starboard side of the "Endicott"'s upper deck near the galley and messrooms. The cabin was not luxurious.

> Here were four bunks, plain steel lockers, a lone porthole, bench and wastebasket. On one of the plywood bulkheads a square bore the stencil: EMERGENCY ESCAPE PANEL   KICK OUT. In the

[6] Albert Glotzer, March 11, 1997.
[7] *Lifeline*, p.39

lockers hung Brooks Brothers suits, Maritime Service uniforms, secondhand topcoats and oilskins. On the little shelves were stowed personal effects of every quality. At night expensive jewelry, money and papers would be jammed into rubber contraceptives, then stowed in waterproof belts against a quick abandoning. Beside the bunks were tacked pin-up girls and pornographic pictures; into the mattresses and the pipes of spring frames went small valuable cargoes for personal smuggling: perfume, pearls, dope, foreign aphrodisiacs and precious stones.[8]

The constant fear of everyone on the Atlantic run was of course the fear of U-boat attack. In fact, since the early summer of 1943 the U-boat threat to Allied convoys had been sharply reduced. Nevertheless, ships were still being hunted and torpedoed, and no crew could take its safety for granted.

No real sense of wartime danger, let alone concern for Noah's safety, appears in the letters from Harold Brown that somehow reached Noah in England. One that survives opens with characteristic Haroldian self-abasement. "Carried a letter addressed to you around in my pocket for 4 days before I remembered to send it. I am a [rat]." England, he went on, must be very interesting. "I have long wanted to visit there—have always liked the English people I have met. After all, there must be something to a place that produced Arise, Arise, the Crystal Spring, etc."

There followed an outburst bitter even for Harold:

> This is just not my world. Whether the time will ever come when this stinking, hypocritical, vulgar music world would crack wide open, I do not know. That is, it must surely come, but how long? Meanwhile, I will simply fill pages with music and strew it all over the god damn place, like Dr. Mabuse.

Noah must have tried to reassure his friend and teacher, and the mail service must have been phenomenal, because less than a week later Harold wrote:

> What you say about my scores for England is pretty true in general—why hadn't I thought of it? Europe is a good possibility for me. This stinking concert world over here will never give me a chance, I am sure.[9]

In this second letter, Harold also comments on his (and Edith's) relief that Noah was "getting back to the Endicott." What this means

---

[8] Felix Riesenberg, Jr., *Sea War: the Story of the U.S. Merchant Marine in World War II*, pp. 88-89.

[9] Harold Brown, letters to Noah Greenberg, December 6, 1944; December 12, 1944.

is tantalizing but unclear. Had Noah started to jump ship but changed his mind? Had he been given orders, later rescinded, to join a worse ship? No one today knows the answer. All that can be said is that Noah was paid off in Boston on January 8, 1945.

On February 20, Noah shipped out again, on the last, longest and most terrifying of his three wartime voyages, aboard the SS. "Woodbridge N. Ferris," bound for Murmansk. Before he left, however, he and Edith regularized their housing situation. They had been subletting the apartment at 215 Second Avenue from another WP comrade. When the comrade returned to take over his quarters, Edith and Noah had to move out, and finding a place in wartime New York was no easy task. But I. B. Hammer and his wife, who owned 215, came to the rescue. They also owned the building at 243 East 14th Street, off Second Avenue, where Hammer's Dairy Restaurant was located. The restaurant took up the ground floor, with apartments above. Three steep flights up, the Hammers told Edith and Noah, was a spacious apartment: large living room, dining room, kitchen, two bedrooms, full bath. The Greenbergs could have it, with one proviso. The back bedroom was already occupied, as it had been since 1933, by a single man of quiet, scholarly habits, known to everybody simply as *der Schreiber*, the writer. What *der Schreiber* was writing, the Hammers were not quite sure, but he wouldn't bother anybody and Noah's music wouldn't disturb him. If Noah and Edith would accept *der Schreiber* as a permanent guest, the place was theirs. They did accept, and for the next six-plus years, the fourth floor of 243 East 14th Street, complete with subtenant, was their home.

Noah's new ship, the "Woodbridge N. Ferris," was a Liberty ship, built in 1943 in Maryland, and as such was familiar territory. But on this voyage, Noah would not be living in the cooks' cabin and earning his pay at the ovens in the galley. This trip, he had signed on as oiler, the job reserved for the second-lowest member of the engine-room department, the lowest being a wiper. It was Noah's job to watch ceaselessly over the many moving parts of the "Ferris'"s machinery, checking for heat and lubricating them where needed. His route took him, oilcan and brush in hand, from the crankshafts at the engine room's floor level, up a ladder and onto a grating to inspect the piston rods and valve gears, back down to the fuel, sanitary, and fresh-water pumps, and then into the alleyway that housed the propellor shaft, to look after the shaft bearings.[10]

---

[10] This description owes its detail to Carse, pp. 162-163.

Why swap the familiar galley for the strange and exceedingly hazardous engine room? (If a ship was torpedoed, the engine-room crew was usually trapped below with no chance of escape.) And why ship out on "the most difficult and dangerous run in the world —through the Atlantic and the Arctic Ocean past the North Cape of Norway—with the submarines . . . out there waiting."?[11] Part of the reason was money. The perils of the Murmansk run meant high pay, overtime, and a war-zone bonus. If he got back alive from Murmansk, Noah as an engine-room hand could count on collecting at least $1,000 and probably more—the equivalent of $8,000-$10,000 in 1990s dollars. But also, given Noah's personality, part of the reason was surely his desire to prove himself, to live up to his idea of himself as a big, tough, strong proletarian as well as a musician and sensitive intellectual—a *mensch* who could get his hands dirty on the job, outface the terror of being blown up or drowned like a rat, carouse and play dollar-a-card stud poker, and still listen raptly to Monteverdi and lead a chorus. Curiosity, too, played a part. As a socialist, Noah wanted to see at first hand the longsuffering socialist motherland.

The Murmansk run owed its beginnings, on July 11, 1941, to President Roosevelt's worry that Stalin, "coldly realistic" and faced with military near-disaster—the invading German armies had nearly reached Smolensk, 120 miles from Moscow—might sue for a separate peace with Hitler. Roosevelt marked on a *National Geographic Magazine* map the area of the Atlantic Ocean for which the U. S. would take responsibility. The president's move would permit Great Britain's overstrained navy to send armed escorts to protect supply convoys headed for Murmansk, the one accessible ice-free port in north Russia. Roosevelt then sent his special assistant Harry Hopkins to Moscow to confirm with Stalin the details of the supply mission. The first convoy, of British and Soviet ships, sailed from Iceland on August 21, 1941.

For U. S. vessels, the route lay north and east along the Atlantic seaboard from their home ports to Halifax, Nova Scotia. From there they would first cross the Atlantic to Scotland and head north from Clydebank to Reykjavik, Iceland. They would then form up in convoy with ships of other nationalities and, under British escort, sail northeast into the Barents Sea, pass between Bear Island and Norway's North Cape and into the Kola inlet and Murmansk.

[11] Robert Carse, *There Go the Ships*, p. 14.

In addition to deck cargo—trucks, tanks, heavy weapons—most U. S. ships carried either live ammunition and TNT or high-test gasoline in their holds. The average speed of the heavily-laden ships was eight knots. The ability to maneuver to avoid torpedoes was almost nil. Of the two great enemies ships and seamen faced on the Murmansk run, it was hard to know which was the more terrifying, U-boat and aircraft attack or Arctic weather.

During the summer, ice would drift down to within 80 miles of the North Cape, forcing the convoys closer to the mainland and bringing them within easy range of Norway-based German aircraft. Daylight, and thus exposure to aerial reconnaissance and attack, lasted for virtually 24 hours. Ships' crews prayed for fog, even though fog greatly increased the chances of collision with neighboring vessels. Winter began in October, with fog and snow, and from December on, hurricane-strength gales were common. Securing deck cargo in howling wind and pitch darkness was nightmarish, and the danger of being iced in was all too real.

U-boats waited for storms to scatter the convoys and separate the merchant ships from their naval escorts, then attacked. Sometimes they trailed vessels that had suffered too much weather damage to continue in convoy, and torpedoed them as they limped back toward Iceland. Sometimes, as in early 1945, they patrolled mainly between Bear Island and the Kola Inlet, risking discovery and sinking to strike at ships on their way home.

Murmansk itself was no refuge. In the late 1930s, according to Robert Carse, a navy base, a weather institute, and a modern city of apartments had grown up to replace the former fishing hamlet. But since 1942, Murmansk had been under constant air attack from bases less than 50 miles away.

> The dock area was mostly rubble and charred beams. But the port was still in operation. The [Hotel] Arctica still stood, and the House of Rest and Culture, and a number of the [1930s] apartment houses. There was a place for foreign seamen called the International Club.[12]

Even in 1945, there was not much more. Worse, incoming ships had to wait for days, sometimes weeks, subject to bomb attacks whenever rain and fog lifted, before they could offload their cargo.

> [T]hey all cleared themselves of their loads of explosives at the ammunition dock three and a half miles upstream from the city. [But] the heaviest shoreside crane handled eleven tons, and the

---

[12] Robert Carse, *A Cold Corner of Hell: the Story of the Murmansk Convoys, 1941-45*, p. 92. The account of the Murmansk run given here is largely drawn from this book.

tanks the vessels carried weighed thirty. The single heavy-duty crane barge was needed to move these and the other bulky cargo pieces. It was a nerve-racking delay for the men. . . .[13]

The war in Europe was winding down, but the U-boats of the Northern Flotilla were prowling the Berents Sea and German aircraft were active. In February and March of 1945, 12 ships were lost to enemy action.[14] The U-boats were still there on May 7, 1945. Indeed, according to Edith (who heard it from Noah) they were "right outside the harbor." But in Murmansk on May 7, the vodka, always in liberal supply, suddenly began flowing like a river in spring. That day in Reims, the Germans surrendered.

[13] *Ibid.*, p. 96.
[14] *Ibid.*, p. 264.

CHAPTER EIGHT

"Now that it's over"
(1945-1948)

On June 17, 1945, the "Woodbridge N. Ferris," John Fabricius, master, discharged its crew in New York. Noah walked down the gangway onto dry land and looked for a taxi to take him home. The Japanese had not yet surrendered. The atom bombs that brought about the end of the war fell on Hiroshima on August 7 and on Nagasaki two days later, with the surrender taking place on August 10. But for Noah, the war was over. An official letter from the United States Maritime Commission, undated but certainly sent soon after Noah's return from Murmansk, asks his draft board to reclassify him as someone who has already seen "substantial continuous service." He kept this letter, along with his ribbons for service in the the Pacific and Atlantic War Zones, for the rest of his life.

The war was over, but Noah's seafaring had scarcely begun.

On a summer evening, probably in late August or early September, Edie, Noah, and "Chips," the "Ferris"'s carpenter, were sitting at the kitchen table at 243 East 14th Street. (Every ship's carpenter since the days of wooden hulls has been nicknamed "Chips.") Noah said to Edith: "Well, now that it's all over and we don't have to be afraid of dying the next day, I can say you missed quite an adventure."

"It's not too late," Chips said. "The 'Gripsholm''s looking for crew."

The Swedish-American Line's flagship passenger liner "Gripsholm," sailing as she did under a neutral flag, was one of the few vessels the belligerents had allowed to sail freely during the war. She had carried Swedish nationals and repatriated diplomats and their families to ports on both sides of the Atlantic. But her crew hadn't seen Sweden for over two years, and now that the war was over and they could get home, they were jumping ship whole-sale in Brooklyn.

Edie, 22 years old, bored and restless, a world at peace stretching before her, exclaimed, "Well, me for the Gripsholm!" Noah shot back, "You get on and I'll get on." And so, the couple shipped out together on the Mediterranean run, Edith in the laundry, Noah as a waiter. "When we pulled out of Naples," Edith recalled,

> some dope spilled cold water on a hot engine and cracked the cast-ing and we spent a month in Italy. They had to send to Sweden for the casting and it took 30 days. They took everybody [the passen-gers, not the crew] off the ship and we limped on one engine into the naval base in Palermo.

A month later, with the engine repaired, the "Gripsholm" set forth for Alexandria. There, Edith found herself helping (or at least per-suaded that she was helping) the Haganah, the secret branch of the Jewish Agency, to arm the future state of Israel. A man named "Elli" claiming to be the head of the Haganah was aboard the "Gripsholm." Elli identified himself to Edith and let her know that he was plan-ning to take advantage of the liner's scheduled stop at Haifa to smuggle both people and material ashore. The lost time caused by the engine breakdown led to the cancellation of the Haifa stop. Elli told Edith that his travelling companion, a Jew who was an officer in the U. S. Army Air Force, had copies of the USAAF training manual for pilots. "We have to get them off," he said. At Alexandria, said Edie, "I wrapped the copies around me, put on a loose raincoat, and the two of them [Elli and the USAAF officer] took me by the elbows and walked me off the boat." Whatever she was carrying, they man-aged to get themselves and it past the police.[1]

The balance of the voyage took the "Gripsholm" to Greece (pre-sumably Athens, though the Swedish-American Lines itinerary does not say so) and to Marseilles. The liner returned to New York and paid off its crew on December 19, 1945.

The writer Patrick O'Brian is best known for his novels of seafar-ing adventure during the Napoleonic wars. He more than once makes his heroes, a British sea-captain and an Irish-Catalan physi-cian and spy, reflect on the simplicity and straightforwardness of life afloat compared with life ashore. For example:

[1] Edith Schor, March 7, 1997

> I cannot tell you what a relief it is,' [John Aubrey] said [to Dr. Stephen Maturin], 'to be at sea. It is so clear and simple. I do not mean just escaping from the bums; I mean all the complications of life on shore. I do not think I am well suited to the land.[2]

Just this sense of refuge from the complexities of his life in New York may well have been behind Noah's decision to stay in the merchant marine and ship out again and again after the end of the war. Love of travel, curiosity, and his lifelong zest for new experience obviously also played a part. So did his desire to identify with working people and to better the lot of his fellow workers. There was also the need to earn a living. Under the Serviceman's Readjustment Act of 1944, better known as the G.I. Bill, anyone who had served 90 days or more in the armed forces received both college tuition credits and modest monthly living allowances. But the G. I. Bill did not apply to merchant mariners. At 26, Noah was old for college: he would be at least 30 before he attained a degree. Music was his calling. But how could he make a start in music at his age, with no formal training and no money to pay for it? Harold Brown, back from Philadelphia, had an answer. Harold, who despite his own excellent training and musical skills was almost starving, had decided to apply for a scholarship at the Yale Music School to study composition with "the monster," as he called the distinguished but notoriously demanding Paul Hindemith. Noah should go there, too.

> Enter the Music School [Harold wrote] as an undergrad Freshman. It will take you 5 years to get your M.A. That seems like a long time, but think, you won't even be as old as I am now when you finish. And you will have an education and degree and connections.

As for how to pay for five years at Yale:

> You can get a scholarship, and earn some money, and maybe your father can help some. Edie will simply have to learn stenography and get a respectable job. They will help.[3]

But the Yale School of Music did not admit undergraduates and had no scholarship funds to speak of. Yale itself did of course admit undergraduates. In 1945, however, hundreds of veterans (many of them former Yale students) were pressing for entry to Yale under the G. I. Bill; and in addition a rigid Jewish quota was in force. Noah

---

[2] Patrick O'Brian, *Post Captain*, p. 88. "Bums" are "bum-bailiffs." In the novel, Aubrey through imprudent investment has run himself into debt and narrowly escapes the bailiffs hired by his creditors to arrest him.

[3] Harold Brown, letter to Noah Greenberg, April 27, 1945.

Greenberg from the Bronx, with his nine-year-old James Monroe diploma, stood next to no chance at all of gaining a place in the freshman class. Had he somehow won one, Edith might have been willing to work, as so many wives did, to help put her husband through college. But then again, she might not. The physical attraction between the two was still strong. But Edith was more mistrustful than ever of Noah's easy charm and his friendships with other women. For his part, Noah was telling friends that he and Edith had little in common and saying, half-jokingly, half-seriously, that he was going to sea "to get away from my wife."

In the event, neither Harold nor Noah tried seriously to get into Yale. On February 18, 1946, two months after Noah left the "Gripsholm," he shipped out for Europe as a wiper on the Alcoa Steamship Company's SS "Lindenwood Victory," It was the first of a series of sailings in 1948 and 1949, on vintage freighters (most of them built during Noah's childhood) with names like "Verendrye," "Yarmouth" and "Elizabeth," the latter not to be confused in any way, shape, or form with the Cunard Line's flagship "Queen Elizabeth II."

Between sailings there were stays "on the beach" that ranged from a few days to seven and a half months. Life ashore was a mixture of Workers Party political activity, energetic socializing, and music. The end of the war had brought many of Noah's friends back to New York. But it was Greenwich Village, not the Bronx, that claimed them. Clara and Rubin Baratz were living on West 14th Street. Clara was working for Armstrong Publications, and Rubin was traveling the world on war relief missions for the United Nations. Avel Austin, out of the SeaBees, took advantage of the G. I. Bill to enroll at Columbia and study for his doctorate. Avel found quarters on West 10th Street, because there "you could get a walkup for forty dollars a month." Harold Brown had been in and out of town since 1944, living wherever anybody would take him in, scraping a livelihood by substitute teaching, spending every extra dollar on piano rental and elaborate sound equipment (well before the advent of hi-fi), and straining every nerve to finish his compositions. Through Harold, Noah met several of Harold's gifted young musician friends from Philadelphia, among them Seymour Barab, Shirley Gabis—she had married Seymour, a cellist, in 1945—and Leonard Bernstein. Noah and Edie also became friends with Eugene Istomin. Between engagements, Istomin "loved to go up to [Noah's] place on 14th Street and always—big, big warm guy—he would be coming back from trips, in that black turtleneck that he wore,"[4] to talk, drink, and listen to music.

The politicals as well as the musicians were back, and whenever Noah was home the Greenbergs' apartment again became a meetingplace for both. Irving Howe, out of the Army and home from Alaska at the end of 1945, found New York "wonderfully un-improved."

> I join the '52-20' club (a year's unemployment insurance at twenty dollars a week). This enables me to contribute a year without pay to our socialist weekly.[5]

Nostalgia and patronization mix in Howe's recollection of becoming one of the regulars:

> [W]e were lucky to have as one of our comrades Noah Greenberg, a lumbering, good-natured fellow who was an accomplished musician. . . . Saturday nights we often wound up at his apartment on East Fourteenth Street, where he would play records of compositions we had never heard of and declaim sternly that among pianists only Schnabel was worth serious consideration, while Serkin was a mere miserable tinkler (a prejudice I've never quite shaken off). Noah would hop and dance around the room like a vast bear, noticing subtleties of performance the rest of us lamely pretended also to hear . . . .[6]

Clara Baratz retains almost total recall of Noah's apartment and the music he shared with friends there.

> The rooms were full of light, and there was a tremendous kitchen, and the long room off the living room was the room with the piano and, yes, the phonograph on which he played Monteverdi madrigals.
>
> Noah never liked to play music softly. He wanted it to be loud, to get the full effect from the speakers. And we were young, we never noticed what time it was. One night, very late, Noah had put on Monteverdi full blast and there came a knock at the door. We were full of fear that we were disturbing someone. And there stood a man in a bathrobe and slippers. Noah talked with him, and after a minute he came back in laughing and said: 'All he wanted to know was, Who wrote the music.'[7]

---

[4] Eugene Istomin, November 3, 1997.

[5] Howe, *op. cit.*, p. 105.

[6] *Ibid.*, pp. 58-59.

[7] Clara Baratz Hancox, December 7, 1997.

Jesse Simons was another returnee who came to listen, but he usually came alone. His marriage to Rickie had broken up while he was in the Army Air Corps. Rickie remained in California for several more years. There she worked as an organizer for the International Ladies' Garment Workers Union in the sweatshops of Los Angeles.

More than once, Edith's and Noah's guests would encounter the strange dweller in the Greenbergs' back bedroom, the individual known as *der Schreiber*. It became clear that the *Schreiber* was engaged in a mighty creative effort of some sort, because he had a habit of wandering into the Greenbergs' part of the apartment during a party and asking whoever was in the vicinity, "How would you describe a floor lamp?" or perhaps a radiator, a parking meter, or a pair of high-heeled shoes. Those present being New Yorkers, intellectuals, and in affable humor were generally more than willing to offer suggestions. The *Schreiber* would listen, nod his thanks, and pad back into his room without further comment.

It was left to another regular at 243 East 14th, the writer, editor, and man-about-Western-culture Dwight Macdonald, to learn who the *Schreiber* was and what he was up to. Years later, in a *New Yorker* profile, he reported his findings. The *Schreiber* as Macdonald describes him was a person with a mission:

> Down on Fourteenth Street . . . there is a man—Daniel Persky is his name—who knows exactly what he wants to be doing, has known it for some sixty-five of the seventy-two years he has been alive, and, what is perhaps more extraordinary still, has done it. Persky's lifelong interest—his 'specialty,' as he would say—has been the Hebrew language. Ever since he was a boy of eight, in Minsk, he has been in love with Hebrew, and ever since he arrived in this country, in 1906, and settled down for good on the lower East Side, he has been sowing Hebrew broadcast, like a Jewish Johnny Appleseed—speaking it, teaching it, writing it, promoting it . . .On Persky's letterhead, there is a Hebrew inscription meaning "The Slave of Hebrew." . . .

Macdonald went on to describe Persky's room as looking like "a junk heap," overflowing with "[m]agazines, books, newspapers, clippings, manuscripts, and letters." Its furnishings were Spartan: "no rugs, no pictures, no curtains or window shades," just one oval table, one chair and a bed.

> Persky's room is actually part of a large front apartment, and a procession of tenants have moved in and out of the other rooms

since Persky dug in, back in 1933. They often used to be members of Left Wing political groups . . .[8]

Macdonald, writing in 1959, was looking back at the 1940s. Edith and Noah were the tenants then, and Dwight himself—everybody called Macdonald "Dwight"—was a left-winger, a Workers Party member (albeit a quirkily individualistic one), and with his first wife Nancy a frequent visitor. Macdonald also supplied the explanation for the occasional appearances of the Greenbergs' eccentric subtenant at parties. Persky was compiling a vast Hebrew-English glossary. Hebrew, to say the least, is not a modern tongue and was even less one in 1945, before the creation of Hebrew-speaking Israel. Persky's quest for turns of phrase that might help him find Hebrew equivalents for contemporary ideas and artifacts was never-ending.

If a faltering marriage was making life ashore hard for Noah, so also was the gradual fracturing of the political belief system on which Noah, Edie, and their friends had based their lives from childhood on. Throughout the war years, not only Trotskyists but anti-Stalinist leftists of all persuasions or "tendencies," to use their own term, had staked their hopes on their deeply-felt belief in the "Third Camp." This held that the Second World War was a battle between contending imperialist camps. Hitlerian fascism was certainly the more evil of the two. Nevertheless, at war-end both the fascist Axis and the bourgeois democracies aligned with the "collectivist bureaucracy" that was the U.S.S.R. would inevitably, by the iron laws of history, lie prostrate. The "Third Camp" would then triumph. A great working-class uprising would sweep away the wreckage of old ideas of governance—Stalinism included—and would bring socialism to the fore everywhere.

It hardly needs saying that these things never happened. After the end of the war, Stalinism entrenched itself not only in the Soviet Union but throughout Eastern Europe, and remained entrenched for more than 40 years. For their part, the capitalist democracies, instead of dying, survived and hugely thrived. There was no working-class revolution. The "iron laws of history" simply failed to prove out. Furthermore, for Noah and Noah's comrades, so many of them Jewish, something else became overpoweringly important. Namely, the evidence of what Hitler had done to the Jews of Europe. The hideous truths of the Holocaust made it impossible to continue to

[8] Dwight Macdonald, "The Slave of Hebrew," *The New Yorker*, November 28, 1959, pp. 57-58.

believe that the war against Nazi Germany had been no more than
an imperialist adventure, and that which camp had won was of trivial
importance.

Said Herman Benson of this time:

> Nothing turned out the way we expected. It was way off from top
> to bottom. I don't say that it was crazy. It wasn't ridiculous. It
> was just absolutely wrong.[9]

The consequence was never wholesale abandonment of the Workers Party. Nor did most members of Max Shachtman's "Children's
Crusade," still young, still full of idealism, surrender their core beliefs in justice, racial equality, workers' rights, and the autonomy
and dignity of the arts. For years after the war, the Shachtmanites
struggled on. "The poorer we got," said Al Glotzer, "the more we
tried to do.

> We pushed ourselves. We pushed the comrades. We maintained
> our income tax [a phenomenal 20% on members' earnings] after
> the war was over . . . But I know, being in the office, that despite all
> that, there was constant decline. A few people leaving here; a few
> people leaving there. The organization was getting smaller and
> smaller.[10]

Max Shachtman himself remained an inspirational leader, fighting the good fight against disillusionment through the 1940s. And
Noah helped. In 1946, indeed, Noah and Shachtman together came
up with a strategy to put Workers Party socialism in the forefront of
New York's brewing anti-Communist political and cultural wars.
This began with a phone call from Noah to his friend from prewar
days Blanche Weiss, now Blanche Saia. In 1940, Blanche had given
up the idea of a concert pianist's career and returned to Hunter College. Now 23 and married, Blanche was still a radical, but she was a
radical wise in the ways of left-wing organizations and shrewdly
skeptical of their leaders' motives.

> [Noah] calls me. . . . He says, 'I'm sitting here, I just finished talk-
> ing to Shachtman, and will you come down?' [To Workers Party
> headquarters.] I said, 'What is it about?' and he said 'Come down,
> we'll just talk together.'
>
> So I came down. It's Noah, it's Shachtman, Noah's the go-be-
> tween between Shachtman and me. So I'm a little bit flattered and
> also wary. Under every Communist is a dictator as far as I'm con-
> cerned.

[9] Herman Benson, in "The Legacy of the Workers Party," p. 5.
[10] Albert Glotzer, in "The Legacy of the Workers Party," p. 13.

Shachtman had something serious to ask her. His idea was that since the war the climate of political thought had changed. In the face of Soviet behavior in Europe, enthusiasm for Russia was giving way to disillusionment. The Communist Party, Shachtman insisted, had lost the hegemony it once had. In this, he saw a great opportunity for socialism—"a Third Front, a new [intellectual] climate."

Noah had recommended Blanche to Shachtman as someone who could put together Shachtman's "Third Front." Blanche was interested, but she refused to go forward until she had extracted from Shachtman an ironclad promise not to interfere with her activities.

On that basis, Blanche formed and for two years ran an organization she called Left Forum. From rented quarters on Second Avenue, it held meetings and sponsored lectures on "the crucial topics that were hot spots," from Existentialism to Chinese-style Communism, in postwar politico-cultural debate.[11] During its brief life, Left Forum was as provocative and defiant of authority as Blanche herself. It was in fact a precursor of the much larger and stronger left-liberal organisations that sprang up to fight the cultural wars: organizations like Americans for Intellectual Freedom and the Europe-based Congress for Cultural Freedom. Noah was supposedly not much interested in political theory. But his role in setting up Left Forum shows him to have been a man ahead of his time.

In late 1948, the leadership committee of the Workers Party decided that it was mere vanity to go on pretending that an organization that had dwindled to two hundred members, unabie to raise the money to run even one candidate for public office, was a true political party. Accordingly, the Workers Party voted itself out of existence—as far as any of its erstwhile members knows, an act unique in American political history—and reconstituted itself as the Independent Socialist League, an organization devoted to furthering socialism by propagandizing in favor of a national labor party.[12]

[11] Blanche Weiss Saia, January 28, 1999.

[12] Neither its outspoken anti-Stalinism nor its Trotskyist tradition of intellectual freedom and internal debate protected the Workers Party/Independent Socialist League from the attentions of the McCarthyite and HUAC witch-hunters. The ISL was placed on the U. S. Attorney General's list of subversive organizations. Only a dogged fight and the efforts of labor lawyer and Washington insider Joseph Rauh won its removal from the list.

As for Max Shachtman, he, like so many other leading lights of the Workers Party, became increasingly conservative—or rather, in his case, increasingly non-liberal—as time rolled on. In the mid-1950s, Shachtman called for "an opening to the right," which meant that socialists should ally themselves with the *(cont.)*

Between watches aboard
the "Washington"
(Courtesy Lucille Dames)

Earlier that year, on January 15, Noah traveled to Newport News to board the United States Lines's SS "Washington," a smallish (7,030-ton) passenger liner, J. Anderson, Master. He signed on as plumber-machinist for what became a total of eight round trips between January and early August on the the New York-Southampton-Le Havre run. On at least some of these trips he had the company of Joe Dames, a slender, precise, thoughtful man, like Noah a Workers Party member and wartime merchant mariner, who had married Lucy Cogan after her divorce from Eddie Riesenfeld and her return to New York.

From April through August, he also enjoyed the companionship of Julius Goldstein. Julius was the kid brother of Noah's close friend Henry Goldstein. A notable wit, described by one of his friends as "a Trotskyist Woody Allen," Julius was living in the Village and taking painting classes at the Art Students' League. "I talked with Noah very frequently. I don't know how the idea became a reality. But I wanted to get to Paris." In 1948, Paris still had claims to be the world capital of art. Was not Picasso there, as he had been from October 1940 to Liberation, rejecting the bribes offered by the Ger-

---

Democratic Party's unionist wing. In the 1960s, he became an apologist for U. S. intervention in Vietnam. In 1972, the year of his death from a heart attack, he supported Henry Jackson's presidential primary campaign.

mans, half-freezing in his studio-flat on rue des Grand Augustins? Had not Matisse, the year before, created *Jazz*, its 20 dazzling color cutouts the talk of artists everywhere? Besides, who needed a specific reason? Julius and Noah too wanted to go because Paris was Paris. "It was one of the beautiful cities of the world and it had great collections of art."

So Noah landed Julius a job aboard the "Washington." "He lied. He said that I was a clothes presser. I wasn't a clothes presser.

> I told the [dispatcher] that I worked for a valet, I was a presser on Park Avenue. It took a lot of chutzpah on my part. Noah had a lot of chutzpah himself. Anyway, there I was and before I knew it I was sailing for le Havre. I had papers saying I was the ship's tailor.

Before long, Julius found himself in trouble.

> The head laundryman says, 'Okay, the stuff is coming in, bellboys are bringing down the suits, there's the machine, start.' I fucked up the first pair of pants, but by degrees I got the hang of it, and [then] a lady sent down her evening gown covered with sequins, and I didn't know a sequin from my hat. I figured you were supposed to steam it, not press it. So I stepped on the pedal, the steam came up, and right in front of my eyes these dandy little bits of molten matter appear all the way through the sides of the buck [the hinged top of the machine]. I pulled [the dress] off and said 'Oy' and went for the head laundryman, and in a classic understatement I said, 'It got screwed up.' And Herman calls in one of the bellboys and says, 'Please take this back to the woman and tell her we don't have the facilities to press this kind of a dress.' The kid went off with the dress and we never heard anything. I was waiting to be thrown in the brig, and it never came off.[13]

The "Washington"'s schedule called for 24-hour turnarounds at Le Havre. United States Lines, after all, was not running the liner to suit the sightseeing wishes of its crew. Accordingly, getting to Paris and back in time to catch the ship—missing a ship was no joke—called for both fleetness of foot and ingenuity of mind.

On one run, Noah was especially anxious to get a fast start. The "Washington" had docked. Julius was watching from the side of the ship as the dock crew began to unload. What he saw made his eyes pop. "Noah and two other guys" had slipped the unloaders (almost certainly French) a carton of cigarettes and were standing in the cargo net atop a pile of freight. When, the dock crane swayed

---

[13] Julius Goldstein, March 18, 1997.

the net high up out of the hold, its human contents swung dizzily back and forth in midair. "Noah's pants and whatnot were all over the place and one guy was smoking a cigar that broke." When the net landed on the dock, "it opened like a flower and these three guys raced for a taxi" to irate shouts from the crowd on deck. Asked why Noah was in such a hurry, Julius dismissed the artistic wonders of Paris with a comic's disparaging shrug. "He probably wanted to get laid."

On another dockside occasion, Noah approached the French official clearing the ship through customs and whipped out a telegram, "an old one I think," from Eugene Istomin. He waved it in the man's face and said loudly, in very bad French, "It's very important that I see this man in Paris right away." Julius, standing nearby, thought this was a "primitive form of argument," but it worked. And when the *douanier* demanded to know who Julius was, Noah shot back, "He has to come, too, because the telegram says it's very important that he be there also." The *douanier* must have been impressed, because he let them both go ashore. This may have been the one occasion during his seagoing days—they lasted until the seas grew rough in October—on which Julius actually did get to Paris, and when he did arrive the City of Light was pitch-dark. "We got to Paris only at night. By the time we got off the ship and caught a train, it was dark already, but I managed to buy some books that I wanted, whiskey and perfume for friends, and it was great."

Paris had art, Paris had girls. And Paris also had music. Edith recalled that Noah would scour the music stores and record shops of Paris and other European cities for the scores and discs Harold Brown had specified. Lucy Cogan Dames half-remembered an Adriatic voyage during which Noah and Joe ran into trouble in a Yugoslavian port, probably Dubrovnik. Their search for phonograph records had led them into a forbidden zone, and they had to explain themselves to the port police before being allowed back on ship.

Such accounts are what gave rise to the apocryphal tale that during his shore leaves abroad, Noah the merchant seaman would go in turtleneck and dungarees into libraries and obscure archives to hunt for the musical rarities that he and the New York Pro Musica would later perform. Asked about this, Seymour Barab, who knew Noah in Noah's merchant marine days, laughed uproariously. "It's a great story. Who am I to say it isn't true?" Bernard Krainis, cofounder with Noah of Pro Musica, was more matter-of-fact. "Noah didn't need to do that. Most of the music was right there uptown in the Forty-second Street Library." As for Noah's sartorial behavior, a photograph taken in a European city—again, probably Dubrovnik —in 1948 portrays him as clad like any tourist in open-necked white shirt, tailored slacks and jacket.

Noah's last trip on the "Washington" began in New York on July 17, 1948, and ended in New York on August 10. 1948. On this trip there were no girls, because Edith herself shipped out as kitchen help on the same voyage. As we shall soon see, Paris glimpsed by night seems to have whetted Edie's appetite for travel abroad. Noah and Edie spent at least part of the rest of August vacationing, but whether in the mountains or at the seashore is uncertain. On September 28, Noah shipped out again, signing on to service the refrigeration plant of the 27-year-old Agwiline freighter SS "Borinquen." The "Borinquen," managed by the New York & Porto Rico Steamship Company, was a fruit boat making the 12-day run to San Juan and return: Noah was discharged in New York on October 11. The trip was Noah's last of the year. He was not done with the sea. He would ship out eight more times before coming ashore for good. Still, in a special sense the "Borinquen" trip was his final voyage as a career merchant seaman.

CHAPTER NINE

GRAND PIANO, "GREAT BINGE"
(1949-1950)

$\mathscr{A}$fter 50 years, Edith cannot recall the exact date, but it was either late in 1948 or early in 1949 that she and Noah found themselves asking each other a very large question. Noah was restless. He was about to turn 30, an age at which young men can no longer persuade themselves that they *are* young men and that the future holds unlimited promise. His seagoing career had brought him to the exalted rank of third refrigeration engineer on a banana boat. His musical activity was confined to collecting and playing records for his friends and teaching part-songs to amateur singers. His life in the movement had turned into an endless round of meetings, bad news and fretful argument.

Edith, who loved him deeply against her better judgment, told him that she would support whatever it was he wanted to do, but that he had to do something other than aimlessly going to sea.

And so, as troubled couples sometimes do when they seek some way to make things better, each idly asked the other: "What would you like best in all the world?"

Noah's answer was immediate and predictable: "A grand piano!"

They both knew that a grand piano was a grandiose fantasy, an expensive daydream like the dream of a career in music. But Noah responded gamely: "And what about you?"

"A trip to Europe . . . as a passenger!"

This too made Noah shake his head, but Edith would not give up on the idea. "We can do it. You keep on shipping out. I'll cover the household expenses out of what I make, we'll bank your pay until we've saved up enough. First, the piano. Then Europe. And we'll go for a long, long time."

Aboard the "Marine Tiger," 1949. At sea, Noah's expenses were minimal
(Courtesy Greenberg family)

On January 9, 1949, after nearly three months ashore, Noah shipped out as a plumber-machinist on the SS "Marine Tiger," a banana freighter notorious as the vessel in which thousands of seasick Puerto Rican emigrants journeyed from San Juan to New York. Noah made three long trips aboard the "Tiger," stopping over in New York for less than 24 hours each time. Clearly, he had fallen in with Edie's scheme: on board, his expenses were minimal.

By spring, they had banked $800, enough for a huge old Steinway grand with fat legs, so massive that it had to be hoisted from the street.

On March 25, however, Noah left the "Tiger." Something had come up, and the Grand Tour with Edie had to wait.

When Noah had come back east, he had left the Seafarers' International Union and joined the National Maritime Union of America, CIO. The NMU was the powerhouse among seamen's unions, with a membership of close to 50,000 and a well-deserved reputation as an unruly organization, its members forever challenging its leadership. Before and during World War II, the NMU was widely considered to be a Communist-dominated union. Joseph Curran and the others at national headquarters in New York did little to dispel the impression. Curran, expelled from parochial school as incorrigible, became a merchant sailor and a headknocking, brilliant labor organizer. He did belong to the Communist Party. But in 1945, he broke with the CPUSA and formed an alliance with a triumvirate of other disillusioned Party members: Jack Lawrenson, NMU vice president and publisher of the NMU newspaper *The Pilot*, Dave Drummond, NMU port agent in New York, and Charles Keith, a seaman and organizer. With the tacit approval of Philip Murray of the CIO, Curran and the Lawrenson-Drummond-Keith trio started and won a war to take control of the NMU from the hard-core Stalinists who dominated the national board.

By mid-1947, Curran was NMU president and he and his teammates had kicked the Communists off the board. But in early 1949, he rigged a trap for his erstwhile comrades. At a mid-April meeting, Curran introduced an amendment to the NMU constitution to bar all "subversives" from membership. It was this maneuver that thrust Noah Greenberg into a bitter and ultimately bloody combat to fulfill Curran's promises of more democracy—always a Workers Party war-cry—by unseating Curran himself.

Since Lawrenson, Drummond, and Keith were the chief "subversives" Curran had in mind, the three men naturally found the amendment not to their taste. On May 2, Charlie Keith led a rowdy special membership meeting at which Curran's "loyalty oath" was voted down by 1,535 to 97. A *Labor Action* article gloating over Curran's defeat was signed by "N. R. Gaden." "N. R. Gaden" was Noah Greenberg.[1] Herman Benson, the paper's labor editor, said of the situation: "We had this enormous faction in the NMU consisting of two people. One of them was Noah Greenberg and the other was another young fellow." His minority status did not dismay Noah.

On May 10, he shipped out again, this time as an engine utility hand on the United States Lines's SS "American Defender," a Liberty ship. On June 7, Noah was back on the "Marine Tiger" as plumber-machinist for four more voyages. This meant that, according to plan, money was building up in his bank account. But except for layovers of 24 hours or less every several weeks, service on the "Tiger" effectively kept him out of New York, away from Edie, and away from the NMU infighting, for the whole of the summer.

On September 9, three days after Noah left the "Tiger" for the last time, *Labor Action* was running an article by N. R. Gaden headlined,

[1]Herman Benson, March 27, 1997; Carl Rachlin, April 9, 1997.

"3-Cornered Fight Looms in NMU Around Curran Regime." In it, Noah carried the fight right to Curran, accusing him of selling out the seamen and making shoddy deals with shipowners.

Noah's labor activities were not confined to reporting. He was working the hiring hall on 17th street between Seventh and Eighth Avenues, greeting fellow-members and passing out *Labor Action*. He was also talking privately with Charles Keith. Of the triumvirate, Keith was the only one who held no official NMU position. He was a dedicated Marxist, but an unorthodox one. (He would later make a fortune in Greenwich Village real estate.)

On Thursday, November 17, the regular New York membership meeting was scheduled for the St. Nicholas Arena, a dingy hall on West 67th Street near Columbus Avenue usually given over to boxing and wrestling matches. Joe Curran flew back from Texas in a chartered plane, making a dramatic arrival in mid-meeting to take over. The meeting quickly turned into a riot. The front-page story in the next day's *Times* was headlined "Seamen Fists Fly as Curran Fights to Cut Off Revolt." The *Daily News*'s front page was a screamer: "RED MOB SEIZES NMU OFFICES." Said Herman Benson:

> [Curran] mobilized a group of I think it was several hundred [outport members] and paid them out of the union treasury and he moved in and physically seized control of the hall . . . and he proceeded to run a mock membership meeting, that is, people screaming, We just say charges presented against Lawrenson are such and such, we're now about to elect a trial committee [to try Lawrenson], all in favor say aye opposed nay, everybody's yelling, motion passed, people start running up to the platform and the police were lined up to keep the [New York] members out so with that kind of mock procedure he expelled [Lawrenson, Drummond, Keith and others] from the union, kicked the shit out of some people at some point and got rid of them.[2]

Herman and others have said that at least once Noah was "roughed up," though not severely beaten, by Curran strongarm specialists. This may have been such an occasion.

Noah had been in daily consultation with Herman Benson and with a young New York labor lawyer named Carl Rachlin. Acting mainly on Rachlin's advice, Noah had phoned Norman Thomas.

[2]Herman Benson, October 8, 1997. Benson's front-page account in *Labor Action*, November 19, 1949, signed with his party name, Ben Hall, is almost as uninhibitedly vivid as this one, remembered 48 years later. Actually, however, Lawrenson, Drummond and Keith were not expelled from the union: the trial committee upheld their removal from office. Expulsion came later.

Thomas was a staunch anti-Communist and the one socialist whose eloquence and unimpeachable integrity had won him the admiration of people of every political leaning. In the mid-1930s, Thomas had been instrumental in forming the Workers Defense League, a Socialist Party organization that offered legal services to workers fighting for their rights against employers, unions, and government. Carl Rachlin was general counsel to the League and on close personal terms with Thomas.[3] He made the introduction, and Noah persuaded Thomas to lead a "Committee of Independent Citizens" to investigate the NMU internal fight. Other members of the committee were Dr. Robert Searle of the Protestant Council, Rev. Marshall Scott of the Presbyterian Institute for Human Relations, Dorothy Day, editor of *The Catholic Worker*, George Rundquist of the ACLU, and Albert Herling of the Unitarian Fellowship for Social Justice. Noah's idea, obviously, was to focus so much public and press attention on the infighting that Curran would have to pull in his horns.

On Wednesday, November 30, the Committee announced that it had found "no substantial evidence of a Communist plot against the union" but "considerable evidence of flagrant violations of the union constitution."[4] It picked its way delicately through the factional minefield, stating only that the use of violence by either side would only make it easier for a Communist power-grab to become reality. At a membership meeting the following night, Curran gained a substantial majority—1,714 to 566—in support of ousting Lawrenson and Drummond. Committee observers were present, but largely to keep an eye on the police.

The Committee did convene a public hearing on Tuesday, December 13. An N. R. Gaden *Labor Action* article reported "a week of terror organized by the [Curran] machine and dished out by a squad of 200 $10-a-day Curran stalwarts." This, the article claimed, led to "embittered silence" in the hiring hall. Whether the membership was terrorized into "embittered silence" or merely resigned to a Curran ascendency, Curran had managed to squelch Noah's effort to recruit rank-and-file members to his caucus.

After Noah's "week of terror" article and the unsigned article on the hearing, *Labor Action* fell silent for more than a month. In fact, there was nothing to cover except an occasional fistfight: serious opposition to Joe Curran's regime had melted away. In the issue of

[3]Carl Rachlin, April 9, 1997.

[4]Committee of Independent Citizens, statement, quoted in *Labor Action*, December 5, 1949, p. 1.

February 6, 1950, Noah roused himself enough to claim that a "new" NMU group was girding itself to fight both Curran and the Communist Party. But his article was mostly a lament. Noah would write once more as N. R. Gaden. He reported a week later on a membership meeting at which the rank and file accepted Curran's changes in the NMU constitution but voted 902 to 829 to reject the findings of Curran's trial committee on Dave Drummond. This was a promising development. But the fight had gone out of Noah's prose. The article ended limply, "What this will mean is hard to say."

We can let Herman Benson write the valedictory for this part of Noah's story.

> At that time [1950] he had an apartment on 14th Street. Because that's where the shift began. I came up to his apartment and he's got this nice apartment and he's playing Monteverdi, right? He's got the Monteverdi on, he's talking about Monteverdi and music of that period, we're talking about that, but the point is, while I'm talking to him the bell rings and up comes a guy from the NMU, one of the seamen, and so we put [Monteverdi] aside and the next thing you know we're plunged back into the great fight in the NMU, but Noah's heart was already out of it. His heart and his head were out of it, and it was pretty clear that he was on his way out.[5]

On March 13, 1950, a Holland-America Line freighter, the SS "Leerdam," weighed anchor in New York and steamed down the bay, bound first for Norfolk, Virginia and then across the Atlantic for Antwerp. Aboard were Edith and Noah Greenberg. As passengers.

---

[5]Herman Benson, March 27, 1997.

CHAPTER TEN

ꝐARIS AND ꝐRADES

(1950)

ꝑeanne Wacker came to Paris in the fall of 1949 to study philosophy. Curiosity and an appetite for intellectual adventure had carried the slender 28-year-old a long way from her Ogden, Utah birthplace. The daughter of transplanted New Yorkers, Jeanne had first gone to Brigham Young University. Then, in a mind-boggling reversal of educational direction, she enrolled at the ultra-progressive Black Mountain College in North Carolina. She roomed with Walter Gropius's daughter Beata and studied drama with Eric Bentley and music with Heinrich Jalowetz, Edward Lowinsky, and Fritz Cohen. In 1946, after one of Black Mountain's periodic faculty upheavals, Jeanne fled to New York and finished her work for the B. A. degree at New York University. There she fell under the spell of yet another brilliant scholar. This one was the acerbic Sidney Hook, once a Communist and still by his own description a "liberal socialist" but since the mid-1930s a fervent anti-Stalinist. Hook was head of N.Y.U.'s Philosophy Department, and Jeanne Wacker soon became one of his favorite students. After a year of graduate school, Jeanne won one of the then-new Fulbright Fellowships for study abroad. In 1949, with the black-market rate for francs at 300 to the dollar, Jeanne could do more than attend lectures at the Sorbonne. She could live decently, indulge a taste for the arts and still spend winter afternoons and spring nights soaking up the existentialism that raged among young Parisians at the Flore, the Deux Magots, the Hotel Montana, and the other haunts of the intellectuals and would-be intellectuals of postwar Paris.

In a word, Jeanne Wacker, bright young American in Paris, was an ideal person to introduce other bright young Americans to the pleasures of a city on the way to recovery. "The bicycle-powered *vélo-taxis* were a thing of the past," according to one account. "In the Tuileries gardens, children [again] enjoyed rides on donkeys or in little carts pulled by goats."[1] The traditional August exodus of Parisians *en vacance* had resumed, another clear sign of emergence from wartime privation. The horrible winter of 1946, when whole sections of the city had gone without heating fuel and frozen pipes and power failures had been endemic, was only a memory.

Jeanne does not remember who among her bohemian friends in New York had written to her that "You must meet Noah Greenberg." But in early April 1950, Noah and Edith, introduction in hand, presented themselves at her flat. "It was love at first sight," Jeanne said of the meeting, "all three of us." The trio went out for a meal, and when the subject of music arose Noah quickly extended an invitation to spend the evening at a pianist friend's. "We went to her apartment," Jeanne said, "and listened to her play through a program she was preparing. It was a delightful episode for me." She and the Greenbergs parted with promises to meet soon again.

Page after page of Edith's carefully labeled photographs make clear which was the Paris she and Noah most wanted to remember. The shot of the Pont du Carrousel from the Louvre might have been taken by tourists from anywhere. So might the one of the French threesome looking intense but chilly in spring sunshine at a sidewalk café in the Place St. Michel. But then there is the view of the cat sitting as if for its portrait in a shop window on the rue du Dragon. (Could it have been taken for Harold Brown?) There is the streetcorner scene on the rue de Sèvres and the even more picturesque shot of the Hôtel de l'Académie and the tabac at the corner where rue Perronet meets rue des Saints Pères. These locales lie at the very heart of Saint-Germain-des-Près, as did the small hotel, its name lost in the mists of Edith's memory, at which they were staying. Noah had clearly visited the celebrated quarter on his hurried shore leaves from the "Washington." Just as clearly, he and Edith loved it.

Over the next several weeks, Jeanne Wacker and the Greenbergs saw a good deal of each other. "We hit it off so well," Jeanne said. "They were going to Italy, so I sent them to friends of mine who were sharing a villa on the outskirts of Florence." But before Edith and Noah left, the question of Jeanne's studying the piano again did in fact come up. Her instruction at Black Mountain had been choppy and unsatisfying, but she loved the instrument. "Well," Noah said,

[1]Antony Beevor and Artemis Cooper, *Paris After the Liberation*, p. 268.

"when we get back I may be teaching, so look me up." Jeanne said she would, and she kept her word.

Of Edith's and Noah's travel through France and Italy, Edith says with breathtaking candor: "It was what made me stop being a socialist. There were the churches and cathedrals and museums and the whole wonderful culture that a mercantile society had created, and we [the socialists] were going to destroy it?" In Henry James's *The Princess Casamassima*, the young socialist revolutionary Hyacinth Robinson, brought up in the London slums, accepts an invitation to Medley Hall, a grand English country house, and undergoes exactly the same transforming revelation.

> The cup of an exquisite experience—a week in that enchanted palace, a week of such immunity from Lomax Place and old Crookenden as he had never dreamed of—was at his lips; it was purple with the wine of novelty, of civilization, and he couldn't push it aside without drinking. He might go home ashamed, but he would have for evermore in his mouth the taste of nectar.[2]

To this day, the taste of nectar remains in Edith Schor's mouth.

For Noah, the cultural delights of Paris and Florence and Rome were only a preliminary to something even more overpowering. He and Edith had had advance notice of a signal musical event, and had planned their trip around it. The event was the Bach Festival that would open on June 2 in the village of Prades, in the Pyrenées-Orientales a few kilometers north of the Spanish border. Leading this homage to Bach would be the renowned cellist and interpreter of the great composer, Pablo Casals.

The genesis of the Prades Festival has long ago become part of twentieth-century musical folklore. The prime mover was Alexander Schneider—Sasha Schneider—second violinist for eleven years with the Budapest String Quartet, excellent musician, bon vivant, and devotee of good food and wine, good conversation, and beautiful women. Schneider had made the pilgrimage to Prades and Casals for a highly unusual reason. As Eugene Istomin put it decades later: "Can you imagine this violinist of all people begging a cellist to help him learn the Bach sonatas for solo violin?"[3]

Casals, like everyone else, found Sasha Schneider delightful and did consent to work with him on the Bach violin sonatas during the summer of 1947. For his part, Schneider tried in vain to persuade

---

[2]Henry James, *The Princess Casamassima*, p. 303.
[3]Eugene Istomin, November 3, 1997.

the great cellist to concertize in North America. Then, acting on the suggestion of Casals's longtime friend the pianist Mieczyslaw Horszowski, Schneider proposed "a Bach Festival next summer [1949], in June or July, in Prades or Perpignan, under your direction." Casals hesitated. A Catalan patriot, in 1946 he had vowed not to perform in public in any country that recognized Francesco Franco's totalitarian regime in Spain. This painful self-imposed silence had changed nothing politically, but it had won Pablo Casals the musician acclaim as a champion of decency and moral integrity on a level with Albert Schweitzer and Albert Einstein. To appear at all, and especially at a festival, might make him seem to be breaking his sworn word. While he brooded, the opportunity for a 1949 event slipped away. But performing at home in Prades, Casals decided, was permissible. So later that year, he gave his consent, and word spread among musicians that Casals would lead a festival in honor of Bach the next summer.

Pablo Casals was one of Harold Brown's great heroes. During the years when Harold was most energetically urging his musical ideas on Eugene Istomin, a recurrent theme was that the gifted young pianist could do no better than to seek out and study with Casals. Even before the Prades event, Eugene had made his way to the dusty small town to meet and play for the master. At Alexander Schneider's invitation, he then took part in the festival, along with dozens of other musicians (including pianists Horszowski, Clara Haskil and his own teacher Rudolf Serkin).

Even before the fact, the Prades Festival had begun to take on a meaning far larger than itself."Pablo Casals was seventy-three years old in the spring of 1950," one of his biographers reminds us, "and through mass communications the nineteenth-century man became a twentieth-century symbol."[4] What triggered this transformation was a photo essay in the May 15, 1950 issue of *Life* magazine . Written by Lael Wurtenbaker with photographs by Gjon Mili of Casals in Prades, the feature was headlined: "Pablo Casals: At last he is preparing to play in public again." There was mention of the two-hundredth anniversary of the death of Bach, but the main theme of Wurtenbaker's copy was that "the musical world's great voluntary exile, Pablo Casals," would soon appear in public again. In 1950, a story in *Life* was the equivalent of a half-hour feature on today's prime-time network TV. Overnight, Casals, already *known*, at least to music-lovers, became a celebrity. For millions of people who cared

[4]H. L. Kirk, *Pablo Casals, a Biography,* p. 453.

little or nothing about music, he would, like Picasso and Thomas
Mann, become an archetype of the artist as sage. The festival itself
took on the aura of a spiritual gathering, the holy month of a secular
religion. Indeed, it was the unpretentious forerunner of today's huge
high-voltage rock exaltations, those circuses that rally thousands and
raise millions for the benefit of the environment, the manatees, the
poor, or some other favored global cause.

The opening concert took place on the evening of Friday, June 2,
in the Church of St. Pierre. Noah and Edith were there. Noah himself wrote an excited description of the scene:

> The visitors were met by a local population that had, for weeks,
> scrubbed this ancient town until it sparkled. 'Bienvenue' banners
> reached across the narrow streets. There were elaborate window
> displays, paying homage to Bach & Casals—One patisserie proudly
> showed a 3 foot almond paste 'cello & bow (edible too). . . . Hun-
> dreds of wooden benches were placed within the church with its
> mixture of Baroque chapels behind Roman arches, enormous
> Gothic nave and gaudy Baroque main altar adorned with multi-
> colored terracotta statues of St. Peter and various other saints. . .

> At 9:30 the musicians assembled on the stage at the foot of the
> altar. A bell tinkled and there was complete silence in the church.
> A nervous Pablo Casals, 'cello and bow in hand, briskly stepped
> forward to the podium. The audience and orchestra rose in si-
> lence (applause forbidden) to greet him. He played the Bach G
> major unaccompanied Suite as only Casals could! with a freedom,
> beauty and passion that one finds so seldom in music today.[5]

The "3 foot almond paste 'cello & bow" duly appears in Edith's
photo album, along with snapshots of the Hotel Salites—27 rooms
and one bath—and other views of Prades. But there are also fine
views of Casals and Sasha Schneider following a rehearsal on June
10. There are pictures of Eugene Istomin seated at a rehearsal piano,
although, curiously enough, Eugene has no recollection of encoun-
tering Edith and Noah in Prades.[6] And someone caught Noah and
Edie on film in the courtyard of the Salites. Edith is serious-faced.
Noah is smiling like a man for whom the gates of Heaven have
opened.

The scope of the Prades Festival, in terms of the amount of Bach's
music performed during the three weeks, is remarkable. In all, there

---

[5]Noah Greenberg, "The Bach-Casals Festival," typescript with handwritten corrections, dated June 21, 1950, p. 3.

[6] This is not surprising: Istomin, by his own account, was "up to his ears" in rehearsals and preparation for the many concerts in which he played.

Edith and Noah, Prades, 1950 (Courtesy Edith Schor)

were six orchestral concerts and six chamber-music concerts. With various soloists, the 30-piece Festival Orchestra led by Casals performed all six *Brandenberg Concertos,* two of the four orchestral suites, six other instrumental concertos, the *Musical Offering,* three cantatas, all six of the suites for unaccompanied cello, all three of the sonatas for viola da gamba and continuo (played on cello by Casals), a large sampling of Bach's other chamber music (e.g., the *Goldberg Variations,* the sonatas for flute and continuo) and several cantatas.

For Noah, Paris, New York, his past life, were of small moment. His own writing makes clear that he was completely wrapped up in—and enraptured by—the marvelous music going on around him. And not only the music itself, but the atmosphere surrounding it: the famous musicians arriving to perform, the celebrities crowding into the church along with ordinary folk, the radio journalists (Charles Collingwood of CBS among others), the recording engineers with their complicated equipment and esoteric shop-talk, which Noah the hi-fi enthusiast would have heard with fascination.

At one point, probably just after the June 10 rehearsal, Noah managed to catch the eye of Sasha Schneider, who spoke with worshipful enthusiasm as one extrovert to another:

> I can't express my great regret that not all the world's musicians can attend these hours of rehearsal to witness our tears of joy over the extraordinary amount of happiness and life [Casals] can give

us. . . .There is never a flat moment. There is always variety. Yes, we can all of us—to the last stand and the last second violin player—ask questions, discuss every little phrase with Maître Casals. We are not afraid to lose our jobs either. We don't even want to 'take five' and we do not worry about overtime. . . . [W]e don't care about not having comforts such as running hot water or electric plugs for our Shik [sic] razors; nor do the girls mind having to go and find their powder rooms out of doors.[7]

Rehearsals, held in the dining hall of the Collège Moderne des Jeunes Filles, were open to the public. Noah attended most of those that took place during the festival, and clearly reveled in them.

What has been accomplished [in rehearsal] is that 'forty musicians' together have approached what Casals does on the 'cello alone. They discussed and were guided to an understanding of the tempi, the material, the amount of movement from upbeat to downbeat, the [establishment] of longer lines, the varying intensity of the climaxes and the overall form. All this was not done pedagogically, however. Casals as a rule played through the movement (he loves the music too much to stop) made a few remarks and suggestions at the end, some discussion, and then a section or the whole movement was done again.[8]

After a few polite remarks about Casals's "kindness and humility," Noah fires off a whole series of interesting statements.

But Casals is just not the person who can turn to a soloist who is playing his portion of the work with an entirely different approach and say 'Look here, our conceptions are different. Play it my way.' This need occurred seldom in the course of the festival, but it occurred. This would not happen with someone like Toscanini. Toscanini always insists, has fired left and right, refused to allow certain conductors to guest conduct because they might spoil what he had molded.[9]

Toscanini's performances, Noah insists, were "usually great." But then he speaks of "a powerful ferocity but just a little too unbending . . . an allegro tempo that runs just a little ahead of being the convincing tempo . . ." In contrast, "[t]he dance movement is always a dance for [Casals] and never an idealized form."[10] Casals's conducting may be less decisive than Toscanini's, he adds, and the play-

[7]Greenberg, *op. cit.*, p. 9.
[8]*Ibid.*, p. 11.
[9]*Ibid.*, p. 12.
[10]*Loc. cit.*

ing of the ensembles under his baton less polished, but his conceptualizations are luminous. Of the performances of the D-minor Concerto for Violin and the final movement of the Fourth Brandenberg, Noah writes, "Who would imagine that such a wonderful approach was possible within the framework of the score?"[11]

At the closing concert, Casals chose as an encore his arrangement of *El Cant des Ocells* ("The Song of the Birds"), a sad medieval Catalan folk song. "The audience, which filled every last nook & chapel, pulpit, organ loft," Noah wrote, "was moved as perhaps no audience ever has been. Certainly not one I've ever seen. An unashamed flow of tears everywhere!"[12]

In setting down what he heard, saw and felt, Noah had in mind something more ambitious than a souvenir journal. The battered twelve-page typescript, heavily edited and augmented in ink, from which the above quotations are taken was intended for publication. On June 23, the last day of the festival, Edith mailed the manuscript from Avignon to a friend, "Billie," in New York. Edith's covering note tells the story:

> We spent the last 3 weeks at the Bach-Casals festival at Prades & Noah was so beside himself that this article was the result. He wrote and asked Phyllis [Jacobson, wife of Julie Jacobson and fellow Workers Party member] to see what she could do about getting it into Commentary or Partisan Review, but we haven't heard from her. . . .[13]

That is, Noah hadn't sent the actual article to Phyllis Jacobson, he had enlisted her services to try to persuade Elliot Cohen or Clement Greenberg of *Commentary* or William Phillips or Philip Rahv of *Partisan Review* to commission it. Now that it was written, and no commitment had been forthcoming, Edith and Noah wanted Billie either to give it to Phyllis or to mail it to Manny Geltman. Geltman, another Workers Party stalwart, had succeeded Irving Howe as editor of *Labor Action.* He too had good literary connections and might help find Noah's piece a good home (The article was never published.)

Edie's offhand comment that Noah was "beside himself" at Prades was close to the truth. He was certainly not alone in feeling transpor-

---

[11]*Ibid.,* p. 13.

[12]*Ibid.,* p. 16.

[13] Edith [Schor] Greenberg, letter to "Billie," June 23, 1950. Edith did not recall working on the typescript or writing this letter, but the material makes it clear that she did both

ted. Casal's biographer, H.L.Kirk, called the 1950 festival "a love feast among musicians,"[14] and there is no doubt that he was right. At the close of the festival, the members of the orchestra addressed an adoring but sincere letter to Casals.

> When we first played together, people from different nations, languages, beliefs, religions, personalities, and styles . . .we had much spirit but little ensemble. . . .With the common aim of trying to understand and interpret Bach under your guidance, we finally really began to play together and each had the tremendous pride of being part of the beautiful collective work. What a lesson this has been.[15]

For Noah, Prades was a defining moment, a turning point. For three solid weeks, he had had before him example after example of what inspiring musical leadership could produce. "Can you imagine musicians getting excited about a performance of the 3rd Brandenberg," Noah wrote, "which they had played dozens of times at rehearsals and 100's of times in the past?"[16] That was what Pablo Casals had made happen. It would be surprising if Noah, being Noah, had not gone to sleep each night with a picture in his head of himself as conductor, smiling, cajoling, teaching, and if need be, commanding eager colleagues in "the beautiful collective work" of making music. He had no idea how he could make it happen—the article was a halting first attempt to get himself and his musical ideas before the public—but from Prades forward, Noah's mind was made up. He would go back home to New York, There, at whatever the cost, he would devote his life to music.

[14]Kirk, *op. cit.*, p. 459.

[15]Letter, Prades Festival Orchestra to Pablo Casals, June 23, 1950, quoted in Kirk, *op. cit.*, pp. 454-455.

[16]Greenberg, *op. cit.*, p. 14.

CHAPTER ELEVEN

$\mathcal{E}$ND OF A MARRIAGE, START OF A CAREER

(1951-1952)

$\mathcal{B}$y the time Edie and Noah arrived in New York, August and the summer were nearly over. The pair spent a few days in Connecticut to decompress, then settled themselves in once again at 243 East 14th Street. There were friends and family to see, gossip to exchange, and tales to tell about their European adventure. But what they themselves called their "great binge" had come to an end. Looming before Noah now was the serious business of how he was going to make a living; and Noah and Edith were not alone in their concern. Noah's mother and father, always convinced of their son's talent, were worried about his future.

Shortly after the end of the war, Lillie and Harry Greenberg had left New York and their needle-trades jobs for Southern California. They had found their way to Elsinore, a tiny resort village on the lake of the same name in the San Bernardino foothills about 40 miles south of Riverside. There they had bought a small variety store, which they ran for several years. They would not return to the East until 1957. But with their son no longer sailing the seven seas, and moreover at loose ends and anxious to begin a new career, Lillie and Harry were eager to be of help. Edith painted a vivid picture of how they enlisted the rest of the family and pressed Noah to give up his dream in favor of good honest work.

> This business about going into music. [Noah's] uncle, Uncle Moniek, was rich. Rema's father. He said to Noah, 'I'll give you a job. In my pocketbook factory.' His mother said, 'Noah, go and see Uncle Moniek.' And his aunt [Branca] said, 'Noah, Uncle Moniek has just the job for you.'[1]

[1]Edith Schor, March 7, 1997.

Edith had some of the details wrong. "Uncle Moniek," Rema's father Morris Davidson, was in the handbag business and was indeed prospering, but as a salesman: he never owned his own factory. According to Rema, Uncle Moniek probably could have landed Noah a job as a junior salesman for one or another handbag manufacturer, or possibly signed him up as his sales assistant and paid him out of his own pocket. With his abundant charm and outgoing personality, Noah would have been a standout success at selling. And he would have a steady job with a weekly salary and a secure future—everything a loving family wants for an only son with a wife to support. What Noah had instead, in the fall of 1950, were two piano lessons a week at five or ten dollars each.

One of his pupils was Jeanne Wacker, back from Paris and now in graduate school at N.Y.U.

> When [Edith and Noah] got back to New York, I did look him up, though I don't remember how or through whom. . . . They were living on East Fourteenth Street, the big vast apartment with the writer in the back room. . . . I trotted over to his house to take lessons, because I lived in the Village also and it was very easy.[2]

Wacker says of Noah that he was an excellent teacher, in large part because he encouraged her not only to work on technique but also to think in large terms about the music she was playing.

> I had never had the opportunity to tackle a whole sonata. My training at Black Mountain was very spotty, and when I came to Noah, pretty soon he had me doing a Haydn sonata, he had me doing easy Bach things out of the Anna Magdalena book, and he had me doing things that had shape, form. He had me doing Czerny also, but I mean I was just so proud of myself when I actually memorized a couple of sonatas for him.[3]

Noah was also giving piano lessons to a woman named Ruth Glazer. But two piano pupils hardly added up to a living. Someone, possibly Harold Brown or another of Noah's and Harold's musical friends, arranged for Noah to meet the composer Elliott Carter. In 1950, Carter was working on his String Quartet No. 1. He was looking for a good copyist to write out some of the parts of the quartet for performance and possible publication. Copying out musical parts from a composer's draft score demands not only a

[2]Jeanne Wacker, October 2, 1997.

[3]Jeanne Wacker, October 2, 1997. Pianists will recognize "Czerny" as Carl Czerny, Beethoven's favorite pupil, teacher of Franz Liszt, prolific composer, and the creator of a classic set of technical exercises for piano.

knowledge of music but patience and manual dexterity. Jesse Simons wrote that Noah was "absolutely superb" at the task.

> Frequently I watched Noah hand print scores. It was a study in contrasts. Noah was big, 6'2", and he had large, thick, heavy hands. With those hands he had run the biggest of lathes. Yet he was turning out scores that were beautiful—he was very precise, delicate, careful and conscientious. I always found it an amazing sight. Unforgettable![4]

Copyists were paid by the page, and a good copyist could earn decent money and in addition gain a foothold in the tight-knit but furiously competitive world of New York classical music. Indeed, it was as a music copyist that Noah first joined the Associated Musicians of Greater New York, better known as Local 802 of the American Federation of Musicians.

Elliott Carter did more for Noah than pay him for his copying. As a Harvard undergraduate, Carter had developed a keen interest in Renaissance music and had begun a collection that included scores from E. H. Fellowes's *English Madrigal School*. During the early 1930s, while studying with Nadia Boulanger in Paris, Carter had become familiar with the work of the musicologists Henri Expert and Charles van den Borren. He added to his collection works from Expert's editions of Orlando Lasso, Claudin de Sermisy, Clément Jannequin, and other French Renaissance composers. He also acquired works from van den Borren's editions of the earlier Franco-Flemish masters Gilles Binchois and Guillaume Dufay. Carter's "closetful" of Renaissance music also included madrigals by Gesualdo and Marenzio and others. It was a treasure-trove, much of it virtually unknown even to scholars in this country "I knew Noah was deeply interested in the music," Carter said, "and he was also very poor. So I pulled out the whole pile and let Noah take his pick."[5]   It was a princely gift.

Still, neither copying nor teaching was music-making, and what Noah desperately wanted was to make music. For her part. Edith wanted Noah to settle down and undoubtedly told him so, which only added to his frustration and fueled his suspicion of her motives. "Noah thought I wanted him to become a handbag salesman," she said of his attitude. But in her bones, she claims, she knew that music, not selling handbags, had to be the answer.

---

[4]Simons, *op. cit.*, p. 17.
[5]Elliott Carter, February 9, 1998.

I said to Noah, 'Look!' I would have *left* him if he'd taken that job. I said, 'Noah, get your family off your back. Go see Uncle Moniek and *tell* him.' And when he came back and said he'd told Moniek he wanted to be in music, I was so happy.[6]

In the end, it was Jesse Simons who found a way for him to "be in music" and, in the process, save himself from the awful fate of life among the handbags.

In 1948, Jesse had quit the socialist movement and, like many other Workers Party dropouts, had gone into union work. His job as Assistant Political Director of the International Ladies' Garment Workers Union had him teaching officials of I.L.G.W.U. locals how to set up voter-registration and get-out-the-vote drives among their members on behalf of the Liberal Party (a brand-new union creation) in New York City's mayoral elections. The work brought Jesse in close touch with local leadership. As well as waging endless war for better pay, working conditions and fringe benefits, the Garment Workers, the "I.L.G." for short, took special pride in its efforts to teach, uplift and provide recreation for its members. Every one of its larger locals had an education director, and it was to these officials that Jesse directed his efforts on Noah's behalf.

Local 22, dressmakers, its membership largely Jewish, was one of the largest and most militant of the I.L.G.'s New York City locals. Through his friendship with Joe Mazur, the education director, Jesse Simons was able to get Noah a job leading a chorus of Local 22 members. Sessions were held at the local's quarters on West 40th Street. "He came in once or twice a week," Mazur remembered. "We paid him $15 a night. Plus cheese and crackers to enhance the experience." Noah led a large group in the union songs and old favorites that everyone knew and could sing even without being able to read music. "He tried to get them into civil-rights and patriotic songs, too," Mazur added. But Noah also worked with a "small coterie" of students who wanted to learn more. He taught them to read music and to sight-read, and "some of them went on to take a serious interest in music." On many nights, Noah would show movies of symphonies and concerts to his choristers and hold discussions afterward. He threw himself into his job with typical enthusiasm, and, said Joe Mazur, "he loved it."[7]

Equally strong was the "Italian" dressmakers' Local 89. Its manager was the flamboyant Luigi Antonini. Vanni Montana, hardly

---

[6]Edith Schor, March 7, 1997.
[7]Mazur, January 30, 1998.

Noah directs the chorus of Local 135 (Cloakmakers), ILGWU
(Courtesy Greenberg family)

less flamboyant, was the education director. Local 89 too boasted a members' chorus, and Noah became its director as well. At various times, he also led the choruses of Local 135, based in Newark, New Jersey and Local 91, cloakmakers', the children's wear local. Joe Mazur also thinks that Noah led the chorus of Local 91, which not only sang for its own pleasure but made appearances at churches and synagogues in the Chelsea district "and got paid" for singing. Each of these other groups would generally meet once a week. Noah would pick appropriate music and conduct the singing. Leading four or five sessions a week brought in a very respectable $60 to $75, or even more, the equivalent of $360 to $450 today. "With I.L.G. and the copying of parts," said Edith, who was also working, "we had finally found a way to earn a living."

On the surface at least, the end of 1950 was a placid few months in Edith's and Noah's lives. Jeanne Wacker mentioned one particularly memorable occasion.

> I remember that Christmas Day was a great day at Noah and Edith's house: this was Christmas 1950, it had to have been. And Noah invited all his good pupils and friends and so on to his house for Christmas Day.

Jeanne had spent the late hours of Christmas Eve with Barbara Anderson "Andy" Dupee, wife of the scholar and critic F. W. Dupee. "At eleven o'clock [we] lifted a glass to welcome Christmas Day." Her party-going continued the next day at Noah's.

> Edith began serving hot buttered Scotch at one o'clock, and we put on the *Messiah* and we all sang along—he had the scores there, of course—and we sang and we drank . . . and we drank and we sang, and then Noah cooked a great wonderful meal. All I know is that he was a very good cook, he loved food and he loved wine and all that. And that was the happiest Christmas I had had since, oh my gosh! I can't remember. Because remember I was alone, my family were in Utah.[8]

Among the "nice interesting people" Jeanne met at Noah's that Christmas afternoon was Julius Goldstein. "And he was smitten," she said with a smile. "Followed me around for a long time." In fact, they liked each other well enough to date for several years.

But all too soon, the fun of the 1950 holiday season was wiped away and forgotten. Shortly after the holidays, Edith came down with the flu. The flu turned into pneumonia and on orders from her doctor Edith went to bed at home, where Noah would be able to nurse her. "The piano was in the bedroom," Edith said. "So for five weeks, Noah was deprived of the piano." Edith regards this as the defining incident. But whether or not she is right, one day in the late winter of 1951 Noah announced, to her bafflement and distress, that after eleven years as her husband he was "not ready for the responsibilities of marriage." Noah's way of proving his point was to move out. It was as if, having broken with his political past and his occupational past, Noah found it necessary to break with his emotional past as well. Edith's world, the one she had tried so hard for so many years to hold together, fell apart. And Noah entered the darkest period of his life.

His first act after the split was to hunt for an apartment in Greenwich Village. He soon found one, a one-room basement flat on Cornelia Street off Bleeker Street in Greenwich Village, far removed from Second Avenue and 14th Street but equally popular with would-be bohemians for its low rent and rickety charm. One of Noah's neighbors was the reviewer and memoirist Anatole Broyard, who settled there in 1948. "The Village, like New York City itself," Broyard wrote, "had an immense, beckoning sweetness."

[8]Jeanne Wacker, October 2, 1997.

It was like Paris in the twenties—with the difference that it was our city. We weren't strangers there, but familiars. The Village was charming, shabby, intimate, accessible, almost like a street fair. . . . We shared the adventure of trying to be, starting to be, writers or painters.[9]

Another familiar on Cornelia Street was the poet Wystan Auden, who lived in the "new but drab building" at Number Seven and could be seen in the neighborhood at all hours. Noah's long friendship with Auden dates from this period.

So too did his acquaintanceship with Dylan Thomas, who as early as 1951 was traveling to the U. S. to read his poetry at the 92nd Street "Y" and indulge his taste for the pleasures of life away from austere postwar Britain. Thomas liked to drink and hold court at the celebrated White Horse Tavern, on Hudson Street near West 11th. Noah's cousin Rema, then a student at City College, was impressed when Noah told her that he often spent evenings drinking with the golden-voiced poet from Wales.

Noah's one room—it had a separate kitchenette and bathroom —was just large enough for the rebuilt Steinway grand bought with Edith's money a year or so before. The availability of the piano meant that he could keep his pupils, and before long he reconvened his amateur singing group, although on a modest scale. One of its members was Jeanne Wacker. The group met every Tuesday night.

I remember being in the basement singing—sight-singing—madrigals and things because Noah had never had a chance to hear this music.[10]

Another participant was Nancy Macdonald. At the time, her marriage to Dwight Macdonald, like Noah's to Edith, was fraying badly.[11] In mid-April of 1951, Nancy and Dwight "more or less" agreed to try a separation over the summer. Dwight was busy editing his poison-tipped *New Yorker* profile of Roger Baldwin, head of the American Civil Liberties Union. He was also seeing his psychiatrist several times a week, boasting about his most recent affair and openly seeking other sexual entanglements. The Macdonalds'

[9]Anatole Broyard, *Kafka Was the Rage*, p. vii.

[10]Jeanne Wacker, October 2, 1997.

[11]Although both Macdonalds engaged in affairs with others (Dwight in particular with Gloria Lanier, who became his second wife), their marriage did not end until mid-June of 1954. From Michael Wrezin's account in *A Rebel in Defense of Tradition*, a biography of Macdonald, the final several years were terrible ones for all concerned.

three-room apartment at 117 East 10th Street, with its tiny kitchen, piles of books and papers and bundles of clothes for refugees—the Macdonalds shared it with their two sons as well—was not the pleasantest of places. Nancy was happy enough to escape to Noah's for an hour or two of song. Indeed, one consequence of her taking part was that she and Jeanne Wacker became good friends.

Noah's cousin Rema remembers being invited to join.

> Noah called me and said, 'I'm having a small group to come over and sing. Do you want to come?' And I said, 'I'm a terrible sight-reader.' And he said, 'Oh, come on, you know you have a good ear, you'll hear it.' He said, 'Sheila's coming.' Sheila Schonbrun. She went to Music and Art. Sheila Jones, she was married to somebody, Schonbrun, and then she married LaNoue [Davenport]. But . . . I remember that he had a number of people who liked to sing, that's kind of how it started! And I said, 'I'm too scared, I'm not a good sight-reader.' So I never went.[12]

Yet another person who did come to sing with Noah was Bernard Krainis, a young man who had developed a passion for old music as intense as Noah's own. Bernie Krainis had dropped out of Noah's high school, James Monroe, at 15, returned a year later, graduated and worked in a machine shop until he was old enough to be drafted. This was in 1940. Only 21 when he was discharged in 1945, Bernie had decided to take advantage of the G.I. Bill and go to college. "I had such a dismal high school record," he said, "that colleges didn't even want to look at me. I started applying to everything north of the Mason-Dixon Line. I got two acceptances, Brigham Young and Denver."[13] He chose the University of Denver because it was closer to home, majoring in anthropology with a minor in economics. But Bernie was also drawn to music. A devotee of Kid Ory- and Jack Teagarden-style Dixieland, he loved to play jazz trombone. He had also taught himself to play the peculiar-looking woodwind instrument his father (a violist in the Radio City Music Hall Orchestra) had given him for his 21st birthday. The instrument, "really primitive" but with an intriguing sound, was a tenor recorder. Bernie's academic performance at Denver was so good that his teachers encouraged him to apply for a Rhodes Scholarship. Instead, he made up his mind to concentrate on the Medieval, Renaissance, and Baroque music of Europe. So he came back to New York to live in Greenwich Village and study with the great musicologist Gustave

[12]Rema Sessler, March 1, 1997.
[13]Bernard Krainis, February 17, 1997.

Reese at New York University.[14] One of the few people in New York who knew anything about the recorder and early music, Bernie learned, was a refugee from Hitler's Germany named Erich Katz. Katz was directing a group of singers and instrumentalists, mostly students of his at the New York College of music, called the New York Musicians' Workshop. His assistant was a 27-year-old Texan who, to Bernie's initial delight, "rapidly picked up my style of playing recorder." The Texan's name was Jack LaNoue Davenport. Among the singers in Katz's group was a bass, Clifford Brayton Lewis, from Glens Falls, New York. Starting in 1949, Bernie became actively involved in the Musicians' Workshop.

"At the time," he said, "I was very interested in singing." Like so many others, he cannot remember who introduced him to Noah Greenberg or how they met. It may have been Jeanne Wacker. Regardless, he was soon making the trip to Cornelia Street on Tuesday nights.[15]

Of Noah at this time, Bernie says simply: "He should have been called Noah Greenberg Enterprises. He was always into something. Did you know he had an interest in a company that sold wire recorders? He tried to sell me a wire recorder."[16] Wire recorders were the cranky alternatives to tape recorders. (Both were World War II German inventions.) The thin magnetized wire on which wire recorders registered sound signals could and usually did get out of hand, resulting in maddening, chaotic tangles. These were virtually impossible to sort out without damage, and one crimp in a three-hundred-foot reel of wire spelled disaster. By 1951, tape had supplanted wire as the medium of choice for professional recordings. But wire recorders were still being sold. To Noah as to other aficionados of early high-fidelity technology, the wire recorder meant that anyone, not only a sound engineer in a studio, could record music. It also meant that anyone with the money to buy one of these devices—they were expensive, but not prohibitively so—could

[14]Gustave Reese (1899-1977) later became one of Noah's most important musicological advisors and one of his greatest fans. Students of music know him as the author of two groundbreaking works, *Music in the Middle Ages* (1940) and *Music in the Renaissance* (1954). Ascetic in appearance, wry in conversation, Reese drew the chart of early music that opened up the repertory to later scholars and performers.

[15]Bernard Krainis, February 17, 1997; D. C. Culbertson, "Men, Women, and Early Winds," in *American Recorder*, November 1996, pp. 7-9; Bernard Krainis, letter to the editor, *American Recorder*, January 1997, p. 21; uncut typescript of Krainis letter dated 28 November 1996.

[16]Bernard Krainis, February 17, 1997.

capture hours of sound on one small reel. The possibilities were captivating, and what Noah found captivating he would instantly try to promote to others, in Bernie Krainis's case without success.

Another friend, and one who both lost and gained by exposure to Noah's special brand of persuasiveness, was Peter Flanders. He had graduated from Harvard in 1948, his college career having been interrupted by two years of military service. A computer scientist in the days when computers themselves were in their infancy, Peter had come to New York to find work and to indulge his twin musical passions, singing madrigals and playing the cello in string quartets. In 1949, non-musical concerns began to go by the board. First of all, he met, fell in love with and married a gifted and beguiling young woman recently back from the West Coast, none other than Noah's friend and Workers Party comrade, Rickie Simons. In 1950, he entered The Juilliard School to study singing and choral directing under Robert Hufstader.

Peter was the proud owner of a whole library of English madrigals, bought years before with a legacy from an aunt. In the spring of 1951, when Rickie introduced him to Noah, Peter cheerfully brought along a stack of scores and joined in leading the singing at Cornelia Street. "What a hustler Noah was," he chuckles. "That summer, he went in the roofing business.

> Somebody must have told him that if you were a salesman for a roofing company and you sold a roof for two thousand dollars, you got five hundred dollars commission.

If you had to sell something, this was a great improvement over what you could make selling handbags for Uncle Moniek.

Pete, still at The Juilliard, needed a summer job. He asked Noah's advice.

> 'It's great,' Noah told me. 'There's nothing to it. You go up in the Bronx and you knock on a door and you tell the lady: Your roof, you know, now's the time to do something about it.'

Five hundred dollars or no five hundred dollars, making cold calls to sell roofs to Bronx housewives was not something for which Harvard had prepared Peter Flanders. Peter expressed his doubts to Noah, who scoffed.

> He said: 'What's the problem? You stick your foot in the door, they can't slam it on you, they have to listen.'

Still, Pete hesitated. "Are there any *non-sales* jobs in that company?"

"Sure, but they're a dollar an hour."

On reflection, a dollar an hour with no selling sounded fine to Peter. Noah put in a word for him, and Peter duly went to work nailing asphalt shingle in the broiling Bronx sun. But suddenly, for no reason that Peter could fathom, "Noah stopped selling roofs and the company went bankrupt." Peter was out of a job. (He soon found work installing rooftop water tanks for Rosenwach & Co.) "It taught me a lesson," Peter said. "The lesson was that the salesman controls things. Without the salesman, there's no business." Noah, he added, was the supreme salesman.[17]

Even so, friends who were watching closely knew that, despite the frenetic pace he was setting, Noah was not a happy man. Indeed, the pace itself was symptomatic of a life gone awry. Copying music by day, leading I.L.G. choruses three, four or five nights a week, leading his own group on Tuesday evenings, teaching piano, trying to sell hi-fi equipment, running up to the Bronx to sell roofing—even for someone with Noah's vitality and endurance, it was too much. And there was more. Jeanne Wacker says she knew that Noah was drinking heavily and going through "a bad time" in late 1951. Jesse Simons was much more graphic.

> At times, he was quite depressed, and would telephone me at 2 or 3 A.M. He had had too much drink and would weep with self-disgust, having kicked some woman out of his apartment who he picked up in a bar. We would talk, and sometimes I went over and made him coffee, or we would walk the streets for hours.[18]

It was in October or November of 1951 that Noah took the melancholy first step toward legally ending his and Edie's marriage. In the 1950s in New York, the only legal ground for divorce aside from extreme cruelty was adultery. Because proving adultery is next to impossible, New York's courts had long held that the only acceptable "proof" was eyewitness evidence on the part of someone other than the spouse. The camera as well as the eye was deemed to bear valid witness. There thus sprang up in New York a sordid little industry of private detectives who could take pictures and women (and some men) willing to have their pictures taken in suitable locations while pretending to engage in adulterous sex. Those who could afford it hired the whole package: the camera-wielding private eye, the room in the dubious hotel and the partner. That way, only the

[17]Peter Flanders, May 29, 1998.
[18]Simons, *op. cit.,* p. 20

one spouse (usually, of course, the husband) had to submit to the humiliation of being caught in the supposed act.

Those who could spared themselves this ordeal by going out of state for a divorce. But only a few states—Nevada, for example—granted divorces recognized by New York's courts. Getting to Reno or Las Vegas and establishing legal residency (in Nevada, this took six weeks) cost far more than Edith and Noah could afford. And Noah was either unwilling or unable to hire a photographer.

So Jesse Simons agreed to lend a hand. On the appointed day Jesse accompanied a wretchedly unhappy Edith to "some fleabag hotel somewhere," and

> we went into a room and there was Noah naked and a woman, also naked but of course hidden by the bedclothes, so Edith could swear before a judge that there was adultery and I could corroborate it.

The event must have struck Noah as an ironic reversal of the excitement of Prades and a sad comment on the present. He may have started to break away from a failed marriage and he may have gained a foothold in music. But Noah was afraid nevertheless that his life was spinning out of control.[19]

[19]Jeanne Wacker, October 2, 1997; Jesse Simons, October 6, 1997, January 23, 1998.

CHAPTER TWELVE

JONI

(1952)

$\mathcal{I}$n the fall of 1950, a 24-year-old singer, Ruth Popeski, left her native Canada for the United States. After study at Toronto's Royal Conservatory and a concert tour of Canada, Ruth decided that to perfect her vocal technique and "further her career" she had to come to New York. She found a place to live and began to work with several teachers, among them Ruth Kisch-Arndt, who coached Roberta Peters, and Sergius Kagan. Ruth Popeski's lyric soprano was warm and appealing, her sight-singing ability and musicianship unusually polished. Before long, she was making a living with her voice: combining appearances at private functions with a steady job in the choir of Temple Emanu-El, the favored house of worship of "Our Crowd," the wealthy German-Jewish community of New York.

Sometime during the late fall or winter of 1950, Ruth's future sister-in-law, Marian Daigon Levine, began to tell her: "You must meet Noah Greenberg."

Marian Levine was a native New Yorker and a onetime radical. She had known Noah before the war as a young comrade in the movement, and had seen something of him as well during his days in the Merchant Marine. "He would come to our house on West 78th Street with [music] manuscripts, and he gave my husband the Baedeker he took with him on trips to Europe." Marian also knew Noah's aunt Bronka Stern, "the other artist in the family." During the 1940s Bronka had danced with the Pearl Lang company. Later, after a knee injury ended her dance career, she had taken up sculpture. Now Bronka's nephew Noah the amateur *musiker* had become a professional. What more natural thing was there than for Marian to try to bring Noah and Ruth together?

In fact, it was Ruth who made the contact.

> I got up the nerve to call him and I went over and sang for him and
> he liked my singing very much. There was just room in his apart-
> ment for his grand piano, with a dictionary of wines and tons and
> tons of Renaissance music. I used to sit on the floor by the piano to
> sing.[1]

Ruth was Noah's very first professional singer. She was a living
revelation of the ease and skill with which a professional, in contrast to the amateurs with whom he had worked since the Harold
Brown days, could sing music of his choosing and mold and shape
it according to his taste. Noah in turn was an enthusiastic and ad-
miring promoter, and endlessly resourceful besides in turning up
music for Ruth to perform. Ruth's agent in Canada had tried to set
up contacts for her in New York, but "they came to nothing. So it
would be three to five auditions a day, a lot of running around, a lot
of disappointments." Noah, however, was always encouraging, and
willing as well to put his promotional talents to work on her behalf.
Before long, Ruth was going to Cornelia Street from her Prince Street
apartment "several times a week" to sing, finding time late at night
and on weekends. "We went through reams of music together, and
he was so generous with his praise and appreciation." She and Noah
were delighted with the arrangement, even though it was bringing
neither of them much money.

> In fact, Noah used to be jealous. I'd get all these club dates for
> twenty-five dollars. You know, a group of folk songs at a meeting,
> a banquet, celebrations, birthdays. I could sing three or four songs
> and go home, whereas Noah had to work [at I.L.G. choral sessions]
> all evening and he'd only get fifteen.[2]

One not-for-pay engagement Noah arranged for Ruth was an
ambitious one: a concert performance of Henry Purcell's Dido and
Aeneas at Dwight Macdonald's apartment. Jeanne Wacker, who sang
in the chorus, remembered the occasion as "quite an event." Dwight,
for some reason, was "swaggering around in a bathrobe" like a gaunt,
goatee'd Noel Coward, until Noah, saying sharply, "Are you sick?"
embarrassed him into changing into proper clothes. As for the performance:

> It was a musical fiasco. Noah recruited some kids from Juilliard
> (probably not top rank) and they squeezed out the [instrumental]

---

[1] Ruth Daigon, February 7, 1998.
[2] Ruth Daigon, February 7, 1998.

Emanu-El, [to sing Belinda to my Dido] and we were off and away. When it came to my big number, 'When I am Laid in Earth,' Noah forgot about the repeat—very important, very gorgeous—and I was left hanging with a few bare 'remember me"s. [Noah] was very apologetic. We laughed about it afterwards.[3]

Noah also arranged an appearance for Ruth at N.Y.U.'s Institute of Fine Arts, then housed in a mansion at 19 East 80 Street. This time, to make up for her not getting a fee, Noah prepared a pre-concert gourmet dinner for Ruth and Arthur Daigon, her fiancé.

[H]e begins with some kind of canapés flavored in wine plus paté also soaked in wine with a special before-dinner drink (wine). The paté had those little black creatures in it that the French hunt for with pigs. . . . Then the main dish was pork marinated in some elegant rich sauce liberally soaking in wine . . . and then he ended up with fruit mixed with heavy cream in a wine sauce.

Predictably, the rich food and wine, an empty stomach and pre-recital nerves took their toll. "Artie walked me around the Village for fifteen minutes," to no avail. Back at Noah's, Ruth was thoroughly and comprehensively sick, felt much better, and went uptown to give a good account of herself at her recital.[4]

Even as he was beginning to work with and find work for professionals, Noah was paying proper attention to his amateurs. A photo dating from this period (the late winter or early spring months of 1951) portrays him in the act of conducting the 22 earnest members of the chorus of I.L.G.W.U. Local 135, cloakmakers, Newark, New Jersey, in a broadcast over the I.L.G.'s own two-year-old radio station, WFDR. (see p.111)

He was also trying to rebuild his personal life.

"I had such a great place," Jeanne Wacker said, with a reminiscent smile, of the flat she called home in 1951.

On Thompson Street, 181 Thompson Street. I had my piano in the kitchen. I had both my piano and my bathtub in the kitchen. This was a great apartment and it had three sort-of rooms. It had a hardwood floor. It had steam heat. . . . I had my private little cubicle toilet and right next to it was the kitchen sink and from the kitchen sink there was a bathtub with an enameled top and that was your workspace. My piano was against the wall, and there was a stove over there, and there was a window, a nice big window, all my rooms had nice big windows, hardwood floors and

[3] Ruth Daigon, e-mail letter, February 7, 1998.
[4] Ruth Daigon, e-mail letter, February 11, 1998.

steam heat and you want to know what I paid for it? Twenty-six dollars a month.[5]

Jeanne's apartment was four flights up, but no one minded. It was a great place to throw a party, "and there were lots of parties." Jeanne's friends from her N.Y.U. philosophy classes would be there. Anatole Broyard might appear from Cornelia Street. ("Don't say anything too much about Anatole. I was one of his beloveds. He was a very charismatic fellow.") So also might some of the painters and dancers Jeanne was meeting; and perhaps Julius Goldstein would show up to drink wine, talk painting, and entertain the other partygoers with the Marx Brothers imitations that were his comic specialty.

At least once, Noah was one of Jeanne's invited party guests. Another guest at the same party was a young woman named Toni Feuerstein, whom Jeanne had met in 1946 or 1947, when both were N.Y.U. undergraduates. Toni's background, like Toni herself, was far from ordinary. She was born in the old Hanseatic League seaport of Danzig. Under the Treaty of Versailles, Danzig, with a population largely German, had been enclosed within Poland's new borders but declared a "Free City." The Feuersteins were one of Danzig's oldest and most respected Jewish families, and deeply proud of a connection with Rabbi Benzion Halberstam, the kingly Bobover Rebbe, head of the Bobover sect of Hasidic Jews and considered by his followers the embodiment of the Besht (Rabbi Israel Ba'al Shem, the founder of Hasidic Judaism). In 1938, when Toni was 12, it was obvious that Adolf Hitler was looking for an excuse to make war on Poland. Danzig became his excuse. He was demanding the return of the city to Germany and a 200-mile road and rail link with Danzig across Polish territory. The world was a year away from war, but for Danzig's Jews, the *Horst Wessel lied* ringing in their ears, the hour was late and the choice self-evident: leave or be swallowed up. Toni, with her mother Paula and her grandmother, were among the fortunate ones. They left for New York and settled in Brooklyn, where Toni's uncle, Jacob Perlow, had come earlier and started a property-management business. Toni's father, Max Feuerstein, soon joined them.

Toni's Yiddish, say many of her friends, was the most beautiful they had ever heard. As a young girl, she was determined never to forget it. But having come to America, she was equally determined to be completely American. "From the day she started to learn En-

[5] Jeanne Wacker, October 2, 1997.

glish, she was determined to get rid of every trace of a foreign accent."[6] What is even more unusual—indeed, almost impossible for anyone older than six or seven—Toni succeeded. Her English was accentless. Her Yiddish, like her childhood in Danzig, went into a separate compartment of her personality, to be opened only on occasion and in the presence of people she trusted.

At 25, Toni Feuerstein had finished high school, gained a liberal-arts A.B. degree at N.Y.U., completed a Master's program in library science at Columbia, spent a year as librarian at a U. S. Army base near Frankfurt, Germany and started a job at the New York Public Library. Along the way, she had sampled matrimony, marrying a Dr. Leon Lefler in April 1944 and divorcing him in September 1945. Though not movie-star goodlooking—nearsighted, she almost always wore thick glasses—Toni was attractive, vivacious, bright, and, when she wanted to be, very funny. There was an edge to her manner that was offputting to some but charming to others. Toni was also, in vivid contrast to Edith, an educated, coolly judgmental young woman, with a thoroughly middle-class upbringing and middle-class manners and values.

"I didn't know Toni that well," Jeanne Wacker said, "and I'm not sure I liked her that much. But we had the same sense of humor about certain things. Anyway, I ran into her in 1951 and I was having a party and I invited her and she came. And Noah was there and I introduced them."[7] As far as Jeanne recalls, there was nothing earthshaking about that first meeting. But by the summer of 1951, Toni and Noah were on familiar terms and spending time together. Indeed, Ruth Popeski and Arthur Daigon went with them on their first date. "[Noah] had the use of the [Lee] Ault house for the weekend, and we were all going to see how the rich lived.

> Toni looked particularly attractive. It was a hot summer day and we were all sleeveless and hatless. . . . Toni . . . was lively and responsive, she smiled and laughed a lot. Well, of course it was their first date, and Noah had probably told her something about us, and she wanted to be pleasant AND she was pleasant.

The Aults, wealthy art collectors were in Europe for the summer. Their home in New Canaan, Connecticut, was made available to Noah and his friends through Lee Ault's accountant, Andreas Esberg, whose wife was a fine amateur pianist and a friend of Noah's.[8]

[6] Jane Greenberg, April 29, 1997.
[7] Jeanne Wacker, October 2, 1997.
[8] I. Meyer Pincus, June 9, 1998.

The house was simply magnificent. The rooms were full of gorgeous painting. I saw a couple of Picassos on the walls plus a lot
of sculpture—Giacometti—and out in their magnificent garden was
[a copy of] Brancusi's *Bird in Flight*. [Arthur and I] spent a glorious
day there and then left Noah and Toni and hitchhiked back to
New York.[9]

Noah and Toni were certainly at The Cloisters together in October of 1951.[10] But Toni was dating other men. At least one of them,
a certain "Richard" or "Dick" whose last name no one remembers,
was serious about her. And Noah, though clearly fancy-free, was
not yet divorced and was also furiously busy building a career. How
much he and Toni were together over the next months is an open
question. But at one point, probably in March, 1952, Toni broke off
contact. For several months, apparently by her choice, she and Noah
neither saw nor spoke to each other.

On April 11, 1952, Ruth Popeski and Arthur Daigon were married in New York. Ruth immediately adopted her married name as
her professional name. Arthur, a doctoral candidate in English Literature at N.Y.U., was understanding and more than tolerant of the late
nights, strange rehearsal hours and odd friends and acquaintances
that were part and parcel of a singer's life. "[Noah] was as fond of
Artie as he was of me," Ruth says, "and showed us great kindness
and warmth." His wedding present to the couple was a song of his
own composing, a pleasant setting in 6/8 time of Wystan Auden's
delicious epithalamium, "Carry Her Over the Water," in which in
sequence doves, winds, a frog, and the bridal couple's carriage horses
"Sing agreeably, agreeably, agreeably of love."[11] Ruth thought it
was "very sweet of him, and terribly touching." In keeping with his
financial condition, too, because "Noah didn't have a farthing to his
name."[12]

On May 12, 1952, in Edith's words, "My time [with Noah] was
up:" their final decree of divorce was issued. Noah's mother Lillie,
Edith added, was the only family member to speak to her at the end

[9] Ruth Daigon, e-mail letter, February 11, 1998.

[10] Toni Feuerstein-Noah Greenberg, letter, July 23, 1952.

[11] One of Auden's few purely lyrical poems, "Carry Her Over the Water" was originally written for his and Benjamin Britten's 1940-41 opera *Paul Bunyan*.

[12] Ruth Daigon, February 7, 1998; e-mail message, February 9, 1998. Noah's setting
of "Carry Her Over the Water" was actually dated March 3, 1952, which was Ruth's
birthday.

of twelve years of marriage. "She said to me on the phone, 'I'm so sorry.' And that was it."[13]

The divorce decree plus Ruth's and Arthur's newlywed happiness clearly prompted Noah to try to renew the relationship with Toni. During the last week in June, he tried repeatedly to reach her by phone at home and at work, even calling a friend, Lillian B., to find out where Toni might be. He settled for a letter. "I'm going away for the summer," he wrote on June 24, "and I thought it would be nice to see you once before I did." He twitted her for being out of town. (She had gone with friends to Fire Island.)

> You certainly picked a bad week for a vacation. All that rain at the beginning of it—and missing a chance to see me at the end of it.

"Well, too bad!" he added wickedly: "Because I think I would have enjoyed seeing you."

He went on to give her his news. He had rented a small house in Amagansett, a seaside hamlet near the eastern tip of Long Island that was a haven for artists, teachers, writers and others rich in summer vacation time but not in dollars. "I plan to stay for at least a month." He urged Toni to contact Lillian, who had been ill. He asked her about her summer rental on Fire Island. "If you care to write me," he ended cautiously, "send it to Cornelia St., it will be forwarded."[14]

A clue to what was blossoming between them exists in the form of a telegram, dated July 9 and time-stamped 9:45 AM, from Toni to Noah in Amagansett. "Have been thinking," it read, "and would like to talk to you too. Please phone me at home Thursday evening."[15] Thursday was July 10. There can be little doubt about the dénoument. At seven in the morning of Monday, July 14, Noah wrote ecstatically to "Darling Toni":

> I'm so deliriously happy! I expected that seeing you and being with you for a day or 2 would be wonderful, but this exceeded everything my imagination could conjure up. Your looks, our love, walking together—the beach, things we talked of, being together.

And toward the end of this first of a score of love letters Noah wrote that summer, he added tellingly: "I'm really at peace with myself for the first time since as far back into my mature life as I can remember."[16]

[13] Edith Schor, March 7, 1997.
[14] Noah Greenberg-Toni Feuerstein, letter, June 24, 1952.
[15] Toni Feuerstein-Noah Greenbrg, telegram, July 9, 1952.
[16] Noah Greenberg-Toni Feuerstein, letter, July 14, 1952.

It was not that everything went smoothly. On Wednesday, July 16, he wrote: "I'm worried about you and that screwball. He might become violent! and chase you down 8th Street with a beer bottle." Evidently, the "screwball" was the Richard who had been courting Toni when Noah first met her. As it turned out, Noah need not have been troubled. On Friday morning, Toni sat down at her typewriter. "Darling," she began:

> Right after I spoke to you last night, Richard called me and kept me on the phone for nearly two hours with his arguments as to why my marrying you would not be a good thing for me, for you, for our children and the world in general. I listened but was not convinced. I still think it's a pretty good idea. And now I feel sure that at least that part of our 'transitional phase' has been cleared up. Pleased?

In a handwritten postscript, she tells Noah amusedly that her despairing suitor had accused her of having spent the weekend in Atlantic City with Anatole Broyard![17]

Over the course of the summer, Toni and Noah spoke on the phone every couple of days and seem to have spent at least some weekends together on Fire Island. Their sunny romance flourished. Only once, at the end of July, did Noah seem to suggest that a cloud might be shadowing it.

> I too am confused [he wrote]. I so want those few days to disappear—but they can't!

Evidently, Noah had become a little too proprietary and Toni, self-possessed as she was—or wanted to be—had pulled back.

> The whole thing really boils down to your not denying the woman in you. I want you to be my woman. Of course there is possessiveness involved. And this is as it should be. I won't crush you with it. . . . I want you to fulfill your role, as mother, as lover, as warm companion. I want to fulfill my role by protecting you, loving you, and being father to your children. . . .

But he seeks to reassure her that he's no Richard.

> And don't allow your present fears to convert my normal urge into a watchdog! *That's really perverse and* distorted. You think I have nothing better to do in my lifetime than stand panting, drooling—guarding jealously and suspiciously my live, 'resisting' treasure?[18]

---

[17] Toni Feuerstein-Noah Greenberg, letter, July 18, 1952.
[18] Noah Greenerg-Toni Feuerstein, letter, July 29, 1952.

Courtship: Toni and Noah
at Amagansett, July 1952
(Courtesy Greenberg family)

By the next weekend, when Toni visited Noah in Amagansettt, whatever had prompted this outburst had blown over. The couple went back, by mail and in person, to making happy plans for the future. This chiefly entailed a summerlong search on Toni's part for a suitable Village apartment. Less important, but by no means inconsequential, Noah the gourmet cook and gourmand eater heeded Toni's admonitions and put himself on a reducing diet.

Cottage cheese (1+ tablespoons a day), protein bread, 1 egg (boiled) (mornings). Lean meat, tuna fish (fresh), lettuce (no oil), buttermilk, coffee (no sugar, no milk), fruit (fresh) for dessert (no beer or whiskey [so far]).

"Please, on the weekend," he added pathetically, "let's have a few nice meals (without bread or potatoes or beer) (but wine)."[19]

---

[19] Noah Greenberg-Toni Feuerstein, letter, July 29, 1952.

CHAPTER THIRTEEN

$\mathcal{F}$ESTINO AND JOHN BLOW

(1952-1953)

$\mathcal{A}$driano Banchieri was Noah Greenberg's favorite Renaissance monk. Born on September 3, 1568 in Bologna, Italy, Banchieri entered the Benedictine religious community of Mount Olivet in 1587 and took his solemn vows three years later. After attaining the priesthood, he served as organist at monasteries in Lucca, Bologna, Bosco, Imola, and Gubbio. Over his lifetime—he died in 1634—his compositions for the church included masses, motets, and settings of the psalms. Banchieri also made notable contributions to music theory. In *L'organo suonarino (1605)*, he laid out precise rules for accompanists to follow when the music consisted only of a bass part with numbers rather than written-out notes. Banchieri is said to have been the first to use the terms piano and forte in composition.

But the monk Dom Adriano Banchieri had a secular specialty as well. He wrote *intermedi* or entertainments, sets of vocal pieces to be performed at the theater or in private homes on special occasions. Banchieri's *intermedi*, their exiguous plots drawn from *commedia dell'arte*, were bizarre, funny and bawdy. One, *La Pazzia senile*, "The Crazy Old Fool," published in Bologna in 1598 and reprinted later in Cologne, was something of a hit. Another, written for a carnival celebration, was entitled *Festino nella sera del giovedi grasso avanti cena a 5 voci miste*: "Entertainment for the Evening of Fat Thursday Before Supper." (*Giovedi grasso*, the Renaissance equivalent of Mardi Gras, was the last night of carnival—*carne vale*, "farewell to the flesh"—before the onset of Lent.)

The only modern edition of *Festino* was published in Rome in 1939, "The Year XVII" of Benito Mussolini's regime. Copies were —and are—hard to find. But possibly as early as 1950, Noah Greenberg

128

had managed to get hold of one. What he saw fascinated him. *Festino* is a set of 20 madrigals, villanelli, canzonettas, and other Renaissance vocal forms. The music is varied, elegant, and straightforward, much less complex and emotional than that of Banchieri's contemporary Monteverdi. Even the burlesques (a contrapunto bestiale, a calves' madrigal, a spindle-vendors' song) are pleasantly melodious. Best of all from Noah's viewpoint, the *Festino* pieces were eminently singable: capable amateurs would find them within reach.

To be sure, *Festino* was not at the forefront of Noah's consciousness in mid- and late August, 1952. Other matters were more pressing. Most important, Toni's long and frustrating search for an apartment had finally met with success. Noah's letter to Toni begun on Thursday, August 21, almost quivers with excitement.

> There is so much to be done and so much has happened in the last week that I feel somewhat overwhelmed. I've put quite a few hours in on the Carter job, but I'll have to finish it in N.Y. (I still have not received the $200 he owes me!)

Then come the big questions:

> Have you gotten the lease? Have you thought about colors. We'll have to consult Julius [Goldstein], perhaps someone else.

Here Noah breaks off. When he picks up on Friday morning, he explains that he took the time out the evening before to play poker, won six dollars, and came home with a "tremendous headache." Then he gets back to business:

> Using the narrow room for a storage & pantry is a good idea. I still can't think about the painting color scheme. I think, however, we'll be able to move in before the 10th. But perhaps you're right about hanging on to your place 'til then, just in case. Mabel [Noah's New York landlady] has rented mine as of the 1st.[1]

The apartment in question was a two-bedroom, fifth-floor walkup at 80 Perry Street, between Bleeker and Hudson Streets in the Village. It would be Noah's and Toni's home, and Noah's headquarters, for the next four years.

The work of moving meant spending the Labor Day weekend in New York rather than Amagansett. In any case, Noah had to be back in the city by September 10. One of his I.L.G.W.U. choruses had already notified him that this was its starting date. Toni, too,

---

[1]Noah Greenberg-Toni Feuerstein, letter, August 21-22, 1952.

had to be back. The job she had landed in August, a three-month stint with Tidewater Oil, researching the company's history, also started in early September. Mrs. Griffith, Noah's Amagansett landlady, had said that he was free to use the house whenever he chose. He and Toni may have taken advantage of the offer later in the fall. But perhaps not: their engagement—Toni loved referring to Noah as her "fiancé"—meant that there were family invitations to extend and accept and many friends to see.

One such occasion still sticks in the mind of Noah's cousin Rema, who was sixteen at the time.

> I remember when [Noah] decided to marry Toni, he was so excited to bring her over, and we were living on Claflin Avenue, which is the West Bronx near Kingsbridge, and he brought her and she was wearing a green velvet dress. I expected to see a movie star, from the way in which he spoke of her, but as far as looks go she was rather ordinary-looking, and she wore pretty thick glasses. But she was extremely charismatic and charming. *South Pacific* had just come out. We had a baby grand and *South Pacific*, and she goes, 'Hey, Noah! this is the kind of music I like,' and she says 'Rema, play it for me!' My sister [Sybil] and I, we looked at each other and I think we were both jealous because he was in love with her and we loved him and we didn't want her to be everything and we got it, because, she didn't even know beans about classical music. But she adored him, and learned, I think, to listen . . .[2]

Almost as soon as the paint was dry, the furniture arranged and the kitchen stocked at 80 Perry Street, Noah started his Tuesday evening singing group in the new location. And soon after that, two other sets of events, seemingly only loosely related, began to unfold.

The first involved Noah's and Harold Brown's friend, the cellist Seymour Barab. After a wartime stint with the band in the Philadelphia Navy Yard, Seymour had gone off to Europe. "This was just the very beginning days of long-playing records. I was over there producing." Seymour traveled from music capital to capital, negotiating with and recording lesser-known (read "inexpensive") orchestras and chamber groups for American record companies. "I worked with René Leibowitz." Known as a follower of Schoenberg and a composer of dodecaphonic music, Leibowitz was also a "contractor," a music freelancer who could put together groups ranging from chamber trios to full orchestras for concerts or recordings.

[2]Rema Sessler, March 1, 1997.

Among Seymour's record-company clients were the two Solomon brothers, Seymour and Maynard. The Solomons owned Vanguard Recording Society, Inc. a label known for excellent sound quality and interesting repertory, though not for big-name performers. (Its "star" ensembles were the Solisti di Zagreb and the Vienna State Opera Orchestra.)

Another of Seymour Barab's clients was Jerry Newman. Newman, a sound engineer, and his businessman partner Bill Fox owned a record shop on Greenwich Street, a few blocks from Noah's and Toni's new home. In addition, Newman and Fox had set up a small recording company, Esoteric Records. Their idea was simple enough. "At the time," Seymour points out, "if you could get musical material cheap and cut a few hundred records and sell them in your store, you could make money.

> It happened that Jerry came to Europe . . . and Jerry and I traveled around and I talked with him, and he was looking for product. He was looking for Renaissance music, and I said to him, 'There's this guy in New York, in the Village, who's doing madrigals with a group.' Why don't you look him up?[3]

In October or November of 1952, Jerry Newman, back from Europe, telephoned Noah Greenberg.

*   *   *

For Bernie Krainis, hunting for music for the recorder at the Forty-Second Street Music Library had proven somewhat frustrating. Sydney Beck, the New York Public Library's music librarian, was a specialist in the English music of the sixteenth through the eighteenth centuries. "If you wanted any music from Beck's period," Krainis said, "it was unavailable, out being bound, whatever."[4] So Bernie had taken to foraging in the non-music divisions of the library. And in the Berg Collection at the Forty-second Street Main Library, he made an extraordinary discovery: the original edition, published in London by John Playfair in 1696, of John Blow's *Ode on the Death of Mr. Henry Purcell.* Its text by John Dryden accounted for its presence in the Berg Collection, which is largely devoted to 18th- and 19th-century English literature. Best of all from Krainis's point of view, Blow had scored the Ode for two countertenors, two alto recorders and continuo.[5] "I knew two recorder-players," Bernie

---

[3]Seymour Barab, February 27, 1997.
[4]Seymour Barab, February 27, 1997.
[5] The term "continuo" or "basso continuo," so important in music of the 16th-18th centuries, refers not to an instrument but to a form of accompaniment. This (*cont.*)

said. "I was one and LaNoue [Davenport] was the other. And I knew of a singer who was a possible countertenor, Russell Oberlin."

As a small child in Akron, Ohio, Russell Oberlin sang all the time but spoke with a stammer. When his first-grade teacher made fun of his speech impediment, Russell's mother came furiously to his defense. The result was promotion to the second grade, and there the teacher encouraged him to sing. The stammer disappeared, and a career began. "I started singing professionally at six," Russell says, "and never looked back." During his school years, he sang mostly at churches. A year after finishing high school, he attended the Chautaqua summer music program, and its director told him that the right place for him was The Juilliard. He graduated from Juilliard at 20, in 1948, a lyric tenor whose musical gifts and blithe temperament were already bringing him many engagements. "All along I was busy. I never had to go out to hunt for work.

> The phone was ringing. I did all sorts of things. At this time, I don't think anybody had ever heard of countertenors. I sang the tenor repertoire. I always looked for music that suited my voice, but it was music for a tenor.

He sang everything, from hymns to show tunes.

> For example, you know Edith Piaf? She did a concert in New York in 1948 and she had this choral group with her . . . [les Compagnons de la Chanson] They had to go back to France, but she had other concerts to give in the U.S. So they put together a group of Americans to sing with her, and I was part of the group. I went to Miami with her. You know, we sang behind a scrim and the band was behind the scrim and only she was out front. And I couldn't figure out why the audiences went berserk for her. I wasn't singing in all the numbers, so I went around to the back of the hall and watched. There she was, in that little *schmatte* of a dress, just a single spot on her, and she'd do a number and just — raise her arm at the right time. And she was terrific.[6]

In 1952, Russell was living in Greenwich Village and busy with engagements all over town, including a regular job in the choir of

---

is built on the bass or bottom line of a piece of music. Sets of numbers written above or below the notes of the bass line tell the accompanist in a kind of shorthand what notes to add to the bass to make the accompaniment harmonious with the main melody. The accompanist, generally a keyboard player or lutenist, reads the numbers and "realizes" the numbers, adding chords, runs and ornaments ad lib. Often, a cellist, viola da gambaist or bass viol player will play the bass line along with the keyboard accompanist, to make it stronger.

[6]Russell Oberlin, January 28, 1997.

The Church of the Ascension, at Tenth Street and Fifth Avenue. The music program at Ascension, led by the exceptional organist, choirmaster, and teacher Vernon L. de Tar, was one of the best in the city. Everybody in music knew that the brownstone church on lower Fifth was the place to go to hear New York's finest young singers. Among the regular listeners were Bernie Krainis and Ruth Daigon. Ruth especially admired the sweetness and effortless upper extension of Russell Oberlin's tenor.

Russell was also part of a group of Juilliard voice students and graduates who sang madrigals under the direction of Suzanne Bloch. The daughter of the composer Ernest Bloch, Bloch was a lutenist-singer who had, in Ruth Daigon's apt phrase, "a stranglehold on the Elizabethan market in those days." On the November night when Bloch's group performed at Times Hall, Bernie Krainis, his copy of the John Blow *Ode* in hand, went backstage. There he found Russell, whom he knew—both were friends of the painter Don Wight— and enthusiastically showed him the music. Russell took a look and said, "Great! Let's do it."

*   *   *

Jerry Newman and Noah Greenberg probably met for the first time in December 1952. Noah made a sales pitch as only he could and the pitch succeeded. He came away with Jerry Newman's commitment to record a performance of the Banchieri *Festino* by a vocal group with Noah as conductor. A formal contract would be drawn up and signed later, pending Newman's approval of the quality of the performance.

"The amazing thing," Seymour Barab said of Noah's feat of persuasion, "was that [Noah] had absolutely no qualifications for this job. He wasn't a [trained] musician, and he was going to conduct this group and rehearse and everything."[7] Barab's appraisal —be it noted that he was speaking as Noah's friend—seems less than fair. Noah had been leading and rehearsing amateur groups, his I.L.G. choruses included, for years. He had read through more Renaissance music, and studied it more closely, than had many musicologists. In any event, Noah's chutzpah, if such it was, did not blind him to reality. Amateur singers, he knew perfectly well, were never going to give him a *Festino* good enough for Esoteric Records to record. He was working with one pro, Ruth Daigon, but one was not enough.

---

[7] Seymour Barab, February 27, 1997.

Noah's first move toward a solution was to call Bernie Krainis and ask: "Do you know any singers?"

As it happened, Bernie did. His acquaintance from the Musicians' Workshop, bass Brayton Lewis, was interested in singing in Noah's group. So were Lois Roman, a young soprano singing in churches in New York, and a 16-year-old High School of Music and Art senior, Sheila Jones. And Bernie and Ruth Daigon both urged Noah, at about the same time, to go to hear Russell Oberlin. He said he would. But at the time, he was actively recruiting another tenor.

Arthur Squires, like Brayton Lewis, was five years older than Noah. For many years, Arthur had combined a deep love of singing with an outstandingly successful career as an industrial chemist.

> During W[orld] W[ar] II, I was obliged to take a holiday from music-making because I worked a routine 57-hour week (and a generous helping of 80- and 90-hour weeks.)

In late 1946, Arthur's wartime ordeal was over. His chemical engineering work at Hydrocarbon Research, Inc. on lower Broadway in New York was still extremely demanding. But Arthur made the time to join the Cantata Singers, a choral group formed by Bach scholar Arthur Mendel. "[Mendel] often gave me small solos. A high point was a performance of [Heinrich] Schütz's *Musicalische Exequien*, in which I had major solo parts (it has several tenor duets)."

In 1950, Arthur also joined the Randolph Singers.

> I don't think Noah ever heard the Randolph Singers, but he did hear the *Exequien*. He called me out of the blue (I think in January 1953) to ask if I would join him and some singers in preparing for a recording of the Banchieri. . . . We met in Noah's and Toni's Village apartment.

At first, Arthur says, he had misgivings.

> [M]any of the singers [Noah] had gathered were just not very good. I think Brayton Lewis was among them (not of course one of the deficient). I do not remember either Russell Oberlin or Ruth Daigon being there at first, but I could be wrong. I don't remember just what led to improvements. Brayton was a lot more forward than I was in those days about speaking his mind. Maybe he told Noah the group just wouldn't do.[8]

Arthur thinks that Brayton Lewis joined Ruth and Bernie in counseling Noah to get in touch with Russell Oberlin.

---

[8]Arthur M. Squires, e-mail message, September 9, 1997.

When he finally did so, later in January, he went to work on Russell with typical Noah persistence.

> I was living on Tenth Street at the time. And one night the phone rang and a man introduced himself and said he was Noah Greenberg. He was putting together a group to make a record. The music was by Banchieri, *Festino*, a group of madrigals, and he wanted to do it one-on-a-line. He'd heard me sing and he wanted me to join the group.

When larger choruses like the Robert Shaw Chorale and the Randolph Singers put a madrigal or two on a program, there might be three or four voices singing soprano, and as many on each of the alto, tenor and bass lines. The result was stronger volume, useful and sometimes essential in a large hall, at the expense of clarity and preciseness. "One-on-a-line" was harder for the singers but much more exhilarating. Still, Russell was less than enthusiastic.

> I said no, I was too busy, I really didn't want to take on more work. I thought that would be the end of it. But he called again. And he called several times. The thing about Noah, he didn't believe in the meaning of the word no. He'd just keep plugging away at what he wanted. He lived just around the corner, he'd say, on Perry Street, and the group was meeting there. Why didn't I just drop over?
>
> Finally, more to get rid of him than for any other reason, I said I'd do it. I went over to Perry Street and there were these people. There was Lois Roman—not much of a voice but a very nice person. And "Cookie" Popeski. Ever hear of Cookie Popeski? That was Ruth Daigon's nickname before she got married. And Sheila Jones and Arthur Squires and Brayton Lewis. They weren't necessarily great singers, but they were very nice people. I liked them very much, and I loved the music, and I liked Noah.[9]

And so, when auditioning was over and serious rehearsals began, the group preparing *Festino* included Ruth Daigon, Lois Roman, and Sheila Jones, sopranos; Russell Oberlin, tenor; Arthur Squires, tenor; Brayton Lewis, bass.

The second rehearsal session, like the Prades Festival two and a half years earlier, was a defining moment, a turning-point, in Noah Greenberg's life.

Rehearsal and turning-point both began with a problem. Sheila Jones was a gifted young soprano, with a strong lower range, but she was a soprano nonetheless. "When we started," Russell said, "I was singing tenor.

---

[9] Russell Oberlin, January 28, 1997.

Sheila was singing the alto line and it just wasn't standing out the way it should. So one day I took Noah aside and said, 'I can do that, sing the alto line.' We tried it, and it was much stronger, the line stood out much more clearly.

Noah obviously knew that Russell's range was exceptional. (It covered two and a half octaves instead of two, and Russell could reach the F above the tenor's usual top note of C above middle C.) But hearing him move upward to an alto part without effort or strain and without switching from a normal voice to a falsetto must have been electrifying. For the first time in his life, Noah was directing a group of singers who could bring to the part-song and the madrigal the same flexibility and responsiveness that Ruth Daigon had been displaying in music for solo voice. And among them was this extraordinary young man who was, as Noah now recognized, that fabulous unicorn among male singers, a true countertenor. It was at that moment, Russell believes, "that Noah decided that he should try to create some kind of permanent group."[10] Russell was absolutely right. The New York Pro Musica Antiqua was about to be born.

CHAPTER FOURTEEN

$\mathcal{I}$NVENTING PRO MUSICA

(1953)

$\mathcal{T}$he letter was dated January 15, 1953. "Dear Sir," it began, "the following when signed by you and us will constitute a complete and binding contract between us."

Its three mimeographed pages spelled out the terms and conditions under which thirty-four-year-old Noah Greenberg and the vocal group he was calling "The Primavera Singers" would make their first two recordings, one of them *Festino*. For Jerry Newman of Esoteric Records, signing up an unknown, untried ensemble involved some—but not very much—financial risk:

> We agree to pay you . . . a royalty of five (5%) per cent of the retail list price in the United States (less the cost of the record cover or album container) . . .

And also:

> We further agree to pay you . . . the sum of forty-one & twenty-five ($41.25) dollars for each singer and/or instrumentalist supplied by you (up to a maximum of seven persons) plus one hundred ($100.00) dollars for your services for each of the two . . . records, and this amount shall be considered an advance against royalties. We also agree to advance to you the sum of $30.00 (thirty dollars) for the purchase of music, and this sum shall also be considered an advance against royalties.[1]

Noah did supply seven performers for *Festino*, including himself as one of the seven. With his separate hundred-dollar fee counted in, the total advance payable to The Primavera Singers for *Festino*—and all the group ever received for it —came to $388.75.

---

[1]Jerry Newman, President, Esoteric Records-Noah Greenberg, letter agreement, January 15, 1953. NYPM Archives, Box 10, folder 1.

For Noah, the Esoteric contract was a clear sign that his hopes and dreams were not only not crazy but could actually yield him a living. He had said no to Uncle Moniek and the world of handbags, and Jerry Newman had proven him right. Furthermore, the contract was an unintentional but perfectly-timed wedding present. On January 21, 1953, six days after it was signed, Toni and Noah were married, probably at City Hall. "I seem to remember," Ruth Daigon said, that "they just announced to everyone that now they were married. . . . Certainly no one I knew attended [a more formal wedding]."[2] A possible explanation of an "official secret marriage" before January 21, 1953 is that Toni became pregnant, or thought she might be pregnant, during the summer of 1952, and so a quick marriage was necessary. The possibility is lent some force by a reference in Noah's letter to Toni (August 3, 1952): "Do you feel pregnant? I hope you are! Even if you really should *not* be." When the pregnancy turned out to be either a false alarm or a miscarriage, the couple would have decided to keep their marriage secret.

Noah, indeed, may have been too busy to celebrate a more formal wedding. In the midst of the *Festino* rehearsals and recording sessions, another project materialized. This one was less inviting than either *Festino* or the group of English madrigals by Thomas Morley and John Wilbye that was to be the second Primavera Singers recording for Esoteric. But Noah had to go to work on it nevertheless.

The twenty-eighth convention of the International Ladies' Garment Workers Union was scheduled to open in Chicago in early May. To commemorate this event, Isidore Nagler, head of the New York Cloak Joint Board, came up with a brilliant idea. The chorus of Local 91, Cloakmakers, under Noah's direction, was one of the best of the I.L.G. choral groups. What could be a more appropriate gift to convention delegates (and a better reminder of the cultural superiority of New York) than a concert of labor songs sung by the Local 91 chorus and captured on one of those fancy new long-playing records?

"Whose bread I eat," the saying goes, "his song I sing." Noah set to work with the Local 91 choristers. To add variety, he enlisted "Gene and Francesca," a duo specializing in union songs sung to

[2]Ruth Daigon, e-mail message, March 12, 1998. According to their elder daughter, Anne Greenberg Donovan, the Greenbergs were married twice. "The official version is that it had something to do wih the religious factor (my mother's parents were religious Jews) and I have reason to believe that there was an official secret marriage and then another one . . ." Anne Donovan, e-mail message, March 13, 1988.

the accompaniment of their two guitars. Noah worked up a program of thirteen songs that started with the *I.L.G.W.U. Anthem* ("Oh, union of the garment workers / To you we ever will be true") and ended with *Hold the Fort*. He brought in Jerry Newman to run the recording sessions and produce and package the product. By early April, the tapes had been made and Isidore Nagler's approval secured. Nagler himself wrote and read the greeting to his "Sisters and Brothers of our great International" that opens the record:

> To us the union is a way of life, filled with ideals and ideas of justice and freedom. In our march forward, song has served to keep up our spirits. The songs which follow express the feelings and aspirations of the Cloakmakers Union and the entire International.[3]

The very first entry in the Noah Greenberg discography is thus not a polished rendering of early music but a long-forgotten ten-inch "LP," amateurish but sincere, entitled *We Work—We Sing*.

*   *   *

Bernie Krainis, meanwhile, had been having his problems. He had his John Blow *Ode on the Death of Mr. Henry Purcell* in hand. He had lined up one recorder-player—himself—and one countertenor, Russell Oberlin. He had already met Jerry Newman.

> I was passing Newman's and Fox's record shop and they had recorder and harpsichord music playing on the outside speaker. It was [recorder player Carl] Dolmetsch and Joseph Saxby. . . . And I walked in and I said to Jerry, 'I can play recorder better than that.'[4]

On that occasion, exercising a degree of chutzpah equal to anything Noah could pull off, he had talked Newman into recording a program of Handel chamber works with recorder.

Bernie went to work on Newman again, this time about the John Blow. Newman agreed to audition the Blow and, if all went well, to record it for Esoteric. Now Bernie sorely needed a second recorder-player and a second countertenor. Having recommended Brayton Lewis and Russell to Noah for *Festino*, he naturally took an interest in the progress of that recording, and in the course of dropping in on rehearsals became familiar with the singing of Arthur Squires. "At that time," Arthur says, "I had a very sweet, clear, absolutely straight voice, no vibrato, not a lot of head voice."[5] It seemed to

---

[3]Isidore Nagler, Greetings, *We Work—We Sing, long-playing record honoring 28th I.L.G.W.U. convention, May 1953.*

[4]Bernard Krainis, February 7, 1997; March 29, 1999.

[5]Arthur M. Squires, December 5, 1997.

Bernie, and to Arthur, too, that with that with a voice like that Arthur might be just the person to tackle the second countertenor part in the Blow *Ode.*

For the *Festino* recording, Noah had retained Blanche Winogron, who was married to Sydney Beck the music librarian, to add keyboard works by Frescobaldi, Gabrieli, Banchieri and Dalza as "incidental interludes." Miss Winogron was a gifted musician, but she was by nature and training a soloist. Also, she played the virginals, a small form of harpsichord. Its delicate tone was more suited to small-scale solo performance than to use as a continuo instrument. For the Blow work as for the Handel recording, Bernie needed someone and something bolder. Possibly through Seymour Barab, or perhaps through Gustave Reese, he met one of the handful of harpsichordists in the city who owned a good instrument and —as important—was willing and able to play non-solo continuo parts.

Herman Chessid fit the bill perfectly. Born in the Bronx and raised in Brooklyn, Herman was a 1948 graduate of the Yale School of Music, where he had studied composition with Paul Hindemith and harpsichord with Ralph Kirkpatrick. He did own a good instrument. It was in fact the first harpsichord built (in 1907) by the pioneering early music devotee and instrument-maker Arnold Dolmetsch (Carl Dolmetsch's father) during the temperamental Frenchman's seven-year stay at the Chickering & Sons piano firm in Boston. Herman enjoyed the challenge of playing continuo accompaniment—it calls for nimble fingers, excellent sight-reading and an ability to improvise—almost as much as he did watching his beloved Brookyn Dodgers play baseball. (One of the reasons Herman became friendly with Jerry Newman was that in an era when few people owned a television set, Jerry was happy to let Herman watch the Dodgers on his TV.)

Cellist George Koutzen was recruited as a second continuo player. Valarie Lamoree, a concert violinist turned soprano (she had sung in *Otello* for Toscanini) had sung on Bernie's Handel recording. She signed up to join Russell and Arthur Squires in the group of songs by Henry Purcell that would make up the record's second side. The one missing musician was another recorder player. As he had intended to do from the start, he approached LaNoue Davenport, now Assistant Director of the Musicians' Workshop. LaNoue, strangely, was tepid. "I don't think he took the project all that seriously," Bernie says. To Bernie's mingled relief and annoyance, LaNoue finally agreed to play on the recording—provided that hisname did not appear. He would hide behind the *nom de disque* John Leonard.

With the personnel lined up, rehearsals could begin. The place: North Baptist Church. The starting time for each session: midnight. Jerry Newman, always on the lookout for handy locations with good acoustics, had come upon North Baptist. It was right in the neighborhood, at the corner of West Fourth and West Eleventh Streets in Greenwich Village. Jerry had made a deal with its minister to use the church as both rehearsal hall and recording studio. As for the outlandish hour, Herman Chessid says, and every working musician will understand: "We started after midnight to cut traffic noise."

Herman was already starting to suffer from the back and neck problems stemming from childhood polio that would seriously interrupt his career. But he remembers the recording sessions as great fun.

> Jerry Newman was a very jovial guy and we used to tell each other jokes during the sessions. Everyone smoked, and we used the collection plate as the ashtray. The minister complained about this, but not to us, he complained to the super. Who told him that if he was renting out his church for something this commercial, what else could he expect?[6]

Noah came to the Blow rehearsals night after night in much the same interested spirit that had brought Bernie to the *Festino* rehearsals. Why not? Everybody was friends with everybody else, and two of Noah's singers, Arthur Squires and Russell Oberlin, were singing for Bernie. In the evenings before it was time to gather at North Baptist, everybody was welcome at 80 Perry Street. Evidently, it was at Noah's and there Russell Oberlin, with incomparable tact, broached the delicate issue of Arthur Squires's vocal range:

> [W]e started working on the Blow and it was really hard for Arthur. He was having all sorts of vocal problems. Just about this time, Charles [Bressler] got out of the Navy. We were old friends.

The young tenor Charles Bressler had come from Kingston, Pennsylvania to The Juilliard, where he had been a classmate of Russell's, and had sung solos with several choruses including the Robert Shaw Chorale. Even at the start of his career, Charles's friends thought of him not only as a gifted singer and (in LaNoue Davenport's phrase) a "fantastic pianist" but as a superb all-around musician.

"I was worrying about Arthur," Russell recalled.

---

[6]Herman Chessid, March 12, 1998.

[S]o I said to Noah, 'Listen, it might be a good idea to have someone understudy for Arthur in case something happens. Charlie
could do it.' So Charles came and we sang it together, and, yes, it
was high for him but he could do it. And poor Arthur heard us in
rehearsal and it broke his heart, but he said, 'I can't do it like that.
Charles should sing it.' Which he did.[7]

Herman Chessid too recalls the incident.

I believe I was in there at that meeting. I remember, I think Bernie
was worried that Arthur would be insulted or something, and
Arthur came along and Arthur appeared to me to be grossly re-
lieved rather than brokenhearted. 'Oh, you must do it, it's your
piece,' [he said to Charles Bressler.] Bernie and I looked at each
other with a sigh of relief.[8]

Arthur Squires himself is completely matter-of-fact about giving
up his part. "The minute I heard Charlie sing, I knew, well hey! he
can do it and I can't."[9] In fact, as Arthur's colleagues willingly at-
test, it was an uncommonly selfless bit of musical behavior.

*   *   *

Edith Schor needed a job. Ill with the grippe and then with pneumonia in the spring of 1951, when Noah had moved out, Edith had
made up her mind to study for a college degree, but she had to support herself as well. Lucy Dames had helped her find work as the
assistant to Neil Handler, head of the Rivers Department of the National Maritime Union. At some point in 1951, she left the NMU for
another, very different organization.

In 1949, the famous Cultural and Scientific Conference for World
Peace was held at the Waldorf-Astoria. It was organized by the Soviet Union, and Soviet delegates were among those who attended.

Among the American sponsors were such diverse individuals as
Albert Einstein, Rexford Guy Tugwell, Leonard Bernstein, Aaron
Copland, Marlon Brando, Harold Rome, Clifford Odets, Lillian
Hellman, Henry Wallace, Frank Lloyd Wright, F. O. Matthiessen
and . . . Harlow Shapley.[10]

In outraged reaction to this display of cultural power, Sidney
Hook, Norman Thomas, and other anti-Communists put together
an *ad hoc* group to mount a rally in opposition. Its sponsors included
Daniel Bell, Clement Greenberg, William Phillips, Philip Rahv, and

[7]Russell Oberlin, January 28, 1997.
[8]Herman Chessid, March 12, 1998.
[9]Arthur M. Squires, December 5, 1997.
[10]Alexander Bloom, *Prodigal Sons*, p. 260.

other rising New York cultural figures. The impulse to organize an intellectuals' response to Communist propaganda outlasted the Waldorf Conference. In Berlin the following year, Hook, the writers Arthur Koestler and Ignazio Silone and the composer Nicholas Nabokov joined two Americans, Michael Josselson and Melvin Lasky, to form the Congress for Cultural Freedom.[11] The C.C.F. soon moved to Paris, where it set about organizing conferences on politico-cultural issues and subsidizing a group of high-toned but strongly anti-Communist journals. Of these, the three best-known are *Encounter* (Great Britain), *Preuves* (France) and *Monat* (Germany).

Back in the U. S., the tireless Sidney Hook brought together yet another group to form a C.C.F. affiliate, the American Committee for Cultural Freedom, with headquarters in New York. The original incorporators of A.C.C.F. were Hook, Elliot Cohen (editor of the Jewish quarterly *Commentary*), William Phillips (coeditor of *Partisan Review*), Richard Rovere (political columnist for *The New Yorker*), George Schuyler (reporter on the *Pittsburgh Courier*), Grace Z. Stone (author under the pseudonym "Ethel Vance" of the anti-Communist novel *Escape*), and James Burnham (Hook's colleague at N.Y.U., former Workers Party functionary and author of *The Managerial Revolution*). Others who joined the A.C.C.F. were "former radicals headed toward the extreme right"[12] like Burnham himself, Max Eastman, James T. Farrell and Whittaker Chambers, and centrist liberals like Arthur Schlesinger, Jr., David Riesman, and Elmer Rice. "New York intellectuals, however, provided the solid center of the organization."[13] One of Noah Greenberg's old Workers Party comrades, Daniel Bell, was an officer. When A.C.C.F. set up its offices, at first at 141 East 44 Street, Room 609, and later at 35 West 53 Street, its first Executive Secretary, at a comfortable $8,500 a year, was Irving Kristol. It was probably Kristol who, needing an office assistant and more than willing to take on a Trotskyist, hired Edith Schor early in 1952. "I was the front office," Edith recalls. "Irv was the rear office." The building at 35 West 53 Street was a few doors down from the Museum of Modern Art. "Somebody on the [A.C.C.F.] board left his

---

[11]Michael Josselson, Estonian by birth, had served in the Office of Strategic Services during World War II and was a cultural affairs officer in the postwar American occupation administration. Melvin Lasky, also an OSS member, had stayed on in Europe writing for *The New Leader* and *Partisan Review*. When their involvement in the anti-Communist "culture wars" broke in the press, both men were named as CIA operatives. Josselson certainly was a CIA agent, Lasky probably was also.

[12]*Loc. cit.*

[13]*Ibid.*, p. 263.

Museum membership card at the office, so A.C.C.F. people could go to lunch at the Museum."[14]

Edith worked for A.C.C.F. until the end of 1952. Kristol himself departed on May 14, 1953, headed for London and the coeditorship of *Encounter* (with the poet Stephen Spender). During this same period, Jeanne Wacker, recommended either by Sidney Hook or James Burnham—she had studied with both men—was there, but, curiously "I don't remember Edith Schor at all." However, Jeanne adds, "memory is a funny thing."[15]

Noah's own relationship with the American Committee for Cultural Freedom and its European parent would always be tangential, more a matter of personal friendships with some of its leading members—Hook, Kristol and the art critics Clement Greenberg and Harold Rosenberg, to name a few—than of any formal affiliation. For example, at about this time (late 1952) Daniel Bell approached Noah, but with a strictly non-political purpose in mind.

> I wanted to learn piano for a very peculiar reason. I'm a sociologist, and one of the things sociologists do is create scales, when you have a scale of utility preferences and things of that sort. And I was very curious about the construction of scales and I always wanted to learn some piano, and I said to Noah, 'You know, why not learn piano? This way, I'll have to do scales and learn about scales and the relationship between notes and scales, and distances and scales, and Noah said, 'Sure,' and I forget what I paid, ten dollars an hour or something like that. And this went on for, oh, almost a year, and then somehow I got busy and lost interest or what, and Noah got very busy, so we stopped.[16]

Still, as apolitical as Noah wanted to be, the A.C.C.F. and its politics, like Noah's own political past, were matters he could never entirely set aside.

*   *   *

With the tapes "in the can" and ready for editing in late March, Jerry Newman scheduled *Festino* and *Ode on the Death of Mr. Henry Purcell* for release in May 1953. It was obvious to Noah and Bernie as they fought off post-recording letdown, that Esoteric Records, scarcely known itself beyond Greenwich Village, could do next to nothing to promote the records. They themselves had few connections. Noah's group at least had a name, The Primavera Singers.

[14]Edith Schor, June 3, 1997.
[15]Jeanne Wacker, October 2, 1997.
[16]Daniel Bell, April 22, 1997.

Bernie's instrumental ensemble had none. On the positive side, both Noah and Bernie believed that they had pulled together unique and exciting performances. Yet it was clear to both men that unless they themselves took action, the records that had cost so much perspiration to produce were liable to moulder in Jerry Newman's and Bill Fox's basement.

Which one of the two broached the idea first, Bernie does not recall. But they swiftly came to an agreement. To garner pre-release publicity for their records, they would team up, pool their resources, and lead their musicians in a live concert performance.

Accordingly, at 1:30 p.m. on March 29, 1953, Bernie, Noah and Toni met at 80 Perry Street, in company with Jesse Simons and I. Meyer Pincus. Mike Pincus was a young lawyer whose wife Miriam had sung in one of Noah's amateur groups. Their purpose was to set up a a corporation that could open a bank account, hire a hall, sign contracts, run ads, have tickets and programs printed, and do all the other business incidental to putting on a concert. Jesse was there because, as he says, "I had a job, and they needed somebody with a job to make them respectable."[17] Mike Pincus amiably agreed to set up The Primavera Singers and St. Cecilia Players of the Pro Musica Antiqua, of New York, Inc. Mike insisted that the corporation seek tax-exempt status as an educational entity, so that Noah and his friends could advise potential supporters that they could make tax-deductible contributions.[18] All five of those present would be corporators and members of the board.

The legal niceties dealt with, the first issue was where and when to play. The rental rates for any of New York's premier concert halls were far too high. Besides, how could unknowns performing music by composers no concert-goer had ever heard of draw a crowd large enough to fill a Carnegie, a Town Hall or a Times Hall? Also, as Noah and Jesse knew from their days of political and union activism, a small hall jammed to the rafters looks much better than a big one half empty. But which small hall? The answer lay beneath their noses. The New School for Social Research, at 66 West 12 Street, boasted an excellent 475-seat auditorium. In use days and evenings during the work week, it was free on some weekends. It was available for a late-afternoon event on the last Sunday of April, the twenty-sixth, and on Sunday afternoons the rent was lowest. To hold the date, a deposit—fifty dollars—was required. Jesse put up the money.

[17]Jesse Simons, March 20, 1997.
[18]I. Meyer Pincus, June 9, 1998.

The next step was to drum up an audience. Greenwich Village in the 1950s *was* in a real sense a village. Noah's, Toni's and Bernie's friends, neighbors, and pupils would certainly show up, as would the friends, relatives, and colleagues of the musicians. New School students and faculty would be interested. Harold Brown and Seymour Barab would be there, and of course Bill Fox and Jerry Newman. Some old comrades from the Workers Party could be counted on. A sprinkling of figures from the music world would come. Sydney Beck would attend because his wife was on the program. Gustave Reese and a few other music historians might appear, drawn by the chance to hear music that they knew only on the printed (or manuscript) page. This would still leave many empty seats to fill, but Noah could draw on his and Jesse's union contacts. Noah's own I.L.G.W.U. choristers were a sure bet for 25 to 30 seats. Some, moreover, would take extra tickets to sell to their I.L.G. sisters and brothers. Jesse Simons sold 22 tickets himself and organized a team to sell more. As for advance publicity, somebody (probably Toni) contacted *The New York Times*, *The New York Herald-Tribune*, and other publications. A single clipping saved by the Greenbergs, undated and with no indication of where it appeared, hints at a promotional effort.

> The latest [early music group] to make its appearance is the New York Pro Musica Antiqua, which was founded earlier this year by Noah Greenberg and Bernard Krainis. The group has already made recordings for Esoteric and next Sunday it will present its first public concert.[19]

The clipping noted the date, time and place of the concert, adding that "[t]he program would be devoted to English and Italian vocal and instrumental music of the sixteenth and seventeenth centuries."

On the day of the concert, April 26, 1953, Bernie and Noah suddenly realized that box offices don't come with built-in supplies of money. Bernie reported that he, Toni and Noah "scurried about the Village on a Sunday morning"—when no banks and very few stores were open— "trying to find enough change...."[20]

The money was found, the box office was opened, the audience filed into the hall and the concert began. "The concert was the long-

---

[19]Clipping, n.d., unidentified publication, in Greenberg family Pro Musica press scrapbook.

[20] Bernard Krainis, letter to the editor, *American Recorder*, November 28, 1996 (uncut version).

est concert in history," Russell Oberlin laughs, remembering. "We were kids, and kids always do that . . . we just went on and on and would be singing to this day."[21] What Russell does not say, but those in the audience do, is that the auditorium crackled with excitement from the opening number straight through to the finale. "It was simply overwhelming," Jesse Simons says, "unbelievable. You could feel the electricity the minute they came on."[22]

The Times's reporter was presumably on the scene, because the bare-bones report in Monday's paper did mention that the concert drew "a capacity audience."[23] It was left to the *Herald-Tribune* to indicate that Noah, Bernie and their colleagues had scored a triumph.

> Old music needs not only to be played; it has to be recreated. And if Sunday's performance may be taken as an accurate indication, both the vocal and instrumental ensemble of the Pro Musica group are eminently able and equipped to bring vigorous life to the music of another day. The Primavera Singers are ideally matched in resonance and timbre, and their work is exact in pitch, spirited as a colt, and hearty in its sonority and color. Their reading of "Festino," a ramblng, a capella renaissance entertainment was both gay and tender, ribald and refined. All told, it was music-making rich and rewarding.

Bernie, LaNoue, Herman Chessid, and George Koutzen fared almost as well:

> [T]hey lack, for a fact, the ultimate in precision. None the less, grace, expressive pungency and charm were a part of all their work. The which reason they, too, were a pleasure to hear.[24]

In the music world, good press is one thing, future success another. But it so happened that in the audience at the New School concert that afternoon was someone who both could and would help put the fledgling ensemble on the cultural map of New York.

[21]Russell Oberlin, January 28, 1997.
[22]Jesse Simons, March 26, 1998.
[23]*The New York Times*, April 27, 1953, p. 19:3.
[24]J[ay] S[.] H[arrison], *The New York Herald-Tribune*, Monday, April 27, 1953, p. 13:2.

CHAPTER FIFTEEN

$\mathcal{A}$T THE "Y"

(1953)

$\mathcal{I}$n 1935, the Young Men's and Young Women's Hebrew Association of New York was looking for an educational director. Founded in 1874, the Ninety-second Street Y, as it has always been called, was the oldest, largest and most august Jewish community center in America. Its board of trustees, largely made up of wealthy, community-minded German Jews, had decided that it should add a dash of education to its mixture of sports, hobby clubs and language and vocational training classes. The decision wasn't an easy one. Some Y trustees wanted the members to go on playing handball and basketball, the staff to go on teaching English to "greenhorns" and nobody else to do much more. Others pointed out that with City College, N.Y.U. and Columbia on the doorstep, all with adult extension divisions, no one would bother with classes, lectures and other educational events at a Jewish Y. But supporters of change like Irwin Edman, professor of philosophy at Columbia, and Rabbi Henry Rosenthal of the Free Synagogue, carried the day. With some trepidation, the board hired William Kolodney away from the Pittsburgh YM-YWHA, where he had developed an ambitious educational program, and brought him back to New York.

Bill Kolodney, thirty-six years old in 1935, was a small man — barely five feet four—with a big mission. First and foremost, he loved the arts. At the same time, like many assimilationist Jews he was convinced that American Jewish communities were too insular. The immigrant experience was over, but Jews were still clustering together as if they were strangers in a strange land. This inwardness, Kolodney was sure, fed suspicion and mistrust on the part of non-Jews, and it cut off Jews themselves from the ideas, values and cultural riches of the world at large. Kolodney wanted to see much more give and take between Jews and non-Jews. His tools were education—he himself had graduated from N.Y.U. and received a M.S. in education from Columbia—and the arts. His professional aim was to broaden the outlook and behavior of secular Jewish institutions like the YM-YWHA.

He started his new job with assurances to the board that his educational goals for the Y were good Jewish goals. "The concept that an ignorant man cannot worship God," he wrote, "is central in Jewish tradition, and knowledge for its own sake Torah L'Shmo, has been widely accepted by the Jewish community."[1] Having sent this soothing message, Kolodney set to work to remake the 92nd Street Y in ways that had little to do with Judaism as such.

Kolodney was abetted in his mission by the Y's superb physical plant. The auditorium in particular was a gem.

> Unlike most auditoriums, the Theresa L. Kaufmann Auditorium is a concert hall with an inclined floor, upholstered seats attached to the floor, no pillars, excellent acoustics, and with clear visibility from every angle. Furthermore, it is air-conditioned. Yet before the various subscription series were introduced, this auditorium was not used 75 percent of the time.[2]

Kolodney's use of the Kaufmann proved that, in addition to being a passionate believer in the arts, he was a brilliant marketer of culture. He was especially interested in attracting young audiences. Almost his first act as education director in 1935 was to launch an art-film subscription series at the Kaufmann, the only one in the city before the Museum of Modern Art opened its film center in 1939. He made sure the prices were irresistible to the impecunious young. (For Y members, admission to films was ten cents, for non-members, twenty cents.) To draw young non-Jews to a Jewish hall, he offered dance groups from colleges of all denominations around the city the chance to demonstrate their work free of charge. To mention one other prime example, the availability of the Kaufmann allowed Kolodney, who loved modern poetry, to experiment with the idea of inviting poets to the Y to read their work before audiences. The idea was a success. Celebrity poets like Carl Sandberg, W. H. Auden and Dylan Thomas would sell out the house. And poetry was a money-maker. At a dollar a ticket, even a half-filled hall would more than cover expenses. Under the direction of John Malcolm

[1]Dr. William Kolodney, "History of the Educational Department of the YM-YWHA," p. 8.
[2]*Ibid.*, p. 88.

Brinnan, and later of Betty Kray, Kolodney's Poetry Center at the Y became one of Kolodney's most enduring creations.

As for music, in the beginning the trustees thought that booking classical-music concerts into the Kaufmann was a foolish idea. Ninety-second Street was much too far from midtown, they said, to attract concert-goers who by habit went to Carnegie or Town Hall. Besides, music-lovers would assume that as part of a "Y", the Kaufmann was a "recreation hall," a gym, with squeaky wooden seats and dreadful acoustics. In any case, non-Jews would feel unwelcome. And who would play at the Kaufmann? Big-name performers were too expensive. Unknowns? The public would never risk its money on the "Y"'s say-so alone.

Kolodney's most effective answer was the low-priced subscription series. Only the wealthy could afford season tickets to the Metropolitan Opera, and most of New York's other musical organizations and concert halls promoted their events one at a time. Subscription series could be designed and marketed in a variety of ways. The simplest was to schedule groups for two, three or more concerts, the programs of which were related, as in the case of the Budapest String Quartet's performances of all of the Beethoven quartets. This, Kolodney saw, would guarantee an audience for an entire bloc of evenings. Subscription audiences paid in advance. By definition, they were also interested enough in a given ensemble or type of music to keep paying for it year after year. The "Y" could thus plan its concert programs ahead, with confidence that individual concerts would be well attended. And a hall that was well booked season after season could afford to introduce new talent, although Kolodney was well aware that the balance between new and established performers had to be carefully maintained.

Most of the classes and lecture series Kolodney established, and the programs he created in modern dance, drama, poetry, and music, are still alive today. Although he was careful not to offend Jewish sensibilities—for instance, he tried to hire only non-Jews to staff the "Y"'s Saturday events—his programs were resolutely humanist and non-sectarian. It took him more than a decade, but by the beginning of the 1950s, as Kolodney himself proudly observed, the "Y"'s

> essential character . . . was changed from that of a neighborhood center with a standard recreational program, meeting the needs only of the Jewish population, to that of a city-wide center reaching all elements of the population. [Furthermore], the new pro-

gram set out to meet the intellectual needs of that element of the
population which found its recreation primarily in the world of
ideas and in the practice and appreciation of the arts beyond the
folk level.[3]

The "Y"'s Number One cultural talent scout was William
Kolodney himself. This fact plus Kolodney's perpetual interest in
the new and unusual explain why he made it his business to be at
the New School auditorium on Sunday, April 26, at 5:30 in the afternoon. What he saw and heard was overwhelming. Within a few
weeks, Kolodney contacted Noah Greenberg with an offer that must
have brought a huge grin to Noah's face. Kolodney would engage
the New York Pro Musica Antiqua not for one but for three appearances at the Kaufmann during the upcoming (1953-54) season, and
would offer Pro Musica as a subscription series. Two of the appearances would be on Monday nights, not the most popular date on
the calendar, and one would be on the Sunday of Christmas weekend, when people might well prefer to stay home. But three concerts! Yes, of course Noah and Bernie would accept. And of course
they would let Dr. Kolodney (Ed.D., Teachers College, Columbia
University, 1949) know well in advance what programs they would
be offering.

This was a breakthrough on a scale that Noah and Bernie had
hoped for but had not dared to imagine. Its implications for the
newly-minted group took the breath away. In Russell Oberlin's
words, "if Kolodney hadn't believed in what we were doing and
offered us a concert series, I'm not sure the Pro Musica would have
held together."[4]

After the New School concert, there was no question in Noah's
and Bernie's (and Russell's) minds: the New York Pro Musica
Antiqua should perform live as well as make records. Now, the
group *had* to be a performing group. It had to stay in existence as
such for at least a full year. To hungry young musicians, that meant
steady work for an eternity. Those who had taken part in the concert—with one exception—could now be formally invited to join
Pro Musica. Of course, they would have to agree not to work with
any competing group. Bernie and Noah would act as managers.
Everybody would share in the profits.

The one concert participant not asked to join was LaNoue Davenport.

[3]*Ibid.*, p. 5.
[4]Russell Oberlin, January 28, 1997.

"LaNoue had taken no part in planning the event," Bernie wrote decades later,

> and since everyone (especially Noah, who was furious) understood that he had insisted on the pseudonym "Jack Leonard" [actually, "John Leonard"] to show his contempt for our efforts, he was not invited to join the group.[5]

"I wish I hadn't done that [insisted on using a pseudonym]," LaNoue said ruefully, also decades later. "I had some foolish idea that as director of the Musicians' Workshop I shouldn't be competing with myself." But the notion that he was contemptuous of the Pro Musica in its early childhood was "all wrong" and "a shame."[6]

Perhaps because they were better established and more interested in solo careers, the instrumentalists were less eager than the singers were to commit themselves to Pro Musica. The continuo players, Herman Chessid and George Koutzen, did agree to make themselves available if bookings came up and no conflicts occurred. Blanche Winogron said carefully that she thought she would take part. The Primavera Singers were far more enthusiastic. All agreed to become members of the group and to go to work on new material.

Noah, exultant, knew that Kolodney's offer threw open a door to the future. He had already sensed the need for Pro Musica, small and specialized as it was, to find its own pathway to advancement. As Russell put it:

> You know Fifty-seventh Street? Where all the agents and managers are, the string quartets and symphonies and everybody? Noah said, 'Fifty-seventh Street has a life of its own. We're not really interested in that. We have to appeal to the intelligentsia.' And that's what he did.[7]

If any New York concert location was a haven of the intelligentsia, it was the Y and the Kaufmann. Regular exposure there would afford Pro Musica a rare opportunity to establish itself and build a following. Success there was critical. To cement a long-term relationship and become a fixture, the little ensemble would have to make its first appearances spectacularly successful. The planning for these would draw on another of Noah's gifts, a real brilliance at planning and organizing concert programs. The first concert, scheduled for October 12, posed no problems. The group could repeat

---

[5]Bernard Krainis, letter to the editor, *American Recorder*, November 28, 1996.
[6]LaNoue Davenport, April 3, 1997.
[7]LaNoue Davenport, April 3, 1997.

the Thomas Morley madrigals and instrumental canzonets it had played at the New School and add works by other Elizabethans if necessary. But what about the other programs?

The theme of the December 27 concert seemed to choose itself. A concert two days after Christmas could certainly be a Christmas concert. As Noah knew, splendid material for a Pro Musica-style Christmas concert had recently appeared. In 1952, the British firm Stainer and Bell had published, as Volume 4 of the "Musica Britannica" series, John Stevens's *Medieval Carols*. The fourteenth-, fifteenth- and sixteenth-century music in Stevens's collection was surpassingly beautiful and full of interest. Best of all from Noah's point of view, few of the carols had ever been performed in public or recorded.

The story may be apocryphal, but after Noah proposed the carols program, some Y board members are said to have raised the issue of whether a Jewish concert-hall was the appropriate setting for a program of Christmas music. Noah and his colleagues, and William Kolodney also, would have thought the objectors hypersensitive: generations of Jewish music-lovers had doted on renditions of the Schubert and Bach-Gounod settings of the *Ave Maria*, on the Mozart and Verdi Requiems and on countless other works based on the Christian liturgy. It was an era, moreover, in which Christmas carols were routinely sung (and prayers offered) in the public schools. Besides, medieval carols were—medieval. They were from long ago, and therefore not at all the same kind of thing as *Silent Night* and *Hark! The Herald Angels Sing*. Old carols, in a word, were music, not religion. If the objection actually was voiced, Kolodney overcame it: Pro Musica's December program was approved.

In any event, the program for the third concert would have offset any objection to the second concert. As Noah explained in an article written later:

> Salamone Rossi, Hebreo, or Schelomo Me-Ha-Adummim, as he was known to his Jewish brethren in the city of Mantua, Italy, was not only the most important Jewish composer of the baroque but one of the musical innovators of his day. Rossi's dates are lost, but we do know that he led an active musical life in northeastern Italy between 1587 and 1628.[8]

---

[8]Noah Greenberg, "Introducing: Salamone Rossi," *The Berkshire Eagle*, August, 28, 1954.

Noah had learned, probably from the composer Hugo Weisgall, who taught at the Jewish Theological Seminary, that Fritz Rikko, a German-born violinist, early-music devotee and Greenwich Village resident, was preparing a new edition of Rossi's works, including a remarkable collection of vocal works for Jewish liturgical use, *The Songs of Solomon*.[9]

As a way of paying Rikko, the Seminary's Cantor's Institute, which Weisgall headed, was funding a series of seminars during which music-history students joined their teacher in transcribing the pieces from microfilms of the original parts. One of the participants was a Columbia University graduate student and instructor in musicology named Joel Newman. As it happened, Joel was also one of Bernie Krainis's recorder pupils. Bernie had told him all about the Primavera Singers and the St. Cecelia Players and their plan to join forces.

> So I was at the first concert at the New School, and oh, boy! Who had ever heard of a countertenor? Who had ever heard Thomas Morley, or Purcell, or a Handel trio sonata? I went back stage afterward and met this huge guy, Noah, and we talked music and he invited me to attend rehearsals at his home. . . .[10]

Noah found Joel not only likeable and knowledgeable but more than willing to help. "Next thing, I attended a rehearsal, and after that Noah would call me at any time of the day or night with a question."[11]

Fritz Rikko's Rossi project soon became Noah's Rossi project, and Joel, to his delight, found himself involved with both.

> Rikko was giving Noah the penciled scores of the Rossi [vocal works] we were putting together, and Noah was giving them to Seymour Barab and Seymour was copying them for the singers.[12]

The copying was tricky work. Hebrew texts, of course, are read from right to left, where musical notation reads from left to right. Putting the right words to the right notes was a challenge, but Seymour got the job done. Joel remembers that for advice on the "underlay," and on Jewish liturgical practice in Northern Italy dur-

[9]Before coming to the U. S., Rikko had been associated with the Schola Cantorum Basiliensis, an early-music group formed in Basel in 1934 by August Wenzinger. Rikko's ambition was to own the score of every trio sonata ever written. His fascination with this musical form is what led him to the work of Salamone Rossi, considered by some historians the first to experiment with it.

[10]Joel Newman, May 4, 1998.

[11]Joel Newman, May 4, 1998.

[12]Joel Newman, May 4, 1998

ing the Renaissance, he and the others called on a Rabbi Feist, "a brilliant scholar," who was the brother of Leo Feist, a leading publisher of 1950s pop music.

As for for instrumental pieces, Joel said, "Noah got Fritz and me together and we produced several sets of trio sonatas. Noah picked the ones he wanted for the concert."[13] Indeed, Fritz Rikko later appointed Joel Newman music editor of the three published volumes of Rossi's instrumental works. And Joel became, in his own words, Noah Greenberg's "captive musicologist" and a key figure in Pro Musica's musical development.

The timing of all of this was exquisitely lucky, and as in the case of *Medieval Carols* Noah was quick to seize upon a piece of good luck. In November 1953, he informed a delighted Bill Kolodney that the February 22, 1954 concert would present instrumental works and settings of Jewish liturgical texts by Salamone Rossi.

Kolodney was not alone in wanting to make the most of Pro Musica's debut. Jerry Newman too was eager. He had released *Festino* early in May, and by the end of June, helped by excellent reviews, he had sold over 300 copies.

Jerry already had the group under contract for a second recording, this one of madrigals by Morley and Weelkes. Then there was the selection of vocal and instrumental works by George Frederick Handel that Bernie Krainis and his colleagues had already recorded. In the wake of the New School success, Jerry, Bernie and Noah decided to package it as a New York Pro Musica Antiqua offering.

The program paired Bernie and soprano Valarie Lamoree in the Handel secular cantata *Nel dolce dell' oblio*. Arnold Black, a friend of both Bernie's and Herman Chessid's, had played the violin and Bernie the recorder in a trio sonata. Bernie had also featured himself in two of Handel's sonatas for recorder and continuo. Herman Chessid was the continuo harpsichordist. Bernie had wanted a second continuo player, one who would reinforce the bass line on a string instrument. Either cellist George Koutzen was not available or else Bernie decided for the sake of "authenticity" and novelty to replace the cello with its earlier cousin the bass viola da gamba. In the 1950s, gambas and gamba-players were in short supply. The one gambist Bernie knew was the wife of a distinguished mathematician. Peter Courant, head of the N.Y.U. research institute that now bears his name, was an amateur pianist and, like his wife Nina, a chamber music devotee.

[13]Joel Newman, May 4, 1998.

Making the Handel record had turned out to be a lively experience. As he had done with the John Blow, Jerry had used North Baptist Church as both rehearsal hall and recording studio. As with the Blow, rehearsals and recording sessions began after midnight. So, as Herman recalls, had certain difficulties.

> Nina Courant was a lovely gracious woman, but she had no business among the professionals, really, and she was an elderly lady, and in this church beginning at midnight and until four a.m. Anyhow, I was improvising [my right-hand part], something I wouldn't do when I got wiser, with a recording. . . .

> Anyway . . . it was late and she [Nina Courant] wasn't exactly with it, she thought she was at home playing chamber music with friends or something, it was the middle of the tape, she looks over at me, she says 'Lovely!' And so we had to do it again. I told her I appreciated, but would you mind saving your compliments 'til after.

Problems of another sort cropped up in the editing.

> The [gamba] part had sixteenth notes, passages. Which had to be fixed. She could play them, but not good enough, not to have all the notes. What Jerry did, he put the headphones on me and at the right moment, the notes she just messed up, I [put in the notes from another take] in time with the rest of the passage. . . No one else could do that if they weren't . . . players. And Jerry coined a phrase—'cause it worked, right?—'Wow! That's a F.F.S.!'

'What the hell is an F.F.S.?'

'A Fabulous Fuckin' Splice!'[14]

Fabulous or not, the splicing didn't always work. To explain away the resulting unevennesses, the liner notes of the Handel recording say blandly that

> [i]n rapid passages, for the sake of balance and clarity, one or the other [continuo] instrument might play only the important harmony notes, or even drop out altogether.[15]

Apart from the Handel and the three earlier recordings (*Festino*, the Blow and the Morley), Jerry Newman taped two other Pro Musica recordings during the spring of 1953. One was a program of English rounds, songs, ayres and madrigals with instrumental interludes. The other was the program of English carols Pro Musica

[14]Herman Chessid, March 11, 1998.

[15]Leon Kaba, liner notes, ES-515, "George Frederick Handel: Music for Ancient Instruments and Soprano Voice." New York. Esoteric Records. 1953.

would be presenting at the Y in December. Both tapes were banked for later release. The carols would be brought out in November, following release of the Morley in October, for the Christmas market. The English program, originally intended as a ten-inch, not a twelve-inch LP, was held for release in 1954.

As a measure of how Pro Musica's fortunes had improved, Jerry was willing to advance nearly $1,500 for the Morley, carols and English programs.

Something else was happening to Noah and Pro Musica that spring. In the mysterious way that word of new talent seeps out, spreads and feeds on itself in New York, murmurs about Pro Musica began to tease the curiosity of the city's arbiters of culture. The murmuring started, naturally enough, in Greenwich Village, where bohemia and a more sedate populace of followers of the arts coexisted and mingled in amiable symbiosis. Noah, bohemian but protean in his ability to charm, had contacts among the cultivated. Even before Pro Musica, for example, he was a welcome visitor at the East Tenth Street home of Judge Julius Isaacs and his wife Betty, both noted in the Village for their interest in the arts. During his sojourn on Cornelia Street, moreover, Noah had met and made friends with a fellow-Villager who was both artist and social and cultural arbiter, the poet James Ingram Merrill.

James Merrill, twenty-seven years old in 1953, was many things. He was one of the finest poetic talents of the postwar generation. He was a figure of note in New York's quasi-underground gay arts community. And he was the son of a very rich man, Charles E. Merrill of Merrill, Lynch, Pierce, Fenner & Beane. Merrill père's genius at selling stock to a broad public had made him a multimillionaire. He was also an incorrigible womanizer and an overpoweringly generous father. "[H]e gives me everything!" groans the young hero of James Merrill's autobiographical novel, published in 1957. "I don't even ask for it! It's been mine since childhood, set up in a trust fund—in twenty trust funds, for all I know! I try to live it down but I can't!"[16] One way James Merrill tried "to live it down" in real life was to be kind, supportive and financially generous in his turn to many people in the arts.

Ruth Daigon remembered that Pro Musica entertained at "a couple of parties in [Merrill's] Village apartment,"[17] a shabby-splen-

---

[16]James Merrill, *The Seraglio*, p. 25.
[17]Ruth Daigon, e-mail message, February 8, 1998.

did duplex with its own garden. Arthur Squires agreed, and added
that Merrill offered "heavy support" to Noah and Pro Musica in the
early years.

> I think I'm on exceedingly firm ground when I'm [saying] that there
> were at least two five-thousand-dollar checks that Noah got from
> Jimmy Merrill simply with one phone call each at some moment
> when it was like a crisis, he just had to have that money. And there
> might have been a third. And this would have been in '53, '54.[18]

Another of New York's notable talent-spotters had no money to
give but did provide maximum exposure. This was Leo Lerman,
culture-vulture and partygiver extraordinaire. Tall, bearded, and
hysterically gay, Lerman was called by some who knew him "the
Elsa Maxwell of Lexington Avenue." His official job was "literary
editor" of *Madamoiselle*, one of the two New York fashion magazines
(the other was Condé Nast's *Glamour*) aimed at young working
women. His real job, at which he excelled, was "to spot what was in
vogue and whose star was rising—or setting."[19] The Sunday night
parties Lerman threw at his five-story brownstone at 1453 Lexington Avenue attracted everybody who was en route to being somebody—including Pro Musica. The food (hunks of American cheese)
and wine "four gallons of nasty red"[20] per party) were dreadful.
But in Ruth's joyful outburst:

> There was one party I will never forget. It was at Leo Lerman's.
> He was a something in the literary world—actually a collector of
> famous people and something of a writer as well. Anyway, to be-
> gin with . . . there was Tennessee Williams serving drinks. When
> he first looked at you, it was on the bias, but the more he drank the
> more direct his gaze became. And I won't ever forget his sitting at
> my feet watching me sing. I had just seen *Streetcar* and was totally
> blown away. . . .
>
> Then Sono Osato, a gorgeous ballerina who was starring on Broad-
> way, came floating down the stairs in some feathered costume, and
> I mean float.
>
> In a corner was Patricia Neal just back from Hollywood (and her
> affair with Gary Cooper) chatting with great enthusiasm to Roald
> Dahl who later became her husband. . . . Then there was Jennie
> Tourel, the marvellous Met mezzo, surrounded by her entourage.

[18]Arthur M. Squires, December 5, 1997.
[19]Gerald Clarke, *Capote: A Biography*, p. 91.
[20]"Leo Lerman," in George Plimpton, *Truman Capote*, p. 45.

New York Pro Musica, Fall, 1953: Left to right: (standing) Brayton Lewis, Elizabeth Kyburg, Bernard Krainis, Arthur Squires, Noah; (seated) Russell Oberlin, Ruth Daigon, Charles Bressler, Lois Roman, Blanche Winogron.
(Courtesy I. Meyer Pincus, Esq.)

Artie and I were dashing around, pointing and laughing until Noah told us to quit it and act sophisticated. Some hope![21]

Noah hated to ask his musicians to sing for their supper, or to perform gratis at a party to butter up prospective supporters. He did ask, though rarely and always reluctantly. But if tastemakers like Jimmy Merrill, who loved music, and Leo Lerman, who loved being au courant, hushed their guests into attentive silence and said, "Noah, how about giving us a couple of numbers?" it was the headiest kind of flattery. More: it was a chance to show off Pro Musica's shining young talent (and Noah's) before a select audience of other tastemakers. It was great free publicity. It was a sure sign that Pro Musica had arrived.

[21]Ruth Daigon, e-mail message, February 7, 1998.

CHAPTER SIXTEEN

GETTING ON THE UPTOWN MAP

(1953-1954)

 $\mathcal{A}$ fter the New School concert, Pro Musica was not heard in public again until October 4. But during the intervening six months, Noah threw himself with his usual energy and enthusiasm into everything that goes into managing a small but bustling arts enterprise. Singlehandedly, he took on the tasks of music director, booking agent, publicist, and fundraising executive. The apartment at 80 Perry Street became Pro Musica's rehearsal hall, music library, business office, and—on many an occasion—communal kitchen. Noah, in brief, was both capitalizing upon and basking in the group's initial success, and he loved every minute of it, even its wilder aspects.

One of these came to pass later that same spring. Wystan Auden, telling one of his friends that he needed a "homier nest,"[1] left 7 Cornelia Street and the West Village for a new flat at 77 St. Mark's Place. The Greenbergs, along with dozens of others of Auden's friends, were duly invited to Auden's and Chester Kallman's housewarming party. Kallman too issued some invitations. The painter Larry Rivers, who lived one flight above the new tenants, gave a graphic account of the proceedings.

> Chester invited a tall, muscular sailor who showed up in uniform, a boy from Iowa, who after three cups of Chester and Wystan's concoction of English tea, white wine, and hundred-proof vodka slipped into a pair of black silk stockings and sheer lace panties and demurely worked a kosher salami into his asshole, singing 'Anchors Aweigh.' Wystan told Chester in a loud stage whisper to 'get that hidee-ola out immediately.' Wystan may have been a snob, but he was not a prude. What he was was a gracious host. His

---

[1] Charles H. Miller, *Auden: An American Friendship*, p. 99.

rage was provoked by the frivolous misuse of the kosher salami brought by Mr. and Mrs. Noah Greenberg of the Pro Musica Antiqua ensemble.[2]

Did Toni and Noah witness this abuse of their housewarming gift? Did they react? Rivers did not say.

In mid-June, six weeks after Pro Musica's debut, Noah was conferring with "the other Greenberg," Clement,[3] about Salamone Rossi's liturgical works and Pro Musica's plans to perform them. As managing editor of the American Jewish Committee's quarterly *Commentary*, a job he held until 1956, Clem Greenberg was always on the lookout for lively stories about aspects of Jewish culture. Rossi certainly was a promising subject. There was indeed a story in a sixteenth-century Jewish composer who wrote music for the synagogue but whose virtuosity on the violin led Duke Vicenzo I of Mantua to exempt him from wearing the yellow patch Jews were forced to wear in public. But Clem Greenberg, ever wary, may have felt the need to distance himself and *Commentary* from Noah's more ardent promotional efforts. He suggested that Noah try these on someone else. On June 20, Noah drafted a letter to the "someone else," addressing him as "My dear Mr. Rabinowitz."

> I am writing you at the suggestion of Clement Greenberg who felt you might be interested in a project I discussed with him a few days ago.

The "project" was the publication and recording of the Rossi works that Fritz Rikko and his seminar students, including Joel Newman, were busy editing. Noah, looking for financial support, sharpened his appeal with a hint of the project's intellectual importance.

> Clement Greenberg said that Commentary would be interested in publishing articles prepared as a result of such [scholarly] findings.[4]

---

[2] Larry Rivers, *What Did I Do? An Unauthorized Autobiography*, p. 110.

[3] Actually, Clement Greenberg's two brothers, Sol and Martin, were likelier candidates for this title, both having been, like Noah, members of Max Shachtman's Workers Party.

[4] Noah Greenberg, draft of a letter to a Mr. Rabinowitz, June 20, 1953. NYPM Archives, Box 25, Folder 3. (There is no indication of the identity of the addressee. He might have been Louis M. Rabinowitz, a wealthy New Haven, Connecticut businessman with a strong interest in Judaica.)

Nothing came of this particular approach, if indeed the letter was ever sent.[5]

On June 25, Noah was drafting another fundraising letter, this one to a "Madame Chareau" to ask for funds to purchase music. Since Noah himself wrote the thank-you letters *to* contributors in the early days of Pro Musica, and since no response can be found in the files, this letter too was probably never sent.

In early July, he and Toni left the steamy city for Long Island and a rented cottage on Fireplace Road in East Hampton, where they spent the entire month. Given the pace of the year thus far, the vacation may have been sorely needed. But as Toni was finding, the last thing Noah wanted was respite from the pressures of success. Indeed, he had good reason to want to press on: soon after their return to New York, they learned that Toni was pregnant.

Rehearsals for the first "Y" concert began in August. Someone pointed out that 1953 was the 350th anniversary of the death of the Elizabethan composer Thomas Morley, whose madrigals, songs, and canzonets made up a considerable portion of the program. One of Noah's strengths as a promoter and program planner was his understanding of the peculiar power of early music to make the past come alive. With this went a shrewd sense of how to turn milestones of cultural history—even those as obscure as the anniversary of a little-known madrigalist—into performing opportunities for Pro Musica. Thomas Morley had written the music for several of the songs in Shakespeare's plays. Like Shakespeare, he had been a resident of the London parish of Little St. Helen's Bishopsgate. The tenuous double link with the Bard lent Morley a touch of literary as well as musical interest. This plus the good offices of Sydney Beck and the growing interest in Pro Musica enabled Noah to squeeze in an afternoon concert, "in Honor of the 350th Anniversary of the Death of Thomas Morley," in advance of the "Y" concert. The place was the main building of the New York Public Library, at Fifth Avenue and 42nd Street. The date, Sunday, October 4, was Pulaski Day. The noise of the bands parading on Fifth Avenue was such that Noah delayed the opening of the concert until things quieted down.

Despite the delay, *The New York Herald-Tribune* was enthusiastic.

> The program when it did come was a beautifully planned, beautifully executed one, where six marvellously ensembled voices, two

---

[5] Noah himself did write an article about Rossi, but this appeared about a year later in *The New York Herald-Tribune* ("Introducing: Salamone Rossi," Sunday, February 21, 1954, Section 4, p. 5). Later still, it appeared, shortened, in *The Berkshire Eagle*. Saturday, August 28, 1954)

recorders, and virginas [sic] offered duets, trios and concerted pieces. . . . For sheer loveliness of tone and finesse in detail and nuance, the Pro Musica Antiqua could scarcely be bettered, and more should be heard of them in concert as well as on record.[6]

The review, however, also referred to the "tiny tones of virginals and recorders and the delicate acapella of the Primavera Singers," and that set Noah's teeth on edge. Something clearly had to be done to erase the impression that Pro Musica was a precious or miniaturist ensemble. Instrumental forces consisting of Bernie Krainis and Bernie's pupil Elizabeth Kyburg, recorders, and Blanche Winogron, virginals, were adequate in a small hall or in a location set up for recording. But now more was needed. Specifically, a violinist to bolster the sound of the concerted pieces and a bass-instrument player to support some of the songs. With an assist from Harold Brown, Sonya Monosoff, a 28-year-old violinist with a certificate from The Juilliard's graduate school and a special interest in the Baroque violin repertoire, was recruited. As for the bass instrument, Noah had been thinking about it even before the Public Library concert. A cellist would have been adequate but inappropriate: in Elizabethan times, the cello had yet to be invented. What Noah wanted was a viola da gamba player. By September 25, with the "Y" concert only three weeks away, Noah had somehow acquired the gamba itself, but he had yet to find anyone to play it. In typical Noah fashion, he turned every ounce of his enormous persuasiveness on a nonplussed Seymour Barab. He handed Seymour the instrument, which had a fretted fingerboard in place of the cello's smooth one, seven strings to the cello's five and no floor spike to support its weight. "You can play this," Noah declared, "there's nothing to it. Besides, I don't have anybody else. You have to do it."

To his own incredulity, Seymour found himself doing it. "Three weeks after I got my hands on a gamba for the first time," he said, still wondering at his nerve. "I was playing it at the YMHA. I put a fingering on every note in the score. Every note. It was horrible." Partly Seymour the musician was accepting a dare. "The gamba is not an easy instrument. I was saying to myself, 'I bet you can't learn [it] in three weeks' and challenging myself to do it." But mostly there was another reason. "You do these things for friends." Seymour went on to develop the point.

> I do think that the proof of friendship is that a friend is willing to make the effort, and Noah got everybody on that wavelength. . . .

[6] *The New York Herald Tribune*, Monday, Oct. 5, 1953, p. 13'.1, 2.

> [He] got out of us what he wanted exactly the same way he got money out of contributors, sheerly on the basis of enthusiasm.[7]

In a word, in music as in every other department of his life, Noah's gift for leadership was the natural outgrowth of his gift for making friends.

Landing the "Y" and the New York Public Library engagements only sharpened Noah's desire to establish Pro Musica in its own niche in New York's musical and cultural life. Noah knew well that a small but influential circle of music scholars, editors, publishers, curators, and educators combined a professional interest in early music with some ability to arrange or pay for performances. In this circle, Emanuel Winternitz was a figure of importance. A musicologist, Winternitz was curator of the Musical Instrument Collection of the Metropolitan Museum of Art. In the days before the Museum's Grace Rainey Rogers Auditorium replaced the old Lecture Hall, in the spring of 1954, Winternitz also booked the concerts held on occasion in the museum's galleries.

On Sept. 29, 1953, a few days before the Public Library concert, Noah found the time to write to Winternitz to invite him to be Pro Musica's guest "at the first of a series of concerts New York Pro Musica Antiqua is giving at the 92nd Street YMHA.

> . . . Our organization consists of a group of professional singers and instrumentalists who devote themselves to the study and performance of mediaeval [sic], renaissance and early baroque music. We were organized at the end of 1952 and have led a rather active music life since. In addition to our inaugural concert (April 26, 1953), we have made six Long-playing recordings for the Esoteric Record Company and have given a series of radio broadcasts. . . . We are especially anxious for you to become acquainted with our work because we know you to be a champion of the music of these times.[8]

Winternitz probably did attend at least the first "Y" concert. Soon afterward—in any event, before the end of 1953—he and Noah met to discuss the vast early-music repertoire and programming possibilities for the fledgeling Pro Musica. But one matter that Noah had meant to bring up at the meeting slipped his mind. It had to do with what the new group should call itself. The name "Pro Musica Antiqua" was by no means original or new. In 1933, Safford Cape, a

[7] Seymour Barab, March 3, 1997. If Seymour's debut as a gamba-player was in fact "horrible," the horror passed strangely unremarked by the critics.
[8] Letter, Noah Greenberg-Emanuel Winternitz, September 29, 1953. NYPM Archives, Box 11, Folder 2.

twenty-seven-year-old American conductor and musicologist working in Brussels, had organized a group specializing in medieval music
and had named it Pro Musica Antiqua. Although not brilliantly
successful, Cape's company was still active, recording and touring,
twenty years later. Noah knew this perfectly well, as did Winternitz
and everyone else with an interest in early music. The situation
made Noah uncomfortable enough to write to Winternitz that he
was prepared to take action.

> We are planning to change our name (New York Pro Musica
> Antiqua) because of the confusion with the Cape group. Safford
> Cape and I discussed the matter when he was in New York. We
> both felt that it was not too late for us to change, since we are es-
> tablishing our reputation now. What we will change it to is an-
> other matter. We must decide very soon. I will notify you as soon
> as we have chosen one. Any suggestions would be most welcome,
> by the way.[9]

But Russell Oberlin tells a somewhat different story, and one with
a different ending.

> We didn't have a name. I remember sitting around and talking
> about this. Noah wanted to call us 'the Primavera Singers and the
> St. Cecelia Players of the New York Pro Musica Antiqua.' I thought
> 'the New York Collegium' sounded classier. Noah knew Safford
> Cape. . . He ran into him on Fifty-seventh Street and told him that
> he wanted to call his group the 'New York Pro Musica Antiqua,'
> and Safford didn't want that at all. Noah came back and told us,
> and he said, 'Well, he can't really stop us. And [Paul] Hindemith's
> already got a collegium.' So we were the 'Primavera Singers and
> the St. Cecelia Players of the New York Pro Musica Antiqua,' but
> after a while we dropped the 'Primavera' and the 'St. Cecelia' and
> just became the New York Pro Musica Antiqua, and then just New
> York Pro Musica.[10]

Because a title cannot be copyrighted or otherwise protected,
Safford Cape could only grin and bear the fact that the younger group
had made off with his ensemble's name.

Emanuel Winternitz was not Noah's only contact at the Metro-
politan Museum. Three days after his first letter to Winternitz, on
October 2, Noah was writing to another Metropolitan staff member.
Beatrice Farwell was working for Sterling Callisen in the museum's
Education Department. She was also an amateur singer, a close

[9] Noah Greenberg-Emanuel Winternitz, n.d. but certainly between October 12, 1953
and December 31, 1953. NYPM Archives, Box 11, Folder 2.
[10] Russell Oberlin, January 28, 1997.

friend of Arthur Squires's, and a devotee of early music. As Arthur Squires recalled:

> I had known Beatrice since about [19]48 and quite possibly '47. She's, you know, even when I met her I knew she was a woman of considerable substance. Her father was Arthur Farwell, the composer. We'd go to the opera together and do a lot of things together. I met her in a pickup group with a fellow that had great trunks of early music, and we'd come together and spend the evening, about eight or ten of us, all—no emphasis on whether you were a good voice or not but always emphasis on being able to read. I deliberately got [Beatrice] into the Cantata Singers so that I could turn over the presidency to her. She was a friend of Noah's through me.[11]

From the start, Beatrice Farwell proved a Pro Musica fan and ally. She had already acquired several of the group's recordings, and had quickly grasped the educational potential of using medieval and Renaissance music as performed by these young, talented, and attractive musicians to draw attention to the Metropolitan's wonderful medieval and Renaissance art. She had evidently phoned Noah (or Arthur) to ask about the makeup of the ensemble and the amount of its fee. Noah began his answer by thanking her again "for auditioning our group (via records)." For a concert at the Metropolitan, he said, he would supply "six singers and three instrumentalists (a chest of recorders, a bass viola da gamba and a portative organ)."[12]

The recorders and the gamba Noah certainly could provide, but the promise of a "portative organ" was sheer wishful thinking. A late medieval version of the organ, a portative really is small enough to be carried. The organist's right hand plays the keyboard, while the left hand and arm work the bellows that supply the air. Representations of this charming instrument abound in paintings, but no actual working portatives existed. Noah was trying to remedy the lack. At the time of his letter to Bea Farwell, he had contacted the Rieger Organ Company and asked it to design and build the first portative organ to be commissioned for at least four centuries. Rieger, however, was running into a great deal of trouble—understandably, given the absence of examples to work from[13]—and in fact never

[11] Arthur M. Squires, December 5, 1997.

[12] Noah Greenberg-Beatrice Farwell, letter, October 2, 1953. NYPM Archives, Box 11, Folder 2.

[13] Noah Greenberg-Prof. Donald G. Loach, Yale University School of Music, letter, Dec. 8, 1953. "I believe I mentioned to you that the Rieger Organ people are building a Portative for our organization, and that we planned to use it at our Christmas concert [at the YM-YWHA]. . It seems doubtful to me that [a portative] will be ready." NYPM Archives, Box 21, Folder 12.

did finish the instrument. But Noah was confident, as always, that the impossible would materialize.

As for the fee, Noah, ever hungry for more work, offered a bargain. "As for the financial question, our fee for a single concert is $500. A second concert, using the same program [as the first], would be only $400."[14] Bea Farwell liked this arrangement. She promptly booked Pro Musica's program of "English and Italian Music of the Early Baroque" for two performances in May 1954. It was the beginning of two long relationships, one between Pro Musica and the Metropolitan, the other between Pro Musica and Beatrice Farwell herself.

The Metropolitan harbored at least one more Pro Musica enthusiast. Two days after the "Y" concert, Margaret B. Freeman wrote to Noah from one of his favorite New York haunts, The Cloisters, where she was Associate Curator. She expressed regret that "for a variety of reasons" she and James Rorimer, the Chief Curator, had had to choose another group for that year's Christmas concert. But, she added,

> We . . . wonder if you have done any commercial recording of medieval music. As you probably know, we present programs of medieval music in recordings twice a week at The Cloisters and are always on the look-out for more medieval material.

She closed with "congratulations on the reviews of your two recent concerts!"[15] This too marked the beginning of a long association, one that would last beyond Noah's own lifetime.

"It pays to fare forth beyond the center of town," The *New York Times*'s Howard Taubman began his review of Pro Musica's first "Y" concert. That is, he added, "if you are in search of a rare, rewarding musical experience. . . ." He went on to name the composers (Morley, Weelkes and Tallis) whose works were performed and speculate that perhaps Shakespeare "had occasion to attend gatherings at which the part songs of Morley were sung.

> They could not have been sung, one would guess, with more modesty and devotion than did the group last night. The six singers of this organization, known as the Primavera singers, sang all together and in smaller units, and they brought a lightness and sweetness of spirit to their work. . . . Of an evening that produced

[14] Greenberg-Beatrice Farwell, letter, October 2, 1953. NYPM Archives, Box 11, Folder 2.

[15] Margaret Freeman-Noah Greenberg, letter, October 14, 1953. NYPM Archives, Box 11, Folder 2.

one delightful piece after another, one remembers best these pieces by Morley: a canzonet for six voices written 'as a reverend memorial of that honorable true gentle Henry Noel Esq'; the air, 'I Saw My Lady Weeping'; two motets and 'Il Doloroso' for two recorders.

Taubman wound up with what was virtually a free ad for Pro Musica, a paragraph giving *Times* readers the dates and themes of the December and February concerts.[16]

On November 5, Dylan Thomas, in the U. S. for a series of readings, was taken unconscious from his room at the Chelsea Hotel on West 23 Street to St. Vincent's Hospital. Four days later, Thomas's life and his fabulous career came to the saddest of endings. He was 39 years old. The heavy drinking for which he was notorious was only partly responsible for Thomas's death. Tests revealed that he was suffering from diabetes, and this in combination with his addiction to alcohol was what killed him.

On the morning of November 14, nearly 400 people crowded into St. Luke's Chapel at Hudson and Grove Streets to hear Rev. W. C. Leach, assistant vicar of the parish, read the lesson from the Fifteenth Chapter of St. Paul's First Epistle to the Corinthians: "O death, where is thy sting? O grave, where is thy victory?" And then, in memory of the brilliant, self-destructive poet who was Noah's White Horse Tavern drinking buddy, the six Pro Musica singers sang two motets, an *Agnus Dei* and *Primavera*, by Thomas Morley. Present to hear them were scores of people prominent in the arts, among them Tennessee Williams, the novelist Dawn Powell, and the poets e. e. cummings, John Berryman, Muriel Rukeyser, Willard Maas, Ruthven Todd and Babette Deutsch.[17]

The group singing that morning was not quite the same as the group that had performed a month earlier at the "Y." The problem that had led to the change was the same one that had led Noah to sign up Sonya Monosoff and appeal to Seymour Barab. Namely, the need to strengthen Pro Musica's sound. Noah and the singers themselves felt that to hold their own with Pro Musica's four strong male voices, the sopranos needed more body. Lois Roman's voice was sweet and pure, but it lacked volume. For Ruth Daigon to try to supply it alone would, in her own words, "make me stand out

---

[16] Howard Taubman, "Elizabethan Music Played at Y.M.H.A.," *The New York Times*, *October 13, 1953, p. 36:3.*
[17] *The New York Times*, Saturday, November 14, 1953, p. 17:6.

and that's NOT what constitutes good group singing."[18] After several of the male singers had raised the issue, Noah quietly began looking for a replacement. And the gods of music smiled on him and sent him Jean Hakes.

Four months earlier, Jean Hakes had graduated from the Yale School of Music, where she had studied voice, and moved to New York. With an eye to a career in teaching, she had enrolled in summer school at Columbia and had taken a day job selling records at Sam Goody's.

> One day a man came in with an instrument under his arm and started talking with me about early music. I said there was a wonderful group doing early music in New York and I sold him one of the Pro Musica records. I don't remember which, but it had Charley and Russell and the whole ensemble on it.
>
> The man asked me how come I knew so much about Pro Musica, and I told him that I'd just come down from Yale School of Music and sung with Hindemith [in the composer's early music Collegium Musicae], et cetera et cetera. He asked me all sorts of questions about my background and where I was living. Then he said that he had written the liner notes for the record I had just sold him.[19]

The man left the store, and Jean has no memory of meeting him again. But the instrument he was carrying, she recalls, was a viola, and her customer may have been Harold Brown, who was at the time a violist in the New York City Center Ballet Orchestra.[20] At all events, a few days later her phone rang. Her caller was Noah, asking her to come down and audition. She was thrilled to comply. "Her voice," said Ruth Daigon, "had a brilliant quality to it." It also had the fullness to match those of Ruth and the men. Noah made up his mind to hire her, but he first had to break the bad news to Lois. According to Ruth, he did so with great sensitivity.

> He went over to her house, had a long talk with her, and explained what the problem was (of course, privately) . . . she probably felt bad [but] she understood and Lois had such good manners . . . she was always invited to the concerts and always came with good grace . . . he did it in the best way possible.[21]

To spare Jean the feeling that she had won her Pro Musica posi-

[18] Ruth Daigon, e-mail message, February 12, 1998.
[19] Jean Hakes, May 10, 1998.
[20] Ruth Daigon, e-mail message, February 12, 1998.
[21] Ruth Daigon, e-mail message, February 12, 1998.

tion at another singer's expense, Noah let Jean understand that Lois Roman had left "because she wanted to go back to teaching school."[22]

For Jean, the events of the late fall of 1953 still tumble around kaleidoscope-fashion in her memory. Out of nowhere, a full-blown singing career had suddenly materialized. She was learning difficult new music. She was rehearsing daily and winning acceptance of her voice and herself into a tightly-knit and exacting group of professionals. She was exposed to the full force of Noah's charm, humor, friendliness and demonic energy. And as if this weren't enough, Jean had just become engaged. Her fiancé, Scott Witherwax, was a Yale man (Class of 1954), which may perhaps explain why he was somewhat less easygoing than Artie Daigon about last-second schedule changes, meals snatched at odd hours (or missed), and rehearsals, up to and including Christmas Day, that started when sensible people were heading for bed.

And then, the days before the December 27 "Y" concert were marred by a happening that even now no one can explain: the eleventh-hour defection of Blanche Winogron.

"In all honesty," Ruth Daigon says, "none of us got to know [Blanche]. She was exceedingly private, exceedingly polite, and a fine musician." (Her performances on the Banchieri and Morley recordings certainly bear out Ruth's view of her musicianship.) But one evening, after a rehearsal,

> she got on a bus and disappeared from our lives. I don't know what happened between Noah and Blanche, and he offered no explanation, he seemed as puzzled as everybody else. It was like an Agatha Christie mystery. It became an 'in' joke after a while: 'If you don't do thus-and-so, I'm going to get on Blanche's bus and disappear.'[23]

Still, despite all the tension, Jean Hakes found the holiday season marvellously exciting. By the evening of December 27, she was bubbling over. But one more disaster—not a very big one—had to be weathered before Pro Musica could take the stage.

> Cookie Daigon asked me to get a dress to match hers, so I bought a black strapless dress. We were all backstage at the "Y," in that miserable backstage with just one bathroom— at least we could go in it one at a time The call came, 'Five minutes,' and I was wearing my engagement ring and I was nervous and excited. Seymour

[22] Jean Hakes, May 10, 1998.
[23] Ruth Daigon, e-mail message, February 9, 1998.

was standing right in front of me and asking me, 'Are you green? You're not scared, are you?' And Russell was telling me, 'Don't worry, honey, there's nothing to worry about.' And I took one deep, deep breath and then another and every one of the fasteners on the dress popped, from my neck all the way down to my tailbone. Well, we were in hysterics, and somebody rushed around and got a needle and thread, and I'm not sure but I think it was Russell who sewed me up.[24]

Whatever the state of Pro Musica's collective nerves after this, the performance prompted Harold C. Schonberg to write in the *New York Times*: "It was an evening that furthered the good impression made by the group at its first concert." Schonberg called the singers "well trained, serious in purpose and possessed of good tonal quality." But then, like a man determined not to succumb to charm, he tailed off to report that "they sang a cappella, or were supported by the slimmest of accompaniments—viola da gamba, played by Seymour Barab, and recorders, played by Bernard Krainis."

Schonberg did also record what appears to have been the only public appearance of Noah Greenberg as instrumentalist in his thirteen years with Pro Musica:

In the absence of Blance [sic] Winogron, the virginals player for the group, Mr. Greenberg seated himself at the little keyboard and took a part in recorder-gamba-virginals instrumental trios.[25]

Three days after the "Y" concert, Noah was again wooing Emanuel Winternitz. In a letter, he broke down the fee of $500 for a single performance. The breakdown included $117 for about seven hours of rehearsal time for "6 singers @ $1.50 an hour, [and] 3 instrumentalists @ $2.50 an hour." The $345 charge for the performance itself covered "6 singers @ $30 ea.,[and] 3 instrumentalists @ $25 each."[26] Bernie Krainis's fee was $30, Noah's, $60. The $36 remaining covered harpsichord transportation and tuning.

Winternitz presumably passed on the information to Bea Farwell for use in preparing her agreements.

Meanwhile, an enthusiastic Bill Kolodney and an equally enthusiastic Noah had agreed to hold another Pro Musica concert at the "Y" that season. This one, moreover, would be one of a kind.

[24] Jean Hakes, May 10, 1998.
[25] H[arold] C S[chonberg], "Pro Musica Antiqua Presents 'Y' Concert." *The New York Times*, Tuesday, December 28, 1953, p. 15:7.
[26]Noah Greenberg-Emanuel Winternitz, letter, December 30, 1953. NYPM Archives, Box 11, Folder 2.

CHAPTER SEVENTEEN

ⱯUDEN, KIRSTEIN, AND BABY ANNE

(1954)

$\mathcal{M}$ore than most poets, Wystan Auden had a professional interest in the interplay of words and music. On this topic, an instructive study in contrasts is offered by Ezra Pound. Pound too loved music and loved to theorize about music and poetry. He wrote of "melopoeia," his term for the musical dimension of verse, and ruminated more vaguely about the "Great Bass," a metaphor for the underlying theme of a good poem. Pound played the bassoon—badly—and even composed an opera —unsingable—based on the life of François Villon. Auden never dreamed of being a composer. (Playing the piano and singing opera arias to his own accompaniment was as close as he came.) But throughout his life, Auden dealt in hard practical terms with the issues of fitting words to music. He did so as opera librettist, first of Benjamin Britten's *Paul Bunyan*, and then, with Chester Kallman, of Igor Stravinsky's *Rake's Progress* and Hans Werner Henze's *Elegy for Young Lovers* and *The Bassarids*. And he did so as lyric poet, as author of dozens of songs, ballads and lullabies, "some of them in calypso and Wild West accents,"[1] some of them in show-tune style, some of them blues.

Nobody remembers how it happened, whether Auden was in the audience at Pro Musica's first "Y" concert, heard the Morley, Weelkes, and Tallis, and dreamed up the idea; whether Auden and Noah together thought it up and presented it to Bill Kolodney; or whether Kolodney himself was the begetter. But whatever the case, in December 1953 the Poetry Center of the YM-YWHA announced "An

---

[1]Edward Mendelson [ed.], *As I Walked Out One Evening* [a collection of W. H. Auden's songs and light verse], Introduction, p. x.

Evening of Elizabethan Poetry and its Music," to be recited by W. H. Auden and played and sung by the New York Pro Musica Antiqua on Saturday, January 30, 1954.

"When Noah Greenberg told us that we would be performing with Auden and that he was coming over almost immediately," Ruth Daigon remembered, "I think all of us went into shock.

> The last time I saw him was in my college text book, and there he was in an old sweater and his carpet slippers which he wore to all the rehearsals. We worked hard. We were motivated.

The event itself was a sellout.

> The auditorium was packed. People were hanging from the rafters, and we were all keyed up. Auden who had come to all of the rehearsals and read from this big beautiful book appeared at the other end of the stage.

The "big beautiful book" was Dr. Edmund H. Fellowes's 600-page *English Madrigal Verse,* from which Noah and Auden had chosen the works for the program. But to the dismay of Pro Musica, on the night of the performance

> we saw no book on the lectern. Evidently he decided to wing it that evening. And he blew it. He forgot some of the poetry, stumbled and really did NOT do a good job.

The musicians were outraged.

> All that awe and respect that we had for him disappeared. This was a performance! You just didn't fool around, especially when so much was at stake. We wouldn't even look at him after the concert because his behavior was so unprofessional. . . . Actually, it didn't make a bit of difference to his audience whether he read well or not. He was Auden, and even a bad performance was an event. We felt a little differently. This was the way we earned our living.

The demand for tickets had been so great that Kolodney had scheduled a repeat performance. Auden must have been abashed, because "the next night, he was a good boy. Came with the book and read from it well."[2]

As well as heightening Noah's and Pro Musica's reputation for doing the unexpected and exciting, the appearances with Auden had profound practical consequences. They were, first and fore-

---

[2]Ruth Daigon, e-mail message, February 8, 1998. Part of the content, including the quoted material, is the text of an earlier message to Edward Mendelson.

most, the occasion that brought Noah into contact with Lincoln Kirstein. Kirstein, at age forty-six, was a figure of great importance on the New York cultural scene. Wealthy and dedicated to making a place in America for contemporary art, he had been only nineteen and a Harvard undergraduate in 1926, when he and Varian Fry founded the avant-garde journal *Hound & Horn*. At twenty-eight, Kirstein had brought George Balanchine to the U. S. to found the School of American Ballet. At twenty-nine, he had been head of the W.P.A. Federal Dance Theatre program. At thirty-one, he had written a seminal essay on the work of the photographer Walker Evans. At thirty-three, he was in South America with funds (from Nelson Rockefeller) to buy paintings for the Museum of Modern Art. At thirty-six (in 1943), after a mysterious imbroglio with the Department of State, he had entered the U. S. Army as a buck private, starting his military career as a driver for General George S. ("Blood and Guts") Patten.

Auden and Kirstein had become friends in the spring of 1945, when the two met in the war-blasted German city of Coburg. Auden was working for the U. S. Strategic Bombing Survey, traveling by Jeep from town to town and using his German to quiz people on the psychological effectiveness of British night bombing, an assignment he loathed.[3] Kirstein, by then a Pfc., was attached to the Third Army's Monuments, Fine Arts and Archives Division and was teamed up with architect Robert Posey in the search for the European art treasures looted by the Nazis.[4]

Two years later, both men were back in New York, Auden to work on his poetry and Kirstein to form, with George Balanchine, the New York City Ballet.

A huge man, six feet five inches tall, Lincoln Kirstein was also a difficult man. Domineering in size and manner, he brought to bear on others a volatile mixture of intelligence, shyness, and sudden anger. Seismically sensitive to others, he could also be both capricious and cruel. He was perfectly capable of getting up from his own dinner-table and stalking wordlessly from the room when a guest offended or bored him. Nicholas Jenkins, Kirstein's friend and literary executor, notes shrewdly that Kirstein was a modernist but one who, like Auden and Pound and T. S. Eliot, distrusted the modern and looked to earlier times and other cultures for aesthetic

[3]George W. Ball, *The Past Has Another Pattern*, pp. 49-50; Charles H. Miller, *Auden: an American Friendship*, p. 86.
[4]Lynn H. Nicholas, *The Rape of Europa*, pp. 331-332 *et passim*.

inspiration.[5]   When Kirstein first heard Pro Musica, at one or the other of the Auden appearances, his imagination was stirred. Pro Musica's music was, of course, both old and new—a paradoxical art form exactly suited to Lincoln Kirstein's rarefied taste. Pro Musica's artists were young and attractive. And Noah's warmth, ambition and passionate commitment struck a spark. Kirstein, who had yearned to be a dancer, knew what it was to be in love with one's own art and with art itself. Quite soon after their first meeting, Kirstein wrote the first of many checks in support of Pro Musica.

Leo Lerman's brownstone at 94th Street and Lexington Avenue was just two blocks north of the "Y." At one of Lerman's celebrity-studded Sunday nights—probably on the night of Pro Musica's Elizabethan concert, December 27, 1953—Noah had met another of New York's cultural luminaries, Goddard Lieberson of Columbia Records. Lieberson was there with his wife, the dancer Vera Zorina, guest ballerina with Ballet Theatre (and former wife of New York City Ballet director-choreographer George Balanchine). Ruth Daigon, wide-eyed as always, described her as "gorgeous. She had this snow white skin, black hair and the most beautiful true-blue eyes. I was fainting all over the place."[6] Noah, however, wasted no energy on swoons. Smiling, waving the hand that wasn't holding a drink, talking animatedly and taking full advantage of a God-given opportunity, Noah was busy making friends with Goddard Lieberson. Even though Noah was in the process of working out another recording deal with Jerry Newman, that night Jerry Newman and Esoteric Records were far away downtown.

Only twenty-nine in 1939, when he joined Columbia as an assistant in the classsical records department, Lieberson in 1949 become executive vice-president and head of all Columbia A&R (artists and repertoire). Under his aegis, Columbia developed the LP record, and Lieberson used it as aggressively to market classical music—contemporary as well as standard repertoire—as to sell pop, jazz, and Broadway show music. Columbia's Masterworks recording artists included conductors Eugene Ormandy, Leopold Stokowski, Sir Thomas Beecham, and Artur Rodzinski. The Chicago, Cleveland, Philadelphia, and Pittsburg symphony orchestras, not to mention the New York Philharmonic, recorded exclusively for Columbia. On Columbia's roster of instrumentalists, along with dozens of

---

[5]Nicholas Jenkins, "The Great Impresario," *The New Yorker,* April 13, 1998, pp. 56, 57.
[6]Ruth Daigon, e-mail message, February 8, 1998.

other virtuosi, were people Noah knew personally and revered: Pablo Casals, Leonard Bernstein, Alexander Schneider, and Eugene Istomin.

But Goddard Lieberson did much more than rely on safe repertoire and established reputations. A man of large, not to say boundless, self-confidence, who once published and gave his friends a book explaining his philosophy of life, Lieberson loved to back his musical judgments,[7] to risk his energy and Columbia's dollars on esoteric material others might dismiss out of hand. The market potential of Noah's current projects must have seemed nebulous, to say the least. Would anybody except scholars buy an LP featuring Jewish liturgical music of the Renaissance? Or a recording of poems read by an Englishman with a tendency to gulp and mumble, plus madrigals and airs by composers with names like Dowland, Jones, and Gibbons? Nevertheless, Lieberson bet on the sheer quality of the product. In February 1954, he offered Noah a contract to record for Columbia "An Evening of Elizabethan Verse" with Auden, the Salamone Rossi program, and a third program to be determined.

In New York's culture bazaar, success breeds success. Soon after the Auden concerts, Noah was contacted by still another cultural entrepreneur, one of the brightest and most up-and-coming of the breed. In 1951, while still a graduate student at Columbia, Jason Epstein had persuaded the executives at the publishing house of Doubleday & Company that a market had come into being for a line of durable paperback editions of books not in the mainstream but of high literary and scholarly merit. Doubleday, to its credit, took a chance on Epstein's sense of the times. It set up Anchor Books with the twenty-five-year-old Epstein as editor, and the quality paperback industry was born. By 1954, more than fifty Anchor titles were in print. Epstein, armed with the power to publish, had become someone to reckon with in literary and artistic circles.

His proposal to Noah and Auden was simple. Capitalizing on the attention paid to the appearances with Auden, Anchor Books would publish a collection of Elizabethan songs chosen by both men. Auden would write an introductory essay on the poetry, Noah one on the music. Noah would score the songs for voice and piano in form suitable for amateur performance. Noah jumped at the chance. Here was a project that would put his name, associated with that of

---

[7]Vera Zorina, May 19, 1998. (She cited as an example Lieberson's decision at dinner at Sardi's after the dress rehearsal of A Little Night Music—but before the show opened—to take a chance on an original-cast recording.)

a renowned literary figure, before thousands of music-minded people.[8]   It would promote Elizabethan music, it would promote Noah Greenberg, and it would promote Pro Musica—as Noah's creation. As part of the deal, Noah arranged a double tie-in with Columbia Records. A note at the end of his introduction informed readers that

> [s]ome of the songs in this collection may be heard on the Columbia record, 'An Evening of Elizabethan Verse and Its Music,' performed by members of the New York Pro Musica Antiqua under the direction of Noah Greenberg.[9]

A note on the record jacket referred listeners to the "Anchor Book, *An Elizabethan Song Book*, edited by Noah Greenberg, W. H. Auden, and Chester Kallman."[10] None of the Pro Musica artists were named in the *Song Book* note, though their names do appear on the record jacket. On both book and record jacket, Noah conveniently neglected to mention that Bernie Krainis was associate music director.

This was not Noah's first effort to assert sole proprietorship and total dominance over the ensemble and its members. On January 28, while he was negotiating Pro Musica's three-record contract with Goddard Lieberson of Columbia, Noah concluded an agreement with Jerry Newman of Esoteric. This one covered a recording of songs of Henry Purcell, specifying that Russell Oberlin be the soloist. The odd thing about this agreement, which Noah signed as president of Pro Musica, is that Russell himself had independently signed an agreement with Jerry a few weeks earlier for the self-same Purcell recording. He had done so quite openly, telling Noah about it. A few days afterward, Noah had come to Russell to urge him to turn over the document "for orderly safekeeping in the N[ew] Y[ork] P[ro] M[usica] A[ntiqua] files."[11] Russell cheerfully complied. In due course, he made the recording, with Seymour Barab and Paul Maynard as the continuo players. But some years later, when Russell thought to recover the contract, "Noah told me that he couldn't find it."[12] Later still, Russell was shocked to learn that Noah had seemingly "lost" the original contract for his solo recording and had sub-

[8]Indeed it would. By 1961, six years after its publication, *An Elizabethan Song Book* had sold more than 60,000 copies.

[9]W. H. Auden, Chester Kallman and Noah Greenberg, *An Elizabethan Song Book*, p. xxix.

[10]Record jacket, *An Evening of Elizabethan Verse and Its Music*, Columbia Records ML 5051.

[11]Russell Oberlin, letter to the author, April 2, 1997.

[12]*Ibid.*

stituted one in which he, Noah, held the sole rights to "direct the recording, edit the tape, and prepare the back-cover."[13] And control the royalties.

The most charitable interpretation of Noah's behavior that Russell can muster is that Noah thought he was acting in the best interests of a young and inexperienced performer. Perhaps; but it is hard not to see a more controlling motive at work. Noah knew well that Russell Oberlin's silvery countertenor lent Pro Musica its distinctive vocal character. As good as the other singers were—and they were very good indeed—Russell was unique.

To protect Pro Musica, to assure its continued success and Noah's own, it was necessary to keep tight rein on Russell Oberlin. If this meant doing something ugly and deceitful, Noah, with the corner-cutting street morality that was part of his makeup, would do it with a shrug and accept it as the price of leadership.

Another incident, described by Ruth Daigon, makes the same point about Noah's fierce determination to exercise control over the marvellous new musical commune of which he was part creator.

> One day we were rehearsing as usual and Noah was cooking a treat for us, *Boeuf bourgignon,* and at one point he went into the kitchen to supervise. Well, while he was gone, we just ran through the song again. He came flying back into the room absolutely furious. Made us quit singing and made it very clear that NEVER were we to rehearse without him conducting us. He was most upset. I can't imagine it was a threat to his musical ability, but honestly we sounded just as good as when he was there. Plus the fact that we were so well rehearsed that every nuance, every breath was bred into our bones. We could easily have sung a concert without him, and maybe that was why he was so disturbed.[14]

On Sunday evening, February 7, 1954, Noah, Toni, Bernie Krainis, Mike Pincus, and Jesse Simons gathered at 80 Perry Street for a New York Pro Musica board meeting. Arthur Squires was asked to join them. The purpose of the meeting was to reorganize the little corporation. Noah and Bernie resigned as officers and were immediately appointed Musical Director and Associate Musical Director. Arthur Squires replaced Jesse Simons on the board and was named president.

Noah and the others had discovered that Arthur was one of those rarest of rare birds, a gifted singer who also possessed first-rate ad-

---

[13]"Recording Agreement, January 28, 1954," between Esoteric Records, Inc. and the New York Pro Musica Antiqua, Paragraph 3. NYPM Archives, Box 10, Folder 3.

[14]Ruth Daigon, e-mail message, February 12, 1998.

ministrative talent. For many years to come, he would be involved in the business and financial affairs of Pro Musica as well as in its music.

The board meeting ended early, probably because others were arriving for a rehearsal, but the board reconvened the next day to deal with a pressing problem. Blanche Winogron's defection had left Pro Musica without a keyboard instrument and, more serious, without a keyboardist. Noah himself had had to fill in at the December "Y" concert, presumably on a borrowed or rented harpsichord. Now at least part of an answer was at hand. In December, James Merrill's father, the Merrill, Lynch magnate Charles Merrill, in response to a request from his poet son, had given Pro Musica fifty shares of stock in the Winn & Lovett Grocery Company. These were worth over a thousand dollars, and Noah went through the formality of asking the board to authorize their sale to provide funds to buy a harpsichord. Whether the money was actually used for that purpose is not clear: not until November did Noah actually order an instrument.

Fortunately, an alternative—and as it turned out, a definitive—solution to the keyboardist problem quickly presented itself in the person of thirty-year-old Paul Maynard. Paul, like Jean Hakes, was a graduate of the Yale School of Music. An organ major, he had studied organ with L. Frank Bozyan and theory with Paul Hindemith. In 1948, his Mus. M. degree in hand, he had come to New York and the post of organist and choirmaster of St. Joseph's Church, at Sixth Avenue and Washington Place in Greenwich Village. His first wife, Patricia Livingston (they had met at Yale, where she was studying harpsichord with Ralph Kirkpatrick), remembers that "before Pro Musica" she and Paul had sung madrigals with Arthur Squires,[15] and it may have been Arthur who suggested that Noah approach Paul.

Paul's pale skin, fair hair, almost invisible eyebrows and benign ascetic appearance created the disconcerting impression that he was some sort of albino saint. He was in fact a true albino, and the poor eyesight characteristic of albinism plagued him throughout his career. But what mattered most to Noah, to Pro Musica, and to audiences was that Paul Maynard was a musician of wide-ranging interests and sympathies and, despite his having to struggle to see the written or printed score, an exceptionally skilled and versatile keyboard player. He made his Pro Musica debut on Monday February

[15]Patricia Livingston, May 29, 1998.

22, 1954, in the Salamone Rossi concert, and became a mainstay of the ensemble, remaining with Pro Musica for ten years.

The Rossi concert itself drew favorable reviews. Noah had shrewdly mixed Rossi's moving settings of Hebrew psalms, prayers, and other religious texts with highly secular songs and madrigals (for instance, *Ghiaccio e foco nell'amata*, or *Ice and Fire in Love*). Joel Newman laughed when he remembered the concert.

> Noah decided to do a wedding ode, for double chorus, and we didn't have that many people, there were the famous six. Okay, this is for eight, so what did he do? He put four of them down on the stage, and in the balcony he had two singers and two instruments. Not to double [the onstage singers] but to play their parts all alone. Up in the balcony, how's he gonna conduct? Here's how he conducted. He conducted the group there [on stage], and the second group didn't have much to sing, it only echoed. And the echo would be sometimes a whole word of the first chorus, [sometimes] a cadence. And he conducted down here [gestures to show Noah's hands low] and then up here [shows Noah's hands up above his head] and we had a lot of jokes about Noah pulling the shades down.[16]

Noah framed the vocal selections with lively four-part instrumental works. Sonya Monosoff found it a bit of a challenge to play softly enough to allow Bernie's recorders to be heard, but she did it. Jay S. Harrison, in *The New York Herald Tribune*, laid on the praise with a trowel.

> A musty page of history had the dust blown from it last night at the YMHA, as Salamone Rossi, a leading Jewish composer who flourished at the end of the sixteenth century, was honored by a program devoted exclusively to his works, The New York Pro Musica Antique [sic], under Noah Greenberg's direction, was the performing group, and to them all praise is due.

Harrison went so far as to call Rossi "a genius of the highest inspiration," whose works "are ravishing in sound, powerfully, blindingly expressive, and of a workmanship rarely matched through time." As for Pro Musica,

> [it] has grown so rapidly in the accomplishment of Rennaissance [sic] ensemble glories that it must be listed among the leading chamber units on the scene.[17]

---

[16] Joel Newman, April 16, 1997.

[17] "Rossi Program," *The New York Herald Tribune*, Tuesday, Febnruary 21, 1954, 18 p.17:5.

The Times coolly agreed that it was

> a charming evening, for everything Rossi composed, it seemed, was tender and lovely and the performances under Noah Greenberg's sensitive direction, had the gentleness, skill and linear clarity for which his group is already noted.

According to the *Times*'s critic, however, Joel Newman's program notes — and, by extension, Jay Harrison's review — decidedly overstated the case for Rossi himself.

> The question of greatness really should not have been raised, for nothing on the program was very deep, very original or even very brilliant.

Rossi, indeed, was no more than a "minor master."[18]

On Sunday, April 11, 1954, at University Hospital, Toni Greenberg gave birth to the Greenbergs' first child, a daughter they named Anne, possibly after Anna, Noah's great-aunt on his mother's side. A week later, when they brought the baby home to Perry Street, Toni was still feeling tired and sore. Noah carried Annie in his arms up the four flights of stairs. Jesse Simons, pressed into service for the occasion, made the ascent lugging a chair that he put down on each landing so that Toni could sit and rest.

The couple was ecstatic about the baby, but in the weeks after Anne was born Noah was also thinking about the summer ahead. Pro Musica played the final concerts of its first (1953-1954) season at the Metropolitan Museum on Monday, May 17 and Friday, May 21. Both performances were sold out, a delicious finale to a year that had proven successful beyond anybody's wildest imaginings. But there was—there always is—the next season to worry about. Bill Kolodney at the "Y" had signed up Pro Musica for three performances over the fall and winter. The Peabody Conservatory in Baltimore and the even more prestigious Folger Shakespeare Library in Washington had booked fall engagements. Margaret Freeman had set aside an evening in late December for a Christmas concert at The Cloisters. And the phone was still ringing. To meet its upcoming obligations, Pro Musica needed new programs and new material. Noah was hard at work on these, but he was eager to have the whole summer to prepare and rehearse the material.

On April 28, 1954, Noah wrote an urgent letter to Lincoln Kirstein:

> I cannot underestimate the importance of this summer undertaking. Upon it hinges the success of the New York Pro Musica

---

[18]"All-Rossi Program at Lexington Ave. 'Y'," *The New York Times*, Tuesday, February 23, 1954, p.25:5.

Antiqua's coming season. . . . The amount of work the group must
do on this schedule is enormous, and it can only be accomplished
during this three-month summer period.

Noah and the others had been plotting this "summer undertaking" since the third "Y" concert in February. It involved finding a
place away from New York City to which Pro Musica's members
could repair *en bloc*, live cheaply, practice, rehearse new programs
of Noah's devising and have some fun.

Everybody agreed that the prospect of spending the summer in
idyllic rural surroundings, with colleagues, friends, lovers and (for
some) wives and small children in attendance, was momentous and
exciting. As a very new member said later,

> It was all of our ideas, really. None of us had much money, we
> were most of us students. . . I guess it was because Tanglewood
> was here and the musical people were here and we thought we
> maybe could give some concerts here and it was just a lovely
> place.[19]

For Noah himself, it would be a grown-up replay of the Cortlandt
summers of his childhood—Camp Machiah over again. Bernie
Krainis described it as "the First Commune."[20] Arthur Squires tied
in the idea with the success he saw arriving.

> [W]e'd already had the plans to go . . . and that was an exciting
> thing. But I really understood that there was no way that — the
> likelihood of [Pro Musica's] taking off, of being significant, was
> just so evident.[21]

Some of the financial help Pro Musica needed it would provide
for itself. A devotee of Pro Musica named Roy A. Rappaport ran the
Avaloch Inn in Lenox, Massachusetts. Lenox was already host to
the hugely popular Tanglewood Music Festival, but Rappaport was
convinced that a dose of early music would help build traffic for the
inn and other local businesses. Rappaport put together a committee, raised a few hundred dollars, rented the Lenox Town Hall and
announced a festival of Medieval, Renaissance and Baroque music
to be held during the last two weeks of August. Pro Musica's share
of the gate might be a couple of thousand dollars. This would be a
nice bonus for what would in essence be out-of-town tryouts of new

[19] Betty Wilson Long, June 19, 1998.
[20] Bernard Krainis, June 12, 1998.
[21] Arthur M. Squires, February 26, 1998.

programs, but it fell far short of the $8,235 budgeted to cover rent, groceries, musicians' fees and Noah's stipend for an entire summer.[22]

"We need about $5,000 [more] for this undertaking," Noah told Kirstein in his letter. "Please forgive me for coming to you again," he added, "but as you can see, we are quite anxious about our present situation."[23] Kirstein's response is not known. He may have written a check himself. He may have asked his sister Mina, who was married to Henry T. Curtiss, to join him: Mina Curtiss would be generous to Pro Musica in years to come. It is also possible that someone other than Lincoln Kirstein—for instance, James Merrill—came to Pro Musica's rescue. Joel Newman, who was by now Pro Musica's official (but unpaid) research assistant, remarks that, during the whole spring of 1954, Noah was immersed in program-making "when he wasn't on the phone raising money. I can't imagine when he ever slept."[24] Seymour Barab testifies to Noah's fund-raising virtuosity.

> I was in on several of his fund-raising sessions and, you know, these people couldn't get their checkbooks out fast enough. I mean, he could *inflame* people. I never saw anything like it.[25]

From whatever source, Noah did raise the needed money. By mid-June, New York Pro Musica was established in its summer quarters and had started to work on the first of its new programs.

[22.] Minutes, NYPMA board meeting, June 4, 1954. NYPM Archives, Box 23, Folder 6. Musicians' fees included forty rehearsals at three dollars per rehearsal for each of twelve musicians ($1,440); six concerts at $40 per concert for each musician ($2,880) and a guest artist's fee of $150 to Rey della Torre.

[23.] Noah Greenberg-Lincoln Kirstein, letter, April 28, 1954. NYPM Archives, Box 2, Folder 6.

[24.] Joel Newman, June 30, 1998.

[25.] Seymour Barab, February 27, 1997.

CHAPTER EIGHTEEN

ꟻIRST SUMMER

(1954)

𝒯hat summer, the summer of 1954, was one that Noah and the members of Pro Musica would remember with nostalgia all their lives.

It began with a departure. Ruth and Arthur Daigon were expecting their first child. "It was the Year of the Babies," Ruth recalls. "Toni and I were pregnant at about the same time. Mine was due in June." Ruth sang with the ensemble through the Salamone Rossi concert in late February and stayed on to take part in the Rossi recording. Then she and Artie decided that it was time for her to step aside—as Ruth thought, temporarily. When she announced that she was leaving, Noah came to her and told her, "When you've had your child and you're ready, come on back."[1] Ruth took Noah at his word and went off happily to await the stork.

Noah turned to Russell and Charles to help him find a replacement. They urged him to listen to the singing of a friend of theirs, a young soprano, Betty Wilson. Betty had grown up, according to her own account, in a "tiny little town in western Maryland." She had sung in its church choirs from the time she was old enough to carry a tune. She had sung in its high school operettas and at the small local college. "I got my degree in three years, and they insisted, all the musical people in my home town, [they] just pushed me." The pushing propelled Betty to New York and an apartment on East 10th Street, which, as she said deadpan, was "quite a change from Maryland."[2] And to The Juilliard, where she studied voice with Lucia Dunham—as did Charles Bressler—and became close friends with

[1]Ruth Daigon, February 7, 1998.
[2]Betty Wilson Long, June 19, 1998.

Russell, Charles, and a third talented young musician who shared their apartment, the harpsichordist Paul Wolfe. When Noah heard Betty sing, he knew at once that her voice, clear and flexible, with a kind of innocence about it, was nicely suited to early music. It also blended extremely well with Jean Hakes's soprano. Betty's musicianship, measured by her ability to sight-read, stay on pitch, and pick up the dramatic sense of what she was singing, was exceptional. Her sense of fun and her love of music were equally strong and infectious. Noah may have made her an offer even before Ruth left, because Betty remembers sitting in on the late February or early March gathering at which everybody decided to summer together in the Berkshires.

With the "summer undertaking" in mind, Noah, Bernie, and Russell drove up to the area to explore the possibilities. Massachusetts resort communities like Stockbridge, Lenox, and Williamstown they found expensive, but there were towns nearby in New York State that drew little or no tourist traffic, and they soon heard of a place in one of these that might be available. The Albany Fresh Air Guild had once run and still owned a summer camp for city children in Canaan, New York, a hamlet some thirty miles south of Williamstown on the western edge of the Berkshires. As soon as they saw the place, they knew they had struck gold.

> It was a big old rambling house and it was perfect . . . for a lot of people. There was a back stairs and a front stairs and several bathrooms, and [many bedrooms], so it all worked out really well.[3]

The kitchen was more than adequate. A building behind the main house would be perfect for rehearsals. There was even a piano of sorts. Best of all, given a little help from Pro Musica's friends, the rent was within reason. By May, Noah had paid the deposit and signed the lease.

In June, Pro Musica's members began making their way, by various means, northward to Canaan. Noah, Toni, and two-month-old Anne came by car, bringing with them a carton containing the scores and multiple copies of the parts for the programs to be prepared. Betty, Russell, and Charles made the journey by rail, enjoying a delightful candlelight supper in the dining car when their train lost power. Jean Hakes, Arthur Squires, and Brayton Lewis arrived soon after. Bernie appeared. The Maynards, Paul and Patricia, brought with them their two very small children. Seymour Barab and Sonya Monosoff rounded out the quartet of instrumentalists. A sign read-

---

[3] Betty Wilson Long, April 28, 1997; June 19, 1998.

*"A sign in antique letter-
ing materialized near
the flagpole"*
(Courtesy Joel Newman)

ing "New York Pro-Musica Antiqua" in antique lettering materialized on the front lawn near the flagpole, in token of official residence. For some days, Noah's used Buick was the group's only transportation. This was both an inconvenience and a threat to survival,
because Noah, in Joel Newman's words, "drove like a maniac," pushing the big six-seater up to sixty-five and seventy on the narrow
country roads and often taking both hands off the wheel to gesture
enthusiastically in the course of self-expression. At length, Russell,
Charles, their friend Paul Wolfe (who joined them on weekends),
and perhaps Bernie pooled their slender resources and bought an
ancient Chrysler for seventy-five dollars. They dubbed the car
"Lillian" and, rattletrap though it was, it took them with greater
safety wherever they wanted to go—to Canaan and Williamstown
for supplies, to Tanglewood for music, to Lenox for a taste of the
local night life, and to various swimming-holes for relief from the
summer heat.

Roy Rappaport of the Avaloch Inn was a major source of comfort
as the group settled in. "His nickname was 'Skip,'" Betty Wilson
recalled, "and he would send a truck over with extra beds or mattresses or whatever it was we needed."[4] It may have been in one of
Skip Rappaport's trucks that Paul Maynard's harpsichord made the

[4]Betty Wilson Long, June 19, 1998.

journey from New York. Jean Hakes remembered that she and four or five of the others unloaded the instrument and chanted Chopin's "Funeral March" as they carried it into the building they were calling "The Barn" where rehearsals would be held.

Another local figure who proved very helpful was the photographer Clemens Kalischer. He had a studio in Stockbridge, had met Noah in New York, and had in fact helped to sell Noah on the Berkshires as a summer haven for Pro Musica. Kalischer, whose work had been on display at galleries and museums for years, now became Pro Musica's unofficial "official photographer." His shots of individual members and of the group at rehearsal were invaluable for publicity purposes. But Kalischer's pictures capture the spirit of Pro Musica in action a thousand times better than routine publicity stills could ever do.

Pro Musica on the move, Canaan NY, summer, 1954. Paul Maynard in white shirt, left, and Bernie Krainis, far right.(Courtesy Joel Newman)

Noah, like a conscientious socialist leader, organized the household arrangements according to his view of everybody's abilities. Noah himself did most of the cooking, and everybody else took on a share of the other chores. Noah appointed Russell, Charles, and Betty to the Food Committee, which meant that they planned the menus and bought the food. "That was another story," Betty said.

> I came from a small farm town and [at home] we always had fresh vegetables. They brought home this pitiful corn from the A&P and I [said,] 'For Heaven sakes, there must be a farm around here somewhere!'[5]

Charlie seized on this with glee and could be heard saying over and over, "WELL! there must be a farm around here somewhere!" But Betty prevailed, and the Food Committee's fresh corn and juicy tomatoes, as well as its eggs and poultry, met even the most perfectionist standards.

Soon, however, rebellion raised its head. At dinner one night, Brayton Lewis announced that in his opinion Pro Musica could eat for less. Brayton had a point, largely because on weekends everybody's friends would come up from New York bearing sleeping bags, camp out wherever there was room, and consume cartloads of food. After a certain amount of debate, Betty, Charles, and Russell tendered their resignations and Brayton became the Food Committee. The appointment was not a success. The first dinner under Brayton's regime consisted of baked beans, Boston brown bread, and, for dessert, chocolate pudding. His colleagues couldn't resist teasing him about this "Brown Meal." Brayton, offended (or pretending to be offended), resigned in his turn and the Wilson-Bressler-Oberlin trio was reinstated.

Skip Rappaport liked Pro Musica so much that the barroom he created in the building behind his inn he dedicated to the group. The bar was decorated like a *bierstube*, with huge sausages hanging from the beams and every imaginable brand of beer on offer. One of Pro Musica's encore numbers was a round, "Five Reasons," a true drinking song the lyrics of which explained the five mighty reasons for imbibing. Skip had music and lyrics inscribed on a big wooden board which he mounted behind the bar and surrounded with sausages. Naturally enough, the popular place became Pro Musica's favorite nighttime hangout.

[5]Betty Wilson Long, June 19, 1998.

Country living was fun, and the fun if anything was heightened by the serious and exciting business for which Pro Musica's members had foregathered, the business of making music.

From February through May in New York, Noah had spent most of the time not filled with concerts and recording sessions on the new programs Pro Musica was to learn and perform. Joel Newman was more than a little awed by what went into the task.

> His musicianship? It was immense. In every way, whether it was to decide the pacing or picking the music in the first place, knowing what piece ought to come where, between what pieces and so on. 'Cause he was at it all the time. I don't know when he went to sleep.[6]

Noah's immediate concern was to expand and add variety to Pro Musica's repertoire. On the face of it, the Morley and Elizabethan programs bore little resemblance to the Banchieri and Rossi programs, but in fact all four were in essence groups of songs and madrigals. And because Thomas Morley and many other Elizabethan composers sought to imitate the ease and elegance of Italian madrigal style, all four programs were Italianate. Noah loved madrigals as he loved earthy catches, rounds and glees, but he wanted to avoid any hint of sameness in his programming and also, as Joel Newman put it, to "get away from Shakespeare." Besides, other and more serious musical forms beckoned. Still focused on England, Noah moved back in time from Morley and his contemporaries to the fifteenth and sixteenth centuries to put together "Court and Chapel Music of Henry V-Henry VIII." Some of the works were by "Anon.," several by Thomas Tallis (known at least by name through Ralph Vaughan Williams's *Fantasy on a Theme by Thomas Tallis*), but many were by composers little-known even today, like Cornissh and Dunstable. To find works for the program, Noah pored over modern editions of Tudor church music in Sydney Beck's Music Division at the New York Public Library and also, with Joel at his elbow, dug deeply into the collected works of the Tudor composers in the music holdings of the Columbia University library.

The music of Renaissance Spain is a world unto itself. It encompasses mocking *villancicos* by unknown street musicians; songs in Castillian and in Ladino, the language of the Jewish *versos* or forced converts to Christianity; the shimmering, ecstatic counter-Reformation Masses and motets of Penalosa, Lobo, Morales, and Tomas Luis de Victoria; and the keyboard music of the blind organist Antonio

[6]Joel Newman, April 16, 1997.

de Cabezon. This music fascinated Joel Newman, who speaks of it with wry irony. "I hated [Spain] because of the Inquisition and what it did to the Jews, so I got crazy for the music."[7] It was Joel who called Noah's attention to the work of the nineteenth-century Spanish music historian Eugenio Anglés. A churchman who spent much of his time in Rome, Anglés brought forth volume after volume of the early music of Spain, including a selection of works dating from the 1480s and 1490s—the era of Ferdinand and Isabella and Columbus (and, as Joel was well aware, of the expulsion of the Jews from Spain).

Joel also led Noah to an obscure sixteenth-century songbook, printed in Rome and known from the location of the one surviving copy (in a Swedish university library) as *Los Cancieneros de Upsala*. In it were printed the parts of a number of two, three-, four-, five- and six-part *villancicos* from the 1550s. Best of all, a Mexican musicologist, Jesús Bal y Gay, had edited an edition of the *Cancieneros* for the University of Mexico. This, like the Anglés collection, was available at Columbia. "From these two books," Joel said, "[Noah] could put together a Spanish program. And the music was a bombshell."[8]

The third of the new programs was devoted to German music. Noah wanted to explore the square-cut music of the late fifteenth-century composers at the court of the Emperor Maximillian. But he had also come across Heinrich Schütz's impassioned setting of the 116th Psalm, "I love the Lord, because he hath heard my voice," with its marvellous alleluia. This and other Schütz works comprised the second part of the program.

What was missing from Noah's sources for these programs was instrumentation. Musicologists were persuaded that instruments accompanied or substituted for the voices in much—though by no means all—Renaissance sung music. But which instruments, and for that matter, which music? It should be underscored that from the medieval through the late Baroque eras (that is, from the twelfth century through the early eighteenth century), composers almost never spelled out what forces were to be employed in the performance of their works. This was particularly true of instrumental works. There were certain exceptions. Works written in the special form of notation known as tablature, for example, were meant only for the solo lute. But broadly speaking, performers had to rely on unwritten rules, on contemporary practices, on musical common

[7]Joel Newman, June 30, 1998.
[8]Joel Newman, June 30, 1998.

sense (and on who was in town) to decide instrumentation. The further back in time one goes, moreover, the more maddeningly vague are the indications of what instruments went with the work at hand.

Noah knew all of this. First and foremost a leader of singers, he nevertheless relished the sonorities and tone colors of early instruments. They were distinctive: different from anything contemporary audiences had ever heard. They made Pro Musica stand out. Noah the showman as well as Noah the serious musician wanted instrumental as well as vocal works on Pro Musica's programs, and he wanted Pro Musica to perform some of the vocal works with instrumental accompaniment. So in Joel Newman's term, "knowing that instruments played with the voices and instruments took vocal music, he cooked it [the instrumentation] up. And he had very varied and exciting programs."[9]

Were Noah's "cooked-up" instrumental treatments authentic? Were they what instrumentation would have sounded like in the fifteenth and sixteenth centuries? On this crucial issue, Bernie Krainis shrugs and laughs. "In 1954, authenticity hadn't been invented yet."[10]

It would be more accurate to say that in 1954 authenticity had been *halfway* invented. Thus, Noah, guided by his singers, absolutely outlawed broad wah-wah vibrato in Pro Musica's vocal practice as being part of a much later (and debased) vocal tradition. He and Bernie and their colleagues insisted on the harpsichord (and soon the organ) for keyboard works written before the invention of the piano. Granted, Bernie played medieval, Renaissance, and Baroque music on a set of recorders of Baroque design: playable modern versions of earlier types came into being only decades after 1954. Even so, Bernie's Baroque recorders were surely more authentic for medieval *estampies* and *saltarellos* than the nineteenth-century multi-keyed metal Boehm flute would have been.

Joel Newman's remark makes it appear as if Noah went blithely ahead, unaided and without regard to what scholarship had to say about the use of instruments in early music. But Noah had read widely and often consulted musicologists, Joel himself and Gustave Reese among them, on instrumentation, tempi, and other aspects of performance. Eventually, as Joel phrased it, "he had a whole support group working for him. He picked everybody's brain."

[9]Joel Newman, June 30, 1998.
[10]Bernard Krainis, February 15, 1998.

One of the key members of the "support group," it seems, was the ubiquitous Harold Brown. At thirty-four, Harold had found a place for himself at New York's celebrated High School of Music & Art. He was teaching mathematics, physics, and beginning violin and coaching an after-school choral group. Harold had looked on with a mixture of delight and chagrin as Pro Musica had come into being. The musicians remember him as being on the periphery of events, attending occasional rehearsals, and dropping in backstage after some concerts as did another of Noah's friends, Dwight Macdonald. But Harold felt he had a highly personal stake in the ensemble and its progress. In later years, he would tell friends that he and Noah, not Bernie and Noah, were Pro Musica's co-founders. Noah, he said, had "constantly" sought his advice on matters of interpretation and performance practice.[11]   In a roundabout sense, the first assertion was true. Without Harold Brown, Noah would have been a very different musician and perhaps not a musician at all. He might never have dreamed the dream of a professional group dedicated to early music, or taken the vibrant approach to early music that made Pro Musica a success. Harold probably was a source of advice on musical issues: he and Noah were in touch throughout Noah's lifetime. Indeed, Noah always acknowledged privately his debt to the older man. What Noah refused to do was to acknowledge the debt openly. He never allowed Harold to claim any connection with Pro Musica. Nor did he use his growing influence as director of Pro Musica to help advance his friend's career. He had his reasons. Harold's inwardness and prickliness—except with very young people he could treat as protegés—were qualities ill-suited to work with seasoned professionals who had minds and attitudes of their own. Harold's unbending adherence to his own ideas was another drawback.[12]   A few weeks of Harold might well have blown Pro Musica apart. Nevertheless, and sadly, Noah's behavior added fuel to Harold's abiding sense of grievance and loss.

For Pro Musica's young musicians encamped in Canaan, learning the new programs was a musical joyride. Rehearsals were held mornings and afternoons in The Barn behind the house, singers

[11]Joel M[eltz] Okenheim, July 1, 1998.
[12]Joel Meltz Ockenheim, later a singer in Harold Brown's Renaissance chorus and a friend, tells the story that Leonard Bernstein had promised Harold a read-through of one of Harold's orchestral works by the New York Philharmonic, with the possibility of a later performance. But "Lenny wanted Harold to change six notes in the piece, and Harold would never do that," so the arrangement fell through.

and instrumentalists together. Everybody would gather, in highly informal dress. Paul Maynard would wander in wearing the red-and-black checked wool lumberjack's shirt he always wore— even in August, Paul was always cold—and seat himself at the harpsichord. Paul, Seymour, Sonya, and Bernie would tune, not always an easy task in wet or sticky weather. There would be some talk about the pieces to be played and sung. Then Noah would begin. Russell, Betty, and Arthur Squires were all persuaded that Noah seldom if ever came to rehearsals with a preconceived notion of what was to be accomplished. Rather, Noah was there, in Arthur's sense of events, "to enjoy the music, to hear it and enjoy it himself, personally.

> And so often in rehearsals, you know, things would happen, they hadn't been planned, they weren't things that Noah had planned out in advance, and maybe after three or four rehearsals of the same piece over a week or a two-week period, the performance would change. But it was because he had heard it, he'd absorbed it, and he understood it better and he began to take a different tempo, speed up here, slow down there, and it took on a life that it might not have had in the first rehearsal.[13]

"We worked," Betty Wilson said, "but it wasn't work." Rather, Noah's improvisatory approach was "exciting and wonderful.

> It was so great in rehearsals. Noah would say, 'Okay, let's try this with the men,' or 'Let's try this with the girls,' 'Let's put it up a fourth, let's take it down a third.' We had *time* to find out how [the songs] sounded and how we wanted to perform them.[14]

Arthur recalled with pleasure other aspects of Noah's approach to the music under rehearsal.

> He was enormously interested in the rhythms. He had this tremendous faculty for choosing the right tempo—and then bending it. And he almost never used ritards the way they're used [in] nineteenth-century Romantic performance. Noah would often ritard in a penultimate phrase, not the last phrase, and then he would *gallop* through the last phrase in an exciting flourish. And I just loved it.[15]

During the course of that memorable summer, various things happened to "jell" Pro Musica, to give it the form and style it would hold for nearly twenty years. First of all was the pressure of the

[13]Arthur M. Squires, December 5, 1997.
[14]Betty Wilson Long, June 19, 1998.
[15]Arthur M. Squires, December 5, 1997.

work itself. Noah had been right when he told Lincoln Kirstein that the amount of work the group had to do was "enormous." Said Betty Wilson:

> We were very busy. Noah was throwing music at us left and right. And that's what made the summer so wonderful. We were together, and we had *time* to really find out how [the songs] sounded and how we wanted to perform them.

The common effort bound the individual artists together, helping to weld them into one cohesive ensemble. "We supported one another," Betty said.

> Jean was having trouble with her breath and Noah liked to hold things out, and I would not be singing, I would be sitting behind, and [the others] would get to the end of whatever they were singing and she wasn't going to be able to hold the note, and she would put her hand behind herself and wave to me and I would pick up the note and no one ever knew.[16]

What Betty meant was that *Noah* never knew—or if Noah did know, he kept quiet, because mastering the music, not the shortcomings of a particular artist, was what mattered to him. Betty, Russell and Charles also kept watch over Arthur Squires's singing. Of all the Pro Musica singers, only Arthur had absolute pitch, meaning that he could instantly identify any note he heard as an A, an E flat or whatever. This, strangely, was a disadvantage in carrying a tune, perhaps because it inhibited Arthur from hearing what the others were actually singing. "We kept nudging him," Betty said. "Mostly it was his vowels. If he had the vowel right he'd be in tune."[17]

No actual decision was made, but somehow it became common ground over the summer of 1954 that Pro Musica was by nature, or perhaps divine order, an ensemble of six singers, four instrumentalists and a director. Despite changes in personnel and the frequent use of guest artists, the core Pro Musica group—Noah later named it the Concert Ensemble to distinguish it from other groups he formed under the Pro Musica label—kept this same form and size for the next two decades.

Then, too, various experiments in rehearsal led to a kind of collective decision that Pro Musica singers would on occasion double as instrumentalists, usually (though not always) playing rhythm

[16]Betty Wilson Long, June 19, 1998.
[17]Betty Wilson Long, June 19, 1998.

instruments—small drums, triangles, the tambourine, handbells, cymbals. "Everybody wanted to do this," Betty said. "It was fun to learn something. Bernie taught me how to play the recorder, and then I played the finger cymbals a lot."[18] Noah also wanted his instrumentalists, however wedded to one instrument, to be able to perform on more than one. This was not an issue with Paul, who played the organ and of course the piano as well as the harpsichord and who would cheerfully learn the medieval precursor of the piano known as the psaltery. Nor did it trouble Seymour Barab, although Seymour the cellist was never enchanted with the viola da gamba. Bernie's recorders comprised a whole family of instruments, from the tiny sopranino pitched like a piccolo to the mellow great bass. But Noah did run into some difficulty in persuading a reluctant Sonya Monosoff to put aside her cherished violin for the treble viol he borrowed in April from Hannah Hammit.[19] According to Sonya, he employed some of the same tactics on her that he had used on Seymour, telling her that the viol would be easy for a player of her calibre, that viol music was sublime, that the group needed the variety. Ultimately Sonya consented, and she agreed to play as well the small three-string medieval fiddle called a rebec. This engaging versatility would become a hallmark of Pro Musica's style. Its impact on audiences was considerable. First, it made many Pro Musica programs into series of small surprises, as performers switched back and forth from singing to playing or did both at once. Secondly, it made audiences aware that such simple instruments as finger cymbals, wood blocks and tambourines, supposedly childish or "primitive," could in fact be used in highly sophisticated music.

By mid-August, Pro Musica was ready to try out its new programs in public, in the series Skip Rappaport had organized for the Lenox Town Hall. For the first of the five concerts, however, Noah cautiously decided to present the *Festino*-John Blow-Morley program, varying it by dividing *Festino* into four parts and interspersing the Morley and Blow works and Paul Maynard's readings of Frescobaldi. The Henry V-Henry VIII program was presented on Saturday, August 21, the Spanish Renaissance program the next afternoon and the German Renaissance and Baroque program on August 28, winding up with Salamone Rossi on Sunday, August 29. Of the initial concert, Jay C. Rosenfeld, the music critic for the local paper, *The Berkshire Eagle*, wrote:

[18]Betty Wilson Long, June 19, 1998.
[19]Noah Greenberg-Hannah Hammit, letter, April 8, 1954. NYPM Archives, Box 21, Folder 6.

Noah & Company, Lenox MA, summer, 1954 (Courtesy Joel Newman)

> The group performs with the individual competence of . . . skilled
> professionals . . . and the zeal and dedication of amateurs. . . . The
> vocalism was doubly enjoyable by reason of the excellence of the
> singers and by the unfamiliar and specialized beauty of the mate-
> rial[20]

An unsigned feature in the *Eagle* of August 27 devoted equal space
to the music of the next evening's German program and to Brayton
Lewis, citing his background with the Robert Shaw Chorale and his
stage appearances in half a dozen musicals including *Finian's Rainbow.*[21] The article did not mention Brayton's endearing blend of high
seriousness and zany behavior. Nor did it point out that one of his
duties that summer had to do with a serious deficiency of the Lenox
Town Hall, that edifice's total lack of restrooms. It had fallen to the
imperturbable Brayton to come to the rescue by laying in a supply

[20]Jay C. Rosenfeld, "New York Pro Musica Antiqua Opens Festival Impressively,"
The Berkshire Eagle, August 19, 1954, p. 17:1.
[21]"German Music of Middle Ages Featured at Lenox Tomorrow," *The Berkshire Eagle,*
August 27, 1954, p. 15:1.

of chamber pots for those of his colleagues afflicted with pre-performance nerves. He let it be known that this responsibility was the cause of some stress. On one occasion, he appeared at dinner wearing a sheet, with one of the pots on his head.

With the last echo of the last encore on August 28, the summer was over for Pro Musica, though not for several of its singers. Charles Bressler, who knew all sorts of people, was friendly with Arthur Claflin, a wealthy New York banker who owned a summer home in Rensslaerville, New York, across the Hudson from Albany. At Claflin's request, Charles, Betty and Brayton, with a few other non-Pro Musica musicians, put on a private concert in a garden at Rensslaerville. That first year, they sang the Brahms *Liebeslieder Waltzes* to a two-piano accompaniment, and followed with a group of madrigals, fleeing indoors, pianos and all, when it started to rain. Later it became a September tradition in Rensslaerville for the trio to put on concert performances of the Gilbert and Sullivan operettas in the little town hall. "The people in the community learned all of the choruses," Betty said, "and then we sang all the parts. And Brayton was giving running commentary."[22]

One more event marked the end of the summer of 1954.

Every year, the musicians at Tanglewood put on a serious reprise of the season called "Tanglewood on Parade." The denizens of the Albany Fresh Air Fund camp found this idea highly appealing. And it was Brayton Lewis who—inadvertantly—supplied a theme for Pro Musica's version. Arthur Squires explained:

> Brayton had a story that he told, and once he'd told it for about the third time we had great fun teasing him. We had a great number of people floating through, significant others and friends and so on. Often the table for dinner would be twenty, twenty-five, thirty people.
>
> ... So we'd egg on Brayton and he'd tell this story, which he claimed was true. Where he lived ... they were doing a whole lot of repairs on the building, so there was a tremendous amount of noise going on. And this woman — Brayton was her neighbor — would lean out the window and [shout] 'Stop that noise! Stop that noise!' and then, finally, after about an hour of that, she yelled out, 'Go back to Russia!' And that was the story. We heard [Brayton] tell it about a dozen times, at least.[23]

[22]Betty Wilson Long, June 19, 1998.
[23]Arthur M. Squires, December 5, 1997.

The day of "NYPMA on Parade," Sunday, August 29, there was a vast audience—perhaps thirty people—in the main room of the house. For the occasion, Arthur Squires played his newly-acquired tenor viol, Charlie Bressler manned the keyboard and Paul Maynard was the recitationist. Their material was Seymour Barab's dodecaphonic setting of a version *in German* of Brayton's tired story. The work, predictably, met with wild applause, but its first performance was also its last.

Dinner that evening, as on most Sunday evenings, would have been crowded and festive. The long table with benches on either side, built to accomodate a platoon of fresh air kids, was just right for Pro Musica and its guests. Noah, Toni, and Bernie sat together at one end, Russell, Charlie, and Betty at the other, with Paul and Patricia Maynard in the middle and everybody else squeezed in wherever they could fit. Huge platesful of food would appear and the food be devoured. Paul would drain his milk—he drank quarts of it a day—and Noah and the rest of the company would put away tumblersful of wine. Noah would preside, the perspiration damp on his forehead, his eyes sparkling behind the black hornrims he now wore, telling stories of his days as a lathe hand in San Pedro and a cook aboard the Liberty ships. Toni might dip into the endless store of dirty limericks this seemingly prim librarian had—astonishingly—collected and committed to memory. On this last Sunday, in all likelihood, the whole group did what had been the Sunday night custom all summer long. "Before [people] left," Betty said, "we would get out what we called the 'grey book.' It was a book of madrigals and we would sing it cover to cover."

Of that first magical summer, Betty said simply, "That was the whole tone of our beginnings.

> It was like we were brothers and sisters. No hanky-panky or anything, we just loved being together and doing whatever. And we loved singing this music.[24]

Arthur Squires, looking back after forty-three years, said with equal conviction, "It was a wonderful time — a wonderful time."[25]

[24]Betty Wilson Long, June 19, 1998.
[25]Arthur M. Squires, December 5, 1997.

CHAPTER NINETEEN

SUCCESS AND INSECURITY

(1954-1955)

℥or Noah, the end of summer and the beginning of the 1954-1955 season marked the start of an odd period in which Pro Musica's success would be dogged by insecurity. The new programs had fared well. The weeks of rehearsing, practice, and concertizing had given Pro Musica the cohesiveness and polish usually associated with string quartets playing the classical repertoire. Pro Musica's youthful members were taking personal delight in what one of them described as "getting out there on that stage and belting it out, making this gift to the audience."[1] Audiences, sensing this, were responding with equal enthusiasm. Critical praise was flowing in. Thus, of the first "Y" concert of the fall ("Court and Chapel Music of Henry V to Henry VIII"), on October 23, *The New York Times* said "[i]n truth, it did seem too soon over." *The Times* also noted the very large audience and ended by calling Pro Musica "one of the city's outstanding musical assets."[2]

Yet, a glance at the calendar was enough to remind Noah that in the classical music business critical success and material success do not necessarily go hand in hand. At the beginning of September, Pro Musica had only eleven concert bookings, seven of them at the 92nd Street "Y," two at The Cloisters, through April 1955. At the then-current rate of three dollars per rehearsal and forty dollars per performance, this worked out to less than $500 for the season for each member and not much more for Noah himself. To keep body and soul together, Noah's singers and instrumentalists, in addition

---

[1]Arthur M. Squires, December 5, 1997.
[2]R[aymond] E[ricson], "Pro Musica Plays English Program," *The New York Times*, Mon. October 25, 1954, p. L31.

to their Pro Musica activity, were going to have to scratch for work elsewhere, teaching, playing in pickup orchestras, singing in churches and synagogues, or taking "day jobs" unrelated to music. Bernie Krainis held group classes in recorder-playing and took on private pupils. The 1950s were the beginning years of the recorder's rise to popularity as an inexpensive, seemingly easy to play amateur instrument, and Bernie himself, thanks in part to the exposure he gained through Pro Musica, would became a leading figure— perhaps *the* leading figure—in the American recorder "movement."

Paul Maynard went back to St. Joseph's. Sonya Monosoff, who had more than once aroused Noah's ire that summer by slipping off to the shed that held the piano to practice her Brahms, gave violin lessons and took on short-term assignments with chamber groups. Seymour Barab had no trouble landing engagements as a cellist and arranger. Of the singers, Russell, Charles, Betty and Jean all found church work and also sang with other New York City choral groups. Brayton Lewis returned to his day job as assistant manager of the British Book Centre, a small shop specializing in hard-to-find British imports, on East 54th Street between Park and Lexington Avenues. Arthur Squires too settled back into a day job, but his was actually a full-time professional career as an industrial chemist at Hydrocarbon Research, Inc., on lower Broadway. "I had a boss," Arthur said, "who was exceedingly forgiving." He was indeed. The scion of a wealthy Texas family, Arthur's boss held a degree in English from Baylor as well as a chemical engineering degree.

> [Mr. Keith] wrote poetry, he fancied himself as a Renaissance man. When I went in and told him that I was going to be off for two weeks in the summer . . . and I was going to be off for three weeks for a concert tour, he'd say 'Knock 'em dead,' and he never docked my pay a penny or reduced my two-week vacation even a day.[3]

Noah himself quickly joined the scramble for outside income. Starting the year before, he had begun developing a Pro Musica mailing list. In mid-September, Toni mailed out a typescript flyer to a number of people on the list, inviting candidates to try out for

> a vocal ensemble limited to 15 singers, which will read and study choral music of the Middle Ages, Renaissance and Early Baroque under the guidance of Noah Greenberg, Director of the N. Y. Pro Musica Antiqua, and Joel Newman, who has done much musicological consulting for the group."[4]

---

[3]Arthur M. Squires, December 5, 1997.
[4]NYPM Archives, Box 35, Folder ii.

The flyer makes no mention of the fees Noah and Joel were planning to charge, but this last edition of Noah's many amateur singing groups was clearly not for friends only. The flyer indicates that the group was to meet at 80 Perry Street, and Joel remembers conducting at more than one session.

> There was one particular piece, a psalm setting by [German Renaissance composer] Melchior Frank, that I really got into, and I remember Noah congratulating me afterward when I really didn't deserve it.

Joel points out that as well as being a source of income, his and Noah's teaching helped expand Pro Musica's reputation and spread the gospel of the beauty and emotional appeal of the little-known Renaissance choral repertory.[5] Developing a study ensemble was also in line with lawyer Mike Pincus's insistence that Pro Musica be set up as a non-profit corporation and that it have an educational aspect. In the 1950s, the Internal Revenue Service regarded with suspicion applications for tax-exempt status from art museums, libraries and other cultural institutions. These, the I.R.S. felt, might or might not truly serve the public. An educational mission, however, was an undeniable public benefit. As such, it would usually gain an organization a "determination letter," an I.R.S. document certifying the recipient's freedom from having to pay Federal income taxes and the parallel right of donors to deduct gifts made to it from their taxable incomes.

After a year and a half, Noah and Toni, and with them Arthur Squires—Arthur was president of the corporation—had learned that a rarefied performing-arts group like Pro Musica would never be able to make its living from concerts and recordings alone. Arthur's business sense and proposal-writing skills would soon prove invaluable in selling Pro Musica's virtues to foundations and other institutional donors. But at the immediate moment, with cash short and the needs pressing, Noah's prowess at raising money from individuals was more important. Early contributors, as we have seen, were New Yorkers. But for nearly a century, the Berkshires had been a playground of the wealthy and well-connected, and that summer Noah had made a great many friends among them. "We used to laugh," Bernie Krainis said:

> Noah would greet [would-be patrons], walking backward, bowing and spreading his arms and smiling broadly. We used to kid him about behaving like an Italian headwaiter.... It was amazing.

[5]Joel Newman, July 31, 1998.

When he was with the rich . . . this big man could somehow make himself tiny, rein in his gestures, balance a teacup and make small talk.[6]

In those uncertain days, no dollar amount was too small for Noah to go after in person. Joel Newman recalls the day on which Noah decided that Pro Musica needed a set of the multi-volume Oxford University Press *Tudor Church Music*. The price: a few hundred dollars.

I have a picture in my mind of Noah sitting at the telephone. We had met these wealthy old ladies in New England. They were old ladies, thin and dried-up, hard-bitten about giving money but they knew they were on to a good thing. Noah called one of them and spoke to her, and she said, Yes, the money would be on its way, and we had our Tudor Church Music.[7]

The good nature and smooth persuasiveness Noah could so easily muster up were very much not in evidence later in September, when Ruth Daigon called. Ruth's baby was now nearly four months old. She was eager to take Noah up on his promise, rejoin Pro Musica, and go on with her singing career. Strangely, however, Noah failed to return her calls. As the days and weeks went by, Ruth's bafflement gave way to anger and a growing sense of betrayal. Not until mid-October, shortly before Pro Musica's first "Y" concert, did Noah let her know, not in person or via a phone call but in a curt typewritten letter, that he had filled her place and was not going to take her back. Ruth was furious, but she was also heartbroken. Not only had she had been Noah's first professional singer, Noah had been her mentor, promoter, and guide to New York, and she and Artie and Noah had been friends and comrades. Furthermore, she had grown to love Russell and Charles and her other Pro Musica colleagues. "I felt as if I was being kicked out of my family."[8]

To Ruth, Noah's behavior was all the more mystifying in the light of his sensitivity when he had had to tell Lois Roman that she would no longer be singing with Pro Musica. Ironically, the very same issue that had led to Lois's dismissal was also responsible for Ruth's. Namely, character of voice. According to Ruth herself, Lois's soprano was too light and too thin to carry well. Ruth's was rich and full—too rich and too full, it seems. Over the summer in Canaan, several of the Pro Musica singers had gone secretly to Noah to ar-

[6]Bernard Krainis, February 7, 1997.

[7]Joel Newman, July 31, 1998.

[8]Ruth Daigon, February 8, 1998.

gue that Ruth's voice was fine for Italian opera and perhaps for Handel but wrong for Pro Musica. Noah may have fought back, but in the end he had given in and agreed to keep Betty Wilson in Ruth's place. He may have come to feel that Betty's voice did blend more smoothly than Ruth's with those of the other singers. But Noah the musician was also Noah the Shachtmanite politician, veteran of a hundred small-scale confrontations. More likely, he had simply been afraid that overruling the complainers would stir up enough discontent to put his precious Pro Musica, shaky as its future already was, in jeopardy. The choice between a promise to a dear friend and the well-being of Pro Musica was no choice at all.

For Noah to go back on his word to Ruth was bad enough: to refuse to see her or even speak with her to break the bad news in person was shameful. Once again, " warm friendly Noah" has to be seen as sadly lacking in loyalty to some of those who helped him when he was getting started, Edith being one, Harold Brown another, and Ruth a third.[9]

Ruth Daigon never heard from Noah Greenberg again. The one person she did hear from, to her considerable surprise, was Toni.

> Remember we both had our babies about the same time. . . . and we had a slight, [a] very slight bond just because we were pregnant together (we were not really meant for each other). But in the fall of the year, that year of the babies and my "resignation," [Toni] did call to see how I was, and I'm afraid I didn't sound overly enthusiastic, I was still recovering [from being fired], but we did speak for a few minutes and I reassured her that I was okay, and that was very decent of her.[10]

Even after more than forty years, the episode leaves a sour taste in the mouth of those who, like Seymour, Bernie, Arthur, and Sonya, knew the circumstances of Ruth's departure. But Ruth herself is both gracious and forgiving.

> I remember Noah for many of the good things that happened. . . . We were all good friends for four years, and he was of enormous help to me in opening up a whole world that I never could have

---

[9]Another explanation is that Noah felt so guilty about his treatment of Ruth that he could not bring himself to look her in the face. But this one merely substitutes cowardice for disloyalty.

[10]Ruth Daigon, e-mail message, February 11, 1998. Another new mother in that "year of the babies" was Noah's old friend Rickie, married (since 1949) to Peter Flanders and spending the summer of 1954 in a Flanders family home up the dirt road that led to the Albany Fresh Air camp. Rickie remembered that "Annie and my son Tony were about the same age and they were both babies that summer."

entered without him. . . . One insensitive act doesn't wipe out the
memory of all the fine times we had . . . like being introduced to
Yonah Schimmel's knishes which gave me heartburn for a week,
and Italian egg creams and prowling the Village with Noah acting
as conductor and interpreter. We had a lot of fun together apart
from the love of music we shared.[11]

Skimpy though it was, the 1954-55 season nevertheless held a few
promising opportunities. One came from out of town. Each au-
tumn, the U. S. officials of the International Monetary Fund played
host in Washington to the combined Boards of Governors of the IMF
and the World Bank. A number of social events for delegates and
their spouses were included in the 1954 schedule of meetings and
seminars. One, on the afternoon of Tuesday, September 28, was a
tour of the Folger Shakespeare Library. Founded in 1932 by Standard Oil executive Henry Clay Folger and his wife, the Folger holds
a matchless collection of Shakespeare's printed works and a superb
collection of other rare Renaissance books and manuscripts. It also
boasts both an elaborate Great Hall and an Elizabethan Theatre
modeled on an innyard theatre of Shakespeare's time. The Folger
was clearly on the IMF agenda to show the cultivated bankers and
economists of the Old World that the U. S., far from being the vulgar
materialist society of stereotype, had its own citadels of high culture. A highlight of the tour was tea and entertainment in the Great
Hall. Pro Musica supplied the entertainment, performing the Elizabethan music program. The engagement was Noah's and Pro
Musica's very first in Washington and Noah's first brush with international cultural politics. Many such encounters would follow.

On October 29, 1954, Noah submitted an application for a study
grant to the John Simon Guggenheim Memorial Foundation. The
application was promptly returned as incomplete, but he resubmit-
ted it, first writing to Wystan Auden, Goddard Lieberson and Columbia University musicologist Paul Henry Lang to ask them to
supply letters of reference.[12] It is possible that Henry Allen Moe,
then secretary and later president of the Guggenheim's board, had
already met Noah and had encouraged him to apply. (Moe, a trustee
of many cultural institutions, including the Museum of Modern Art,
was an influential figure in New York cultural affairs.) This move
too was a significant first. Apart from being a source of money, it
was important to Noah in two ways. For one thing, as his friend
Rickie Flanders observed:

[11]Ruth Daigon, e-mail message, February 10, 1998.
[12]NYPM Archives, Box 7, folder 5.

Pro Musica in rehearsal, 1954. Standing (l-r): Noah, Jean Hakes, Arthur Squires, Russell Oberlin, Brayton Lewis, Charles Bressler, Betty Wilson. Seated (l-r): Bernard Krainis, Martha Blackman, Sonya Monosoff, Paul Maynard
(Courtesy of the Music Division of The New York Public Library for the Performing Arts Astor, Lenox, and Tilden Foundations)

[Noah] was uneasy about not going to college. All auto-didacts are uneasy about it, because first of all there's all the business about formal training and credentials, and second of all there is some element of truth in the notion that [college] is the best way of learning a body of material.[13]

A Guggenheim Fellowship would reassure Noah the "auto-didact" that his years of immersion in early music and musical practice had made him a man of authentic learning — a genuine scholar, on a par with academic musicologists like Gustave Reese and Paul Henry Lang. Furthermore, Noah the shrewd student of advancement knew that just as it's easier to get a job if you already have a job, so is it easier to land a grant if you've already landed a grant. A Guggenheim Fellowship, even a modest-sized one, would pave the way for other, more generous awards.

The summer of 1954 had seen the beginning of activity on another front, the acquisition of musical instruments. Today, the manufacture of "authentic" medieval, Renaissance and Baroque instru-

[13]Rickie Flanders, March 15, 1997.

ments is a kind of American cottage industry. It sometimes seems as if every town and village in the land has its bearded, bluejeaned specialist in harpsichords or viols or minstrels' harps or krummhorns or even serpents. There are directories of early-instrument builders, and the quality of their output is often very high. In the 1950s, however, only a few brave souls in this country were grappling with the vexatious problems of making instruments the sounds of which might not have been heard for centuries. These eccentrics were almost all harpsichord-builders. For instruments other than harpsichords, the only sources were in Europe. Communicating with these sources was often difficult—to say the least—bargaining with them tricky and between bargaining and actual delivery the financial positions of both parties both slender and subject to unpredictable change, usually for the worse.

For Noah, who had declared to Edith five years earlier that the one thing he wanted most in all the world was a grand piano, a Pro Musica instrument collection would be both useful and a status symbol. More than a symbol, indeed, it would be a tangible proof of stability, a sign that Pro Musica (and Noah) had arrived. Developing a collection of instruments appropriate to the particular periods and styles of early music was therefore to become a major theme of Pro Musica's offstage life. Its archives are full of letters and documents that chronicle this unending preoccupation—hagglings with the artisans who made and repaired instruments, low cries of exultation at discovering new and more reliable suppliers, exasperated pleas for prompt delivery, excuses for tardy payment, and promises on both sides to do better next time.

Thus, on May 15, 1954 Bernie Krainis, as director of Pro Musica's instrumentalists, had written to Hermann Moeck Verlag in Celle, West Germany, to order a "chest" of three viols. The idea was that Seymour would play the bass, Arthur Squires the tenor, and Sonya the treble, freeing Pro Musica from having to rely on borrowed instruments. Moeck, an old established music house, did not manufacture viols itself, it contracted out what few orders it received. Time went by, the summer season opened and nothing was heard from Moeck and somehow the price for the set jumped from $158.25 to $236.50—plus $58.00 for three sets of strings for each instrument. The transaction, not surprisingly, was never consummated.

Fortunately, Bernie turned up another and less dilatory source. On January 3, 1955, he wrote to Eugen Sprenger in Frankfurt am Main, asking for information on viols. On January 26, Sprenger, who did make his own instruments and who clearly wanted business, wrote back giving prices and enclosing a copy of a letter from Paul Hindemith in praise of a Sprenger viola d'amore. Bernie promptly ordered a treble viol. Sprenger wrote back on February 8, thanking him for the order but asking: Where's the fifty-dollar deposit? By February 20, Sprenger had received the check and had started on the viol. The total cost for the viol, a bow, a case and shipping via air express was $149.75. The instrument actually arrived in April.

Noah, meanwhile, had arrogated to himself the task of buying a harpsichord. For this project, he already had money in hand, the proceeds of the sale of Charles Merrill's 1953 gift of stock. And he had a special set of needs in mind. Note that in the mid-1950s, harpsichords were even rarer than those who played them. The few harpsichordists well-enough known to go on tour—Wanda Landowska was one, Ralph Kirkpatrick another, Noah's friend Sylvia Marlowe a third—could never count on finding playable instruments in the cities and towns on their schedules. They were obliged to travel with their harpsichords. To the pressures of nightly performance this added a set of nightmarish logistical difficulties, those attendant upon the repeated crating, shipping, insuring, local haulage, tuning and maintenance of a large, complicated, fragile and unstable keyboard instrument.

For one American harpsichord builder in particular, John Challis, the miseries of the artists represented an intriguing opportunity. Challis had learned his craft as an apprentice in the Haslemere, England atelier of Arnold Dolmetsch. Back in the U. S., he had set up shop first in New York, then in Detroit. There he had begun experimenting with highly unorthodox materials in an effort to produce a harpsichord that sounded well but was sturdy enough to withstand the rigors of travel and stable enough not to require top-to-bottom adjustment and retuning at every stop on its owner's itinerary. One of Challis's favored materials was aluminum. Hideously anachronistic to purists, aluminum was sturdy, lightweight (at least, no heavier than hardwood) and impervious to changes in temperature and humidity. At one time, Challis was using slabs of aluminum for pinblocks, desisting only when it became clear that without special and expensive bushings the tuning pins set into the pinblock would loosen in their holes and throw the entire stringing disastrously out of whack. Some Challis harpsichords (including one commissioned by the virtuoso Fernando Valenti) were built on aluminum frames. Others had wooden frames but aluminum soundboards: the latter, immune from warping and cracking, were meant to impart strength and rigidity to the whole instrument.

Pro Musica had yet to go on tour, but Noah had already booked a few out-of-town concerts and was hoping for many more. Besides, even at home in New York the group's rented harpsichord was constantly on the move—up and down the four flights of steps at 80 Perry Street and in and out of the "Y," the Grace Rainey Rogers, The Cloisters, and wherever else the group was rehearsing and performing. There was constant worry about its durability (and playability). Even if it took every last dollar of the Merrill gift, it was time for Pro Musica to buy its own harpsichord. Noah wanted this one to be resonant—he hated "tinkleboxes"—yet small and compact enough to be moved easily and rugged enough to withstand the hard knocks of the road.

And so, in late September 1954, Noah opened negotiations with John Challis for a Challis "portable harpsichord." On November 4, Challis wrote him back, thanking him for his seventy-five-dollar deposit. A month later, having heard nothing, Noah wrote to ask—politely—for delivery as soon as possible. Again nothing. On January 26, 1955, Noah wrote pleading for delivery during March. Challis sent him back his own letter with a scribbled note on the bottom to the effect that he would try. On February 4, Noah wrote that "we are fortunately in a position to pay you for the instrument now. I would appreciate a commitment from you on delivery during the month of March." Challis's February 8 reply sounded a placating note, but as for a commitment:

> It is possible that I may have an exchange portable [an instrument that somebody was returning to Challis in exchange for a different instrument] by April or perhaps a bit before then.

On February 13, Noah wrote, with grinding teeth but still politely,

> Would it be possible for us to take the exchange portable by April and use it for our projected tour until the [one] you are building for us is ready?

Challis did what undependable but indispensible craftsmen invariably do in situations like this one. He put off answering until he could put it off no longer, and then came up with a brand-new story. Six weeks later, on March 25—Noah's hoped-for March delivery, of course, had long since become a dream—Challis wrote:

> I had hoped that an order cancellation would help you out . . . by April 1, but as luck would have it they found funds and it leaves

you out. The best thing now is about May 1st. But what about lunch in New York?

The saga finally ended in early June, when Challis notified Noah that the harpsichord was "ready and can be sent in about a week." By then the two men were on the best of terms and Noah was inviting Challis to "drop in on us at Lenox [Massachusetts]" during the summer. The harpsichord, complete with aluminum soundboard, was duly shipped from Detroit. Bernie Krainis picked it up in a borrowed station wagon at the Albany airport. The Challis proved to be well worth the delay, lasting through hundreds of concerts and countless vicissitudes of travel before Noah ordered it sold.[14]

---

[14] The Greenberg-Challis correspondence is in NYPM Archives, Box 21, folder 4. In fact, the Challis harpsichord was sold in 1963.

CHAPTER TWENTY

ON THE MONEY TRAIL

(1955-1956)

Over the next three seasons, nothing (or very little) seemed to change for Pro Musica. Each summer, its members, like a small transhumant tribe, migrated to the Berkshires to work and play. Each fall, Pro Musica reappeared in New York to present the new programs Noah had devised and the group had prepared and tried on summer audiences. Each season, Noah booked a few more—and more prestigious—out-of-town engagements. Pro Musica became a favorite at Chicago's Ravinia Festival and at Castle Hill in Ipswich, Massachusetts, and a fixture at the Coolidge Auditorium of the Library of Congress in Washington. Each season reaped a harvest of favorable reviews. (Very few were unfavorable.) Each season had its fundraising successes and its moments of financial panic.

And yet, everything did change.

Between early 1955 and early 1958, the New York Pro Musica grew from a well-regarded local ensemble into an internationally famous group. Noah himself went from self-taught pioneer of early music to respected musicological authority, sought after as lecturer and educator as well as practicing musician. Appearances on NBC-TV's educational show *Omnibus* made him something of a minor-league cultural celebrity. And these were the years that saw the transformation of "downtown Noah," Greenwich Villageite, devourer of knishes, and frequenter of the White Horse Tavern and the Cedar Bar, into "uptown Noah," paterfamilias, respectable dweller on New York's Upper West Side and steady customer (along with many another hungry musician, scholar and writer) of Sheila Chang's unforgettable Broadway restaurant The Great Shanghai.

Money had much to do with this upward shift in Pro Musica's fortunes. So did music. Pro Musica in these years reached a remarkable peak in its performances. And of course Noah himself was a prime mover—indefatigable, unstoppable, making friends and grabbing opportunity by the forelock at every turn of the road.

*   *   *

The 1954-55 season ended with a disappointment. At the "Y" in February, Wystan Auden had joined Pro Musica for a second time in two evenings of "English Verse and Music," featuring Noah's and Bernie Krainis's reconstruction of a masque by the Elizabethan-Jacobean composer Thomas Campian. The April "Y" concert dates were the last of the series. For these, Noah, inspired by the success of the Auden programs, put together a parallel event, a program featuring the poetry of the French Renaissance master Pierre De Ronsard (1524-1585) and musical settings by La Rue, Jannequin, Sermisy, and other sixteenth-century French composers. Noah persuaded Goddard Lieberson's wife Vera Zorina to be the "Auden," the onstage reciter of the Ronsard verses. Zorina, a conscientious and cultivated artist, threw herself into the project.

> I worked on Ronsard very hard. It was especially difficult because the French was archaic French and I struggled to master the pronunciation. Also, I memorized the verses. If you read from a book on stage, you are always looking down at the page and your rapport with the audience is lost, so I always memorized.[1]

Bernard Krainis laughed when he remembered the occasion.

> Yeah, because we had such great expectations. It was such a great idea. It exactly followed up the Auden stuff, and Noah was terrific on follow-throughs. This was going to top the Auden thing because of the celebrity-big name Zorina.... There were these big expectations, big star — and it bombed.

The reason it bombed, Bernie added, is that the snobbish French community in New York City refused to believe that the German-born Vera Zorina could speak acceptable Renaissance French and do justice to Ronsard's poetry. "[The French] stayed away in droves," and for some unknown reason Pro Musica's usual audience also stayed away. "I mean, you could shoot moose at the 'Y' both nights."[2]

A story in *The New York Times* two weeks later (on Saturday, April 25) did much to cushion any sense of letdown. The headline read: "248 Get $968,000 in Study Grants," and the story named the New

[1]Vera Zorina (Birgitta Lieberson-Wolfe), March 26, 1998.
[2]Bernard Krainis, August 13, 1998.

York-area winners of Guggenheim awards. Among them was Noah Greenberg, who received $3,500 to "continue his studies of Medieval and Renaissance music." As a 1955 Guggenheim Fellow, the auto-didact from the Bronx was one with such pillars of scholarship as Dr. Arthur Holly Compton of Washington University in St. Louis, Nobel laureate in physics (and one of the fathers of the atom bomb) and Dr. Stanley K. Hornbeck, former director of the State Department's Office of Far Eastern Afairs.[3] The prestige of the award was such that Noah could easily brush aside the fact that the Guggenheim trustees had granted him only about two-thirds of the $4,700 he had asked for.

Noah's search for money to live on blended well with his need to prove himself academically and his genuine interest in music education. The mixture of motives fed his eagerness, despite a crowded schedule, to accept an invitation to join the faculty of the Mannes College of Music. Founded in 1916 as the David Mannes School of Music, it was run for many years by members of the Mannes and Damrosch musical families and was in fact a pioneering center of the study of early music. As early as the 1920s, the French tenor Yves Tinayre, a specialist in medieval French vocal music, was on the Mannes faculty. And both Sydney Beck and his wife Blanche Winogron taught there in the 1940s. Mannes had been reorganized in 1953 as a degree-granting college and was looking to expand its programs and enlarge its faculty, both on a very limited budget.

Noah was appointed "director of choral conducting." His primary duty was to lead the Mannes School Chorus in once-weekly sessions. But as was his wont, he also put together a smaller group of Mannes students to work more intensively on the early vocal repertoire. This, according to music theorist Carl Schachter, a fellow faculty member at the time, was more of a success than the larger chorus.

> As a rule, music-school choruses don't do very well. Piano majors, violin majors, don't want to sing, they want to practice their instruments. Voice majors want to work on the voice repertoire, and voice teachers sometimes tell their students that choral singing is bad for them. The smaller group was more focused.[4]

Throughout the mid-1950s, Noah made a weekly trip to to the College, then housed in three adjoining brownstones at 157 East 74th Street, to lead the all-school chorus for an hour and direct the smaller

---

[3] *The New York Times*, April 25, 1955, p. 18:5.
[4] Carl Schachter, August 21, 1998.

ensemble for an hour and a half. After 1958, the time he gave to his Mannes post diminished, but Noah's association with Mannes would last until 1963; after Noah's death Toni would find work at Mannes as assistant to the president of the college and would eventually serve on its board of trustees.

Within weeks of the Guggenheim award announcement, the new Guggenheim Fellow was hot on the trail of more money. This time, the prospect was the Rockefeller Foundation. The proposal for a Rockefeller grant was dated May 30, but comment from Arthur Squires, who wrote the proposal, strongly suggests that he and Noah had been in touch with Rockefeller officials well beforehand. The idea behind the proposal was to allow Noah to stop running Pro Musica "out of his hat." The apartment at 80 Perry Street was bursting at the seams with books, music, and people, not the least of the latter Anne Greenberg, now an active two-year-old.[5] Pro Musica's wants were many and its resources, even counting Noah's $3,500, were slender. There was urgent need to set up a proper office, to hire secretarial help and to put Pro Musica on a businesslike footing. The need was equally pressing to add to and house Noah's and Pro Musica's collection of books on music, scores, part-books and bound editions of composers' works. Pro Musica was also in dire need of adequate rehearsal space. Said Arthur:

> It was ever so clear and the man at the Rockefeller organization made it very clear — we desperately needed some money — the Rockefellers were quite happy to receive a proposal that really only set up an office.[6]

Arthur's proposal was a thoroughly workmanlike presentation. It covered Pro Musica's background, reputation, and importance and its concert schedules, current budget, and plans for the future. It was not timid in what it sought. The proposal called for a contribution of no less than $56,000. Noah had already had considerable success in attracting foundation support and would have more success in the years ahead. For example, the Irwin S. Miller Foundation (Miller was chief executive officer of Cummins Engine Corp.)

[5]Charlotte Nelson, "Noted Musical Virtuoso Lectures on Renaissance Music-Making," *The Wayne Collegian* [student newspaper of Wayne State (Michigan) University], Tuesday, March 20, 1956, p. 4. "[H]is authoritative library . . . now threatens to crowd him out of the apartment where he lives with his wife and daughter."
[6]Arthur M. Squires, December 5, 1997. Nearly a year later, on April 2, 1956, Noah wrote to Lincoln Kirstein with the needs outlined in the Rockefeller proposal. These included a lecture hall/studio, two rehearsal studios, a library and an office. NYPM Archives, Box 2 [new numbering], folder 6.

was making yearly contributions of $1,000. James Merrill's Ingram Merrill Foundation gave $2,000 a year. The Doris Duke Foundation had been giving Pro Musica $500 a year and would continue to do so for many years. The Audrey S. and Thomas B. Hess Foundation (Hess was the publisher of *ArtNews*) made steady annual gifts of $250. Max Ascoli's private foundation had contributed $250 to $500 per year since 1955. (Ascoli was the editor and publisher of *The Reporter*.) Still, the size of the Rockefeller Foundation request propelled Pro Musica out of the eelymosenary minor leagues and into a completely different category. The response, when it came nearly a year later, was correspondingly impressive. The Rockefeller grant, payable in installments over five years (1957-58 through 1961-62), totalled $46,000. In current (2000) dollars, this was the equivalent of nearly $375,000.

In the spring of 1955, however, the outcome of Arthur's proposal lay far in the future. Noah was still relying on smaller gifts and for the most part on the generosity of private donors. He was constantly adding new names to the list of his friends and Pro Musica's patrons. Some, like Corning Glass heiress Ursula Corning, art collector Ben Heller, and Dorothy Norman, culture-loving wife of a Sears, Roebuck & Company heir, Noah had met in New York. Others, notably Mrs. W. Murray Crane and Lawrence Bloedel, had come to Pro Musica's 1954 concerts in the Berkshires. Mrs. Crane, the widow of Murray Crane of the Crane Paper Company of nearby Dalton, had been the namegiver and financial backer of the progressive Dalton School in New York and one of the founders of the Museum of Modern Art. Bloedel, a Williams College alumnus, had retired from the family lumber business in Washington State and now split his time between the Berkshires and New York City. In 1947, he and his wife Elli had purchased the Field Farm in South Williamstown from John D. Rockefeller's daughter Alta and her husband and lived there for much of each year in a spectacular modern home. The Bloedels, ardent collectors of art, fell in love with Pro Musica and Noah and became dedicated supporters.

It may have been through the Bloedels or through Lawrence Miller, whose family owned *The Berkshire Eagle*, that Noah made his arrangements for the summer of 1955. The Albany Fresh Air Fund house in Canaan was not available, but another property was a definite possibility. This one was an imposing villa called Fernbrook, on West Mountain Road in Lenox, Massachusetts, home of the Tanglewood Festival. Fernbrook had been empty since January 1954, when its occupant, a putative German count named Robert Metz, had died in Chicago. Metz was a singularly unpleasant character who usually swaggered around Lenox whacking a riding-crop against his shiny boots, but who sometimes appeared in *lederhosen* and Alpine hat. He was reputed to have reduced his imported German estate workers to virtual slavery. He was also supposed to have half-starved the Great Danes he kept in cages in the cellar of the house. After Metz's death, it came out that he had never been Fernbrook's owner. He had held only a life interest in the property under the will of his first wife, Elizabeth Gates Ross, who had died in 1946. The true owner in 1954—also Elizabeth Gates Ross's legatee—was Paul Schmidinger, the Fernbrook gardener. The main house, approached by a sweeping circular drive, stood amid gardens and manicured grounds (including a swimming-pool). Its living and dining rooms were on a grand scale, it boasted twelve or thirteen bedrooms and a music hall, complete with minstrels' gallery. The place, indeed, was something of a white elephant. Schmidinger, who lived quietly in a cottage on the estate, was more than happy to lease it to Pro Musica for the summer.

Encamped in its mansion, Pro Musica set to work on the new programs Noah had prepared during the spring. There was only one change in the makeup of the ensemble. Seymour Barab, who had supported Noah from Pro Musica's very beginnings, had left after the last "Y" concert to pursue his career as cellist and composer. Fond as he was of Noah and the others, Seymour claims that he was never a devotee of early music. "Beethoven talks to *me*," he declares, "but those guys [early music composers] were talking to . . . to the angels."[7] Seymour's replacement was one of the most extraordinary of all of Pro Musica's instrumentalists. Martha Blackman, born in Chicago, had studied cello at The Juilliard School under Leonard Rose and in 1953 had gone to Germany on a Fulbright Fellowship to study the viola da gamba. In New York in 1955, she appeared as gamba soloist with Arthur Mendel's Cantata Singers and with Margaret Hillis's ensemble. Martha was friendly with a number of Pro Musica's artists. Beautiful to look at, she was so gifted a gambist (despite her unorthodox technique)[8] that when Seymour resigned it was a foregone conclusion that Noah would recruit her.

[7]Seymour Barab, February 27, 1997.

[8]A distinguishing feature of the viola da gamba is a fingerboard fretted like that of the lute and the modern guitar. Frets affect both intonation and string timbre, and help to give the gamba its characteristic silvery sound. According to her close friend Morris Newman and other Pro Musica instrumentalists, Martha Blackman played an unfretted gamba, at least during the early years of her Pro Musica membership. This may have cost her some tone quality, but it allowed her to do some "cello-like things" with the earlier instrument.

As he had in 1954, Noah had worked up three new programs. Two of these focused on master composers of the Renaissance, Claudio Monteverdi and William Byrd. The third was thematic: "The Virgin in Medieval and Renaissance Music." Noah often professed a special affinity for Monteverdi, jokingly insisting to his friends that "I'm Monteverdi," because "Monteverdi," like "Greenberg," translates into English as "Green Mountain." At all events, the Monteverdi program became one of the most frequently repeated of all Pro Musica programs. As the centerpiece for the singers, Noah picked the six-madrigal cycle *Lagrime d'amante al sepolcro dell'amata* ("The Tears of a Lover at the Tomb of the Beloved") for six voices a capella. Betty Wilson was the soloist in *Amor—Lamento della Ninfa*, a dramatic work for mixed voices and instruments that owes much to Monteverdi the opera composer. Betty and Jean Hakes teamed up in the exultant *Et Resurrexit* from the 1610 *Vespri della beata vergine*. But perhaps the most memorable works on the program were two duets, *Chiome D'oro* and, from the posthumous Ninth Book of Madrigals, *Zefiro Torna*. The latter is a marvel of musical "affect", its lyrical sweetness plunging into deep sadness and the sadness in turn melting into the bright ending. As sung by Russell and Charles, with Paul, Martha Blackman, and Bernie (playing the bass recorder) as continuo accompanists, *Zefiro Torna* became one of Pro Musica's most brilliant accomplishments. More than forty years later, those who know it from performances or recordings still regard it with awe, as unsurpassed and unsurpassable.

The chief work on the William Byrd program was his Mass for Five Voices. Byrd, a recusant Catholic in a savagely anti-Catholic era, almost certainly meant this Mass for use by small gatherings for worship in secret. The Gloria is appropriately exultant, but most of the movements are contemplative rather than flamboyant: this setting is music for the inner life. A number of Anglican anthems—Byrd wrote for the Established Church as well as for his own outlawed one—several instrumental works (including two for viols), a group of songs, and a cluster of carols and hymns for Christmas rounded out the program.

"The Virgin in Medieval and Renaissance Music" was performed only once during the summer and not at all afterward. It seems to have been one of Noah's rare errors in musical judgment. Almost certainly, some of the works in the program were "recycled" and used in other programs.

Pro Musica's offstage life during the summer was as ebullient as ever. One memory shared by several Pro Musica members is of a swimming party at a vast abandoned quarry near Lenox. The three inseparables, Russell, Charles, and Betty, set themselves afloat on a huge log, paddled their way offshore, then, teetering on their improvised raft, produced a rendition of the *Rheinmädchen* music from Wagner's *Siegfried*, the sound reverberating off the quarry's towering granite walls.[9] Weeks later, for the 1955 end-of-season "NYPMA on Parade," Joel Newman wrote a prodigious masque about the problems of the Food Committee, basing the music on a rousing 1940s hymn.

Even though Pro Musica was living in Lenox, its 1955 Berkshire concerts were given in the Stockbridge Town Hall. Throughout the summer, their publicity was excellent. *The Berkshire Eagle* provided voluminous and adulatory coverage of both personnel and performances. After the Monteverdi concert on August 20, Milton R. Bass wrote: "Surely this is the kind of *a capella* singing we will get in heaven from that famous choir."[10] Audience response was equally strong, but the novelty of early music may have been wearing off, because ticket-buyers grew fewer as the summer wore on. Not until Pro Musica returned to New York in September did audience size begin to match critical praise. The October 22 Town Hall concert (of Spanish and German Baroque music) was sold out, and *The New York Times*'s reviewer wrote that

> this devoted group of artists soon made it clear that you can no more patronize such giants as Schuetz, Isaac or Victoria than you could patronize Haydn or Brahms.[11]

Following the "Y" concert devoted to William Byrd on January 23, 1956, also sold out, the same *Times* reviewer abandoned restraint. Byrd, wrote Edward Downes, was "revealed [as] a composer of breathtaking power and delicacy." As for Pro Musica itself:

> Fortunately, the adventursome Mr. Greenberg commands a virtuoso ensemble. That is, his ten singers and players have, in addition to individual brilliancies, the capacity to become one in musical impulse.[12]

[9]Bernard Krainis, February 17, 1997; Arthur M. Squires, December 5, 1997; Betty Wilson Long, June 20, 1998.

[10]Milton R. Bass, *The Berkshire Eagle*, Sunday, August 21, 1955.

[11]E[dward] D[ownes], "Versatile Group Plays Pre-Bach Works," *The New York Times*, Monday, October 24, 1955, p. 23:1.

[12]Edward Downes, "Works of William Byrd Are Presented," *The New York Times*, Monday, January 23, 1956, p. 22:1.

The 1955-56 season ended out of town, with a concert at the Detroit Institute of the Arts. This had been booked not by Noah himself but by an agent, David Libidens, and is an indication that Noah was turning to professional help in marketing Pro Musica. Libidens's tenure as Pro Musica's representative, however, was shortlived. By fall, Noah had been approached by Ronald Wilford of David W. Rubin Artists Management. Wilford thought Noah "a genius."[13] Given time, he felt that he could turn Pro Musica into a major attraction. He remained Pro Musica's agent through 1958.[14] In 1958, however, Ronald Wilford moved from the Rubin firm to CAMI, bringing Pro Musica with him.

One other episode of the 1955-56 season both sheds light and casts shadow on Pro Musica's rise to success.

In his May 1955 Rockefeller Foundation proposal, Arthur Squires included in the section on Pro Musica's budget mention of an exciting venture.

> Under the auspices of the International Exchange Program of the American National Theatre and Academy, an eight-week tour of Southern Europe and the Near East is planned for the Spring of 1956. This tour will be undertaken at financial arrangements which will just cover artists' expenses.[15]

The American National Theatre and Academy (ANTA) had been founded in 1935 under a special federal charter. But not until after the war did ANTA come into its own, when actor-director Robert Breen took it over and made it into a foundation, funded by both government and private support, to promote American theater. Internationally, ANTA, working with the State Department, became the main sponsor of cultural exchanges between the U. S. and Europe and thus a key player in the cultural and ideological Cold War. For Pro Musica, barely three years old, to have been chosen to tour

---

[13]Ronald A. Wilford, September 28, 1998.

[14]NYPM Archives, Box 9, folder 15. The issue of management in Pro Musica's early years is somewhat confusing. For some part of 1955, Columbia Artists Management Inc. seems to have been representing Pro Musica on a case-by-case basis. Thus, on May 11 Schuyler Chapin, then at CAMI, was writing to Noah about the costs and benefits of touring. In September, Chapin was asking about CAMI's fee for arranging a Pro Musica appearance on the television program "Omnibus." Later, in October or November, Ronald A. Wilford signed Pro Musica to a contract with David W. Rubin Artists Management. Later still, Noah wrote to William Judd at CAMI regretting that the Pro Musica board had not chosen CAMI as manager.

[15]Proposal to the Rockefeller Foundation, May 31, 1955. NYPM Archives, Box 27, folder 1.

Europe under the aegis of ANTA was an extraordinary honor. It was a financial boon and a free trip abroad for the artists and a testimony to Noah's and the ensemble's musical excellence.

Bureaucracies move slowly, and no public announcement of the ANTA tour was made until late in the fall of 1955. Then *The New York Times*, on Thursday, November 24, ran a concise but fairly detailed account:

> A three-month, ten-country European tour by the Pro Musica Antiqua will take place April 1 through June 25, 1956. The announcement was made yesterday by Robert W. Dowling, chairman of the Exchange Program of the American National Theatre and Academy, under whose auspices the tour will take place.
>
> The group will present fifty-five concerts in England, France, Italy, Spain, Portugal, Greece, Yugoslavia, Austria, Germany and Switzerland.
>
> The Pro Musica Antiqua, six singers and four instrumentalists under the direction of Noah Greenberg, performs music of the thirteenth through seventeenth centuries.[16]

As late as Monday, December 5, Noah was writing excitedly to an acquaintance in England that

> We recently received news that the International Exchange Progam of the American National Theatre and Academy are sponsoring us on a tour of Europe this coming Spring.[17]

But soon thereafter—indeed, within days—Noah received word from ANTA that the tour had been canceled. Why? No written explanation survives in Pro Musica's archives, but word seems to have filtered back to Noah that Pro Musica was regarded as too specialized to appeal to audiences overseas. Noah was understandably infuriated by the sudden cancellation. Among many other considerations, it meant a huge loss of income. At this late date, finding spring bookings to replace fifty-five cancelled appearances was impossible. In the event, Noah would have to struggle to arrange two. He was even more disturbed by the obvious shallowness of the reason given: ANTA and the State Department had had months in which to evaluate Pro Musica's suitability for an overseas tour. It was all too likely, given the climate of the times, that the real reason lay elsewhere.

---

[16]"Pro Musica Will Tour," *The New York Times*, Thursday, November 24, 1955, p. 41:7.

[17]Noah Greenberg-William L. Smoldon, letter, December 5, 1955.

To try to find out, Noah and Toni reached out to friends from Noah's political past.

In the mid-1950s, the liberal anti-Communist American Committee for Cultural Freedom found itself in an odd position vis-à-vis the reactionary anti-Communist forces led by Senator Joseph McCarthy. Sidney Hook, Irving Kristol, Elliot Cohen, and other A.C.C.F. intellectual cold-warriors wanted to be seen as toughly anti-Communist, but they also liked to think well of themselves as liberals. They therefore recoiled from McCarthy, characterized him as a demagogue who did anti-Communism more harm than good, and sought to distance themselves from the junior Senator from Wisconsin and his tactics. One of their ways of asserting that they were the *right* kind of anti-Communists was to set up an A.C.C.F. committee to look into instances where people had been mistakenly or falsely accused of being Communists or Communist sympathizers.

Through one or another of his contacts, (perhaps his old friend Daniel Bell, but more likely Sidney Hook himself), Noah learned of the existence of the A.C.C.F. committee. Directly or indirectly, he brought the facts of the cancelled tour to its attention. References in the A.C.C.F. archives make clear that the committee did indeed take up the matter. "Pro Musica tour cancellation" appears on a master list of cases given committee consideration. The actual case file appears to be missing. But one powerful piece of evidence of the committee's activity does exist. It is a letter dated January 12, 1956, from Sol Stein, Irving Kristol's successor as A.C.C.F. Executive Director, to Maxwell Rabb. Rabb at the time was President Eisenhower's cabinet secretary and the White House contact man for minorities.

> I have just been advised [Stein wrote] that you were informed by the State Department that the Pro Musica Antiqua case that Irving Ferman had spoken to you about was not a matter of 'security,' but rather of a determination by the appropriate committee in the State Department to cancel the projected and publicly announced tour of Pro Musica because that group had too narrow an appeal.
>
> We have twice been able to ascertain that the story told you by the State Department is inspired more by the needs of diplomacy in discouraging inquiries into the matter than by an accurate portrayal of the actual basis for the reversal of the decision. The real story is as follows:
>
> During the final consideration of the contract between the State Department (ANTA) and the Pro Musica Antiqua group, the cultural presentation staff of the International Educational Exchnge

Service made, as is the custom, a pro forma inquiry into the backgrounds of the persons to be sent on tour. In this connection, it was ascertained that Mr. Noah Greenberg, director of the group, had in the past been an anti-Stalinist Schachtmanite [sic]. This made him a 'controversial' person. The officers of the State Department concerned with this matter felt that with a wide choice of groups it would be advantageous not to get involved with a group in which there was someone who was 'suspect,' not [sic] matter how foolish the reasons. As a result, the decision was made to cancel the projected tour. Therefore, it can be said that the reversal of the original decision to send the group to Europe occurred because of 'security reasons' rather than the diplomatic reasons given by the State Department to you.

I have twice ascertained the above to be the truth of the matter.

We had hoped that the Pro Musica Antiqua tour would give cultured Europeans the impression that America has not only the popular Negro culture of Louis Armstrong and 'Porgy and Bess' but also a strong, however limited, interest in serious musical scholarship and performance.[18]

Whether Rabb or anyone else replied to Stein's acerbic letter is not known. But the cancellation stood. Pro Musica did not go on tour.

[18] Sol Stein-Maxwell Rabb, letter, January 12, 1956. Stein sent a blind carbon copy of this letter to Noah Greenberg. The copy is in the possession of the Greenberg family. The A.C.C.F. archives are housed in the Tamiment Institute/Ben Josephson Library at the Bobst Library, New York University. Because Folder 23, the folder containing the "New York Pro Musica cancelled tour" correspondence, is missing, full details of A.C.C.F. efforts are lacking.

CHAPTER TWENTY-ONE

865 West End Avenue

(1956)

$\mathcal{I}$n the spring of 1956, Russell Oberlin was in the market for a car. He knew exactly which model he wanted. He had his heart set on a two-door MG, the classic British sports car, the canvas-topped convertible with the broad leather strap across the hood. It would be perfect for his needs. The only problem was that the dealer didn't happen to have the MG in stock and didn't know when he'd be able to get one. But he did have something else—a Jaguar XK140 sports coupe, black, with a red leather interior. "My family thought I was crazy," Russell said, "but I had the money and I said to myself, 'What the heck, I need a car, why not go for it?' and I bought it."[1]

Russell's love-affair with his new Jag, like that of so many Jaguar owners, was tinged with frustration and anguish. (Until Russell had a non-Jaguar mechanic shape a waterproof wrapper for the distributor head out of an old inner tube, the Jag simply wouldn't go in the rain.) But he did need a car, and one that would get him from place to place in a hurry. Pro Musica was once again spending the summer in the Berkshires. Noah's search for a large place to rent had led him to the Delta Phi fraternity house on South Street in Williamstown, vacant when Williams Collage was not in session, and by early June the group was in residence.

Noah had booked four Sunday afternoons at South Mountain in Pittsfield. But with the rug pulled out from under the ANTA European tour and Berkshires audiences alarmingly scanty, Noah found it necessary to hunt elsewhere for business. Some he found locally. Noah and Nikos Psacharopoulos, resident director at the

[1]Russell Oberlin, February 27, 1998.

Williamstown summer theater, had met socially, and each was interested in the other's work. On Nikos's schedule this year (1956) was a production of Shaw's *Saint Joan*. Noah put together a group of fifteenth-century English, French, and Italian works, and Pro Musica taped it for use in the play. In return, Nikos's Williamstown Theatre Foundation sponsored a Pro Musica concert at Williams College's Adams Theater.

At almost the last possible minute, Noah did land additional bookings. Lincoln Kirstein, who had a summer home in Westport, Connecticut, was a trustee of the American Shakespeare Festival, held each summer in nearby Stratford. On April 2, Noah wrote to sound out Kirstein about possible Pro Musica appearances at the Festival. Russell Oberlin, in fact, had already signed a separate contract to sing at Stratford. The music for his solo songs in *Much Ado About Nothing* and *The Merchant of Venice* would be written by none other than Virgil Thomson.

Russell's independence irked Noah, but he had so little work for Pro Musica that there was nothing he could do to stop the young ambitious countertenor from seeking outside engagements. Nor had he been able to hold his violinist. In March, Sonya Monosoff dropped out of Pro Musica altogether. Married, interested in the classical as well as the pre-classical repertoire and not enamored of the viol, she preferred to freelance. To take Sonya's place, Noah plucked 36-year-old Paul Ehrlich from the violin section of Thomas Scherman's Little Orchestra Society. The son of a Brooklyn doctor, Paul Ehrlich came from a musical family. His brother, Jesse, a cellist, was a highly successful studio musician in Hollywood. Exceptionally versatile, he had studied both violin and flute, and in addition played clarinet, oboe and recorder. He also played and taught the guitar. It was Paul's private boast that he could get music out of anything: the older and more battered the instrument, the more tuneful he would make it sound. At Pro Musica, Paul would play the viol, the rebec —Noah loved its shrill, scratchy sound—the recorders, and the one-keyed, soft-voiced Baroque flute.

*   *   *

For Toni and Noah, the spring of 1956 brought a change of a bigger, more momentous kind than the change in personnel. On the strength of his Guggenheim Fellowship and his Mannes College appointment, and doubtless anticipating Rockefeller Foundation funds, Noah began to hunt for new quarters. His search brought him to the Upper West Side. In some ways, this seems odd. From his days in the movement, Noah had always lived downtown, and he especially loved the Village. Toni too had become a downtowner. Seymour Barab recalls that when Noah broached the possibility of a move, "I want you to know that Toni screamed and kicked and hollered about moving above Fourteenth Street."[2] Still, there were reasons to do it. Starting in the late 1940s, the white exodus to the suburbs was emptying the apartment houses of the West Side. As West Side neighborhoods grew poorer, they grew drab and dangerous. But the apartments the lawyers and doctors and business people were leaving behind were large ones, with big rooms and thick walls and high ceilings and generous kitchens. The buildings had elevators: on the Upper West Side, there was no need to labor up four or five flights of steep stairs with a baby on the hip and a couple of heavy bags of groceries to lug besides. Musicians loved these apartments. The soundproof walls meant that they could pound or strum or sing away to their hearts' content without infuriating their neighbors. The side streets might be dangerous, but the avenues were safe, nearby buses and subways ran all night, and the rents were within reach.

865 West End Avenue, the twelve-story building at the northwest corner of 102nd Street and West End, was then, and is now, solid and substantial but not pretentious. Through a door off its lobby is a ground-floor space long since divided into several doctors' offices but in the spring of 1956 a single commodious room. On most floors, there are four apartments to the floor. Apartment 10A is a classic Upper West Side layout. The front door opens on a long hallway, with the kitchen and a maid's room immediately on the right. Further down the hall, also on the right, are the dining and living rooms, the latter with its windows overlooking 102nd Street. Off the hallway to the left are two bedrooms, the larger a corner room with its own bathroom. At the very end of the hallway, there is a third small bedroom.

The ground-floor space rented for $183 a month. By the grace of New York City's rent-control statutes, the rent for Apartment 10A, if Noah's and Toni's daughters remember correctly what their parents told them, was $185 a month.

What arguments—if any—Noah needed to persuade Toni to leave Perry Street are easily imagined. Annie was already a toddler and would soon be a grown-up little girl who needed a room of her own. After a fifth-floor walkup, a building with doormen and elevators

[2]Seymour Barab, February 27, 1997.

offered obvious advantages. The maid's room could later serve as quarters for the domestic help Toni wanted and needed. There was room off the kitchen for a washing-machine and a dryer. As for Noah's priorities, the kitchen was small, but roomy enough to allow him to keep his cooking skills alive. The living-room and dining-room, connected by wide glass doors, would be ideal for family get-togethers, parties, and informal entertaining. Best of all, the space on the ground floor would become Pro Musica's office, library, and rehearsal studio. Instruments, books, scores, files could be housed there, leaving Apartment 10A free as the Greenbergs' private home.

It is possible that the office was set up first, but by the early summer of 1956, Noah, Toni, and Anne were living in Apartment 10A. Anne remembers that her father's grand piano was installed a corner of the living-room, along with Noah's big red leather wing chair and that design icon of the 1950s, a "butterfly chair," its tubular wrought-iron frame supporting an orange canvas sling seat. On the walls, along with other works, including at least one painting by Julius Goldstein, were two small oils that Toni had bought years before from a fellow-student at N.Y.U. named Helen Frankenthaler. One had cost Toni ten dollars. The other was more expensive. Toni had had to buy it on time, giving Frankenthaler five dollars a week until the full price, fifteen dollars, was paid off.

*   *   *

Not until mid-July did Noah nail down a schedule of four Monday concerts at the Shakespeare Theatre in Stratford. These were welcome indeed, but they posed a severe logistics problem. The dates were the last three Mondays in August and the first Monday in September—and on each occasion Pro Musica was performing the day before in Pittsfield. The two towns were nearly 100 miles apart as the crow flies, and much further apart than that on the narrow and congested Route 7 that linked them. By the end of the summer, Russell's XK-140, as well as Noah's red Chevrolet convertible and the other Pro Musica cars, knew the trip by heart.

The summer's new programs were only two in number, not three: "Music of the German Reformation and Baroque" and "The Old Testament in Early Music." Even these were not entirely new, some works in each of them having been drawn from earlier programs. But the new works Noah and Joel Newman had picked were, as usual, demanding. One of the most taxing was not part of either of the new programs, but an addition to Pro Musica's "Tudor and Elizabethan Music." This was Orlando Gibbons's extraordinary *London Street Cries*, a work for voices and viols. For the viols, Gibbons had written a three-part fantasy of the type known as an *In nomine,* from the scrap of plainsong or Gregorian chant that, played slowly by the tenor viol, is the core of its structure. The fantasy was a workout for Pro Musica's trio of viol players, Martha Blackman, Paul Ehrlich, and Arthur Squires.

Interwoven with the fantasy was a madrigal, a medley of a dozen or more of the marvellous musical cries that were the advertising commercials of Elizabethan London.

> Hot apple pies hot . . . hot pippin pies hot . . . Ha' ye any old shirts to mend . . . New oysters / New Wellfleet oysters . . . Will ye buy any ink, will ye buy any ink? / Very fine writing ink, will ye buy any ink? . . . If there be any who bears news / Of a grey mare with a white mane and tail / She halts down right before / and is stark lame behind / And was lost this thirty-first day of February / Let him go to the crier / And he shall have well for his hire . . . Sweep chimney sweep / Sweep chimney sweep / Sweep chimney sweep with a hoop derry derry derry / Sweep chimney sweep. / From the bottom to the top / Sweep chimney sweep / Then will no soot fall / In your porridge pot / With a hoop derry derry derry sweep

Out of this melange of song and string music in performance would suddenly soar Russell's pleas for the miserables of the city: "Poor naked Bedlam / Tom's a-cold" and "Have pity on us poor prisoners of the Marshalsea / For Christ Jesus' sake / Give us meat."

London Street Cries was given its first performance at the Adams Theater on Sunday, July 19, 1956. Like *Zefiro Torna,* it became one of Pro Musica's most celebrated numbers. The work was so complicated that things could all too easily go wrong. On one occasion, Charlie Bressler, distracted by some outside event, began singing: "Cheep swimmney cheep / Cheep swimmney cheep . . ." The others, listening, began laughing so uncontrollably that, to Noah's fury, they had to stop and start again—a betrayal, in his mind, of the compact between Pro Musica and its audience. But when *Street Cries* went well, as it almost always did, it delighted audiences with its moving musical panorama of Elizabethan life.

Despite ample publicity and splendid reviews, the 1956 summer season was one of small audiences and financial deficits.[3] Pro Musica did return once more to Williamstown. but the 1957 summer season would be its final summer in the Berkshires.

---

[3] According to Arthur Squires, Pro Musica ran up expenses of $8,000 and brought in only about $3,000 in ticket sales, leaving a deficit of $5,000.

Noah opened the 1956-57 New York season with the Monteverdi program at Town Hall. The *Herald Tribune's* Jay S. Harrison once again let his enthusiasm show freely. Monteverdi, he wrote, "will become outmoded only when sentiment and depth and passion become outmoded, too." As for Pro Musica, it was unnecessary "to cite given numbers or point to any single member of the ensemble — choosing one is simply to sacrifice another equally as fine."[4]

The season rolled on, with back-to-back performances at the "Y" in October. Then, on November 3, the New York Pro Musica Baroque Trio, consisting of Bernard Krainis, recorder, Paul Maynard, harpsichord, and Martha Blackman, viola da gamba, gave a concert of Baroque music at Carnegie Recital Hall (now Weill Hall), the small chamber-music auditorium at Carnegie. On the program were sonatas for recorder and continuo and solo works for Martha and Paul as well. On the surface, the event seemed a pleasing extension of Pro Musica's programming. In fact, it mirrored Bernie's growing disenchantment with Noah's leadership and with the direction in which Noah was taking Pro Musica. Bernard Krainis, it must be remembered, had spent years acquiring the technique and interpretative skill to reinvent the recorder as the virtuoso solo instrument it had been two centuries earlier. At this point, the rich Baroque literature for recorder and continuo and for recorder and other instruments and continuo had barely been touched. Bernie was eager to explore this repertoire, as soloist and as chamber player in collaboration with his Pro Musica colleagues.

In contrast, Bernie felt, Noah had not much interest in Baroque instrumental music and little concern for the careers of Pro Musica's instrumentalists. Thus, Paul Maynard, a brilliant harpsichordist, waas receiving almost no opportunity to show off his talent. Sonya had left for much the same reason. Bernie too felt that what he had to do onstage was often elementary and undignified—"comic relief," he called it in his unhappiest moments. He had not been shy about expressing himself, and Noah said, "Sure, work with Paul Maynard and Martha and do a concert." Perhaps a separate Pro Musica Baroque group would be the answer. Bernie would wait and see. Still, Noah had plans that were diverging more and more sharply from Bernie's idea of what Pro Musica should do and be.

[4]Jay S. Harrison, "Pro Musica Antiqua Opens Year With Monteverdi Bill," *The New York Herald-Tribune*, Thursday, October 11, 1956, p. 13:7,8.

CHAPTER TWENTY-TWO

⌂ANUSCRIPT EGERTON 2615

(1953-1958)

⌂round 1870, a music manu-
script, British Museum (later British Library) MS Egerton 2615,
attracted the attention of a pioneering scholar of medieval music,
Charles-Edmond-Henri de Coussemaker. The manuscript contained
an eleventh-century work from the Cathedral of Beauvais in northern France. The work was an example of liturgical drama: one of
the hundreds of augmentations of the liturgy that had grown up in
medieval churches to dramatize and interpret the Word of God. This
one was drawn from the Biblical Book of Daniel. Its title was *Ludus
Danielis (The Play of Daniel)*. Coussemaker included it—text, stage
directions, and a single line of neumes, the early notation in which
plainchant was recorded— n his immense compilation *Scriptorum
de musica medii aevi nova series*, the four volumes of which appeared
between 1864 and 1876. After that, nobody did much about *Daniel*
for nearly the next hundred years.

It was in the pages of Coussemaker, in the early 1940s, that a British schoolmaster and dedicated scholar of medieval music, William
L. Smoldon, first encountered *Daniel*. The play intrigued Smoldon
for several reasons. One was that the secular element in it seemed
to him very strong—much stronger than in other liturgical dramas.
Most of the characters in *Daniel* are human, not divine, and they
display a surprising range of emotion: pride, fear, love, envy. There
is even emotional conflict, as King Darius is seen to agonize over his
decision to obey the law which altereth not and cast Daniel into the
lions' den. An English-language version of *Daniel*, Smoldon thought,
would be gripping enough to be a splendid theatrical project for the
boys of his school, Stratford Grammar School.

Hesitantly, Smoldon began to transcribe the neumes into modern
staff notation and prepare a score in which the syllables of the text

were matched up with the proper notes. As he worked, he puzzled over how to make English and plainchant go together. He also found himself entangled in one of the knottiest questions confronting the scholar of medieval music: whether instruments were ever used in music performed as part of the liturgy. Musicological opinion was against the idea, but some of the *Daniel* music was so tuneful. . . . Smoldon became convinced, at least for the present, that instrumental accompaniment was not only appropriate but necessary.

He said as much in his chapter on liturgical drama in *The New Oxford History of Music*. And according to Smoldon himself, it was this account that first sparked Noah Greenberg's interest in the drama.[1] In fact, Noah had come upon Smoldon's chapter and had begun thinking about *Daniel* at least as early as February 1953, a month and a half before Pro Musica itself was formed. He wrote an enthusiastic letter to Smoldon. Smoldon, an eccentric in the glorious tradition of gifted, absent-minded, faintly dotty English eccentrics, responded warmly.[2] It was the beginning of a correspondence and a friendship that would override doubts and disagreements over the interpretation of music and would last until Noah's death.

Noah was especially delighted to learn that Smoldon was working on transcriptions of two of the *Daniel* songs. But Smoldon as headmaster of his school was busy with other things. Not until late 1954 did he send Noah the transcriptions, along with English translations of the original Latin texts. Noah, no expert himself and wanting an expert's opinion, turned the transcriptions over to a man whose knowledge of medieval music he had already tested.

Rev. Rembert Weakland, O.S.B., was twenty-seven years old in 1954.[3] The young Benedictine had been ordained just three years earlier—when he still had a year to go to complete a major in piano at The Juilliard School. "The Benedictines have been wonderful to me," Weakland said of his religious order in 1995. Indeed, his superiors encouraged him to go beyond Juilliard and study music history at Columbia under Paul Henry Lang and Erich Hertzmann. Seated next to him in Hertzmann's class was Joel Newman, who had by then become Noah's "house musicologist." That winter

---

[1]William L. Smoldon-Noah Greenberg, letter, October 24, 1958. The Greenberg-Smoldon correspondence on *Daniel* cited in this chapter is in NYPM Archives, Box 4, folder 4.

[2]William L. Smoldon-Noah Greenberg, letter, February 14, 1953.

[3]The Most Reverend Rembert G. Weakland, O.S.B., April 8, 1995. Since 1978, Father Weakland has been Archbishop of the Roman Catholic Archdiocese of Milwaukee. He will be referred to throughout this text simply as "Rembert Weakland."

(1954), Noah had started to put together the program he called "The Virgin in Medieval and Renaissance Music." To contrast with the works of Renaissance composers like Josquin Desprez and Cristobal Morales, he planned to present several of the medieval Marian antiphons. These four great works of responsive chant in honor of the Virgin probably date from the second half of the eighth century. They have been sung daily in monasteries as part of the Divine Office since the thirteenth century, and are sung in churches as part of the service on August 15, the holy day of the Feast of the Assumption (commemorating Mary's bodily ascent into Heaven), and also at Christmastime.

Noah felt that the program notes for the antiphons—indeed, for the entire program—should be written by someone deeply versed in liturgical music Joel suggested his Benedictine classmate and friend Rembert Weakland. To Noah's delight, Weakland turned out notes that were lucid as well as authoritative (and delivered on time) and also gave Noah good advice on which versions of the antiphons to use.

Accordingly, when Smoldon's transcriptions of the *Daniel* songs arrived, Noah asked Weakland to review them. Weakland was happy to agree. Like Smoldon, he looked up the play in Coussemaker, but found the Coussemaker *Daniel* "unsatisfactory," so he wrote to the British Museum for a clear photocopy of the original manuscript, Egerton 2615. With this in his hands, he re-examined Smoldon's transcriptions and, as he put it, "got fascinated."

What fascinated Weakland was that the metrics of the texts were very emphatic, even though the neumes suggested a kind of "arrhythmic Gregorian droning."[4] To try to resolve the disparity, Weakland went back to Coussemaker. In Coussemaker's huge *Scriptorum*, a treatise called *Anonymous 4* was devoted to twelfth- and thirteenth-century secular music. Beginning early in 1955, Weakland had used *Anonymous 4* to help him determine the rhythmic values of the two *Daniel* songs.

Noah, meanwhile, had shown Smoldon's work to Gustave Reese. Joel Newman recalls the scene when Noah, with Weakland's ideas in mind, reached Reese by telephone to ask his opinion of how the songs should sound.

---

[4]Rembert Weakland, April 8, 1995.

> Reese was humming away in monotonous, droning fashion and Noah was sitting at his desk banging his hand down ONE two three ONE two three to get the rhythm across.[5]

Reese nevertheless encouraged Noah to push forward with *Daniel*. Reese may have known that Smoldon was not a decisive personality. He was also somewhat timid about his lack of formal scholarly credentials. Accordingly, he would be skittish and would need reassurance. In late February 1955, Noah wrote to Smoldon that "[i]f it is feasible we would like to present the Beauvais-Daniel play in its entirety." But he prefaced the bold proposal by saying "I am writing to you at the suggestion of Gustave Reese." Invoking Reese's name was a way of hinting that American musicologists would look kindly on Smoldon's efforts.[6]

Within days, Smoldon shot back an answer: "As soon as possible I shall be sending to you a manuscript acting copy of the 12th century music drama Daniel." He added, "It is quite obvious that the whole work was steeped in orchestral sound."[7] On the last day of March, Noah reiterated his desire to put on a full-scale production of *Daniel* in the "Spring [of] 1956."[8]

Suddenly, however, matters stalled. On June 11, Smoldon wrote to apologize for not sending the *Daniel* as promised.[9] A month and a half later, on July 28, he wrote "I am about to send you the acting copy . . ."[10] He did so, but now it was Noah's turn to slow things down. Smoldon's *Daniel*, a typescript speckled with corrections in green ink, was in English. It made no attempt at interpreting rhythms. And it called for musical accompaniment, largely in the form of trumpet fanfares, by a force of ten or eleven instrumentalists playing modern instruments. On August 5, Noah wrote that he had been unable to raise the money for a production. And furthermore, he added:

> Concerning your transcription, we would like it understood that our performance . . . [can]not be limited to your orchestration. . . . It would not be practical for us to undertake the project if we had to hire 6-7 outside musicians, to supplement our own troupe.[11]

[5]Joel Newman, June 30, 1998; September 7, 1998.
[6]Noah Greenberg-William L. Smoldon, letter, February 23, 1955.
[7]William L. Smoldon-Noah Greenberg, letter, February 27, 1955.
[8]Noah Greenberg-William L. Smoldon, letter, March 31, 1955.
[9]William L. Smoldon-Noah Greenberg, letter, June 11, 1955.
[10]William L. Smoldon-Noah Greenberg, letter, July 28, 1995.
[11]Noah Greenberg-William L. Smoldon, letter, August 5, 1955.

Smoldon wrote on August 23 to say that Noah "should be getting an English copy of *Daniel* almost as soon as this letter. . . . Don't take my orchestral demands too seriously."[12] But a month later he was waxing colder. "Now that you've got Daniel in front of you, I'd like to say something more." The "something more" was considerable hesitancy about instrumentation, the very issue on which he had been so certain in February. He waxed colder still in October, telling Noah that he was struggling with transpositions and certain rhythmic problems.

Noah wrote on November 7 with cheery news.

> It looks as though we will be able to present a full dress version next Christmas. [1956] The first performance would be to an invited audience at a large private home here in N. Y. The subsequent performances would be at the Cloisters of the Metropolitan Museum of Art. I could not imagine a more perfect setting in the United States.[13]

But in this same letter, Noah let drop the word that he had plans to include three—not two—*Daniel* excerpts in Pro Musica's December appearances at The Cloisters. (These of course would be concert, not theatrical, performances.) What Noah failed to mention is that these excerpts would not be taken from Smoldon's version of *Daniel*.

Rembert Weakland, meanwhile, knew that he was swimming in murky musicological waters. So he had cautiously submitted his own partial transcriptions to his Columbia professor, Erich Hertzmann. It may have been at Hertzmann's suggestion that Weakland also sent copies to Oliver L. Strunk, a leading authority on medieval music, at Princeton. Weakland's transcriptions retained the original Latin texts and were unequivocally clearer and more vigorous rhythmically than Smoldon's. With the blessing of Strunk, Weakland showed the finished transcriptions to Noah. Weakland recalls that Noah grew excited and said, "Let's do it all!"[14]

Tactfully, Noah informed Smoldon in December that there would be some "deviations" from Smoldon's versions in the Cloisters presentations.[15] The "deviations," of course, were the Weakland transcriptions.

[12]William L. Smoldon-Noah Greenberg, letter, August 23, 1955.

[13]Noah Greenberg-William L. Smoldon, letter, November 7, 1955.

[14]Rembert Weakland, April 8, 1995.

[15]Noah Greenberg-William L. Smoldon, letter, December 5, 1955.

Smoldon's letter of February 2, 1956, must have produced a sigh of relief on Noah's part. In it, Smoldon asked Noah to return the acting copy of *Daniel*. Smolden had been giving William Gilman Waite's 1954 book *The Rhythms of Twelfth Century Polyphony* a careful reading. He had also been discussing *Daniel* with his old friend Thurston Dart of Jesus College, Cambridge. "Bob" Dart, harpsichordist, teacher, and major figure in British early music circles, had reservations about Smoldon's approach. All of this was makng Smoldon rethink his views.[16]

Noah answered two weeks later, sending back Smoldon's acting copy "with regret" but adding:

> I fully understand your caution. The responsibility of re-acquainting the world with a work of art not presented for 700 years is indeed a great one.

He also told Smoldon that tapes of the Cloisters excerpts were on their way and invited Smoldon to be "merciless" in his criticism.[17]

Smoldon's response came in early May. "What a rhythmic riot [your Daniel] is! Most successful, I thought." This, if less than enthusiastic, was at least not the voice of someone who felt betrayed. "I'm beginning to wonder if I'm very much use to you in the matter," Smoldon said later in the letter, but he urged Noah to go on with *Daniel* even if their ideas differed. He himself would continue to work on his edition of the drama for the Plainsong and Medieval Music Society of Britain.[18]

At about the same time, Rembert Weakland was on his way from New York to Milan, where he was preparing to spend the year studying Ambrosian plainchant. But he took MS Egerton 2615 with him and "in Milan I did the whole play."[19] Noah and Pro Musica were in Williamstown working on—among other things—the "Old Testament in Early Music" program, scheduled for performances on September 2 and 3.

On August 3, Noah wrote to thank Weakland effusively for sending him the first half of *Daniel*.

> What a pleasure it is reading the work as you have transcribed it. I cannot tell you how glad I am that our final decision was to per-

---

[16]William L. Smoldon-Noah Greenberg, letter, February 2, 1956.
[17]Noah Greenberg-William L. Smoldon, letter, February 15, 1956.
[18]William L. Smoldon-Noah Greenberg, letter, May 4, 1955.
[19]Rembert Weakland, April 8, 1995.

form it in the original Latin. The sound of the piece is so different
— the stride and pace of the conducti is so much more exciting.[20]

He wrote again in October, telling Weakland as he had told
Smoldon a year earlier that "[w]e are going ahead with plans for a
series of performances of 'Daniel.'" This time, however, the plans
were far more definite. There was no more talk of a "tryout" in a
private home: all the performances would be held at The Cloisters.
Also, "we have definitely decided to use your Latin version." This
decision of course raised the question of how a contemporary lay
audience would follow a music drama sung in medieval Latin. Noah
had already formulated the answer: there would be an English narration "interspersed throughout." Furthermore, he had decided on
the form of the narration and had picked the narrator.

> [W]e would like the narrator's part to be in verse and in keeping
> with the spirit of the play. I wrote to W. H. Auden asking him if he
> would be interested in doing this. He is acquainted with 'Daniel'
> since I showed him W. L. Smoldon's realization two years ago. He
> was quite taken with it at the time and I'm sure he will offer to
> write the narrator's role.

Noah enclosed a check for $100 as an "'advance' against against
royalties on performances of your wonderful edition of *Daniel*." [21]

In a December 12 letter, Noah told Weakland that he has met with
Margaret Freeman of The Cloisters to make plans for the production. He added that Lincoln Kirstein had agreed to be the producer
and asked Weakland for "any suggestions as to casting, scoring, etc.
I would appreciate them."[22] Over the months that followed, Noah's
letters to Weakland became a sporadic commentary on what might
be called the philosophic aspects of the production.

On the practical aspects, an enormous amount of work lay ahead.
Noah and Kirstein had to find a director and work out with their
candidate the myriad details of casting, characterization, staging,
lighting, set design and costuming. Here Kirstein's years of experience with the the American Ballet, and his obsessive interest in the
details of stagecraft would prove invaluable.

One of Noah's first and hardest tasks was to persuade the members of Pro Musica that mounting a full-dress production of *Daniel*

[20]Noah Greenberg-Rembert Weakland, letter, October 13, 1956. This and subsequent
letters in the correspondence were supplied by and are used with the permission of
Archbishop Weakland.
[21]Noah Greenberg-Rembert Weakland, letter, October 18, 1956.
[22]Noah Greenberg-Rembert Weakland, letter, December 12, 1956.

made sense in the first place. Joel Newman makes no bones about his reaction. "I thought Noah was crazy. Who the hell was going to sit through an hour and a half of chant?"[23]   Arthur Squires admits that he was skeptical.

> We did excerpts from *The Play of Daniel* in a concert at The Cloisters about a year before the actual production, maybe a year and a half. . . . And I was totally unimpressed. And I think most of the musicians were, too.[24]

Most of the singers were troupers who had been dressing up in costume to sing ever since their first appearances as angels in their Sunday School Christmas pageants. They might have reservations about whether *Daniel* would "play" or not, but they had no problem at all seeing themselves onstage in medieval garb. The instrumentalists were another matter. In conventional opera and virtually every other form of instrumental performance except marching bands, the members of the orchestra are seated comfortably in the pit or off by themselves elsewhere. But Noah wanted the instrumentalists in *Daniel* to put on fancy dress, grab their instruments, and do their playing right in the middle of the onstage action. Bernie Krainis for one wasn't sure about this. A proud young man, and one eager to establish himself as a serious soloist, he felt certain that he would look "silly." And what about Paul Maynard? Surely Paul wasn't expected to stumble nearsightedly around the stage in costume carrying his harpsichord, which in any case would be ridiculously anachronistic?

"Noah," Bernie has said many times, "could outtalk anybody."[25] Whatever other arguments Noah may have used to sell the *Daniel* idea to his colleagues, the presence of Kirstein as backer, the challenge of recreating medieval instrumental music and Noah's promise that Pro Musica's *Daniel* would be neither undignified nor dull were by themselves persuasive. All four Pro Musica instrumentalists cast aside any doubts and took part in the show.

By the end of February 1957, Noah's Williamstown friend Nikos Psacharopoulos, three years out of Yale Drama School and already on its faculty, had agreed to direct *Daniel*. Robert Fletcher of the Ballet Theatre had been retained as costume and stage designer. Noah had also enlisted a friend from his days in the movement, the Columbia art historian Meyer Schapiro, as an "artistic advisor" on

[23]Joel Newman, September 7, 1998.
[24]Arthur M. Squires, December 5, 1997.
[25]Bernard Krainis, February 17, 1997; August 13, 1998.

design issues. In mid-May, Noah wrote to Rembert Weakland in London that "Prof. Meyer Schapiro and Auden are both in London *now* and they would both like to meet with you to discuss 'Daniel.'"[26] Whether or not Weakland did meet with the others is not clear, but Noah himself, "by a streak of luck," was able to be in London in early June and would hold the meeting himself. "I am most concerned with the narration," he told Weakland beforehand:

> . . . it can change the character of the play if it is improperly written. It should be quite unobtrusive, short and kept separate (rather than intertwined) from the drama and music. It is unfair, in a way, to place such restrictions on a poet of Auden's stature. However I am certain he will understand the problem and see the 'Daniel' play as a whole.[27]

Lincoln Kirstein played to perfection the role of grouchy put-upon patron. But his wealth (and that of his sister Mina Curtiss) and his willingness to spend made the difference between a pedestrian production and a spectacular one. Noah had told William Smoldon that he was unable to afford extra instrumentalists. But now, with Kirstein's backing (and with Rockefeller Foundation money in the bank), he could not only afford the extra instrumentalists, he could hire more singers and even acquire a few rare instruments as well.

One in particular he had long coveted. He told himself that it would be indispensible in *Daniel* and he asked Bernie to try to find one. And so, on February 22, in response to Bernie's letter of inquiry, organ-builder Josef Martin in Cologne wrote condescendingly:

> In the field of gothic and renaissance music I am rather an expert here in Europe and I am offering you my work, once by advising you about the types of instruments suitable for your musical intentions; on the other hand I am also able to make true style copies of portatives in my workshop. . . . For [music from Dufay's chansons to Ockeghem and Obrecht] a portative without sordunpipes is necessary—compass a"-f".
>
> An electric blower for the portative (the instrument is held on the knee) is out of question: the left hand of the player works the bellows and so has a certain influence on the sound. (The electric blower would have to be built into a little table on which the portative would be standing, but, as to the style, still would be a wrong disposition.[28]

[26]Noah Greenberg-Rembert Weakland, letter, May 16, 1957.
[27]Noah Greenberg-Rembert Weakland, letter, May 20, 1957.
[28]Josef Martin-Bernard Krainis, letter, February 22, 1957. NYPM Archives, Box 21, folder 12.

Patronizing he might be, but Martin clearly possessed real expertise. Better yet, he could deliver. "You could have a portative in the middle of October," he said at first. But Noah himself took over the correspondence and put on the heat. In mid-May, Martin wrote, "I shall be happy to make the small portative for you, and will have it ready by the sixth of July."[29] He was as good as his word. The portative arrived in Williamstown in time to make an appearance in the concert of Sunday, July 23. "It is a beautiful little instrument," Noah wrote Martin, "and we are very pleased with the sound." It also aroused some curiosity. "Many people in the audience came back stage after the performance to see the instrument and ask questions about it."[30]

Smoldon's trumpet fanfares, according to Joel Newman, raised the thought in Noah's mind that trumpet music of some sort would be appropriate for the opening of *Daniel*. This prompted a search on Joel's part for a suitable buisine, or straight trumpet, and one of Noah's Williamstown friends thought he knew where one could be found. It was found, in fact, propped up in a corner of the office of the redoubtable S. Lane Faison, at fifty a star professor of art history at Williams College and since 1948 director of the college's Museum of Art. The trumpet belonged to a lady who had left it on permanent loan to the Williams museum. Would Faison countenance a loan from the Museum to Pro Musica? Ralph Renzi, the Williams information director, helped gain Faison's consent. The trumpet, after all, was a precious artifact, the oldest of its kind in the United States.

Noah's instrumentation for *Daniel* also called for other rare instruments, a vielle, two minstrel's harps, a psaltery and a bell carillon. The provenance of the vielle and the minstrel's harps is unknown. The psaltery was ordered from the Dolmetsch Workshops in England. The bell carillon came from much closer to home. In the spring of 1957, the music teacher at The Brearley School, one of New York's best and most exclusive private girls' schools, had invited Bernie Krainis to come to the school to teach a recorder class. Bernie was intrigued to notice in the music room a set of Whitechapel handbells. Handbell-ringing, a Brearley tradition, is an exercise in which each participant holds one or two bells and must be alert to

[29]Josef Martin-Noah Greenberg, letter, May 18, 1957. NYPM Archives, Box 21, folder 12.
[30]Noah Greenberg-Joseph Martin, letter, July 23, 1957. NYPM Archives, Box 21, folder 12.

ring—a gentle shake is all that's needed—each time a tune calls for the bell's particular note. The bells can also be hung in a wooden frame and tapped lightly with a padded stick. When Noah wanted a "chime of bells" for *Daniel*, Bernie knew where to borrow one.

In creating the instrumentation, Noah was guided by more than a simple desire to replace Smoldon's twentieth-century trumpets with suitably medieval instruments. He wanted to justify his belief that the use of instruments in a church, questioned by many musicologists (including, at times, Smoldon himself) was appropriate. He found support for the practice in the writings of music scholar Edmond A. Bowles, and probably also in discussions with Meyer Schapiro, who would have pointed out with Bowles that medieval iconography, and church sculpture in particular, abounds in imagery of musicians playing instruments of the types Noah was using. Besides, the frequent ecclesiastical inveighing against the practice as sinful and corrupt may simply have meant that a great deal of instrument-playing was going on in medieval churches.

One other factor shaped Noah's instrumentation. As a later reviewer wrote,

> It was an imaginative idea to associate different characters [in *Daniel*] with some of the percussion instruments: the queen with finger cymbals, Daniel with small cymbals, the envious counsellors with sleigh bells, and so on.[31]

For Noah, the spring and summer of 1957 were a whirlwind. A "Y" concert in April was followed by a recording session. In London for a week in June, Noah was back in the U. S. in July and in residence with Pro Musica in Williamstown preparing new programs —when he was not racing down to Stratford, Connecticut to lead the ensemble in a second season at the Shakespeare Festival or in New York with Toni and Anne with "the house in a mess and everything . . . just too complicated"[32] and up to his ears in *Daniel*. There were ominous signs that the pace was too exhausting even for Noah. One was a sudden ferocious outburst of temper. Pro Musica was living and rehearsing at 123 East Main Street, another large and elaborate Williamstown mansion. As was his wont, Noah had set forth a set of rules for proper behavior, one of them being "No Ball Playing" on the grounds. Noah's pal Julius Goldstein was up for the weekend, and when Julius absent-mindedly committed the sin of

[31]"Thirteenth-Century Proto-Opera," *Times Literary Supplement*, February 5, 1960, p. 76.
[32]Noah Greenberg-Rembert Weakland, letter, July 23, 1957.

tossing a ball to someone, Noah lashed out at him with a vengeance. Bernie listened, appalled, as Noah "ate Julius up one side and down the other, yelling and screaming." Nobody, Bernie thought, and certainly not the mild-mannered Julius, deserved treatment like that. The episode made Bernie wonder about what was happening to Noah. Later, he commented that "Noah really lost it that summer."[33]

---

[33] Bernard Krainis, August 13, 1998.

CHAPTER TWENTY-THREE

ᴀN 11TH-CENTURY "SMASH HIT"

(1958)

$\mathcal{B}$y the beginning of September (1957), Noah had in hand a score of *Daniel* with the various sections transposed into the keys in which they would be sung. He had had this put on Multigraph master sheets—plain-paper copiers were far in the future—so that he could run off as many sets as he needed. This meant that the singers could begin practicing. To meet his casting needs, Noah had hired four additional male singers, Jerold Sien, Alan Baker, Alva Tripp, and Gordon Myers. One, Gordon Myers, would eventually join Pro Musica on a permanent basis. It also meant that Noah could start Stuart Gardiner on his part of the production. Gardiner was music director of the Church of the Transfiguration ("The Little Church Around the Corner") at 29th Street and Fifth Avenue. He had agreed to lend Noah seven of his boy choristers and to teach them the *Daniel* music and how to sing it.

Only Noah's copy of the score had the instrumentation indicated, because, as he told Rembert Weakland, "there will be much experimenting before the performance."[1]

On October 1, Noah convened a meeting of Pro Musica's board of directors at 865 West End Avenue. This was a very different board from that which had met at Perry Street in April 1953. As the list of attendees reveals, it was coming to be a very different Pro Musica as well. Noah, of course, was there. So was Toni, and so was attorney Mike Pincus. Arthur Squires, who had joined the board as president in February 1954, was also present. Jesse Simons had long since resigned, and Bernie Krainis, though officially still a board member,

---

[1] Noah Greenberg-Rembert Weakland, letter, September 2, 1997.

was absent. But four newer board members were at the meeting.[2] Their credentials tell the tale of growth and change.

One of the newcomers was Arthur Squires's friend Beatrice Farwell, daughter of the composer Arthur Farwell and a member of the Education Department of the Metropolitan Museum of Art. A second was Thomas Colby, III, a wealthy friend of Noah's. Noah had talked Colby into heading a special committee to raise funds for Pro Musica instrument purchases. Another moneyed friend of Noah's, Marcus Rottenberg, was the third new member. The fourth, who chaired the meeting, was Richard F. French. Dick French, several years older than Noah, was a Harvard graduate with a doctorate in musicology. In 1952, as his non-tenured Harvard teaching appointment was drawing to an end, he found himself by happenstance lunching with Tillman Merritt, head of the Music Department, and Merritt's friend Paul Hindemith, composer and head of the Yale School of Music. Hindemith expressed dissatisfaction with his American publisher, Associated Music Publishers. A.M.P., a subsidiary of Broadcast Music, was the U. S. distributor for many major European music houses and was publisher in its own right of foreign works in editions by American editors. Things were not as they should be at A.M.P., Hindemith observed. Perhaps if Dick were on the staff, the situation would improve.

Armed with a letter of recommendation from Hindemith, Dick landed a job with A.M.P. In the fall of 1952, after a pleasant summer at the University of Indiana, he arrived in New York, found himself an apartment and went to work. "I was paid," he said happily, "to go to concerts."[3] And to offer publication contracts to composers and arrangers for promising works.

During the spring of 1954, Noah approached Dick with a handful of arrangements, probably of English madrigals. Dick looked them over and agreed that they were publishable. Further, he sensed the market potential in a series of arrangements of early-music vocal works suitable for performance by amateurs as well as professionals. Over the years, some 50 of these appeared under the New York Pro Music Editions label.

Some of the arrangements Noah made himself, some were made by Joel Newman, and some, Noah parcelled out to various Pro Musi-

---

[2] The minutes of the meeting or meetings at which they were elected are missing from the Pro Musica Archives, so the times at which they joined the board cannot be dated.

[3] Richard F. French, September 24, 1998.

ca members. The fees and royalties were modest, but the A.M.P. editions helped spread the word about Pro Musica among amateur singers and the growing ranks of recorder players.

"The way I got on the board," Dick said, "was a conspiracy between Noah and Arthur Squires. They would invite me to join, whereupon Arthur would immediately resign as president and I would be drafted."[4] Dick's memory of the sequence of events is not quite correct. Arthur actually stayed on as Pro Musica's president for nearly two years before Dick succeeded him. But it is certainly true that Arthur Squires, skilled in mathematics, was graphing what Pro Musica's continuing success would mean to him.

> I discovered that if you make a log[arithmic] plot of the number of concerts versus the number of years, I think that in 1953 we might have had four, the growth curve was exponential. . . . What happened was, toward the end of the 56-57 [season], I knew that 57-58 was my last year, because the projection from 14 concerts in 56-57 was going to be 45 concerts [in 1957-58], and I knew the *Play of Daniel* was in it and there was no way I could do 70 [in 58-59]— not and keep a nine-to-five job as an engineer.[5]

It is equally true that the idea behind electing Dick French to the board was to try to free Noah, even before Arthur left, from the impossible burden of managing a successful arts organization and at the same time being the creative impulse behind its success. Dick French's knowledge of the music business, academic connections, calm efficiency, and whimsical sense of humor were strong marks in his favor. For his part, Dick liked Noah, loved early music and felt he would enjoy the challenge of helping to put Pro Musica's business affairs in order.

From this period on, "Noah's hat" stopped being Pro Musica's office address. The real office files began to fill up with the paperwork attendent upon success. The little organization became a party to sheaves of contracts, with singers,[6] instrument-makers, theater people (for *Daniel* and its successors), record companies, and presenters. A river of correspondence began to flow, covering everything under the sun from musicological detail to what women sing-

---

[4] Richard F. French, September 24, 1998.

[5] Arthur M. Squires, December 5, 1997.

[6] Pro Musica's singers and instrumentalists all belonged, first of all, to Local 802, American Federation of Musicians, and Pro Musica contracted with the union for their services. Because *The Play of Daniel* was a work for musical theater, the singers also had to join the American Guild of Musical Artists, and separate contracts for them had to be concluded with AGMA.

ers who left Pro Musica should pay if they wanted to buy their concert dresses. Lecture invitations came in almost weekly, to be accepted or turned down. Tax and accounting forms proliferated. Pro Musica began to buy insurance and, as instruments were lost or damaged, to file insurance claims. An attempt was made to assemble scrapbooks of reviews. There is a whole separate river of correspondence about money—begging letters, grant proposals, last-ditch pleas, formal acceptance letters, thank-you letters.

Toni Greenberg could and did cope with some of this flood of paperwork. Later, as treasurer, she would write the checks, look after cash flow, and badger Pro Musica's artists about travel and rehearsal schedules. But Dick French knew the outside territory better, knew the people whose egos needed to be soothed and those who needed a nip at the heels to move them along. And Dick knew money. Better than Toni, Dick could deal with debtors and creditors and donors and foundation executives. Above all, he could try to interpose himself—when Noah would let him— between Noah and the scores of people who absolutely, positively had to speak with, meet with, deal with Noah Greenberg.

There was particular need for a Dick French to take on such duties in the fall of 1957. *Daniel,* for one thing, was soaking up virtually every minute of Noah's time. As Noah wrote to Weakland in early November, "this project has been swallowing me whole."[7] Other Pro Musica appearances, like the "Y" concert of November 9, were receiving too little of his attention.

Even more important, at least as far back as mid-1955 Noah had concluded that to hold together financially and artistically, Pro Musica had to begin to tour extensively. Possibly at the suggestion of Pro Musica's then booking agent, Ronald Wilford, Noah had gone to the dominant firm in the business, Columbia Artists Management, Inc., for "advice" on setting up a touring program. On May 11, 1955, Schuyler Chapin, who would one day be general manager of the Metropolitan Opera, but who was then a lowly CAMI artists' representative, wrote Noah outlining the costs and possible returns. (One of the heaviest costs would be the salary and expenses of a road manager to accompany the ensemble, look after the instruments and music, work with presenters on publicity and ticket sales, and see to stage arrangements.) Chapin's advice: have money in the bank to offset the heavy initial expenses. One of the wish-list items in Arthur

---

[7] Noah Greenberg-Rembert Weakland, letter, November 8, 1957.

Squires's May 30 Rockefeller Foundation proposal was a fund to help meet the cost of putting Pro Musica on the road.

Pro Musica had in fact gone on the road briefly in January 1957, prompting the first of dozens of newsy, wistful letters that Toni and Noah wrote to each other when Noah was on tour. In this one, Toni wrote:

> It was absolutely brilliant of you to call—I wanted to hear your voice so badly. Only trouble, it was over so fast and now it's still four days to go. . . .
>
> One good thing about this separation is that I'm <u>almost</u> caught up with all the NYPMA detail work. <u>And</u> with the New Yorker though tomorrow being Thursday I doubt if I'll stay ahead very long.[8]

But the "NYPMA detail" was mounting up faster than Toni, with a small daughter to raise and other family obligations, could handle it. If Pro Musica were to embark on extensive tours, and these were in the planning stages, Noah would be away from the office and hard to reach for weeks on end, and unable to deal with any but the most important phone calls, letters, requests, and policy matters. Although Dick French himself could only devote part of his time to Pro Musica affairs, his presence and earnestness would be a godsend.

Another issue was preoccupying Noah as the preparations for *Daniel* gained momentum. This one was Pro Musica's recording arrangements. However amiably he and Goddard Lieberson got along in person, Noah was far from amiable about the quality of Columbia's Pro Musica recordings. The first one, of Elizabethan verse and its music, had been by far the poorest. There were glaring differences in sound level and quality between Auden's recitations and Pro Musica's performances. According to Joel Newman, who was there, the Columbia producer and sound engineer, in an effort to achieve balance, made Pro Musica set up at the far end of the studio, distant from the microphones. When Noah raised an objection, he was told in no uncertain terms to do it Columbia's way. The result was that Auden's voice came over harsh and loud, while Pro Musica's playing and singing was blurry and soft. The second and third recordings for Columbia, the Monteverdi and Salamone Rossi disks, were of better sound quality, but the treatment Pro Musica received in the studio left Noah seething. Nor was his temper improved when he saw the Rossi record jacket. The designer had used

---

[8] Toni Greenberg-Noah Greenberg, letter, January 10, 1957.

four pages of the seventeenth-century edition of *The Songs of Solomon* as cover illustration. So far, so good; but he had placed them in such a way as to make the chief element of the design a cross—not the ideal image for a recording of Jewish liturgical music.

Then, even though Vera Zorina was married to the president of the company, Columbia had displayed no interest in recording the Ronsard program for which Zorina had spoken the poetry. Noah began looking for another record company. He tried Westminster and Angel, to no avail. But in the fall of 1956, Noah's luck had once again asserted itself. Israel Horowitz, whom Noah had known since both were schoolboys, had left his job as a reporter covering the record industry for *Billboard* magazine and had joined Decca Records as Director of Classical A&R (Artist and Repertoire). Decca's classical department, Horowitz says, "did some very good things, but it was not a *big* operation." (Its budget was miniscule and its only major star, apart from the Trapp Family Singers, was the guitarist Andrés Segovia.) Horowitz himself had no record production experience. "I had been in a recording studio only twice, as a visitor." But he had studied violin, classical music was his passion, and "I guess I was a fast learner."

Horowitz lost no time in approaching Noah.

> I got [to Decca] the latter part of 1956, and . . . our first contract was in March of 1957. The first record we made [with Pro Musica] was a Christmas album. We weren't even stereo then, it was a mono album.[9]

The album, "Music of the Medieval Court and Countryside for the Christmas season," recorded in April 1957, was also something of a first for Decca. Mort Nassiter, "an art director but more than an art director," was the person responsible for the design and packaging of Decca's classical albums. Horowitz quickly gained his support.

> I said, We've got to do something special, something that will accomodate the extra annotation that [this music] deserves. Mort was also an enthusiast, and it wouldn't have happened without him.[10]

Instead of relying on a simple sleeve, the two created an album in the form of a lavishly illustrated folder with a colorful front cover. Inside, a four-page insert listed the performers and the program and

[9] Israel Horowitz, April 15, 1997.
[10] Israel Horowitz, April 15, 1997.

supplied detailed program notes written by Noah's friend Saul Novack, professor of music at Queens College.

But this album, ambitious as it was—it sold very well—was by no means all that Horowitz had in mind.

> I knew that [Noah] was then working on *The Play of Daniel*. I had wind of it, I knew about it, because I knew what was happening.

Horowitz was, as he put it, "interested in *The Play of Daniel* at that time," but Noah was cautious. His experience with Columbia had been chastening.

> He wouldn't commit. 'Let's see what happens with [the "Court and Countryside" album]. . . . I think he had faith [that] I [wasn't] trying to pull wool over his eyes, get him, use him or exploit him, but he wanted to see what Decca would do.

Horowitz negotiated "an option of sorts, to be decided,"[11] on Pro Musica's next recording, which Is hoped would turn out to be *Daniel*.

On Sunday, November 3 (1957), Noah held the first read-through of *Daniel*. Aside from a few minor changes, he pronounced himself "very pleased with the results."[12] The "Y" concert on November 9 temporarily interrupted the *Daniel* preparations, but Noah was able to schedule several rehearsals in November. The first full-scale run-through, of two hours, took place at The Cloisters on December 1. The singers rehearsed at The Cloisters two weeks later. There was a two-week timeout, as Pro Musica's members scattered for the holidays and for out-of-town musicmaking. (On December 27, for example, Martha Blackman led her five-person Viol Study Group, later named the Pro Musica Viol Consort, in a program of English viol music in New Haven at Yale's Woolsey Hall.)

Noah's frantic schedule was not allowed to cut short the Greenbergs' holiday entertaining for the family. This year as every year, the Christmas tree Toni and Noah installed in one corner of the living-room outraged Noah's Aunt Dora, who made no bones about her feelings. "It was the greatest conversation," his cousin Rema said.

He would start in, 'Dora. It has nothing to do with that [the birth of Jesus and Christianity] It's a pagan —'

'Paygan, shmaygan, it's a Christmas tree!'

Rema was quite sure that Toni and Noah had no desire to slight, much less deny, their Jewishness.

[11] Israel Horowitz, April 15, 1997.
[12] Noah Greenberg-Rembert Weakland, letter, November 8, 1957.

It was because of the symbolic nature, of the green in the middle of the winter, all of that. But it was *Christian* symbolism, and my mother thought it was terribly disrespectful.

On Saturday and Sunday, December 28 and 29,[13] Pro Musica rehearsed *Daniel* for a total of nine hours at the Church of the Transfiguration. Needless to say, not everything went smoothly. At one rehearsal, nobody remembered to bring a full score. After the first of the seven episodes, Nikos Psacharopoulos, the director, looked blankly around and said, "What comes next?" prompting a certain amount of undisciplined laughter.[14]

The Cloisters, closed to the public on Mondays, became available on Monday, December 30, for final rehearsals and, starting at two in the afternoon, the dress rehearsal. Then, on the bright afternoon of January 2 (1958), came the premiere performance, the first of seven at The Cloisters.

The impact of *Daniel* on New York's normally hard-bitten critics was remarkable. The music critic Edward Downes, reviewing the drama for *The New York Times* on January 3, called the production "superb . . . a rare conspiracy of imagination, scholarship and showmanship. . . . The story alone is moving . . . The music, which combines Gregorian chant, Gothic conductus [processional music] and echoes of folk dance and song, contributes immeasurably to heighten the emotional tone." The costumes, Downes went on, "were obviously a labor of love in their rich execution as well as the dramatic flair for color and the sense of style that unified the whole ensemble."

As for audience approval, Downes felt it necessary to remind *Times* readers that "[a]ll performances are sold out and there were voices in the audience yesterday pleading . . . for an extension of this year's run."[15] The plea was answered, at least in part. The Cloisters, as part of the Metropolitan Museum of Art, could not be closed to visitors indefinitely. But the Met's telephones, and Pro Musica's, were ringing off the hook. It seemed that everybody in New York wanted tickets.

Noah, always concerned about Pro Musica's own following, was especially disturbed at the situation. On January 4, Pro Musica sent out an embarrassed but exultant card to its loyalists:

---

[13] Rema Sessler, March 1, 1997.

[14] Joel Newman, April 16, 1997.

[15] E[dward] D[ownes], "Medieval Drama Sung at Cloisters," *The New York Times*, Friday, January 3, 1958, p. 15:3.

The Metropolitan Museum of Art

The Cloisters

THE PLAY
OF DANIEL

A TWELFTH CENTURY MUSICAL DRAMA

ON THE AFTERNOONS OF JANUARY 2, 3, 4, & 6

1958

The New York Pro Musica

NOAH GREENBERG, DIRECTOR

The "smash hit's" unassuming program
(Courtesy of The New York Public Library [Astor, Lenox, and Tilden Foundations])

A key moment in The Play of Daniel
(Courtesy of The New York Public Library [Astor, Lenox, and Tilden Foundations])

The New York Pro Musica deeply regrets that no tickets were available to the general public for *The Play of Daniel* at The Cloisters this week. Performances of *Daniel* were engaged by the Metropolitan Museum of Art, which first offered tickets to its own members expecting to make those remaining available to the general public. Actually all performances were sold out within days after the Museum membership was notified.[16]

Pro Musica made hasty arrangements for a series of additional performances at the Riverside Church, at 122nd Street and Riverside Drive. In its vast nave, Riverside could seat 2,500, but more than 9,000 requests for tickets came in for the first performance at Riverside, scheduled for January 19. The church's Committee on Religious Drama had to schedule two additional performances for January 26. Even so, hundreds who would have paid any price to see and hear *Daniel* were denied the opportunity. They would have to wait at least a year.

Brooks Atkinson thought the wait would be worth it. Indeed, the *New York Times's* first-string drama critic, had fallen under the same spell that had enchanted the rapt crowd at The Cloisters that wintry afternoon. On January 26, Atkinson wrote: "Everything about this

[16] Announcement card, January 4, 1958. NYPM Archives, Box 50, folder 9.

hour-long invocation to glory has been done with reverence, grace and the craftsmanlike skills of medieval art. . . . Nothing so fine as this has been done in New York in recent memory."[17]

The aftermath of *Daniel* was not without its comic moments. One, came when Noah opened Lincoln Kirstein's letter of March 9 (1958):

> If we do [*Daniel*] again, we should have some more small boys and various improvements, including the lion masks remade. . . .

Kirstein enclosed a check for Nikos Psachoropoulos, but added, "if he expects to get 100 dollars for every performance of the play, he is mad." Then he came to the nub of the matter:

> The costumes, designs, manufacture, properties and furniture came to $26,576.83, and as a matter of academic interest, and I will be paying for them at the rate of $3,000 a quarter-year for ever as far as I can see: not that I grudge it, but when you figure costs, don't forget this item, too.

He signed himself grumpily, "As usual, Lincoln."[18]

Then there was Carl Miller's prideful letter to the *Yale Alumni Magazine.* Carl, a close friend of Dick French, was a 1948 graduate of the Yale School of Music and president of the school's alumni association. He wrote:

> By a slight juggling of statistics, it can be said that out of 29 singers, instrumentalists, actors and directors concerned [in *Daniel*], 16 came under the direct influence of either the School of Music or the School of Drama. . . .

Carl proceeded to enumerate all of the Yale folk involved, from Robert Montesi, Mus. B. '54, who played the buisine, to Converse M. Converse and Rex Robbins, both of the Yale College class of 1957, who played the all-important roles of Daniel's two lions.[19]

More serious, on the evening of January 6, after the four o'clock performance, Margaret Freeman of The Cloisters wrote one of the most touching tributes to Noah of the many that he received.

> Our Romanesque Hall looks awfully empty today, and the whole place seems terribly quiet. And what is strange is that I am not at all sure that I like it that way!

[17] Brooks Atkinson, "Daniel a Hit," *The New York Times*, Sunday, January 26, 1958, Section 2, p. X1:2

[18] Lincoln Kirstein-Noah Greenberg, letter, March 9, 1958. NYPM Archives, Box 2, folder 6.

[19] Carl S. Miller, letter to the editors of *The Yale Alumni Journal*, NYPM Archives, Box 51, Folder 1. The letter appeared in the April 1958 issue.

It was, as you well know, a wonderful production and I am proud to have been a small part of it. I do hope that the performance at Riverside Church goes off equally well, and that the audience leaves with delight and wonder on their faces — as they did here — and that at least one old lady will say: 'I am glad that I have lived long enough to see this.'[20]

On January, Noah wrote to William Smoldon:

I must again tell you how sorry I am that we did not work with your version, but frankly, we all felt it comes off much better in the original tongue. Auden wrote a magnificent piece —very simply, very moving, sermon-like.[21]

Smoldon sent Noah congratulations and wrote again on January 16 to ask, with characteristic diffidence, if he should withdraw his *Daniel* text from publication by the Plainsong and Medieval Music Society. Noah encouraged him not to do so: his *Daniel* appeared in 1960.

In March 1958, Israel Horowitz finally persuaded Noah to allow Decca to record *Daniel*. In October of that year, Noah sent Smoldon a copy of the just-released recording. Smoldon wrote to thank him, and added:

Already it seems to me that the problem of accompaniment has been met most brilliantly, the singing beautiful and tasteful and the whole beautifully reproduced. . . . I am glad to think that I had something to do with setting you to the task which has ended with this magnificent result.[22]

It was a selfless and touching comment from the man who started the whole project. It was not, however, Smoldon's final word. That would come more than twenty years later, fourteen years after Noah's death.

[20] Margaret Freeman-Noah Greenberg, letter, January 6, 1958. NYPM Archives, Box 50, folder ix.

[21] Noah Greenberg-William Smoldon, letter, January 8, 1958. NYPM Archives, Box 4, folder 6.

[22] William Smoldon-Noah Greenberg, letter, October 24, 1958. NYPM Archives, Box 4, folder 6.

CHAPTER TWENTY-FOUR

℧HINKING BIG

(1958)

On February 19, 1864, one Justus Henry Rathbone met with a few friends in Washington, D. C. and founded The Knights of Pythias. A fraternal organization dedicated like so many others to "friendship and the love of peace," the Pythians in their heyday in the 1920s numbered over a million nationwide. Many local chapters put up elaborate halls or "temples" to handle swelling future memberships. But the increases never materialized and, indeed, after World War II membership began to decline: the Pythians in 1998 had a membership of less than 200,000. In city after city, the grand temples themselves were sold or leased to whoever might have need of elaborate facilities with high ceilings and expansive floor space.

The Knights built their temple in New York City in the 1920s, a massive structure at 135 West Seventieth Street, between Columbus Avenue and Broadway. By 1950, the Pythian Temple was much too much clubroom for the chapter, and the officers were leasing the facilities to outsiders—including Decca Records.[1]

Israel Horowitz explained:

> "They had a ballroom." They called it a ballroom, [but] it was a theater type of thing without fixed seats. Wood. With a balcony and a stage, a lot of space. And Decca had an exclusive on the use of this as a recording studio and we had our equipment there permanently in a small room.

Entertainment companies other than Decca used the Pythian ballroom. The pioneering TV show "Rock Around the Clock" origi-

---

[1]The Pythian Temple is now (2000) "The Pythian," an expensive condominium development.

nated there. But the ballroom was ideal for certain types of classical recordings.

> [I]t was problematic [except] for relatively small forces, in terms of an orchestra maybe forty-five or fifty pieces. . . . The best Segovia recordings were made there.

Over Christmas, Noah had made up his mind to trust Decca. That left it up to Horowitz to persuade his executive vice president, whose background in classical music was skimpy and whose knowledge of medieval liturgical drama was, in Horowitz's word "zilch," that an expensively-packaged recording of an hour-long medieval liturgical drama would be just the right thing for the forthcoming Christmas season, ten months away.

> Anyway, I told him, we even worked out a budget. . . . So he asked me how much it's going to cost. It'll cost four thousand dollars. Ah! That was the whole *Play of Daniel*. Talent cost, what we paid out, whatever the deal was or the minimum down payment or advance for royalties.And he said, 'How many is it going to sell?' And I said, without any experience, "Oh, the first year, I think we'll do five thousand.'

Horowitz's boss made a point of noting the forecast in his reminder file. But he okayed the project.[2] So on Wednesday, January 29, 1958 and on the following Friday and Tuesday, the cavernous, dusty Pythian ballroom became the scene of Decca's taping sessions of *The Play of Daniel*.

Well beforehand, it was clear that Noah had bet on a winner. What had begun as an exercise in theatrical esoterica, to be given before a select audience in a private home, had become a "smash hit": the term is Noah's own[3]. Furthermore, Daniel clearly had what theater people refer to as "legs": i.e., durable popularity. There was every reason to suppose it would become a fixture of the New York Christmas season, like Lionel Barrymore's Scrooge in the radio version of *A Christmas Carol*, or like *The Nutcracker* ballet half a generation later. Daniel, in a word, would be a classic. It would also be a moneymaker, a production that would be an assured source of income for years to come. Noah the impresario was delighted. So also was Noah the expansionist visionary. The success of *Daniel* meant that Pro Musica would have to broaden its reach. In addition to being a concert ensemble, it would have to become, at least for a time each year, a theatrical company. Costumes, props, stagecraft, and acting would

[2]Israel Horowitz, April 15, 1997.
[3]Noah Greenberg-Rembert Weakland, letter, January 23, 1958.

have to become part of the group's stock in trade. But what of that? Noah's grand plan for Pro Musica already called for a set of separate but overlapping organizations engaged in teaching, research, and publishing as well as musical performance. One of these, Martha Blackman's Viol Study Group, was already in being. Others would take shape during 1958 and 1959. *Daniel* would fit in smoothly with this up-to-date version of what Bernie Krainis, with mingled admiration and disdain, called "Noah Greenberg Enterprises."

Still, *Daniel* was not allowed to dominate everything. Eight days before recording began, Pro Musica was in Washington giving a concert at Dumbarton Oaks. Four days after the final recording date, Noah was directing an Italian Renaissance program at the "Y." And on Friday, February 14, Pro Musica made its Boston debut before a capacity audience at Jordan Hall. The program was headlined as "medieval" but was in fact a sampler of English, French, and Italian Renaissance works borrowed from other programs. It was repeated on March 10 at an outdoor concert at Vizcaya in Miami. The warm damp weather made an ordeal out of tuning the viols and the harpsichord, but the *Miami Herald*'s music critic was more than happy to overlook the difficulties, calling the group's work "meticulous, inspired, completely tasteful, of the highest artistic quality."[4]

Back in New York at the end of March, Noah convened a board meeting for April 13. Its main purpose was to discuss compensation. There had been rumblings from the artists about money in 1957, when the first installment of the Rockefeller grant, $18,000, had come in and had promptly been spent on setting up the 865 West End Avenue office. Certainly the office was important, Bernie and others agreed. But Pro Musica had been set up as a kind of cooperative—or so people dimly remembered—with the idea that the profits from its activities would be split more or less evenly among the participants. Wasn't there a way that some of the Rockefeller money at least could wind up in the hands of the people who had put Pro Musica on the map? And what was Noah himself making out of the Rockefeller grant?

Arthur Squires and Dick French both remember instances in which they tried to explain the difference between money earned from concert fees and recordings and money contributed to a tax-exempt organization for organizational purposes.[5] Everybody would nod that,

[4]Doris Reno, "Gifted Performers Play in Open," *The Miami Herald*, Tuesday, March 11, 1958, p. 7-B.
[5]Arthur M. Squires, December 5, 1997; Richard F. French, September 24, 1998.

yes, the organization did have needs of its own and that meeting these would make everybody's life easier. But carpeting and drapes were hardly essentials of musical life, and especially after *Daniel*, wasn't there a lot of money sloshing around . . ?

At the April 13 meeting, the board approved a payment plan that Noah and everybody else hoped would quiet the murmurings. Arthur, still president and still of course active as singer and viol player, was given the job of presenting the plan and also explaining Pro Musica's finances to his fellow artists. He did this in a memo dated June 21, 1958 and addressed "To Artist Members of Pro Musica":

> This note will give you an approximate advance accounting of the money you will earn during the 1958-59 concert season . . . This is the first year it has been possible to give such a reasonably accurate advance accounting.

Each artist would be paid $50 per straight concert engagement, $60 per concert on which Pro Musica paid no manager's commission—this covered engagements at the "Y" and The Cloisters—and $25 per seminar in connection with a concert.[6] In addition, during tours artists would be paid $20 a day for days of travel between concerts or other open days. As for Noah, "Conductor's fee is double, except that in case of per diem allowance, where conductor's per diem is same as artists'."

Arthur (using input from Noah, Toni, and Dick French) estimated that during the 1958-59 season Pro Musica would be giving thirty-six regular concerts, six concerts at the "Y" and The Cloisters and three seminars, and that there would be fifteen open days. On this basis, each artist would earn a total of $2,535. "These figures," the memo quickly added, "do not include probable *Daniel* performances, for which every effort will be made to establish higher fees." Nor did they include rehearsal fees and record royalties. Including the latter, earnings per artist would be about $3,000, or roughly—very roughly—$20,000 in current (2000) dollars. Years later, Arthur was at pains to point out that "one of the remarkable aspects of Pro Musica [was that] we never paid less than union scale."[7]

Arthur next edged onto more dangerous ground, giving estimates of Pro Musica's income and expenses for the 1958-59 season just begun. From its forty-two engagements, Pro Musica would earn

---

[6]Noah was thinking in terms of engagements that combined teaching sessions or workshops with concerts.

[7]Arthur M. Squires, December 5, 1997.

$41,950, or almost exactly $1,000 per engagement. Artists' fees (Noah's included) would absorb $30,100; travel would cost $6,500; harpsichord cartage, $750; and publicity and manager's expenses, $3,000. This left a surplus of only $1,600 for the organization.[8]

Finally, Arthur wrote, "You may be interested in a consolidated accounting of concert income since Pro Musica began." This covered the period from April 1953 (the date of the New School concert) to the end of the 1957-58 fiscal year. It showed that Pro Musica had net earnings from concerts (after payment of manager's fees) of $55,005.

It had paid out $41,593.50 in fees to its artists, $9,088.89 to cover travel costs, $1,315.27 for harpsichord cartage and $2,419.94 for publicity and manager's expenses. Total expenses were thus $54,417.60. This left a five-year surplus "spent on organization expenses" of $587.40.

Who, reading these figures, could say that Pro Musica was a wicked capitalist employer, wringing profits from the sweat of its workers?

No one did say that, but the murmurings continued. Some members felt that their livelihood was at stake and that Arthur, whose earnings from his job in chemistry were substantial, couldn't see that $50 a concert wasn't much of an income. Besides, Arthur's accounting made no mention of the sums received from the Rockefeller Foundation and other contributors. Most of that money was spent on books and music for the library and on developing the instrument collection, but the absence of an explanation fed suspicions that Noah was putting some of it in his own pocket.

Also, the very existence of the pay plan was a sign of how far Pro Musica had retreated from being a gathering of partners toward being an organization with a boss and employees. Newer members like Paul Ehrlich were less annoyed by the shift than those who, like Russell and Bernie, had been present at the creation and who felt themselves more or less coequal with Noah. Russell in particular had steadily been receiving invitations to perform as a soloist. As early as 1955, he had turned down William Kolodney of the "Y," who offered him a solo concert.

[Kolodney] said, 'What about doing some folk music?' I said, 'I love folk music, but I don't know any. I'd have to find an accom-

[8]Memorandum, "To Artist Members of Pro Musica," June 21, 1958. NYPM Archives, Box 4, folder 7. Pro Musica's fiscal year ran from June 1 through the May 31 of the following year.

panist and start looking through material, and I'm very particular about what I sing. It would be quite a project.'

Noah heard about this—I wasn't keeping it a secret—and he didn't like it. I was his singer, which is what he wanted.[9]

Audiences, Kolodney felt, wanted to hear more Oberlin. So he suggested that Noah add lute songs to Pro Musica's Elizabethan programs. Noah agreed, and two of John Dowland's most exquisite songs, "Flow My Tears" and "In Darkness Let Me Dwell," became featured solos for Russell.

But in 1958, Russell was far from feeling that he had to be "Noah's singer" alone. The winter before, he had sung the tenor solos in Fritz Reiner's Chicago presentation of Handel's *Messiah*. Now, as a free agent, he signed a contract with Beverly Merrill. A wealthy Greenwich Villageite, Miss Merrill wanted to use her money to make a lasting contribution to the arts. At the suggestion of music historian Savile Clark, she decided to devote herself to the recording of rare early music. Noah, who had known her as a neighbor on Perry Street, tried mightily to persuade her to operate under the auspices of Pro Musica, but Miss Merrill resisted his blandishments and set up entirely on her own. Russell's contract called for him to record thirteen Dowland songs for her Expériences Anonymes label. Jerry Newman of Esoteric Records was the sound engineer. Russell's accompanist was Joseph Iadone, who had gone from being one of the greatest of jazz bassists to becoming a master—indeed, in the 1950s the only American master—of the lute. Noah did not think well of this arrangement, but he could do nothing to prevent it.

Bernie too was growing more restless. Nowhere in the pay plan was there anything extra for him as "associate director." Parading around The Cloisters and up and down church aisles in *Daniel* costume was a very different thing than appearing on a concert stage in white tie and tails.

Belonging to Pro Musica was a mark of distinction, a source of steady work and the best possible platform for a recorder-player who wanted to teach as well as perform. Bernie was reluctant to leave, but he was unhappier than ever with Noah's leadership style and not at all pleased about Noah's schemes to branch out in multiple directions.

Arthur Squires himself was concerned, albeit for very different reasons. As dearly as he loved singing, Noah, and Pro Musica, Arthur

[9]Russell Oberlin, January 28, 1997.

had concluded that the future Noah was mapping out for the ensemble was not a future in which he, Arthur, could wholeheartedly take part. Arthur's interest in large-scale industrial chemistry went far beyond the day-job level, and it was in this field that he was determined to make his career. Sooner than he had anticipated, during the very same spring weeks in which he was writing the memo about pay, Arthur let Noah know that he could no longer stay on as a full-time member of Pro Musica.

There was no need, however, for Noah to start shopping for a new male singer. Arthur's replacement was already at hand. In fact, he was an old friend of both men. Gordon Myers, born in 1918 and raised on an Iowa farm, had graduated from Cornell College in his home state in 1941.

Gordon, a baritone whose range allowed him to sing tenor and bass parts, sang his first solo in the fourth grade and began studying singing seriously "as soon as my voice cracked." He came to New York in 1941 to audition for and win a Juilliard Fellowship in voice. In the Army for four years, Gordon made a hit singing Frank Loesser's war song "The Ballad of Rodger Young." On his release in 1946, he came back to New York, The Juilliard, and the Martha Dodd Singers, subsisting for nine months on the ninety-three dollars a week he had earned by singing an advertising jingle. There followed many jobs in singing, choral conducting and radio announcing. In 1952, Gordon's wife, the soprano Harriet Hill, began singing with the Randolph Singers. David Randolph often turned to Gordon when he needed a baritone soloist, and through the Randolph Singers Harriet Hill and Gordon met Arthur Squires.

At Cornell College, Gordon had studied with Francis German, a Juilliard graduate and an outstanding voice teacher. Shortly after Gordon's postwar return to New York, German too came east and opened a New York studio. Gordon continued to work with German and Arthur began to study with him as well. When Arthur joined Pro Musica, he introduced everybody to everybody else. In July 1957, Noah invited Gordon to sing the baritone part in Thomas Tallis's Mass for Four Voices, which Pro Musica was performing at Stratford on August 19. Gordon accepted, even though it meant interrupting a West Coast vacation to fly east for rehearsals and the concert. A few weeks later, Noah invited Gordon to sing the role of Darius in *Daniel*. And when Pro Musica left New York for concerts at Tanglewood on July 17 (1958), at Chicago's Ravinia Festival on July 23 and 24) and elsewhere in the midwest through August 1, Gordon made the trip and Arthur stayed behind. It was the first of

Gordon Myers as Darius
in a later performance of
Daniel *at Spoleto in 1960.*
(Courtesy Gordon Myers)

eleven tours and some 300 concerts in which Myers sang with Pro Musica.[10]

Letters from Toni kept Noah in touch with the small realities of family life.

> Sam took Annie and me to the Great Sh[anghai] for dinner tonight —very pleasant. We had shrimp with oyster sauce, jantza (spelling?) and a noodle dish which was superb. He insisted on treating us! . . . If Julius [Goldstein] is free tomorrow, maybe I'll go see 'Marjorie' [Morningstar] with him.

Toni signed off with love—and a postscript urging Noah "if you get Ravinia check, please send at once, because we're getting low."[11]

The next evening, July 23, Julius Goldstein did indulge Toni in one of her and Noah's favorite pastimes.

[10]Gordon Myers, *I Sing — Therefore, I Am*, pp. 1, 21, 23, 24-39, 79, 97.
[11]Toni-Greenberg-Noah Greenberg, letter, July 22, 1958.

Julius and I . . . had dinner together and then saw 'Marjorie Morningstar.' Some movie!!! I will tell you all about it next week.[12]

Noah took advantage of the two-night stand in Chicago to set up a meeting with his chum the harpsichord-builder John Challis. Challis suggested that the two meet at the Palmer House. "The rooms are airconditioned and as the town might be boiling hot, it will be as comfortable as anywhere with the aid of a bottle of whiskey for comfort."[13] As it happened, each man wanted to ask a favor of the other. Noah was perennially frustrated by the difficulty and expense of moving Pro Musica's Challis harpsichord from concert location to location. Plans for more extensive touring would only add to the problem. If Challis harpsichords in private hands could be made available in at least some of the cities and towns on Pro Musica tours, it would save a lot of time and money. Could Challis help?

For his part, Challis needed publicity. An article about him in the culture section of *The New York Times* would help him sell more harpsichords. Did Noah have any friends on the paper?

Both men promised to do whatever they could, and both men tried. But it was Challis, not Noah, who did most to keep his promise. In September, Noah wrote to apologize for not doing more to interest *The Times* in a Challis story, and also to beg Challis to supply a harpsichord for Pro Musica's October 27 concert at Cranbrook Academy, in Bloomfield Hills near Detroit. Challis responded that "we can manage somehow," but added a word of caution.

Important! Tell no one around here I'm loaning you the harpsichord, but no one! Otherwise I'm hounded by people who always want to borrow.[14]

Meanwhile, a more serious issue had presented itself. Before leaving for the midwest, Noah took the time to draft a long letter to the members of Pro Musica's board. The subject was "the problem of finding a new concert management."

Ronald Wilford has done a superb job for our organization and we were quite happy with him. . . . He has booked over thirty dates for us for next season (excluding New York).

But Wilford was leaving David W. Rubin to head a theatrical division at Columbia Artists Mangement and was giving up all of his attractions except the brilliant French mime Marcel Marceau.

[12]Toni Greenberg-Noah Greenberg, letter, July 23, 1958.
[13]John Challis-Noah Greenberg, letter, July 8, 1958.
[14]Noah Greenberg-John Challis, letters, September 22, 1958, September 30, 1958; John Challis-Noah Greenberg, letter, October 2, 1958.

Noah then gave a remarkable analysis of Pro Musica's standing as an attraction.

> The concert giving aspect of Pro Musica has grown to the point where we are considered a major attraction in the concert field. Our fee places us in the category of Virtuosi di Roma and I Musici and is higher than the fee of the Budapest Quartet.

In Noah's mind, this meant that a manager specializing in chamber ensembles could not book Pro Musica because its fee was too high. Also, and interestingly,

> We do not need a management such as Barrett because his specialty is getting 'prestige' dates for his artists and we have plenty of those (as a matter of fact, this is one of our problems—Library of Congress, Dunbarton Oaks, Eastman School, various museums—these we have always had) and what we need most are regular concert booking in large cities.

Pro Musica, Noah felt, had to choose between two alternatives: S. Hurok and Columbia Artists Management. Because Sol Hurok was out of the country, a meeting with him was impossible. But CAMI was eager to talk, and Ronald Wilford arranged a conference with CAMI's president, Fred Schang.

One of Noah's biggest worries was that Pro Musica, "thrown into this large commercial apparatus," would be given short shrift and would lose its identity. Schang was able to reassure him. Schang in person had handled Margaret Field-Hyde's English Singers, the Virtuosi di Roma and the Paganini and Festival String Quartets, and well understood how to look after small distinctive ensembles. Better still,

> His son, Chris Schang, Jr. has long been a fan of ours, seems a very sincere and enthusiastic young man and will be responsible for handling us in the Schang office. He has a fair knowledge of early music, thanks to Yale and Hindemith, and is being groomed to take the old man's place.

Noah's "other major concern" was that

> Columbia, eager to get as many dates as possible for us, would throw us into the Community Concerts circuit for 8-10 weeks at a time, a fate worse than death.

Community Concerts, Inc. a CAMI division, specialized in bringing classical music to untaught audiences in out-of-the-way places. This provided work for CAMI's clients and live performances for those who otherwise could never hear them. But Community Con-

certs often had to be given in school gyms or auditoriums with dreadful acoustics and no facilities for the artists. And the fees for appearances were drastically discounted. So Noah had reason to be wary.

> I told Mr. Schang that we were interested in being handled only on
> a straight sales basis and that we would only agree to Community
> engagements as fill-ins between regular concerts. Very practically
> this means, we have a date at the Toledo Musum on Monday and
> Ohio State University on Thursday. We would accept a Commu-
> nity date in between. This he accepted without reservation.

Also, Noah dreaded being on the road for months on end.

> I stipulated three booking periods, late fall, mid-winter and mid-
> spring -all 3-4 week periods. This, too, was acceptable, I'm happy
> to say. My suggestions on program format were acceptable, also.

As far as Noah was concerned, the search for a manager was over.

> What remains now is for us to notify Columbia that we would like
> them to draw up a contract which would include many of the ques-
> tions I mentioned above.

Board members could pass on any suggestions of their own to
Arthur, who would reach Noah on tour. But in effect, Noah was
asking the board to ratify a *fait accompli*.[15]

Also interesting is the tone of Noah's discussions with Schang.
This is no timid artist knocking shyly at a manager's door. Noah is
rather the seasoned, self-assured personality, conscious of success
and convinced (and able to convince the hard-bitten Schang) that
even greater success lies ahead.

A week later, on the eve of his departure, Noah passed on to Arthur
a draft of a memo for the board outlining his plans for the fall and
beyond. These show clearly that Noah was Thinking Big. *Daniel*
had taught him that he could bring together and coordinate large
forces with striking result. He wanted to go on painting with a broad
brush. To present major medieval and Renaissance choral works,
like the Masses of Ockeghem, Obrecht, Josquin, and Morales he had
studied for so long with Harold Brown. To experiment with instrumental accompaniment as he had in *Daniel*, and also to explore larger-
scale instrumental music—the immense, untouched literature for
viol consort, for example, and the great body of early Baroque works
for court masques, festivals and civic occasions. For such grand
purposes, Pro Musica's six singers and four instrumentalists were
simply not enough.

---

[15]Noah Greenberg-members of the NYPM Board, letter, July 10, 1958. NYPM Archives, Box 4, folder 7.

The first realization of his plan was the Pro Musica Motet Choir. This all-male vocal ensemble would "model itself on the chapel choirs of the XVth and XVIth centuries" and "comprise between fourteen and twenty-four voices, according to the music's requirements, and solo singers [would be] drawn from the Concert Ensemble."[16] In fact, Noah had already lined up an engagement for the group, which had been started but had barely rehearsed, at St. Thomas Church on Fifth Avenue in Manhattan. Now he said:

> I plan rehearsals through the months of October and November (about eight) with full complement of instruments and singers. . . . I would very much like to make a Josquin recording following the November 30 concert.[17]

In the same draft memo, Noah made mention of his ambitious plans to have Pro Musica offer classes in choral singing and to continue Martha Blackman's beginner's and advanced viol study groups. He also outlined his design for a "Wind and Brass Ensemble Study Group" to induce "players of professional standing" to set aside their modern trumpets and trombones, oboes and bassoons and try to master shawms, sackbuts and other so-called "loud" instruments of the Middle Ages and the Renaissance. This would bear fruit within months as the Pro Musica Wind Ensemble.

Noah knew that he was spreading himself very thin indeed and that others would want to share the limelight.

> I think we should take up the question of these ensembles appearing under auspices other than ours and agree on some formula such as 'Viol Ensemble of the New York Pro Musica, Martha Blackman directing.'[18]

But Noah could never bring himself to let this happen. Until his death in 1966, every concert and recording of every Pro Musica ensemble was billed as "Directed by Noah Greenberg."

For Bernie Krainis, Noah's grand plan was more than a little horrifying. The original idea of Pro Musica as a small collegial group of gifted musical equals was slipping away. In its place would be Pro Musica the institution—big, impersonal, diffuse, and of doubtful musical quality. Bernie was perturbed enough so that at some point

---

[16]The description is drawn from the liner notes of the Decca recording DL 9410, Josquin Des Pres.

[17]Noah Greenberg-Arthur M. Squires, draft memorandum for the Pro Musica board of directors, July 18, 1958. NYPM Archives, Box 4, folder 7.

[18]*Ibid.*

during the year—it might have been in April or May, in the wake of Arthur's money memo, but it was more likely in September, at the beginning of the 1958-59 season—he led a delegation of his colleagues into a cards-on-the-table meeting with Noah to present their grievances. Bernie, remembering, said ruefully:

> Noah was brilliant, absolutely brilliant. He tied us up in knots. His basic approach was, How can you do this to me? I've worked and slaved to get us where we are, and now you turn on me.[19]

Noah's reproachful manner—Joel Newman called it "the guilt trip tactic"[20]—worked like a charm. According to Bernie, Noah's experience in Trotskyist labor infighting is what made him more than a match for Pro Musica's musicians. In any event, the budding protest movement collapsed. But individuals quietly began making their own plans.

In an effort to stave off one possible defection, Bernie approached Noah after the meeting to warn him that, "Look, we're going to lose Russell." Noah's brusque rejoinder was the classic answer of every boss faced with a threat of desertion: "Nobody's irreplaceable." Events were to prove Noah right. And yet, events were also to prove him wrong.

[19] Bernard Krainis, August 13, 1998.
[20] Joel Newman, September 9, 1998.

CHAPTER TWENTY-FIVE

$\mathcal{N}$EEDED: NEW VOICES

(1958-1959)

$\mathcal{A}$s if in defiance of Bernie Krainis's gloomy prognostications, Pro Musica's 1958-59 season got off to a strong start. There was one change. Jean Hakes, after four seasons, had resigned. Pregnant with her first child, Jean would have found touring very difficult. Her husband, Scott Witherwax, was pressing her to leave. She was also one of those who had confronted Noah over money and other issues, and this may have played a part in her decision.[1] The parting seems to have been amiable, however, because several years later Noah was recommending Jean warmly to Yale Teacher Placement and Jean, responding, sent Noah her "warmest love."[2]

Noah's remarkable luck with sopranos continued to hold. He was able to enlist Bethany Beardslee as Jean's replacement in time for the summer 1958 concerts. A Michigan State University graduate, Bethany had been a voice scholarship student at The Juilliard, making her concert debut at age twenty-two in 1949. She had appeared as a soloist with Arthur Mendel's Cantata Singers, but was also keenly interested in contemporary vocal music, of which she later became a leading interpreter. "I knew Betty and Russell and Charles from Juilliard," she said, "and Noah had already tried to get me to join [Pro Musica]."[3] More than Noah's charm, the lure of steady work, travel, and the chance to sing with friends were what persuaded her to accept now. Pro Musica's first "Y" concert, on October 18 (works of the early German Baroque), was sold out. On

[1]Gordon Myers, October 27, 1998.
[2]Noah Greenberg-Yale Teacher Placement, letter, September 2, 1964; Jean Hakes-Noah Greenberg, letter, September 1964. NYPM Archives, Box 2, folder 1.
[3]Bethany Beardslee, October 28, 1998.

Sunday, November 9, *The New York Herald-Tribune* ran an article by Jay S. Harrison in anticipation of the second "Y" concert on November 15. The centerpiece of the highly favorable article was Noah's capsule history of Pro Musica. In this, Noah, faced with discontent on Bernie's part, astutely gave much credit to Bernie and the other instrumentalists. Thus:

> One of the people in our [amateur] vocal group, Bernard Krainis, was very interested in instrumental music: he got together an instrumental group. That was the start of Pro Musica.

Noah also stressed versatility, leading Harrison to conclude that

> It is not unusual . . . to find a Pro Musica man alternating between the violin, recorder, wooden flute, rebec and treble viol.

In fact, it was highly unusual: only one "Pro Musica man," Paul Ehrlich, could play all of these instruments at professional level.

Paul Maynard, too, came in for high praise.

> [W]e needed a harpsichordist who was a specialist. We found one in Paul Maynard, who realizes all of our continuo parts. A lot of people, of course, know what to do with a Bach continuo—but what about Monteverdi and Schuetz and giants like that? That's where Maynard, who is also also an excellent organist, came in. Besides, he also learned to play the psaltery.[4]

Of the instrumentalists, only Martha Blackman went unmentioned.

Two weeks later, Noah's Pro Musica Motet Choir made its debut. On a bitter night, St. Thomas Episcopal Church, the handsome brownstone Gothic church at Fifth Avenue and 53rd Street, was filled nearly to capacity for the "free" concert. (St. Thomas's vestrymen specified that there could be no charge for admission to "God's House," but Pro Musica was allowed to solicit a free-will offering.) Noah had put together and rehearsed a chorus of five countertenors, four tenors, two baritones, and two basses. The program included works by Dunstable, Dufay, and Obrecht, with Josquin Desprez's *Missa Pange Lingua* as the longest, most complex offering. Russell, Charles, Gordon Myers, and Brayton Lewis sang solos.

Accompanying the singers in some passages were several instrumentalists. One of them was Joel Newman's brother Morris, a professional bassoonist who also played the recorder and took a keen

---

[4]Jay S. Harrison, "Music's Past Meets the Present," *The New York Herald-Tribune,* Sunday, November 9, 1958, Section 4, p. 5:3-6.

interest in other early wind instruments. A month and a half earlier, in mid-October, Noah had roused Morris (who lived a few blocks away) out of bed with a phone call.

> He woke me up, 'Come over.' 'Tomorrow,' said I.... He says, 'I've got a whole bunch of instruments I want you to try.' So I came in. [Noah had] ordered—without telling anybody, the usual Noah stuff—he had ordered a cartload of instruments from [the German maker] Steinkopf, Stonehead, right? who later on sold his whole operation to Moeck. And there were three shawms, there were two cornetti, there were krummhorns. I tried the krummhorns, tried to keep from laughing, it's a kazoo, it's not a good kazoo, they have a range of a tenth if you can play them, if you can't they have a range of an eighth. There were no guides, there were no fingering charts, the charts that Steinkopf issued didn't work at all.
>
> Anyhow, I played them, I spent the whole day there. And then I played the shawms, for which [Steinkopf] had sent reeds that didn't work. Immediately, the problem with the alto and the tenor [shawms] was [that they] really needed [something] close to a bassoon reed.
>
> So I said, 'Yes! Okay.' And he said, 'Okay, what should we do?' And I said, 'Let's hire a brass band and a double-reed band to start off with.'

This, however, had to wait.

> I wanted good players, players I knew, [but] we were right in the middle of the season, it was impossible.

Morris's friend, the trombonist Arnold Fromme, did agree to take part in the November 30 St. Thomas concert, playing a tenor trombone. Morris himself played the alto shawm.

> [T]here was supposed to be someone who later backed out on the tenor shawm and also a bass shawm was there, it didn't work at all. I mean, no one could play it. We couldn't use it . . . I knew the bass fiddle player Ken Fricker . . . so Ken played because we couldn't trust the bass and we couldn't trust the tenor, and we had trouble finding people.[5]

Paul Maynard took charge of the regal, a portable reed organ with a buzzing timbre like that of the group of krummhorns Noah had bought but could not find people to play.

Chorus and instrumentalists were placed in the loft at the rear of the nave, so that, as critic Howard Taubman observed, "[t]he gath-

[5]Morris Newman, November 5, 1998.

ering that filled the pews was obliged to crane its necks if it wished
to see as well as hear." But both Taubman in *The New York Times* and
Allan Hughes in *The Herald-Tribune* were laudatory. Taubman found
the program "fascinating." Mercifully unaware of the pickup character of the instrumental accompaniment, Hughes wrote that "the
entire evening . . . was one of revelation and great beauty."[6] Noah's
dream of "a brass band and a double-reed band" playing his newly-
acquired wind instruments was still some months short of fulfillment. Morris Newman would put his friendships and credibility
on the line and struggle mightily to help make the dream a reality.

Audience demand for *The Play of Daniel* had grown so strong that
the Romanesque Hall of The Cloisters was now too small and its
availability too restricted to meet the need. During the summer of
1959, Noah had begun to shop for a more suitable location. His first
thought was Riverside Church. As he told Arthur Squires in a memo:

> Kirstein, Wilford and I have met with the Riverside people and
> have discussed the possibility of five perfomances in the Nave.
> Wilford is negotiating this and he has the exact figures which cover
> payroll, a Pro Musica %, amortization of Kirstein's costumes,
> agents fee, and preparatory costs. They will notify us before La-
> bor Day. . . . [7]

For whatever reason, these arrangements fell through, but Noah
soon located another setting. The Chapel of the Intercession of Trin-
ity Parish, far uptown at Broadway and 155th Street, is one of the
most beautiful of New York's Episcopal churches. Bertram G.
Goodhue, who also designed St. Thomas and St. Bartholomew's
churches, designed the Chapel in English Gothic style, with an open-
timbered painted roof, and thought it his finest work. Ross
Parmenter, reviewing *Daniel* in *The Times*, called it "wonderfully
appropriate" for liturgical drama.[8] Thus, even though the nave
seated six hundred people, it was not so large that those processing
down the aisle had to take giant steps to reach the transept exactly
when the music reached its end.

Daniel was given six performances at the Chapel, starting on
Monday, January 5, 1959 and continuing each evening through Sat-

---

[6]Howard Taubman, "Music: Sacred Program," *The New York Times*, Monday, December 1, 1958, p. 38:1; A[llan] H[ughes], "Male Choir at St. Thomas," *The New York
Herald Tribune*, Monday, December 1, 1958, p. 12:1.

[7]Noah Greenberg-Arthur M. Squires, draft memo for NYPM board, July 18, 1958.
NYPM Archives, Box 4, folder 7.

[8]Ross Parmenter, "Chapel Uptown Provides Setting For Pro Musica's 'The Play of
Daniel'," *The New York Times*, Tuesday, January 6, 1959, p. 30:2.

urday, January 10. The production was essentially the same as it had been at The Cloisters, though inviting small touches were added. The chapel was lighted in part by candles standing in the arches of each of the five bays of the nave. At the end, when Russell came forward in "the rainbow wings and the robe of Sassetta pink"[9] of the Angel of the Annunciation, all other lighting was extinguished, leaving the audience to listen by candlelight to the final Te Deum.

Around the first of the year, Fred Schang of Columbia Artists Management "inherited" Pro Musica, fully booked for the 1958-59 season, from Ronald Wilford. At that point, Wilford remembers, Schang said, "I don't want to see them, I don't want to hear them." Schang was terrified lest Pro Musica not be everything Wilford assured him it would be.

Wilford, ageless, dry of wit, very much a power at CAMI after forty years, and as unsentimental a judge of talent as the music business can boast, looks back at Noah almost with awe.

> Noah was unique. He had a completely musical mind. A blend of musicianship, historical research and entrepreneurial instinct. He knew the five 'W''s — Who [to perform], What, Where, When and Why. He had passion.

Wilford made another interesting point about Pro Musica.

> Everything was a story. Noah was a story, a guy from the Merchant Marine leading a music group. How Pro Musica got started was a story. Oberlin was a story. The instruments were a story. The music was a story.

But, he added, all of the promotional potential of these "stories" would have been useless had the music not been so gripping. Under Noah, Wilford said with evident gusto, "[Early music] wasn't dry. It was wet. Wet and juicy."[10]

*   *   *

In early February, Noah made yet another effort to deal with Pro Musica's chronic harpsichord-moving problem. His approach this time was to acquire a second harpsichord. With two, he told the Pro Musica board, he could "leapfrog" the instruments from place to place on tour, always having one on hand and one awaiting Pro Musica in the next city or town. The board approved a purchase, and Noah duly contacted Frank Hubbard in Boston. At age 38, Hubbard combined nearly twenty years of study and research with

[9]*Ibid.*
[10]Ronald A. Wilford, October 30, 1998.

exceptional shop skills. First with his partner William Dowd and then, starting in 1958, on his own, Hubbard was leading what Ralph Kirkpatrick called "the major revolution of this century in harpsichord building . . . simply a return to seventeenth and eighteenth century principles of construction."[11]

The order Noah placed with Hubbard called for an instrument quite different from Pro Musica's sturdy workhorse of a Challis. What Noah asked for was Hubbard's model of an Italian virginals, a compact version of the harpsichord with strings that run parallel to the keyboard instead of at right angles to it and a different (though interesting) quality of sound. One considerable advantage of the virginals was its portability. The Hubbard instrument weighed less than 40 pounds. Even with its separate stand, it would be easy to move by car and comparatively inexpensive to ship by air. All told, it was a good choice for an instrument to take on tour. Noah was eager to have it in hand in time for Pro Musica's summer concerts. But Hubbard, like John Challis, was busy with other projects, not unduly worried about schedules and deadlines and amiably immune to pressure from a customer.

Noah placed his order by telephone in late February. On March 1, Hubbard wrote to Noah, wondering why Paul Maynard didn't use his own Hubbard harpsichord on tour and delicately but firmly asking for money. "My memory is quite shaky and I am not quite sure how firm your order is. Our terms are $100 deposit with the order and balance on delivery."

On March 4, Noah confirmed the order by mail, enclosing a $100 check and begging Hubbard for a packing box, which Hubbard had said he was reluctant to take the time to build.

Hubbard waited more than a month to respond, but on April 8 he did so, thanking Noah for the business and promising delivery by "the beginning of August." He also offered Noah a canvas carrying case and also promising a wood packing case.

On June 12, Hubbard wrote Noah with good news. "I hope to have your virginal [sic] finished by July 1." He invited Noah to come by his Tremont Street shop on July 10, when Pro Musica would be in the area, and take his pick of the two virginals he was completing. But something about Hubbard's letter must have made Noah nervous, because on June 17 he wrote to ask if the virginals could be used at Pro Musica's concerts at Castle Hill, Ipswich, on

[11]Ralph Kirkpatrick, "Forward," in Frank Hubbard, *Three Centuries of Harpsichord Making*, p. v.

July 10th and eleventh. Hubbard responded tartly ten days later that

> While I hope to have your virginal finished early in July I make it a matter of policy never to allow a concert to become contingent upon my performance.[12]

Hubbard did help Noah locate an instrument that Pro Musica could borrow for Castle Hill. But Hubbard's haughty "matter of policy" seems merely to have been a cover-up for the inability, common among harpsichord-builders, to keep promises or meet deadlines. Not until late September would the virginals arrive in New York.

Noah had other reasons to be worried during the spring of 1959. In March, the dire happening that Bernie had been predicting for months came to pass. Russell Oberlin told Noah that the current season would be his last with Pro Musica. "He'll never leave," Noah had assured Morris Newman. "He loves the music too much." Now he was leaving, and leaving behind an empty spot that would never quite be filled. "Noah didn't want to lose me," Russell said, "but he couldn't very well stand in my way. And he didn't."[13]

---

[12]Frank Hubbard-Noah Greenberg, letter, March 1, 1959; Noah Greenberg-Frank Hubbard, letter, March 4, 1959; Frank Hubbard-Noah Greenberg, letters, March 18 and June 12, 1959; Noah Greenberg-Frank Hubbard, letter, June 17, 1959; Frank Hubbard-Noah Greenberg, letter, June 27, 1959. NYPM Archives, Box 21, folder 4.
[13]Russell Oberlin, January 28, 1997.

CHAPTER TWENTY-SIX

A FRIENDLY BEAR AT 40

(1959)

On Thursday, April 9, 1959, two days before Anne Greenberg's fifth birthday, Noah himself turned forty. He was no longer the trim, jaunty merchant mariner of a decade before. Still less was he the bushy-headed would-be intellectual, pipe in mouth, of his late adolescent photographs. He had put on weight—too much, Toni kept telling him—and he was beginning to grow a paunch. His dark hair, thinning since his twenties, had almost given up the struggle, and Noah was nearly, though not quite, bald on top. As always, his jet-black eyebrows lent definition to his face. The black hornrims he wore made him look deceptively mild-mannered and scholarly. But his big bulky frame and self-confident bearing gave him an impressive presence, and his vitality and zest for life were as apparent as ever. "Being around Noah," declared Morris Newman, echoing the sentiments of many others, "was like being around a big friendly bear."[1]

At forty, the bear had every reason to be friendly. Professionally, Noah was at the top of his trade and at the peak of his extraordinary career. Pro Musica itself was of course the best evidence, and now recognition was catching up with accomplishment. The musicological establishment had admitted Noah (there were a few dissenters) as one of its own, electing him to the Council of the American Musicological Society. Noah's and Wystan Auden's *An Elizabethan Songbook* had sold so well as a paperback (60,000-plus copies) that Doubleday was bringing it out in hardcover format. Oxford University Press was about to publish a handsome edition of *The Play of Daniel,* based on Rembert Weakland's transcription and "edited for

---

[1]Morris Newman, May 29, 1998.

Noah and daughter Anne, c. 1959
(Courtesy Greenberg family)

modern performance by Noah Greenberg." With board approval, Noah was paying himself a salary as music director of $3,000 a year, up from $2,600 the previous year. He had received nearly $8,000 more for conducting Pro Musica in concerts. Still leading the student chorus at Mannes College, Noah was beginning to add to his income by lecturing: at the end of April, he would speak on *Daniel* at Union College in Schenectady. In all, he was earning a modest but quite respectable middle-class income of about $15,000.

Less modest were Noah's musical plans for the future. He was preparing to embark with the Pro Musica Concert Ensemble on tours meant to bring the delights of early music to thousands of new hearers in this country and Canada. The Motet Choir was already in being. Martha Blackman was running into trouble with the Viol Consort, but Noah had no idea that the trouble was serious. The Wind Ensemble, off to a halting start at St. Thomas Church a few months earlier, was gathering steam. Morris Newman had recruited two fine oboists, Melvin Kaplan and Ronald Roseman, to learn treble and alto shawm respectively. Noah had persuaded Gilbert Cohen and Robert Meyers to join Arnold Fromme in the trombone section. (Gil Cohen later became the bass trombonist of the New York Philharmonic.) In September 1958, Noah, on Jean Hakes's recommendation, had reached out to Robert Montesi. "I hear you're a great zincke [cornetto] player," Noah had begun on the phone. As a seventeen-year-old trumpet student, Bob Montesi had indeed played cornetto in Paul Hindemith's Collegium at the Yale School of Music. He had then done a three-year stint with the Air Force Symphony and was now making a nice living as a trumpeter with the Radio City Music Hall Orchestra. Noah first asked Bob to arrange and play the spectacular trumpet calls in *Daniel*. Almost in the same breath, he had held out the idea of Bob's playing cornetto in the nascent Wind Ensemble, and Bob, captivated by Noah, was delighted to join.

Not everyone was so agreeable. Of one other person Noah took on, Morris Newman says only:

> He never came on time for anything. And he never learned his part and he never learned to play and he bullshit the entire time and he was insulting. . . . And finally I went to Noah and I said, 'Listen Noah, I can't handle this guy. Either you can have me or you can have him.' And Noah said, 'Oh, you can't make me do that,' and I said, 'Yes I can. You've hired him, you can fire him.' It was terrible, [Noah] was so sweet, it broke his heart but I made him fire him.[2]

Some of the group's members were so busy as freelancers on modern instruments that they had little time to practice on Noah's old instruments, and rehearsals were hard to schedule. But in the spring of 1959 Noah was planning to have the Wind Ensemble take part in a number of fall concerts.

He was also looking hard for new large-scale projects with which to follow *Daniel*. Somehow, perhaps through Wystan Auden, he came across *Magnyfycence*, an allegorical morality play by the Tudor poet laureate John Skelton. Skelton had been tutor to Prince Henry, later Henry VIII. In the play, obviously aimed at Henry, Magnyfycence, an openhanded prince, is led astray by Lyberte and Felycyte and nearly ruined by wicked counsellors like Courtly Abusion and Crafty Conveyance, but is rescued by Good Hope, Circumspecyoun, and Perseverence. Skelton's simple edifying plot and rough-and-tumble versifying offer abundant opportunities for musical interludes. Noah was enthusiastic as only Noah could be. He approached Lincoln Kirstein about producing *Magnyfycence*. Kirstein thought it wasn't a bad idea, but he was busy promoting things Japanese, including an American tour of the Gagaku Dancers, and turned Noah down in typical Kirstein fashion by listening and saying nothing rather than by giving him a flat "No." Noah backed off and turned to other ideas, but he never gave up the idea of a Pro Musica

[2]Morris Newman, November 4, 1998.

Magnyfycence, with actors speaking the lines and Pro Musica supplying instrumental and vocal music by Tudor composers. Noah
would furnish the music. Kirstein would act as producer.

In May, he came up with another ambitious project. "I have been
looking at the so-called 'Coventry Plays,'" he wrote to Rembert
Weakland. The Coventry Plays form one of the five great groups of
English "miracle" or "Mystery" plays, the others being the York,
Towneley, Chester, and Wakefield cycles.

> If, let us say, we did portions of the Mary cycle in this collection, I
> would like to use a company of actors and a company of musi-
> cians. Where the rubrics call for a liturgical piece, we would per-
> form it either in plainsong or in 15th century English polyphony.
> Where music is appropriate in and between scenes, I would like to
> use the 15th century polyphonic carols. All processions should be
> with music.[3]

Six months later, Noah was still contemplating "*Ludus Cov.*"

> I think a good company of actors, and a good director, can make
> the verse quite understandable to a modern N.Y. audience. There
> will be some modernization necessary, but to revise all of it would
> mean robbing the medieval flavor from the plays. Also—I think it
> is harder to read than listen to. But this is in its formative stages .
> . . .[4]

And the Pro Musica production of the Coventry Plays remained
in its "formative stages" forever.

Ten years had gone by since Noah's last hurrah as an active "political," his losing battle against Joseph Curran for democracy in the
National Maritime Union. Those fires were banked, but Noah stayed
in contact with many old friends from the Trotskyist days. He was
on amiable terms with unreconstructed left-liberals like Manny
Geltman, Irving Howe, and Meyer Schapiro (who remained an ardent socialist until the day he died). Being Noah, he was also on
amiable terms with Sidney Hook, Sol Stein, Irving Kristol, and Jason Epstein, all of whom had rejected socialism in favor of capital-
ism, hardline anti-Communism, and law-and-order conservatism.
And being Noah, he was on the friendliest terms of all with Dwight
Macdonald, who had turned his back on ideology—for the moment
—and was employing his considerable talents in deploring middlebrow culture in essays in the most middlebrow of magazines, *The
New Yorker*.

[3]Noah Greenberg-Rembert Weakland, letter, May 20, 1959.
[4]Noah Greenberg-Rembert Weakland, letter, October 29, 1959.

Noah was emphatically not in sympathy with his neoconservative friends' growing, thinly-disguised distaste for the blacks and Hispanics who were making New York City uncomfortable for the white middle class.[5]   Always wary of lending his name to charitable or cultural causes, Noah did do so for the NAACP Artists' Committee to end segregation at concerts. Indeed, he did more. At whatever cost in bookings in the south, he insisted that CAMI append a "Discrimination Rider" to every Pro Musica contract. This read:

> The party of the first part [the institution presenting Pro Musica] hereby agrees that there shall be no segregation or discrimination practiced because of race, color or creed against any player or against any patron as to admission to or seating in the auditorium of the performance covered hereunder.[6]

But Noah certainly did believe with Hook and Kristol (and many others, left, right and center) that Stalinism had to be fought on the cultural as well as the politico-military front. Noah was very willing to do his bit in the "culture wars"—as long as Pro Musica's artistic reputation was not compromised.

Still, the odds are that friendship rather than ideological affinity gave rise to a couple of strange connections between Pro Musica and the Hook-Kristol-Stein "liberal anti-Communist" camp. Thus, in June 1959, Pro Musica's secretary, Susan Thiemann, resigned to devote more time to her musicological studies.[7] Noah's and Toni's old friend Jeanne Wacker, now Mrs. Thomas McMahon, was between jobs and in need of money, and Noah promptly hired her as Sukie's replacement. The brilliant Jeanne McMahon had been one of Sidney Hook's prize students. She was not only a good secretary, her personal address book was a who's-who of New York liberal intellectuals (many of them also friends of Noah's), from Nancy and Dwight Macdonald to James Merrill, from Mary McCarthy and Hannah Arendt to Alfred Kazin and Reinhold Niebuhr. By the end of the year, Jeanne was speaking up in board meetings: it was her idea to ask Dwight Macdonald to help Pro Musica "get a plug in the special column on Christmas gift suggestions in The New Yorker" for the Dec. 27 benefit performance of Daniel.

At the same meeting, Dick French, now board president, informed the board that Jeanne had "taken on an assignment from the Con-

[5]For evidence of this distaste, see Bloom, Prodigal Sons, pp. 331-337.
[6]NYPM Archives, Box 19, folder 3.
[7]She did so with considerable success. Susan Thiemann, later Susan T. Sommer, pursued a career in music librarianship and is at this writing (2000) chief of the Music Division of the Library for the Performing Arts at Lincoln Center.

gress for Cultural Freedom in Paris." The C.C.F., founded in 1950 in Berlin by Sidney Hook et als, was the major worldwide forum for intellectual anti-Communists.[8]

Jeanne's "assignment" called for her to work one day a week.[9] Noah obligingly let Jeanne use her desk in Pro Musica's office for thirty-five dollars a month. (But cut Jeanne's salary by 20 per cent to reflect the loss of her services.[10]) This arrangement lasted through 1962. Jeanne cannot remember what it was that she did for C.C.F., but she does say that she and Noah "never discussed politics."

Another oddity was Pro Musica's relation with the Farfield Foundation. This was a tax-exempt foundation set up by Julius Fleischman and a handful of his wealthy friends. The friends were a remarkable group. On Farfield's board were Whitelaw ("Brownie") Reid, owner of *The New York Herald-Tribune*, William A. M. Burden, investment banker and president of the Board of Trustees of The Museum of Modern Art, Cass Canfield, editor-in-chief of Harper & Row, Godfrey S. Rockefeller of the National City Bank branch of the Rockefeller family, Donald Stralem, a wealthy book collector, and Milton C. Rose, director of the William C. Whitney Foundation.[11] Farfield, with offices on East 52nd Street, made gifts to various cultural organizations, including the New York City Ballet. It may be that Kirstein, who knew Bill Burden well from their work at The Modern, suggested to Noah that he submit a grant proposal to the Farfield, and Farfield did make at least one contribution (of $2,500) to Pro Musica.

The Farfield Foundation, however, was notable for reasons other than its charitable endeavors. In 1966, Farfield was revealed as being one of two major foundations (the Hoblitzelle Foundation of Texas being the other) that served as a front for the clandestine funneling of millions of dollars of C.I.A. money into the Congress for Cultural Freedom and, indirectly, into the A.C.C.F. John Thompson, Farfield's executive director during the 1960s, actively promoted Pro Musica's participation in events sponsored by the Congress for Cultural Freedom.[12] But in 1998 he laughingly brushed aside the

[8]See p. 233.
[9]Jeanne Wacker, October 2, 1997.
[10]Minutes of NYPM board meeting, December 7, 1959. NYPM Archives, Box 23, folder 1.
[11]This Foundation had been established by Whitney heir Michael Straight, who after an association with Anthony Blunt and the other "Cambridge Communists" in the 1930s, was always under pressure to demonstrate his loyalty to the U. S.
[12]John Thompson-Noah Greenberg, letters, February 5, 1962 and February 13, 1962.

notion that Noah and the Pro Musica had had anything to do with the C.I.A. aspect of Farfield's operations.[13]

Did Noah know that the Congress was a creature of the C.I.A., or that Farfield was a C.I.A. front? Probably not, although he was shrewd enough to have guessed, as some of his friends did guess, at some kind of U. S. Government involvement in the Congress. If Noah had known, would he have cared? The odds are that both the artist and the anti-Stalinist would have smiled. The Yiddish expression that covers the case is simple: *Nehm' das Gelt unt geh'*—take the money and run.

If politics was only a flickering concern of Noah's at forty, family life was of steady and absorbing importance. In February 1956 and again in early 1957, Noah had traveled to California, taking Anne with him, to visit his parents in Elsinore and introduce them to their only granddaughter. Lillie Greenberg's heart condition was serious enough to require her to use an electric invalid cart in the store, so that she could stay off her feet as much as possible. At fifty-seven and fifty-six, Lillie and Harry Greenberg had put enough money by so that, with what they would realize by selling the store and their house, they would be able to retire. Sometime after Noah's and Anne's visit in 1957, they did manage to sell their Elsinore property. They came back East to Shrub Oak Park in northern Westchester County. In 1942, Lillie's sister Dora Davidson and her family had built a bungalow in Shrub Oak, the last to be developed of Westchester's radical-left communities. The Greenbergs bought and settled into a modest frame bungalow with a small back-yard terrace, two houses down from the Davidsons.

Noah's cousin Rema Davidson saw a good deal of Noah, Toni, and Anne in those years. Twenty-three in 1959 and not yet married, Rema worked for Noah, doing odd jobs and selling tickets for *The Play of Daniel*.

> It was a great part-time job, because the venues were so wonderful. At The Cloisters [in December 1957] and the Church of the Intercession on 155th Street [a year later].[14]

But the big family excitement of Noah's fortieth year came exactly three weeks after he celebrated his own birthday. On April 30, Toni gave birth to a second daughter. It had not been an easy pregnancy. Early in the first trimester, Toni had been confined to bed for

NYPM Archives, Box 35, folder vii, Box 34, folder vi.
[13]John Thompson, November 12, 1998.
[14]Rema Sessler, March 1, 1997.

several weeks.[15] But the new arrival, Jane, weighed a healthy eight and a quarter pounds and was greeted with delight by everybody except five-year-old Anne. Anne, like most other five-year-olds, was intrigued with the idea of a baby sister and willing enough to play surrogate parent, but not one hundred per cent certain that Jane was such a good arrangement. "Our newcomer, Jane, is a wonderful child," Noah wrote to Rembert Weakland when the baby was six months old. "Toni and I are very pleased. Anne is still a bit suspicious about the whole development."[16]

Anne, in fact, was going through a rather stormy childhood. The strongminded daughter of two strongminded parents, she was friendly and charming and extremely bright, but not always docile and willing to please. Anne's cantankerousness, in typical small-child fashion, was mostly directed at her mother as the parent largely responsible for her upbringing. Toni Greenberg prided herself on being organized, disciplined, and coolly self-possessed. She was determined to bring these traits to bear on the task of raising her daughter. But Toni, by all accounts, was also sharp-edged and possessed of a sharp tongue. She often lost control and snapped at Anne or aimed a sarcastic comment in her direction—techniques that, as every parent knows, seldom lead to domestic tranquility.

The situation was complicated by Toni's devoting so much of her time and energy to Pro Musica's business affairs, although she tried hard to do the office work after Anne had gone to bed. Nor was Anne's lot—or Toni's—made easier by Noah's frequent absences and by the furious pace of his professional life, and of his and Toni's social life, whenever he was at home.

Predictably enough, Noah, when he was at home, was the special, sought-after parent. And Noah loved being Anne's Daddy. On Sunday mornings, when Toni's idea of happiness was to sleep late and luxuriate in bed with the *New York Times* and *Herald-Tribune*, Noah and Anne would jump into Noah's car and head north on the West Side Drive and the Henry Hudson Parkway to Riverdale, the westernmost section of the Bronx. There they would stop at the home of Noah's old friend Rubin Baratz and his second wife, Cherito, for the classic brunch of scrambled eggs, lox, bagels and cream cheese. Then they would get back in the car and work their way downhill and eastward through the Bronx to Van Cortlandt Park South and

[15]Toni Greenberg-District Director of Internal Revenue, letter, October 3, 1959. NYPM Archives, Box 73, folder ii.
[16]Noah Greenberg-Rembert Weakland, letter, October 29, 1959.

Gun Hill Road. Their ultimate destination was the Bronx Zoo, where they would spend the afternoon together.

Anne also remembers later, less idyllic car trips with Noah.

> We would take a load of old clothes and put them in the car and drive down to The Bowery and the Lower East Side. And my Dad would stop the car and we would simply put the clothes out on the sidewalk and leave them there. 'Don't worry,' he would say, 'the people will get them who need them. And they won't have to go to some shelter or church to beg for them, either.'[17]

It was a lesson in poverty, and in her father's tenderness toward the poor, that Anne would remember forever.

After seven eventful years, Noah's relationship with his wife was still as much love-affair as marriage. In some ways, it was an odd match, this pairing of the warm outgoing boy from the Bronx with the detached self-sufficient librarian from Danzig. Toni was not everybody's cup of tea. Some of Noah's Pro Musica colleagues admired her braininess but found her not easy to like. Bernie Krainis said of her that she was "very, very smart" but that there was some "J.A.P. [Jewish-American princess] in her."[18] Arthur Squires, who as Pro Musica president worked closely with her, was more forthright.

> You know, I would have to say that I really didn't like Toni a lot. She wasn't one of my favorite people. [She] always struck me as more than a little bit spoiled and somewhat demanding.[19]

Arthur's comments are reminiscent of Ruth Daigon's remark that "Toni and I were not really meant for each other" and that Toni, very pleasant at first, "grew more and more distant, a trifle icy"[20] after she and Noah were married.

In contrast, Dick French, who also worked closely with Toni, had a much more favorable view of her. "She was diligent, effective, and totally devoted to Noah."[21]

Toni Greenberg did have a sharp tongue and, surprising in someone so controlled, a tendency to blurt things out without stopping to think. Rubin Baratz recalls an incident at one of the Baratz's Christmas parties in Riverdale.

---

[17]Anne Greenberg Donovan, June 11, 1997.
[18]Bernard Krainis, February 176, 1997.
[19]Arthur M. Squires, December 5, 1997.
[20]Ruth Daigon, e-mail message, February 11, 1998.
[21]Richard F. French, September 24, 1998.

We happened to have a German woman—at that time they didn't have an established mission at the U.N. [where Rubin was working]. So Toni turns to Cherito and says, 'Who invited that Nazi?' She'd never met her before, had no idea who she was, except that she spoke with a heavy German accent. And my wife turned to Toni and said, 'Toni, I'm sorry, I'm going to have to ask you to leave.' And Toni rushed to Noah and began to cry. And so Noah said to Cherito, 'What happened?' Cherito said, 'She insulted a guest of mine. If I invite someone to my party I don't expect they'll be insulted by other guests for no reason at all.' She didn't say what [Toni] said or anything, but Noah said, 'Toni, apologize to Cherito.' He didn't want to leave! So, still sobbing, Toni said, 'I'm sorry, Cherito.' And they stayed as if nothing had happened. . . .'[22]

Noah's matter-of-fact reaction suggests that outbursts of anger or sarcasm on Toni's part were not all that rare. He put up with them because he loved her, as she bore with his fast driving, overindulgence in food and drink and consuming immersion in his work, because she loved him.

Indeed, despite the wide differences in background and personality, Toni and Noah had much in common. The list would have to include rapid-fire intelligence, delight in language, books and wordplay, fondness for the visual arts (especially painting and the movies), broad-gauge Jewishness that had everything to do with family and culture and nothing whatever to do with religion and— not least—mutual sexual attraction.

"Darling . . ." Noah is writing from upstate New York. The letter was written well after 1959 (none from that year have been saved), but the sentiments are those of the happily-married forty-year-old. Noah comments on the weather (freezing) and the mood of the ensemble ("Even Gordon [Myers] smiled.") He speaks well of the budding musicianship of his cousin Michael Davidson, Rema's kid brother. And then he says:

It is getting harder and harder to go away on tour. We must plan each one from now on so that either I come home in the middle or you come along for a week. The children are getting older and it will be easier to do as each year passes.

He asks her to "kiss the girls" and closes with "All my love."[23]

[22]Rubin Baratz and Clara Hancox, May 19, 1997.
[23]Noah Greenberg-Toni Greenberg, letter, February 8, 1963.

CHAPTER TWENTY-SEVEN

SCOUTING OUT EUROPE

(1959-1960)

On March 25, the Wednesday before Easter Sunday of 1959, a nineteen-year old music major in his senior year at Hunter College had just finished lunch and was headed down the long corridor from the basement cafeteria to the men's room. As he was about to enter, he heard a voice urgently calling his name. "Robert! Robert! Don't go in there!" It was the assistant to the dean. The young man, mystified, asked, "Why not?" and heard an even more mystifying answer. "You've got to go to Carnegie Hall."

Being young and, as he said himself, "a bit of a smartass," the young man asked, "Why? Are the bathrooms at Carnegie better than the ones here?"

"No, no," was the impatient reply. "Leonard Bernstein's office called and you've got to go over to Carnegie right now. Here's a dollar for a cab."

The young man grabbed the dollar, got into a cab and went.

And I get [to Carnegie Hall] and they take me up to a little room, and Lennie Bernstein is in it. And he plunked a score, 'Here,' he said, 'can you sight-read?' I said, 'Yes.' So I sight-read in German Pontius Pilate, which was a countertenor role, not too high, going up to high C as I remember, 'Weiss' du ich das ich wacht haben dich die Kreutzigen,' gorgeous music that the 18-year-old Handel wrote in the *St. John Passion*, right? So I sing this, he says, 'Fantastic!' He brings me downstairs and I'm onstage and he's at the harpsichord conducting. I stand up and I sight-read this thing . . . the Schola Cantorum was there with Hugh Ross, and Margaret Khalil and [the bass-baritone] and David Boyce was the Evangelist. And they're standing and I do my thing and Lennie is saying, screaming over to anybody that would hear him, I'll never forget it, he says, 'Listen to this guy sing! Look at the line that he's doing. How amazing!'

Leonard Bernstein had engaged Russell Oberlin to sing Pontius Pilate. When Russell developed a bad sore throat three days before the performance, Bernstein was sunk in gloom. "What are we going to do? I need a countertenor and the only one in the world is sick." One of the tenors in the Schola Cantorum, Joe Porrello, spoke up. "There's a tenor that sings up that high that's replaced Russell [before], we've worked together." His name? "Robert White."[1]

Robert White had indeed replaced Russell before. Noah had heard Bobby White in the 1958 Musica Viva production of Monteverdi's *Orfeo* at the "Y," (in which Charles Bressler had also appeared) and had called him. "Can you sing up high?" he asked.

I said, 'Yeah, what do you mean?' And he tried me up a way, and there it's a kind of reinforced high, high tenor sound and it was very beautiful and I negotiated it. . . .[2]

In a word, Noah had discovered a backup countertenor. When Russell had to miss a spring 1958 Pro Musica concert at Caramoor in northern Westchester, Bobby White stepped in. Then, in March 1959, Russell, irreplaceable Russell, had given notice that he was leaving. But no sooner had he done so than the backup had burst onto the musical scene, wowing Leonard Bernstein and drawing rave reviews for his Carnegie Hall debut in the Handel *St. John Passion*. Noah wasted no time in asking Bobby to join Pro Musica as its regular countertenor.

I was . . . very excited because I had a real paycheck coming in. In today's numerical dollars it was a pittance, but in those days it was a very hefty sum, and to come out of college and all of a sudden — to be booked in the major major concert posts around the country . . . Ah, it was fabulous, we were the hottest thing — I was part of [it, and] the music was divine.[3]

Thus Robert White became part of Pro Musica in time for its *annus mirabilis*, the 1959-1960 season.

The year of wonders began on October 18, with a program of works from Germany at the "Y." A week later, Pro Musica left on a tour that swung from Cambridge, Massachusetts as far west as Minneapolis, then circled back by way of Pennsylvania, upstate New

---

[1]Robert White, June 9, 1998.
[2]*Ibid.*
[3]*Ibid.*

York and Washington. In all, the group performed at fourteen locations in twenty-six days.

In *The Washington Evening Star* of November 21, music critic Irving Lowens, who had known Noah for many years, pulled out all the stops. The Pro Musica's Monteverdi concert at the Coolidge Auditorium of the Library of Congress was "perhaps the most anticipated concert of the current season." Pro Musica itself was

> a magnificent company . . . under the direction of one of the most creative practical musicians of our time, Noah Greenberg. . . .This is a phenomenal ensemble. . . . The whole was a cooperative venture, a treat from beginning to end.[4]

Back in town, they repeated the Monteverdi program at the "Y" on November 29 and immediately began preparing for six performances of *Daniel*. In these, Russell made his last American appearances with Pro Musica.

It was on the fall tour that Noah, helping to slide the harpsichord into the rear of a rented station wagon, slipped and badly hurt his back. The injury, diagnosed in New York as a slipped disk, was serious, and so painful that for months Noah had to wear a corset in order to conduct. It also persuaded Noah to hire a "band boy" to travel with the group on its winter tour to California and the Far West. His job would be to look after Pro Musica's instruments, shipped from New York, drive the instruments and Noah from place to place and handle further shipping arrangements as needed. The prize candidate was a lanky, friendly, capable 31-year-old Princetonian, Robert Long. Noah hired him and handed him the American Airlines airbills, a check to cover airfreight costs, and a rendezvous for the next day in San Francisco. The next day, Noah himself flew west on TWA.

The following evening, Pro Musica presented the Monteverdi program before a packed house at the main Berkeley auditorium. The concert went extremely well, number smoothly succeeding number through the intermission. Backstage, Bernie Krainis approached Noah with a request. Bernie had a solo in the second part of the program, a sonata for alto recorder by the eighteenth-century Italian composer Francesco Veracini. The singers would be performing beforehand, and their music stands would be set up in front of Bernie. What about taking a few seconds to move the stands clear, so that the audience would have a good look at Bernie as he played?

[4]Irving Lowens, "Pro Musica Offers Thorough Treat," *The Washington Evening Star,* November 21, 1959, p. A9:1-2.

"Noah threw another of his temper tantrums," Bernie said, "and as far as I was concerned that was the end of the line." Intermission drew to a close, everybody went on for the second half and Bernie played his sonata—on a cleared stage. After the last work on the program, Monteverdi's *Litany of the Blessed Virgin*, and the encores, Bernie again came face to face with Noah backstage. There was no yelling or screaming, as there had repeatedly been in the past. But Bernie's resentment had finally crystalized.

> I said, 'Noah, you're going to have to get yourself another recorder player.' Bobby White was standing there in the wings and his jaw was hanging down, he was completely stunned. He'd never heard anything like this, ever.[5]

Noah said nothing. Later, he asked Bernie if he planned to play out the remainder of the tour. "Of course," Bernie said: to do anything else would be to hurt Pro Musica and let down his colleagues. And beyond? For over a year, there had been were serious signs that a European tour was in the cards.[6] Bernie hesitated, but only briefly. In his heart, he knew he had to break with Pro Musica and pursue his own career, and the time to do it was now.

Bernie and Noah were much too professional to allow the tension between them to affect Pro Musica's performances, and Pro Musica's first tour of the west was a critical success. For most members, it was a marvelous experience as well. Pro Musica saw a great deal of California at its most beautiful. The first week took the company from Berkeley and Stanford in the San Francisco area through the Napa Valley to Angwin and a concert at Pacific Union College, with post-concert parties or receptions nearly every night— including one at the home of Bernie Krainis's sister-in-law and another given by Bernie's sister. Then it was east to Davis near Sacramento, back to Palo Alto for an appearance at Stanford and northward up the coast to Eureka. On the way, Noah scheduled a stop at Sebastopol, a small town on the Russian River, where his Uncle Solomon Sogenstein— "Schloime," to the family—ran a poultry farm. Pro Musica spent the afternoon and early evening of Monday, January 11 relaxing with Schloime in the sunshine before pushing northward through redwood country to Eureka.

[5]Bernard Krainis, January 24, 1998.
[6]See Noah Greenberg-Katie Kassimati, letter, December 16, 1958: ". . . we have been forced to postpone our projected tour for one year, as the State Department found that the expenses of sending *Daniel* to Europe ran beyond their budget for the coming year. We are now setting our plans for the following summer, 1960 . . ." NYPM Archives, Box 50, folder xix.

The second phase of the tour Pro Musica spent in the south. The group performed at no fewer than ten California high schools and art centers in a row, from Beverly Hills High to Whittier High School in Richard Nixon's birthplace, under CAMI's Community Concerts program. Noah may have had his misgivings about Community Concerts, but the artists thought they were a fine way to see Southern California and make some money besides.

Pro Musica played in Los Alamos, New Mexico on Thursday, January 28, and flew from Albuquerque to Tucson, Arizona the next day. The group had three days to explore the city before a Sunday night concert.

By this time, Bobby White had bonded firmly with Charles Bressler, Betty Wilson, and Bethany Beardslee; and Bob Long with all four. In one of their explorations of the city, four of the five friends (Charles was elsewhere) found themselves outside the open gates of a massive old stone building built around a central courtyard. They sauntered in and, relishing the quiet and the acoustics, the three who were singers started to sing the beautiful anonymous villancico *Si la noche haze escura*. As the music gained volume, heads appeared at the upstairs windows. When the singers noticed that the windows were barred, it dawned on them that they were serenading inmates of the county jail. They sang on and were rewarded with enthusiastic applause.[7]

On Wednesday, February 3, while the company was en route to Waco, Texas, the story broke in *The New York Times* that ANTA and the U. S. State Department would sponsor a major Pro Musica overseas tour. Over a two-month period, the group would present *The Play of Daniel* at ten locations in England, France, and Italy, including Westminster Abbey and the Festivale di due mondi in Spoleto.

Why the State Department reversed itself and decided that Noah was no longer a "controversial person" is an open question. Perhaps it was because of representations on Pro Musica's behalf by the American Committee for Cultural Freedom. Perhaps it had occurred to somebody at State that veteran Trotskyists like Noah hated Soviet Communism more bitterly than did even the most fervent right-wingers. Or perhaps it was simply that, with the McCarthyites discredited, more relaxed attitudes had prevailed. Whatever the reason, Noah was taking nothing for granted. In answer to a letter of congratulation from Rembert Weakland, he wrote:

---

[7] Betty Wilson Long, April 28, 1997; Bethany Beardslee, December 9,

It was nice of *The New York Times* to announce our European tour with the *Daniel* play—but there are still many bridges to cross on this project. It looks pretty good so far but I am still not counting on it.[8]

This nervous reply was written on February 15, two full weeks after the *Times* story appeared. But whatever his doubts, Noah wasted no time in making his preparations. Back in New York from Waco on February 5, the first thing he did after breakfast the next morning, a Saturday, was to call Russell Oberlin to invite him to join the tour. This made good artistic as well as good promotional sense. Even though Robert White would also be on the tour, Russell was identified with *Daniel* and his presence and artistry would bolster interest in the production. Russell said yes, as anyone knowing Russell would have guessed he would, for the adventure and for the sheer joy of raising his voice in places like Westminster Abbey and Spoleto.

But Russell was not Noah's only problem. He was facing even more urgent personnel problems. The first was that of replacing Bernie Krainis. To solve it, Noah had only one real option, and he may well have acted on this while he was still on the road. Certainly, by February 9 in New York he had reached LaNoue Davenport and asked him to join Pro Musica as its recorder-player. LaNoue had always wanted the job, and in experience, proficiency, and musicianship he was exceedingly well qualified. He accepted at once. Very soon, he and Noah began to confer about making another change. Did LaNoue know anybody who could replace Paul Ehrlich? As Morris Newman recalls,[9]

LaNoue thought that one of his own students should be the replacement. Shelley Gruskin, a New Yorker, had graduated from the Eastman School of Music, had studied recorder with LaNoue, and was teaching the instrument at the New York College of Music. Like Paul, Gruskin was a flutist as well as a recorder-player and an experienced concert musician.

Whatever the reasons for Paul's dismissal, at some point before the Pro Musica board meeting on May 10, Noah let Paul know that his contract with the Concert Ensemble would not be renewed for the 1960-1961 season. He would be engaged for the 1960 Christmastide *Daniel* performances at St. George's Church in New York: Shelley Gruskin's skills did not extend to proficiency on the rebec.

[8]Noah Greenberg-Rembert Weakland, letter, February 15, 1960.
[9]Morris Newman, November 4, 1998.

Out west, Bethany Beardslee too had told Noah that she would be leaving at the end of the spring tour in May. She was expecting her second child, and Godfrey Windham, her composer husband, felt as did Jean Hakes's husband that Bethany should stay close to home to raise their children. At times, Bethany had also felt uneasy about being "under-rehearsed." Betty, Russell, Charles, and the other first-generation Pro Musica members, of course, had rehearsed intensively. They knew the repertoire, they knew one another's styles and they knew what Noah wanted. But, Bethany said,

> When I joined, I had to learn a great deal of music. I really worked hard on those songs. But we actually learned some of the pieces as we did them [onstage].[10]

Interestingly, Arthur Squires also voiced this same charge.[11] Part of the reason was Noah's faith, naive or not so naive, in his singers. Their skill, and his own conviction, led him to believe that they could do virtually anything he asked of them, to demand that they do it and to be hurt when they failed to deliver.

Bethany's decision meant that once again he had to enter the soprano market. On the morning of February 11, he held auditions for three sopranos. One of them, Carolyn Backus, impressed him favorably, but he made no decision until the 24th, when he called Carolyn to offer her the job and then called Bethany to let her know who her successor would be.

All of this was taking place amid the usual whirl of Noah activities: Wind Band rehearsals, a sitting for publicity portraits, a lunch with Sydney Beck, a meeting with Nancy Tuttle of ANTA, a call to Israel Horowitz of Decca about a recording date for the German program, a meeting with Leonard Bernstein, a reception for composer Marc Blitzstein, dinners with the Elliott Carters, with Jeanne Wacker McMahon and Julius Goldstein, and with Russell Oberlin, post-concert parties, and Wystan Auden's annual birthday celebration. At length, on the night of Friday, February 26 Noah shook himself free of his schedule and, with Dick French, flew off to London, Paris, and Rome on a 10-day trip paid for by CAMI (with a seven-hundred-dollar assist from James Merrill), to survey the various loca-

---

[10]Bethany Beardslee, December 9, 1998.

[11]Arthur M. Squires, December 5, 1997. For three concerts in November 1960, Arthur filled in for Charles Bressler, who was singing with the New York Philharmonic. "I breezed through the Mennonite [college] concert [at Goshen College, Goshen Indiana], but I was as under-rehearsed going into those two Chicago concerts as I have ever been in my life. [Noah] just didn't give me enough rehearsal time."

tions, win friends and influence people and nail down the plans for the Pro Musica *Daniel* tour.

In London, Noah's first task was to carry out the numerous instructions Toni had given him. Anticipating the usual tourist stomach troubles, he bought himself Enterovioform. Next, he placed a call to Lusia Arendt, Toni's oldest and closest friend from their childhood days in Danzig. The Arendts—Lusia was married to Jurek Arendt, a physician—were away for the weekend, so Noah turned his attention to a second set of orders. During the tour, Toni and the children would be based in London. Noah should locate an

> English hotel—near parks—2 or 3 rooms, bath kitchenette (hot plate will do—not to actually cook but fix Jane's meals), approx 23-28 [dollars a] week, must have good hotel restaurant to serve meals upstairs—central heating if possible.[12]

He tried at least five hotels. Two of them (the Atheneum Court and the Earl Court Hotel[*sic*]) drew flat "No"'s. Three others (The White House, The Royal Court and The Dolphin Square) were possibles.

His family chores done, Noah turned to business. At five o'clock, he met Denis Stevens, musicologist and director of the Ambrosian Singers, at the headquarters of the Plainsong and Medieval Music Society. At six, Noah joined Jeremy Noble, a Renaissance music specialist and one of the staff critics for *The Times of London*, for drinks, followed by dinner at eight. The next day, Sunday, was reserved for flying visits to many of the possible locations for *Daniel*. On Monday, Noah toured Westminster Abbey in the company of Denis Stevens and Sir William McKie, organmaster and master of choristers. A meeting with William Glock of the BBC followed, after which Stevens took Noah to lunch at the Garrick Club.

Noah was even busier in Paris. CAMI had put Noah in touch with Anatole Heller of the Bureau Artistique Internationale, to see if Heller could arrange concerts for Pro Musica in addition to the thirty-three *Daniel* performances. (He could.)

On Tuesday, March 1, Noah lunched with Heller, and later the two of them spent the entire afternoon with the incomparable Doda Conrad. Doda, a bass-baritone and a man of good looks and charm, was the son of the great Polish soprano and teacher Marya Freund. Before the Second World War, he had joined the group of singers led

---

[12]Pencilled entry in Noah Greenberg's engagement diary, Saturday, February 27, 1960.

by Nadia Boulanger to perform at the private musicales of the celebrated Princess Edmond de Polignac. In 1937, Doda sang the bass part in the historic recording of Monteverdi madrigals that Boulanger directed for HMV. At the outbreak of war, Doda rendered signal service to the harpsichordist Wanda Landowska, helping her move from St.-Leu outside Paris to the South of France and trying (vainly) to preserve her instrument and music collections from being looted by the German occupiers. What he did during wartime is uncertain, but in 1945 Doda Conrad bobbed up—in the uniform of a captain in the U. S. Army!—as one of the people in charge of the Munich Collecting Point set up by SHAEF to gather and safeguard fine-art treasures appropriated by the Nazis.[13]

Now, fifteen years later, Doda was artistic director of Fondation Royaumont, a privately-funded cultural center at Royaumont, a ruined thirteenth-century Cistercian Abbey founded by Louis IX and located some 18 miles north of Paris. Doda and Noah had in common an unabashed love of cultural spectacle. They had been in correspondence since June 1958 about the possibility of a performance of *Daniel* at this historic site.

The next day (March 2), Doda gave Noah, Dick French, and Anatole Heller a tour of Royaumont followed by lunch. That afternoon at five, Noah met with several State Department cultural-affairs officers, including Mme. Yvonne de Casa Fuerte of the United States Information Services, to whom Noah had written in February at the suggestion of his friend, the harpsichordist Sylvia Marlowe. The idea was to build up interest in *Daniel* and in Pro Musica itself. Mme. de Casa Fuerte and her colleagues were duty-bound as culture warriors to promote and publicize U. S.-sponsored cultural events in their host country, but of course they could do so with varying degrees of enthusiasm. Noah was determined to turn them into Pro Musica devotees, and by his own account he succeeded.

At six-thirty, Noah rejoined Doda Conrad, and the two dined with the fabulous Geneviève Thibault, Comtesse de Chambure, a leading scholar of Renaissance music and one of the most influential patrons of early music in France. Her approbation was an endorsement worth its weight in gold.

"Dinner at Boule d'Or," Noah noted in his diary, and whether in praise of the food or of the Comtesse's company—or both—he added four checkmarks.

[13]Lynn Nicholas, *The Rape of Europa*, photograph, p. 406.

On March 3, Noah visited the church of St. Germain-des-Prés to measure the famous old Romanesque-and-Gothic church as a location for *Daniel*. At two in the afternoon, he was at Sainte-Chapelle, awarding it four large and enthusiastic checkmarks as a possible venue. He then accompanied Heller on visits to several Paris theaters: Heller was planning to book the Pro Musica Concert Ensemble for a Paris engagement separate from *Daniel* and wanted Noah to let him know which would be the most suitable. Dinner that night at the Restaurant Mediteranée on the Place de l'Odéon, in the heart of St. Germain-des-Prés, rated only three checkmarks. The next morning, Noah caught the airport bus for a flight to Rome. He met there with representatives of Giancarlo Menotti's Festivale di due mondi and, although no Rome engagements were planned, he took the measurements of the Romanesque church on the Piazzo del Grillo. An overnight trip to Florence on Saturday, March 5, afforded a chance to look over the church of Santa Trinità, begun in the eleventh century, with its Ghirlandaio fresco portraits of the Medicis, where *Daniel* would be performed. That evening, Noah dined with the composer Luigi Dallapicola, an advocate of twelve-tone music who was also a passionate admirer of Monteverdi and Gesualdo.

Back in Rome on March 7, Noah went shopping for toys for Anne and Jane and bought himself a hat. He had originally planned to go on to Lisbon via Madrid, but no Portugal bookings had been forthcoming, so he cancelled his Lisbon flight and instead flew back to Paris for a final meeting at the U. S. Embassy with cultural-affairs officer Steven Morris, Doda Conrad, and Anatole Heller. On March 10, the scene set for the tour, he was back in New York.

CHAPTER TWENTY-EIGHT

ℙRO MUSICA INTERNATIONAL

(1960)

"[ℙro Musica] sailed on the *Queen Mary* from New York on May 18 [1960] at 12:59 p.m. Daylight Saving Time." Thus Gordon Myers, a man in love with exactitude, on the beginning of the *Daniel* tour. Gordon was also—he still is—a man in love with the good things of life.

> Many details of our first Atlantic crossing have slipped from memory. I *do* recall that three times a day we could order *anything* we desired from the menu, and as *much* as we wanted. I handled this crisis with very little difficulty, . . . On the *Queen Mary*, I ate almost everything within reach.[1]

Even though Noah, a formidable trencherman, built up his appetite by swimming with Anne in the *Queen Mary's* pool, he could not compete with the appetite that Gordon had developed as a farmboy in Iowa.

Aboard the Cunard liner with the rest of the company was Bob Long. As on the western tour, so now: Bob was entrusted with the complicated responsibility of seeing to the transportation of baggage, instruments and people, a job he would handle with aplomb. But Bob was also on his honeymoon. In the course of the western tour, he and Betty Wilson had become more than companions. They had fallen in love. Two weeks after Pro Musica's return from Texas, to the wistful sorrow of Julius Goldstein, they were married.

Before Pro Musica left New York, someone—almost certainly John Phipps, who was managing the tour in England—had placed an ad in *The London Times* of May 9 that read: "Fire-eaters, sword-swallowers, preferably with ecclesiastical experience, required May-

---

[1]Myers, *op. cit.*, p. 81.

SPANISH MUSIC

DECCA RECORDS

of the Renaissance

NEW YORK
*Pro*Musica

NOAH GREENBERG, Musical Director

The fifth of Decvca's many NYPM recordings, released in April 1960, shortly before the group left for Eujrope.

June." The ad produced a nice ripple of publicity for Pro Musica and *Daniel.* It also produced, in time for the first performances in England, at Wells Cathedral near Bath in the southwest, one fire-eater and one sword-swallower. Their duty was to lend color to the opening procession.

> To blow petrol into a flame on cue, as the fire-eater did, was no problem. But for the [sword-swallower], who usually took his time . . . "on cue" was not so easy.

Gordon watched as the sword-swallower, before the first performance,

> lubricat[ed] his throat with what I assumed was a medicinal liquid which he carried in a small and shiny container tucked in among the folds of his tunic.

Unfortunately, the lubricant failed to work. The sword-swallower, try as he might, couldn't open wide enough to swallow the sword. And so,

> he whirled with his back to the audience and thrust the blade down his shirt front. Noah was so angry he fired the guy.

Gordon tried to intercede, but Noah would have none of it, "shouting at me something that sounded a lot like, 'Mind your own blankety-blank business.'" The finale was a sorrowful note from the sword-swallower to Gordon a few days later, to the effect that a heavy cold and swollen glands, not charlatanry, were the cause of his inability to perform. He had since recovered, but "you get no second chance in this theatrical business."[2]

Wystan Auden, in residence at Oxford, lunched with Noah at the famous Mitre before the 2:00 p.m. rehearsal at St. Barnabas Church. Auden took the role of the monk-narrator and read his own narration during the several performances at St. Barnabas. But as was not uncommon with Auden, he underplayed his lines so much that even the singers, thoroughly seasoned by now, had trouble judging their entrances. The English actor John Westbrook, who delivered the lines at performances elsewhere in England, was much more effective.

Pro Musica moved on to London on June 3, with peformances of *Daniel* scheduled daily from June 6 through June 11. On June 7, Noah called on Yehudi Menuhin in Highgate at four o'clock, and at seven dined at the Garrick Club. That season, indeed, London clubland opened its doors to the visitor from New York. Noah took tea at the Reform on June 8, and on Saturday, June 11, Denis Stevens gave Noah and Toni cocktails at the Garrick before a party thrown by Toni's friends the Arendts. There was time for shopping, too, in particular for Noah to buy himself a pair of black "formal" shoes for his full-dress appearances with the Concert Ensemble.

That same week, something extraordinary befell Russell Oberlin. "We were doing *Daniel* at Westminster Abbey," Russell said, "and I got a call from John Phipps.

> 'Covent Garden [the Royal Opera] wants you to sing on their stage.' 'What's it all about?' I said. He said he didn't know, they'd just asked him to tell me. I said: 'I don't audition, and we're in Westminster Abbey. If they want to hear me, they should just come over.' 'No,' he said, 'they want to hear you on their stage.'

[2]*Ibid.,* p. 82.

Again I said no, but he called later and said, 'You know, I really think you shouldn't pass this up.

Russell asked Phipps what "they" wanted him to sing. "Anything you like," Phipps told him.

So I got hold of Paul Maynard and hired some rehearsal room and we rehearsed Handel. We went over to Covent Garden and they were renovating it. They were always renovating it. The place was full of scaffolding and workmen making noise. We went onstage and got set up, a couple of lights onstage and the house dark. A workman was talking on the telephone with somebody and he said we could start whenever we liked and the workmen would stop.

So we started and they did stop and listen. I sang some Handel. Then a voice came from deep in the house: 'Do you have any Purcell?' I had *Music For A While,* and I sang that. Then this portly man came down the aisle and it was Sir David Webster, the Director of Covent Garden. He said, 'Thank you so much, I enjoyed it very much indeed, we shall be in touch with you again, you can be very sure of that.'

Covent Garden was indeed in touch with Russell again. Sir Georg Solti, the new music director, offered him the part of Oberon in Benjamin Britten's opera *A Midsummer Night's Dream,* a part intended by Britten for the English countertenor Alfred Deller but sung with distinction by Russell at Covent Garden and later in the U. S. and Canada.[3]

The next stop for *Daniel* was Italy. But Anatole Heller had booked the Concert Ensemble for a single performance at the Salle Gaveau in Paris on Tuesday, June 14. Noah, Toni, and Anne flew in from London a day earlier. Noah's first act was to telephone the Boule d'Or, the "four checkmark" restaurant on the Place de la Bastille to which he had been introduced in March. Noah, Toni, and Doda Conrad dined there in style that evening.

The day of the concert, Gordon Myers found himself in the grip of a male singer's nightmare.

I asked the [hotel] concierge if he could get my tails pressed. . . . [B]ecause he spoke some English, I felt sure he understood that I needed them back by 6:00 p.m. . . .

I recall vividly asking him for my tails at around 6:00. . . . His face went white. He dashed out and ran across the street only to find that the clothes presser had closed shop for the day. . . .

[3]Russell Oberlin, January 28, 1997.

I called Noah Greenberg's room. Toni, his wife, said he was soaking in the tub and could not come to the phone. She suggested I
call the lady who was managing us in Paris for Columbia Artists.
She listened to my problem and suggested that I call Doda Conrad.

Doda came to the rescue—more or less. Five minutes before concert time, Doda arrived backstage at the Salle Gaveau with his own
set of tails.

I hastily zipped open the little canvas bag and it was apparent that
he had not escorted his tails to the cleaners for a very long time. In
spite of a rising and persistent aroma, I pulled on the pants as fast
as I could. Doda was over six feet tall. Betty [Wilson] helped me
to pull the pants up as high as possible and she pinned them to my
shirt. . . . I squirmed frantically into the coat before walking out on
stage, Doda's tails slapping at my heels.[4]

Gordon's ordeal notwithstanding, the concert, a combined Flemish and Spanish program, was a great success.

In Spoleto, the problem was of an entirely different order. The
Spoleto Festival staff had made arrangements to use the small but
beautiful Church of S. Eufemia for the eight scheduled performances
of *Daniel*. His Excellency the Bishop of Spoleto, however, had grown
increasingly restive about this use of one of his churches. Who was
this Greenberg? What was this so-called liturgical drama all about?
The bishop finally announced that for the arrangement to hold, he
would have to approve the production in advance. So no more than
an hour after arriving by bus from Rome on the morning of Wednesday, June 15, the *Daniel* cast had to put on a hasty impromptu performance for the bishop, his chancellor and a few other high dioc-
esan officials. Gordon Myers chronicled the event:

Although some were absent, most of the cast and crew reassembled
to give the "command" performance. . . . The bishop and his en-
tourage, quite simply, were a terrible audience. They stood up,
walked around, talked out loud among themselves, and were, by
far, the most discourteous audience we had ever encountered. And
when we finished, they left without saying a word.[5]

Seemingly, no one ever told Gordon that the bishop was delighted
with *Daniel*, not to say ecstatic. Not only did he reiterate his permission to use the church, he spread the word among the *prominenti* of
the town that they should not, they must not, miss the drama. The

[4]Myers, *op. cit.*, pp. 86-87.
[5]*Ibid.*, p. 88.

Spoleto performances, for which Pro Musica, with State Department permission, waived its fee, were among the best of the tour.

Another highlight came a few days later, in Florence. A group of the singers gave a special concert in the New Sacristy, the creation of Michelangelo, of the Church of San Lorenzo, the so-called Medici church. Said Robert White:

> Four of us went and stood in front of *Night* and *Day* [the wonderful figures adorning the tomb of Giuliano dei Medici] and sang for the Mayor of Florence and a hundred of the best people in the city.

The work Bobby and the others sang was the "Monodia," the *Lament on the Death of Lorenzo,* composed by Heinrich Isaac in 1492 to the Latin text of Poliziano. Years later, Bobby would tell friends, "You know, one of the great moments of my life was standing in that spot [to sing]."[6]

The schedule called for two *Daniel* performances at Santa Trinità on July 1 and a Concert Ensemble performance (the Flemish-Spanish program) at the Teatro Communale in the Palazzo Strozzi the next day. But the Florentine response to Pro Musica was such that Noah had to add a second Concert Ensemble performance on July 4, this one largely of works of Monteverdi.

From the start, the consensus had been that the Auden narrative for *Daniel* should be delivered in the language of the country in which the particular performance was being given. This meant that translations were needed. The Italian translation posed no problems—except that the young actor in the role of the monk spoke so quickly that the singers and musicians had to sweat to make out their cures.

In France, the translation issue was complicated by Doda Conrad's insistence that he should take over the monk-narrator's role, at Royaumont and at St. Germain-des-Près. Noah was more than agreeable. During Noah's February stay in Paris, Doda had proven himself a friend and a stout supporter of the tour. A polished performer, he would make a fine monk. Noah had already commissioned a translation of the narrative from Yves Bonnefoy of Harvard, who had been recommended by several of Noah's French contacts. At Noah's behest, Bonnefoy sent on the translation to Doda. After some weeks, Doda wrote to Noah in New York that he, Doda, was amending the translation. Noah, alarmed, wrote back urging him to be in touch with Bonnefoy. Doda later said that he had tried but failed to reach Bonnefoy and had therefore entrusted a revised translation to a friend of Doda's, Gérard Doscot. By the time Noah unraveled

Doda's machinations, it was too late: the *Daniel* programs, with Doscot's credit, had already gone to press. Luckily, M. Bonnefoy understood and forgave, rightly heaping his coals of fire on Doda's head, not Noah's.[7]

Noah and his family arrived in Paris on Tuesday, July 5, two days ahead of the company. The evening of their arrival, he and Toni dined at Lapérouse, the temple of gastronomy on the quai des Grands-Augustins. *Daniel* rehearsals began at Royaumont on the morning of July 8. For some reason, the Saturday performance had to be rescheduled, so that both performances at Royaumont were given on the afternoon of Sunday, July 10. Noah was in his glory on Monday, being interviewed for French radio at five o'clock and holding a press conference at six before rehearsal at eight. The party after the July 12 opening performance at St. Germain-des-Près began at 10:45 p.m. at a private home on the rue du Dragon, a short block from the church.

The next day, Noah lunched with Nicholas Nabokov. As well as being a prolific composer, Nabokov, a onetime employee of the U. S. Military Government in Berlin, was a doughty veteran of the anti-Stalinist culture wars and the Secretary-General of the Paris-based Congress for Cultural Freedom. Four days later, Noah had drinks with another C.C.F. stalwart, François Bondy, editor of the journal *Preuves*. Almost certainly, Irving Kristol or Daniel Bell had provided the introductions: the night of April 4, Noah had been at Kristol's party for Bell and would have told both friends about his forthcoming Paris sojourn.

The French tend to bridle—to say the least—at efforts by the non-French to appropriate or exploit aspects of French culture. It was thus extraordinary, and probably due to Noah's own promotional efforts and obvious good will, that Radiodiffusion-Télévision Française presented a combined broadcast-telecast, live from St. Germain-des-Près, of the July 16 performance of *Le jeu de Daniel*, *"drame liturgique de Beauvais."*

Back in London on Tuesday, July 19, Noah spent the next two days making contact with key figures in the British early-music community. He tried repeatedly to telephone Ralph Vaughan Williams's widow. He also called Margaret Field-Hyde, director of The English Singers, the pianist Rosalyn Tureck (a famed interpreter of Bach), and the American musicologist Joseph Kerman. He reminded

---

[7]M. Yves Bonnefoy-Noah Greenberg, October 26, 1960. NYPM Archives, Box 50, folder xvii.

himself to set aside two tickets to an upcoming *Daniel* for Thurston Dart. "Bob" Dart at 39 was two years younger than Noah and a major figure in the British early music movement. An organist and harpsichordist, Dart had not yet taken up his professorship of music at Cambridge. Since 1956, as keyboard soloist and leader of such pickup groups as The Jacobean Ensemble and The Philomusica of London, he had been recording a pathbreaking series of the works of the major Elizabethan and Jacobean composers for the London/ Oiseau-Lyre label.

Having twice reminded himself, Noah did remember to stop off at Lewis & Sons on Jermyn Street, a "bespoke" tailor of renown, to pick up the striped trousers he had ordered a month earlier. On July 21, however, he had to postpone lunch with Sir William McKie of Westminster Abbey in order to catch an 11:30 bus to St. Albans in Hertfordshire, twenty miles north of London. Three performances of *Daniel* were given on successive evenings in the Lady Chapel of St. Albans Abbey, a thirteenth-century addition to the eleventh-century abbey foundation. The first evening after the performance, the Dean gave a dinner for the company. Gordon Myers also remembers drinking good English ale at The Fighting Cocks, an ancient establishment that billed itself as "the oldest inhabited licensed house in England."[8]

Noah returned to London after each performance. He had his luncheon with Sir William McKie on Friday, July 22 at that august center for the scholars, ecclesiastics and intellectuals of Britain, The Athenaeum. On Saturday, he bought stiff collars to go with his formalwear and hurried off to 75 Harley Street near Cavendish Square for a morning meeting with Margaret Field-Hyde. And on Sunday the twenty-fourth, after the third *Daniel* at St. Albans, he called at 10 Hanover Terrace at four o'clock, in time for tea with Mrs. Ralph Vaughan Williams.

The last *Daniel* performances of the tour were given at St. Nicholas Chapel in King's Lynn, Norfolk, a late medieval (fifteenth-century) church. In the audience on Wednesday, July 27, were Benjamin Britten and Peter Pears. On Thursday, Elizabeth, Britain's beloved "Queen Mum," was driven from Sandringham to attend the performance and greet the cast afterward.

The extra cast members and the *Daniel* stage crew went back to London by bus and flew home. Noah rented a car and drove Toni and the girls to Wroxham on The Wash, where they spent the night.

[8]Myers, *op. cit.*, p. 92.

Anne and Jane Greenberg
and friend, Dartington, 1960
(Courtesy Greenberg family)

The Concert Ensemble, however, boarded the first of two trains for the journey from King's Lynn, via Cambridge and London, to Totness in Devonshire. Near Totness is Dartington Hall, a beautiful thousand-acre estate. Dartington's modern history is intriguing. A Yorkshireman named Leonard Elmhirst and his wife, the idealistic Whitney heiress Dorothy Straight, bought the rundown estate in 1925 and spent many Whitney millions on restoring it.

As a coda to the tour, John Phipps had booked two concert-ensemble performances at Dartington's six-week International Summer School of Music. These were given on Saturday, July 30 and Monday, August 1. On August 1, the BBC recorded Pro Musica's Flemish-Spanish program and a Dufay work for later broadcast.

On August 2, the Concert Ensemble went up to London by train on the first leg of its trip back to New York. Toni, Noah, and the children, however, spent a few more days in England. Noah squeezed in visits to William Smoldon and Denis Stevens before the Greenbergs flew to Amsterdam, rented a car and drove first to Hamburg and then north into Denmark for some winding-down and relaxation. They would not be home until the end of the month. As Noah wrote, deadpan, to his new friend François Bondy: "Toni and I had a very nice few weeks in England and then we spent two weeks in Denmark to rest up."[9]

[9]Noah Greenberg-François Bondy, letter, August 26, 1960. NYPM Archives, Box 50, folder xii.

How important was Pro Musica's first European tour? In terms of its impression on European artistic and cultural circles, quite important. Noah's appraisal, in a letter to Rembert Weakland, was probably accurate.

> The overall effect of The Pro Musica and *The Play of Daniel* on Europeans was truly wonderful. Of course it is true that there was an element of doubt and slight suspicion before each initial appearance. I suppose the Europeans had a perfect right to be dubious about the idea of an American Company presenting a Medieval work, but all this hesitation disappeared as soon as the play started. The overwhelming reception from the press and most of the scholars was indeed gratifying.[10]

On the financial side, an audit conducted months later reveals that Pro Musica collected $10,636.90 in income from the tour, while incurring expenses of $104,810.17.[11] The State Department, of course, knew perfectly well that the cost of sending *Daniel* to Europe for over nine weeks would far exceed the fees Pro Musica could charge. Not money but cultural prestige was its concern. The best measure of State Department satisfaction is that its Cultural Affairs officials placed Pro Musica high on the list of candidates for future tours.

In terms of Pro Musica's reputation, the tour was a spectacular success. The organization gained recognition as something completely unlike the stereotypes of American cultural activity and behavior. A critic attending one of the King's Lynn performances put the matter adroitly:

> [*The Play of Daniel*] gives a valuable chance to adjust Norfolk's distorted view of American civilisation, by presenting a little-known facet of American culture: the preoccupation of many intellectuals with medieval art, and their perfectionist approach to its presentation.[12]

As for Noah, the tour cemented his reputation as a significant figure in the international musical community. Not only did it gain him the friendly respect of the Bob Darts and Jeremy Nobles and Denis Stevenses of the early music movement, it brought him to the attention of Yehudi Menuhin and Benjamin Britten, Ursula Vaughan Williams and Giancarlo Menotti. These were notables in a wider world of culture as well as in the smaller universe of music, and they would not forget him.

[10]Noah Greenberg-Rembert Weakland, letter, September 6, 1960.

[11]Most of the expenses were payroll costs: salaries for performers and staff totalled $83,198.38.

[12]Anonymous critical article, quoted in Myers, *op. cit.*, p. 95.

CHAPTER TWENTY-NINE

$\mathcal{A}$ WOLF BY THE EARS

(1961-1962)

$\mathcal{O}$n the evening of Thursday, August 18, 1960, the Greenbergs dropped off their rental car at Schipol Airport near Amsterdam and boarded a KLM Royal Dutch Airlines flight for New York. Back at 865 West End Avenue on Friday, Noah phoned Lincoln Kirstein and Chris Schang of CAMI to report on the tour. That evening, he met Dick French to be briefed on Pro Musica business affairs. His breathing-spell was over, and it would be long before he allowed himself another. Pro Musica's first European tour had gained Noah success on something approaching a grand scale. But as the somber folk saying warns, he who succeeds has a wolf by the ears.

Noah's wrestlings with the wolf were exhilarating but unending. The first and most chronic of his problems was musical talent. Herman, Seymour, Ruth, Sonya, Jean, Bernie, Arthur, Russell, Paul, Bethany—the list of those who had made Pro Musica a waypoint on their musical journeys was long. Pro Musica's membership remained stable throughout the three-week fall tour and a highly successful *Daniel* season. But new departures were in the making.

In February 1961, Noah had to report to his board that no fewer than three members of the Concert Ensemble were leaving. Lutenist Joseph Iadone, with whom Russell Oberlin had recorded in 1958, had replaced Paul Ehrlich for the 1960 fall tour. Joe Iadone's technical brilliance and fierce perfectionism are legendary to this day. A virtuoso lutenist would have added a new dimension to Pro Musica's repertoire. As Noah knew, the solo lute literature was vast and virtually unexplored; and the lute, not the harpsichord, had been the chief accompanying instrument of the Renaissance. But the connection was not to be. One problem, and probably the biggest one, was that Joe Iadone hated to fly. As the board minutes delicately put it, he was "unable to adjust to the rigors of travel."[1]

Another issue may have been that Joe's meticulous attention to musical detail clashed with Noah's more relaxed style. Morris Newman called Joe "an awesome person . . . very unforgiving if you did anything that he didn't approve of musically. Thank God he approved of me. . . ."[2]   He may not have approved of Noah. In any event, he would leave before the 1961 spring tour.

Even worse news was Martha Blackman's resignation. Martha's personal charm and magnetism, like her musicianship, were undeniable. But hers was a complex personality. "When she was right," Bernie Krainis said, "she was wonderful. Smart, funny, with it."[3] Morris Newman, who knew her well, called her "monstrously gifted — supremely musical."[4]   Bobby White said, "I got along fantastically with Martha."He held up two fingers, "We were like that.

> She was wildly, meanly closed, and at the same time she was so entertaining and so intelligent . . . she was like a big sister.[5]

Yet Martha suffered from some serious disabilities. One was what is now called "performance neurosis": a stagefright so crippling that Martha might try to lock herself in the ladies' room before a performance and defy her colleagues to fetch her out. Or be miserably sick to her stomach in front of everybody in the dressing-room, then walk onstage with elegance and play as if she hadn't a nerve in her body or a care in the world.

Another of Martha's problems was a kind of insouciant unpredictability. She would invariably show up for rehearsals, but not always on time. She would prepare her solo pieces at the last possible minute. Sometimes she was, as Bernie said, funny, witty and charming. At other times, she would lapse into withdrawn silence or flare up in anger. Bethany Beardslee thought that Martha suffered from depression and that her mood-swings might have been caused or aggravated by medication.[6]

Still, Martha was exquisitely skilled, and her gifts as soloist and continuo player were such that losing her was painful. Nor, seem-

[1]Minutes, Pro Musica board meeting, February 9, 1961. NYPM Archives, Box 23, folder ii.

[2]Morris Newman, November 4, 1998.

[3]Bernard Krainis, February 17, 1997.

[4]Morris Newman, November 4, 1998.

[5]Robert White, June 9, 1998.

[6]Bethany Beardslee, December 9, 1998.

ingly, did Martha leave Pro Musica with friendly feelings. As leader of Pro Musica's viol study group, she had had charge of a set of viols owned by Pro Musica. She returned them only reluctantly, several months after resigning. Then, later in 1961, Martha started to claim that Pro Musica owed her more than a thousand dollars for teaching the viol study group. Noah, Toni, and Dick French were appalled. They were certain that whatever fees Martha had earned had long since been paid out of tuition receipts. Martha admitted that she hadn't kept the books too carefully and could present no proof, but she insisted nevertheless that she was owed $1,065. Despite lengthy explanations and pleas for understanding, Martha actually filed suit against Pro Musica for that amount. Rather than go to court against a troubled former star, Pro Musica settled the case in 1962 for $750.[7] Long before, Noah had swallowed his anger and disappointment and had written Martha off as one who "was incapable of working with professionals, in spite of her great talents."[8]

The third person who left in the spring of 1961 was Betty Wilson. Like so many other Pro Musica sopranos, Betty dropped out because she was pregnant. Her departure too was a blow. As well as owning a lovely voice and knowing how to use it, Betty had a musician's ear for the timing, intonation, and phrasing of the ensemble as a whole. Because of this, and because of her sunny, steady temperament, her influence on the group extended beyond her singing. Also, Betty represented continuity. Almost from the beginning, as Noah had developed new material, she had been there to interpret it as he liked it and to help others perform it in "Pro Musica style."

As in the past, Noah shrugged off the losses and set about finding replacements. A note in the Pro Musica archives indicates that he auditioned Stanley Buetens, one of the few professional lutenists in the U. S. But he seems to have decided not to hire any lutenist at all except on a guest-artist basis. Several years later, Noah would acquire an archlute or chitarrone, a large bass lute used as a continuo instrument, but what plans he had for it would die with him.

Barbara Mueser was Martha's successor for one season. Judith Davidoff filled in for Barbara on one occasion in March 1962.[9] Then,

[7]Minutes of Pro Musica board meeting, November 4, 1961. NYPM Archives, Box 23, folder ii. Correspondence, legal matters. NYPM Archives, Box 8, folder xxiii.

[8]Noah Greenberg-Grace Feldman, letter, TK, 1961. NYPM Archives, Box 1, folder xii.

[9]Judith Davidoff, January 22, 1999. The appearance was at a concert of works by Elizabethan composers at Goodrich Chapel, Albion, Michigan. Ms. Davidoff's train from Boston had to be flagged down to allow her to debark at Albion.

when Barbara decided that she could not tour, starting in the fall of 1962 Judith became Pro Musica's full-time gambaist. Like Martha, Barbara and Judith were charter members of the group—in the beginning truly a tiny club—of gifted women string players who had begun to specialize in the viol and its music. Barbara was a native New Yorker and a graduate of Barnard College. She studied cello with Luigi Silva, then became intrigued with the viola da gamba and traveled to Basle to study the gamba with Eva Heinitz and August Wenzinger. Judith Davidoff had majored in music at Radcliffe, graduating in 1949, and had also studied at the Longy School in Cambridge.

Barbara's and Judith's approach to the gamba was more orthodox than Martha's. The fingerboard of their instruments were fretted in proper Baroque fashion. They grasped their bows, outcurved ones rather than incurved cello bows, with the palm and fingertips up (i.e., underhand), in keeping with Renaissance and Baroque tradition. Martha Blackman's style was distinctive and exciting, but both Barbara and Judith more than lived up to the her standard.

Sheila Jones had sung with Noah's amateurs when she was sixteen, and at seventeen she had taken part in the *Festino* recording. Sheila Jones was now Sheila Schonbrun, with a degree in music from Queens College and several years of concert experience. Like Betty Wilson, Sheila was musician as well as singer. As Betty's successor, she had a shrewd understanding of what Noah was all about:

> [It was] not only the musical conception, the vitality and the sonorities, but it was his business sense and his representation, his understanding of how important it was to keep building an audience all the time, and he was masterful at it, he was just so full of enthusiasm and energy, and he was always reaching out to people and he kept at it, he knew you had to keep at it, you know, any patrons, he kept after them and he did it in a totally reasonable, not a toadying way at all, he believed in what he had to offer so he just exuded that.[10]

With Barbara and Judith in place of Martha and Sheila in place of Betty, Pro Musica was still Pro Musica. In the fall of 1961, Noah led the Concert Ensemble through the midwest and southeast and presented exciting new programs (works by Heinrich Isaac and Ludwig Senfl, works of early Tudor composers, sixteenth-century Flemish works) at the "Y" in New York. "The music," said Robert White, "was fantastic during those years."[11] But even as the critics praised

[10]Sheila Schonbrun, April 3, 1997.
[11]Robert White, June 9, 1998.

his singing, Bobby White himself was having second thoughts about his vocal career.

At a Decca recording session a year earlier, in October 1960, Bobby and Charles Bressler had sung the tenor duet "Habe deine Lust" from Heinrich Schütz's *Kleine geistliche Konzerte* of 1639. The record, *Music of the Early German Baroque*, had been well-received. But for Bobby, the result had been disquieting.

> Charlie had this lovely resonance to his tenor voice, I remember, it was up front. And I listened to me in the playbacks and my voice was way down in the throat when I'd sing in the tenor range at all. And I realized I was losing my voice.[12]

Before the 1961 fall tour, Bobby had auditioned for conductor Léon Barzin and had sung one number in the countertenor range.

> That man [Barzin] was so prescient. He said, 'Look, you can do that magnificently, that high voice. But it's not your real voice. It will ruin your real voice if you do it. You'll make money very quickly. And you'll make a name. But it comes with a curse. You will become very well known very quickly. But you will then have to live it down, you will never be able to escape. . .'

Bobby sang the countertenor roles of Prince and Angel in the four December 1961 performances of *Daniel*; and he sang countertenor throughout the Concert Ensemble's five-week 1962 winter tour. But Barzin's comments and what he had heard in the playback earphones were haunting him. And so, at the end of the tour in March, he broke the news to Noah that he was leaving at the end of the season. This was by no means a simple proposition, because Bobby's feelings about Noah were not simple.

> [Noah] was a wonderful musician. He conducted us and it was always a very free kind of thing, but I knew what I was doing with him. He was an earthy, earthy man, but highly intelligent [and] a bit formidable. I was a little scared of him, he was this big guy and I was a kid. And then again I wasn't [scared], because I knew he respected me. He could be dismissive of me because I was a young kid, but he always thought I had a lot of talent, so I knew he liked me. You know what I mean? . . . I never felt comfortable with him, but I loved being with him.

Noah's reaction was likewise not simple. As Bobby remembered the interview, "He almost started to go ballistic," but he caught himself. Sopranos, gambaists, lutenists, as rare as the good ones are, were easily findable by comparison with countertenors. So Noah softened his tone. "He was begging me," Bobby said. 'Oh, but you've made such a name for yourself. You've created a niche.'" That, of course, was exactly Bobby's problem. "I said, Noah, I don't want a countertenor career, A, and, B, I certainly don't want a niche career, whatever I do."[13]

With Russell and Betty gone and Bobby White on the way out, perhaps it was inevitable that Charles Bressler too would quit Pro Musica. By common consensus, Charlie was an "incredible musician."[14] Also by common consensus, he was the freest of Pro Musica's free spirits, an uncloseted gay man in a closeted era, and an irrepressible wit who could turn his own rare musical mistakes into hysterical comic turns. "He could just wipe you out," LaNoue Davenport said.

> You know the Monteverdi *Chiome d'oro*? Well, there's an eight-bar introduction and that's repeated. And so we'd been doing it twenty-five times on tour and Charlie's attention must have wandered. And we played the introduction once and Charlie went: "CHIO — !" and stopped. Like that.

The freeze in mid-song, plus the droll look of alarm on Charlie's face, proved impossible to ignore. "[O]ne by one the instrumentalists started chortling and they couldn't control themselves. . . . Finally, I think, I was the only one left playing."[15]

Charlie could always be counted on to supply a slightly surreal one-liner. Gordon Myers told of one flight between two midwestern cities, "on a small plane which made a number of stops on the way.

> As one might guess, we seldom sat together—and after two or three 'local' stops the stewardess asked, 'Are you all part of a group or something?' Charles Bressler spoke up in his ringing tenor voice,'Yes, we're the football team from Sarah Lawrence [then an exclusively women's college] going down to play Ohio State!'[16]

Then there was the performance of *Daniel* put on, Bobby White recalled, for Canadian television.

> I had to play the portative organ. . . . At one break, when I was . . . in the satrap's clothes, the gay deceivers, as Charlie called them, I

[13]*Ibid.*

[14]Sheila Schonbrun, April 3, 1997. The same opinion was voiced in slightly different terms by, among many others, Russell Oberlin, Robert White, Bernie Krainis, and Albert Fuller.

[15]LaNoue Davenport, April 3, 1997.

[16]Myers, *op. cit.*, p. 97.

remember Charlie in his white robe *Daniel* costume . . . ran over to where I was sitting and sat down at the little portative that could just gasp a single line of music out. And Charlie, who was such a good keyboardist anyway, he started pumping furiously with the left hand and the right hand's going [Bobby whistled a frenzied downhill arpeggio and repeated it], he's doing the Widor. The toccata [one of the huge organ works of Charles Henri Widor, intended for the grand organ of St. Sulpice], and you can see the thing coming apart, you know? I said, 'Charlie, Charlie, you're playing the Widor on that portative?' And Charlie without missing a beat goes, 'Well, it's the king of the instruments, isn't it?'[17]

Offstage, according to LaNoue, this enormously gifted man "could get himself in plenty of trouble. With guys. A couple of times, Noah had to bail him out. Charlie was wild. Really wild."[18] Wild or not, he had been a mainstay of Pro Musica from the day in 1953 he took over the second countertenor part in Blow's *Ode on the Death of Mr. Henry Purcell.* Noah announced Charlie's resignation at the board meeting of April 14, 1962, along with that of Bobby White. Charlie did agree to appear at one or two New York concerts and in the winter *Daniel* performances. But after his departure, only Brayton Lewis and Paul Maynard of the original group remained. The idea of a Pro Musica in which the same people would sing and play together season after season was dead.

Noah, ever resourceful, accepted the situation. His response was to try to build a "farm system" in which new talent could be screened, trained, given paying work, and kept on tap to fill places in the Concert Ensemble as these opened up. This was one of the ideas behind the Motet Choir, the Viol Ensemble, and the Wind Ensemble, although these groups were also meant to stand on their own. It was very much the idea behind a new group that Noah had helped to form in the fall of 1960. The Abbey Singers were professional chamber singers and as such known quantities. Noah brought them together because Young Audiences, Inc., which was booking groups to sing in public schools, could find them work—the pay was an exceedingly modest twenty-one dollars per person per performance —and he himself could draw on them at need.

The talent in this "talent pool" was exceptional. The five original Abbey Singers were Sheila Schonbrun, soprano; John Ferrante, tenor; Arthur Burrows, baritone; Marvin Hayes, bass-baritone; and the twenty-seven-year-old mezzo-soprano, Jan DeGaetani. All except

[17]Robert White, June 9, 1998.
[18]LaNoue Davenport, interview, April 3, 1997.

DeGaetani were currently singing for Noah, in the Motet Choir, in *Daniel*, as guest artists with the Concert Ensemble, or in some combination of these. Within months, Sheila would replace Betty in the Concert Ensemble and John Ferrante would become the next singer to figure in Noah's unceasing search for another Russell Oberlin. The tenors David Dodds and Earnest Murphy joined the group in 1962, and Murphy too would move up to the Concert Ensemble. Jan DeGaetani stayed with the Abbey Singers for several years on her way to her brilliant and broad-ranging career.[19]

Sheila said of Noah's farm-system efforts: "One of his purposes, I think he was sort of like Duke Ellington, was to create a living for these musicians. He would have loved to pay everybody the same," she added, but he felt that he had to pay his regulars more per performance than he did his guest artists. One way to to equalize the imbalance was to try to find the latter extra work.[20] To broaden the Abbey Singers' appeal, he chose pieces for the group outside the realm of early music. Their one record for Decca, *Five Centuries of Song* (March 1963), began with Weelkes and Byrd and ended with Ernst Toch's delicious spoken "Geographical Fugue" and Aaron Copland's "I Bought Me a Cat."

*   *   *

If labor was one unending problem for Noah, money was another. The hard fact was that Pro Musica's income, outgo and financial condition were maddeningly unpredictable. Thus, at the begining of the 1959-1960 season, finances were shaky enough to persuade Noah to consider doing something he detested, putting his musicians on parade to raise money. In June, he suggested to the board "a party at the St. Regis Roof [the ultra-fashionable nightspot atop the Hotel St. Regis] with the Pro Musica ensemble performing between courses." Lining up the guests (and givers) would be a committee of Noah's wealthy women friends and supporters: Ursula Corning, Mrs. John Barry Ryan, Mrs. Murray Crane, and Lucie Rosen.[21] Nothing came of this grotesque idea, even though

---

[19]Philip West, February 4, 1999. Jan DeGaetani was married to West, the oboist, orchestrator, and teacher who replaced Mel Kaplan as treble shawm player with the Pro Musica Wind Ensemble and Renaissance Band. In fact, West and DeGaetani met at 865 West End Avenue. He was there for a Wind Band rehearsal. "Everybody was there and Jan came in for an Abbey Singers rehearsal and Noah said, 'Hey you guys, do you know Jan DeGaetani?' and that smile [of hers] flashed and— boom." Jan DeGaetani died in 1989.

[20]Sheila Schonbrun, April 3, 1997.

[21]Minutes, NYPM board meeting, June 17, 1959. NYPM Archives, Box 23, folder i.

"Pro Musica's finances were in very bad shape."[22] Noah and the board decided instead that a benefit performance of *Daniel* would be more dignified. Eight Daniel performances were to be held at St. George's Church on Stuyvesant Square. The evening performance of Sunday, December 27 was set aside for the benefit, with an impressive sponsor list[23] and tickets priced at fifteen, twenty, and twenty-five dollars instead of their usual price of three dollars. The benefit brought in nearly $5,000 and other contributions during the season came to $13,068.68. Still, Pro Musica lost nearly $10,000 in 1959-1960, and only the final $8,000 of the 1957 Rockefeller grant kept the organization more or less solvent.

Even in a banner year, Noah would be nervous about money. At the beginning of the 1960-61 season, Noah told his board that the summer European tour had been a smash success. But, he said, "although Pro Musica is successful, it is in desperate need of funds."[24] He was not entirely wrong. In 1960-1961, Pro Musica undertook 36 out-of-town engagements, performed three times at the "Y" and once each at the Metropolitan Museum and the Cloisters in New York, gave seven performance of *Daniel* in Chicago and five in New York, and made one appearance on television. The Concert Ensemble brought in $71,889, the equivalent of over half a million 1998 dollars. *Daniel* had gross revenues of $25,228. The two together thus grossed $97,117. But Concert Ensemble costs, largely payments to the performers and travel expenses, came to $66,110, and commissions to Columbia Artists Management were $8,985. So the Concert Ensemble actually ended up $3,206 in the red. *Daniel* did better, netting $7,299. The Motet Choir lost about $400.

In all, Pro Musica earned $4,093 and raised an additional $13,151 in contributions. But operating expenses—e.g., Noah's salary, office overhead, publicity, insurance—came to $16,500, eating up most of what had come in and leaving a year-end surplus of only $1,022.

In 1961-1962, the pattern was roughly similar. The Concert Ensemble and *Daniel* together netted over $10,000 on gross receipts of $121,603. The Motet Choir again lost money—$951—but contributions totalled over $17,000, almost enough to cover operating ex-

---

[22]Minutes, NYPM board meeting, Sept.9, 1959. NYPM Archives, Box 234, folder i.
[23]The list included such musical luminaries as Leonard Bernstein, Elliott Carter, Aaron Copland, William Schuman, and Virgil Thomson. Other notables were Wystan Auden, Thomas B. Hess, James Rorimer and Vera Zorina. Most of Noah's wealthy women backers also lent their names.
[24]Minutes, NYPM board meeting, Oct. 12, 1960. NYPM Archives, Box 23, folder i.

penses of $17,510. The result was a surplus of $10,401. However, $6,000 of this amount had been earmarked by donors for the purchase of organs, and Noah immediately laid out the money.

In 1962-1963, Pro Musica played 45 out-of-town concerts, performed three times at the "Y" and once each at the Morgan Library, Washington Irving High School, and Columbia University in New York, put on six New York performances of *Daniel,* and toured Europe for over a month in the summer. The Concert Ensemble made money. Receipts came to $91,913, and expenses and CAMI commissions totaled $85,996, leaving a gain of $5,927. *Daniel* grossed $21,457 but netted precisely $55.42 after expenses. Again the Motet Choir lost money (even after receiving a $3,500 grant). Oddly, its deficit was $951, as it had been a year earlier. Pro Musica's music thus brought in a mere $5,031. This year, fortunately, miscellaneous receipts and contributions of about $28,000 pushed total income up over $35,000, enough to cover operating expenses that ran close to $22,000 and generate a surplus of over $13,000.

The point is that the busier and and more successful Pro Musica became, the more it cost to operate and the larger the sums it had to seek from outside contributors. Once again, it is Noah versus the wolf, and it explains why, despite the other pressures on his schedule—and despite his own reluctance—Noah had to devote so much time and energy to the thankless, embarrassing tasks of fundraising.

In Noah's diaries and letters and in Pro Musica correspondence, there are hints, at first vague and insubstantial, that health was more of an issue in Noah's life than this big gourmandizing bear of a man liked to admit. Almost the first demand Toni made of Noah during their courtship in the summer of 1952 was that he cut down his smoking and drinking and lose weight. When a mutual friend lectured him on his overuse of butter in cooking, Toni wrote that she was "Delighted repeat delighted."[25] He was to lose "fifteen pounds off [his] middle." A few days later, Toni asked in a letter "how's your weight reduction plan program coming????"[26] But evidently, more than dieting was involved. On Wednesday, August 6, Noah wrote cryptically:

> Went to the doctor today. . . . The pain didn't go away — and I had cut down on my smoking (1/2 pack a day). The Dr. said the muscles in that area were strained. So I feel lots better about it now.[27]

---

[25]Toni Feuerstein-Noah Greenberg, letter, July 18, 1952.
[26]Toni Feuerstein-Noah Greenberg, letter, July 21, 1952.
[27]Noah Greenberg-Toni Feuerstein, letter, August 6, 1952.

From this, it seems Noah had been experiencing some chest pain, grounds for a certain amount of apprehensiveness, especially in the light of his mother's weak heart. But nothing came of the episode, and for years the record is silent on the issue of Noah's health.

The back injury Noah suffered in the fall of 1959 was a serious one, enough to put him in a corset for many weeks.

His friend the music critic Irving Lowens commiserated with him months later.

> This slipped disc business is hell on wheels, I understand—and it seems to be an occupational disease of conductors. Stay away from it, yes? This is one possession just not worth hanging on to, even though you may be fond of it. [28]

Like many sufferers from back pain, Noah learned to live with the condition. Aspirin helped. A long soak in a hot bath to ease his aching back muscles became a regular part of his pre-concert routine. Whatever trouble it caused him, his slipped disk never led him to cancel a concert or lecture.

Noah's style of life was hardly conducive to good health. Where food and drink were concerned, moderation was not his way. A two-pack-a-day smoker, he preferred unfiltered cigarettes. His voice was hoarse from smoking and his breathing notably heavy. Like many smokers at the time, Noah made sporadic efforts to cut down or quit, but he never broke himself of the habit.

Also, Pro Musica's constant touring carried with it all sorts of health hazards, from head colds to perpetual fatigue to psychological stress. Noah, wisely, went out of his way to make Pro Musica tours more than mere endless trudgings from college town to town. La Noue Davenport remembered with zest Noah as tour chauffeur:

> The conversations we used to have driving! We'd be driving, oh, backing off the steering wheel, going 78 miles an hour, smoking cigarettes. . . .[29]

Sheila Schonbrun said that being on tour with Noah was exciting in and of itself.

> And also, when we went to Hannibal, Missouri, he arranged for us to tour Mark Twain's home. He wanted to do it, and he arranged for things like that all the time.[30]

---

[28]Irving Lowens-Noah Greenberg, letter, April 6, 1960. NYPM Archives, Box 47, folder xix.

[29]LaNoue Davenport, April 3, 1997.

[30]Sheila Schonbrun, April 3, 1998.

Noah's stamina was extraordinary; but even so, as he entered his forties, touring stopped being a picnic. His old friend Jesse Simons remarked on the toll it exacted:

> On returning from concert tours, Noah would be exhausted. He told me that after out of town recitals, he had to attend parties because it was there he would meet past and potential contributors. Those attending these late-night parties were important in the cities where they lived, and wanted to have Pro Musica in their homes. They insisted on having the Director, and there was no way for him to avoid it. 'I must go.' he'd say, 'Even if I'm tired, sweaty and want to take a shower and take off my shoes and tuxedo.' I recall there was a year, maybe a year and a half [1960-1961], when Noah had a terrible back problem. Nonetheless, he went on tour. It was extremely hard on him. Even when Noah was taking drugs for the back pain and when all he wanted to do was to lie down, he nonetheless went to these social affairs.[31]

Gordon Myers recalled one tiny but revealing episode. At a concert at the University of Buffalo in November 1962 the tempi in one number began slowing and slowing.

> We [the singers] looked at each other, wondering what the hell was going on. And there's Noah, standing in front of us reaching in his shirt pocket for a cigarette! All of a sudden he woke up and realized where he was and started to conduct again. He had been in another world.[32]

This is the behavior of a tired man. Yet even when the wolf seemed to be winning, Noah would never, never let go.

---

[31]Jesse Simons, *op. cit., p. 27.*
[32]Gordon Myers, February 11, 1999.

CHAPTER THIRTY

ℋIS MOST POWERFUL PATRON

(1963)

𝒪n August 1962, Noah was faced with a sudden moment of panic. Tenor David Dodds, who was directing the Abbey Singers, wrote to Noah, who was vacationing with the family: "a matter of the direst urgency has arisen within the last 48 hours; we have lost our countertenor (the new one, that is) to the medical profession, sort of."[1] That is, countertenor Herbert Coursey had suddenly decided to leave and enroll in medical school. Noah had already drafted John Ferrante to take Robert White's place in the Concert Ensemble. Should John come back to the Abbey Singers for Abbey's fall season? On Noah's advice, Dodds immediately put up notices inviting auditions from countertenors, but Noah did "lend" John Ferrante to the Abbey Singers for some fall concerts.

The Abbey countertenor search, however, was only a distraction. Throughout the late summer of 1962, Noah and Dick French were preoccupied with two much larger projects. One, scheduled for the following summer, was a second ANTA-State Department-sponsored tour. This one would take Pro Musica to Eastern Europe and the Soviet Union. The other was a Sacred Drama program to be carried out with St. George's Church. Under this scheme, St. George's would commission three new Pro Musica productions of liturgical dramas (in addition to *Daniel*) and provide the physical setting and some office space and services for Pro Musica during the Christmastide presentation of each. Pro Musica would raise the production money and share the box-office receipts with St. George's.

[1]David Dodds-Noah Greenberg, letter, August 11, 1962. NYPM Archives, Box 47, folder iv.

The scope of the Sacred Drama program meant that Noah and Dick would have to try to raise money on a very large scale. Dick suggested that a serious effort should be made to seek support from the Ford Foundation.

Noah's first contact with the Ford dated back to the very beginning of Pro Musica in 1953. Somewhere, he had made the acquaintance of the French-Canadian soprano Eve Gauthier. Mme. Gauthier's enormous repertoire included Javanese and Indian music, the songs of Igor Stravinsky, works of George and Ira Gershwin, and even early music. Among Mme. Gauthier's other acquaintances was Dyke Brown, a Ford Foundation vice president. In February 1953, she suggested to Noah that he write Brown, and promised to tell Brown to expect the letter. Noah, optimistically, dated his letter on Valentine's Day. Brown wrote back a month later, dashing his hopes.

> the Foundation does not presently have a program which includes music and the fine arts, and there is little likelihood of our undertaking activities in this area in the near future.[2]

In March 1958, a few weeks after *Daniel's* brilliant premiere, Noah had written to Robert Hudson of Ford's Educational Television and Film Division about the possibility of a film. Hudson had answered, but nothing had come of Noah's approach. (Not until 1965 did National Educational Television shoot a kinescope of *Daniel* for presentation on Christmas Eve of that year.) Nor had other efforts in 1958 and 1959 borne fruit. But Noah and Dick had learned that Edward F. D'Arms, a senior Ford grants officer, had attended several concerts and had expressed enthusiasm for Pro Musica.

On September 29, 1962, Noah and Dick offered the members of Pro Musica's board their "preliminary thoughts about an approach to the Ford Foundation."[3] Their ideas were bold, almost outrageously so. They were planning to ask Ford for an amount equal to about $2,500,000 in current (1999) dollars.

> The Foundation, it is hoped, may provide money for the Drama project with St. George's Church ($300,000-$350,000) for presentation of the dramas in the United States outside of New York, for the purchase and maintenance of larger office and rehearsal space, and for the endowment of the overhead expenses of Pro Musica, including rehearsal costs, additions to the library and instrument

[2]Dyke Brown-Noah Greenberg, letter, March 10, 1955. NYPM Archives, Box 27, folder 2.

[3]Minutes, NYPM board meeting, September 29, 1962. NYPM Archives, Box 23, folder ii.

collection. It is also hoped that certain support might be had for one or two foreign tours of the Pro Musica ensembles and drama projects during the term of the grant.[4]

On December 1, 1962, Noah told the board that he and Dick had "had conference with Mr. Lowry of Ford Foundation.[5] Noah Greenberg had met his last and most powerful patron.

W. MacNeil Lowry was not born to wealth, had a distaste for it and never acquired it. Indeed, he never earned more than a modest executive salary. McNeil Lowry was a child of the midwest and was in many respects a walking embodiment of its virtues: honesty, frugality, plainspokenness, a sense of obligation to others. By the time his and Noah's paths crossed, Lowry had been many things— teacher, magazine editor, reporter, government official, Navy intelligence officer, Washington bureau chief of a string of midwest newspapers. Able, energetic, and personable, he had done well in all of these jobs. He had made influential friends wherever he went. His friend James Reston of *The New York Times* helped find him work (at the World War II Office of War Information and, after the war, at the International Press Institute.) His friend Milton Eisenhower tried to hire him at the University of Pennsylvania. His friend Hubert Humphrey, no mean connoisseur of networking, thought that Mac Lowry was one of the best-connected people he had ever met.[6]

In 1936, Henry Ford had set up the Ford Foundation to handle his and his family's personal charitable endeavors.

After Henry Ford's death and that of his eldest son Edsel in the late 1940s, the Ford Motor Company went public and the Ford Foundation found itself in possession of 88 per cent of the shares, thereby becoming the behemoth among American foundations, with a net worth of nearly a billion dollars.

In October 1953, Mac Lowry joined the Ford Foundation. Within two years, Lowry was presenting to a dubious board of trustees a proposal for a new program, "the humanities and the arts."[7] A year later, the Ford's new president, Henry Heald, threw his influence behind Lowry's proposal. In March 1957 Mac Lowry became Ford's Arts and Humanities program director.

Lowry's approach to giving away arts dollars was unorthodox. Instead of sitting behind a desk to read grants applications, he in-

[4]*Ibid.*
[5]Minutes, NYPM board meeting, Dec. 1, 1962. NYPM Archives, Box 23, folder ii.
[6]Hubert Humphrey, quoted in Joan Simpson Burns, *The Awkward Embrace*, p. 303.
[7]Burns, *op. cit.*, pp. 309-314.

dulged his reporter's urge to find out in person what was going on in the arts. He spent most of his first two years at Ford traveling the United States, questioning hundreds of painters, dancers, theater folk, and musicians he met. Lowry stoutly refused to be lobbied by Ford trustees or anyone else on behalf of an applicant or program. He was determined to deal only with the creative people themselves.

> I do not either in my office or on a field trip begin discussions or even visitations except with the artist or artistic director and send out in advance warnings against the convening of board members or committees.[8]

Most unusual for a "philanthropoid"—the coinage is Dwight Macdonald's—Lowry detested playing it safe.

> I have also been interested in putting philanthropic dollars where they would do the most good. And this hasn't made me very popular with some very potent people in New York who are the boards of the Metropolitan Opera, the Lincoln Center, the Philharmonic Orchestra, the Metropolitan Museum, and so on.[9]

What Lowry did want to support was:

> [the] small group in the performing arts led by someone who really is motivated and capable of professional standards and aesthetic standards.[10]

In brief, everything about Mac Lowry made him the perfect patron for a gifted, striving organization, artistically successful but chronically underfunded, like Pro Musica.

In December 1962, Noah was busy with *Daniel* rehearsals and performances. He was also preparing the Motet Choir and Wind Ensemble for joint concerts at The Cloisters on January 2 and 3, 1963 (one day after the final *Daniel* at St. George's). Nevertheless, he found time to join Dick French at a meeting with Mac Lowry on Friday, December 7. The seven Pro Musica appearances in the New York area during the remainder of January meant that Dick French met most often with Lowry and refined, in talks with Edward F. D'Arms, a report that went to Ford on January 8, 1963.

"The purpose of the report," Noah and Dick repeated to the board on January 26,

> is to obtain subsidy to expand certain activities of Pro Musica, to acquire necessary capital assets to do so; so that the income to the

[8]Quoted in Burns, *op. cit.*, p. 274.
[9]Quoted in Burns, *op. cit.*, p. 315.
[10]Quoted in Burns, *op. cit.*, p. 288.

artists may be substantially increased and the minimal excess profit
from the expanded activities may enable Pro Musica to handle an
annual operating budget of $40,000 instead of the current $25,000.

One matter Dick's report did not cover was the role of St. George's
Church. Frederick A. O. Schwarz, a vestryman of St. George's, had
suggested that Pro Musica ask Ford for $7,600 to cover expenses at
St. George's for each year in which one of the four sacred dramas
would be put on, plus $2,600 for every other year. St. George's min-
ister, Rev. Edward O. Miller, later raised the $7,600 figure to $10,000.
This was exactly the sort of piggybacking that annoyed Mac Lowry,
although he was much too astute to say so directly. Instead, he

> emphatically and repeatedly stated that the Foundation could not
> even run the risk of being accused of contributing to operating
> deficits (which was effectively the case with St. George's). . . .

Accordingly, Pro Musica dropped mention of St. George's from
its proposal.[11]

On February 7, Noah and the Concert Ensemble set forth by Avis
rental car on a tour that took them first to the midwest and Canada
and then, at the end of the month, to the deep south. The first day
was ghastly. As Noah wrote to Toni:

> We did not arrive here until 1:30 AM last night. A terrible wind
> and then it started snowing around Syracuse. Visibility was quite
> poor and we had to drive at 30-40 MPH. I was so exhausted when
> we arrived![12]

The concerts went well, but the stress of touring mounted as the
tour wore on. In Winnipeg,

> [t]he sponsors here have arranged all sorts of C[anadian]
> B[roadcasting] C[orporation] interviews and I'm furious with them.
> They tried to insist that the entire company appear (without pay)
> and I turned them down. . . .
>
> Everyone is getting along fine — even John F[errante]. I saw both
> Carolyn and Gordon smile yesterday, believe it or not.[13]

Noah had found time in Minneapolis-St. Paul to look in on the
Guthrie Theater, then in course of construction. He also visited both
the Art Institute and the Walker Art Center in search of paintings by

---

[11]Minutes, NYPM board meeting, Jan. 26, 1963. NYPM Archives, Box 23, folder iv.
[12]Noah Greenberg-Toni Greenberg, letter, February 8, 1963.
[13]Noah Greenberg-Toni Greenberg, letter, February 15, 1963.

some of his favorite American artists, but "[they] had two special shows on and all the regular stuff was out of the galleries." In this same letter to Toni, he also sounds a theme he had raised earlier.[14]

> Being away from you is especially difficult this time for some reason. Seems to get harder all the time . . .[15]

A homesick Noah slipped away from the tour on Thursday, February 21 and caught a plane to New York. During his two-day visit, he, Toni, and the girls managed to take in one of Noah's all-time favorite movies, the Marx Brothers' *Duck Soup.* Then it was back to the midwest.

On February 25, in DeKalb, Illinois, Noah first learned of an important change in plan—and some tricky management maneuverings. Since January, Noah had been working with Leverett Wright of Columbia Artists Management and Frank Siscoe of the State Department on yet another ambitious project, a Pro Musica tour of the Soviet Union. The Russians and the State Department were eager to have Pro Musica go. Siscoe complicated matters, however, by asking Wright if CAMI would allow Pro Musica to make the tour as part of a crisscross arrangement with the Barshai Chamber Orchestra. The Barshai was represented by Sol Hurok, and it was Hurok who had approached Siscoe with the idea. Because exchange arrangements resulted in lower management commissions, Hurok seems to have hoped that CAMI would turn down the deal. That would pave the way for Hurok to approach Pro Musica directly with the exchange idea. Wright, however, told Siscoe that CAMI would permit Pro Musica to tour under an exchange agreement, thereby robbing Hurok of what Noah called his opportunity "to undermine our faith in CAMI."

But as Noah wrote to Toni,

> the Russians wanted us in the Fall <u>not</u> August — so it is postponed until Spring 1964 or Fall 1964. . . . I am delighted that it has turned out this way, frankly.[16]

He was not eager to give up his August even for the excitement of travel to the Soviet Union. The delay would also afford him precious time to plan the program, pick the right personnel and fit the tour into Pro Musica's schedule.

---

[14]In the letter of February 8, 1963. The relevant passage is quoted in Chapter Twenty-six, p. 281.

[15]Noah Greenberg-Toni Greenberg, letter, February 15, 1963.

[16]Noah Greenberg-Toni Greenberg, letter, February 25, 1963.

A few days later, Noah commiserates with Toni over the discovery of a cyst—benign—in her breast. He rejoices that "it is only 2 weeks now, darling" before the tour draws to an end. They would be grueling weeks, however, because of drives of hundreds of miles between engagements. In this letter, written from Memphis, Noah also touches on an all-too-familiar problem.

> The countertenor audition came off on Tuesday [in DeKalb]. My fears that [Thomas] Norager [in medical school in Chicago but reconsidering a singing career] was not professional enough were confirmed. He's got the range and he reads well, but he must study to develope [sic] his vocal technique. He's coming to New York in June and I'm going to . . . help him along.
>
> Ferrante came to see me after the audition and assured me that now he wanted to stay. That he's discovering things he can do that he never knew about his voice. It has shown in the last few weeks (with breakdowns all along). I'm afraid we must take him to Europe. What we replace him with will not be an improvement and can only mean lots of work.

One other observation set the stage for an extraordinary experience to follow.

> Perhaps I'm paranoid, but the Southerners we deal with seem hostile. The fact that we book in as the New York Pro Musica immediately dubs us. Nobody has been tarred and feathered yet, but they are not very cooperative. That famous Southern warmth is somehow missing. And they look at us as though we were strange.

Noah knew—the whole nation knew—that five months earlier, on October 2, 1962, after lengthy negotiations had failed, three thousand troops had been called in to quell rioting on the campus of the University of Mississippi. Armed U. S. marshalls had escorted James H. Meredith through jeering mobs to be the first black to enroll at Ole Miss.

Now Pro Musica was going there to perform. "I'm very curious about Oxford," was Noah's terse comment.[17]

His curiosity was more than satisfied. Pro Musica arrived in Oxford at about 3:00 p.m. on Thursday, February 28. Noah immediately phoned Ray Kerciu, an instructor in the University's art department whose name had been given to him by the Dean of Fine Arts at Northern Illinois University. Kerciu was waiting for Noah.

> He's a very close friend of Meredith and he and his wife were in fact bringing Meredith to [our] concert. I sat with [Kerciu] for one

---

[17]Noah Greenberg-Toni Greenberg, letter, February 28, 1963.

hour and heard the hair-raising description of what is happening
on this campus and the way M. conducts himself. Who [Meredith]
sees, what he's like, who fraternizes with him, the administration's
attitude, the faculty, etc.

In this letter, deliberately written as a chronicle of events, Noah
told Toni what happened next.

At 5 PM (after walking around campus) we went into the cafeteria. 2 minutes later Meredith became part of our chow line (5 people
removed). He's a wiry, short, well-adjusted-looking, lightskinned
Negro. He waited in line . . . ignoring those around him and equally
ignored. We got our food and found a large table, and then Ray
Kerciu went back to get M. to take him to our place. The surrounding tables were jammed with students and when he sat down with
us there was no noticable [*sic*] reaction, not even silence. It was as
though they had all agreed to ignore his presence. This is the current attitude here, apparently —'Ignore the nigger—let's bide our
time.'

Noah found Meredith "a very impressive guy," with a "great sense
of humor" which "has probably made the ordeal bearable."

[W]hen he speaks ideas he is very penetrating. For instance, he
explains the phenomenon of only one Mississippi Negro applying
to Ole Miss this way. 'I left home at 16. I was away from home for
11 years. Now every Negro down here has a white man who is
responsible to see to it that he's taken care of and learns how to
keep his place. This is the system—but they couldn't keep tabs on
me because I wasn't here.'

In a note hastily added the next day in New Orleans, Noah explained why he had waited to mail the letter.

I'm sure the local people [in Oxford] tamper with the mails. They
all *hate* the gov't & Kennedy. The marshalls & soldiers are call [*sic*]
Kennedy's Koon Keepers. Everyone (pro & con Meredith) says M.
would be dead in a matter of hours if the gov't pulled out.[18]

Nobody in the Ole Miss cafeteria had said or done anything overtly
menacing. Nevertheless, for Noah and his Pro Musica colleagues,
Yankee outsiders, to seek to break bread with James Meredith took
a certain measure of courage.

On a much lighter note, Noah the gourmet mentions that Pro
Musica's New Orleans sponsors took him out t to dinner at Brennan's
(home among other delicacies of Bananas Foster) and then to

---

[18]Noah Greenberg-Toni Greenberg, letter, February 28/March 1, 1963.

Preservation Hall to hear New Orleans-style Dixieland "played by real old-timers."

> [A]fterward] they wanted to know if I considered it music! They were really shocked to hear that I liked both the music and the performance. They couldn't understand that one could like Mozart and this also.[19]

The tour continued. Pro Musica gave two concerts in Florida, then moved into Georgia for two more, one of them at Spelman College in Atlanta, the Rockefeller-supported college for black women. The day of an appearance at the Medical College of Georgia in Augusta (Monday, March 11), Noah was reading Hannah Arendt on non-violence and Wystan Auden on Oscar Wilde in *The New Yorker* and asking Toni's opinion of both writings. Then he abruptly changed the subject. Mac Lowry had just reached Noah with the incredible news that the Ford Foundation had awarded Pro Musica $465,000.[20]

---

[19]*Ibid.*

[20]Dick French recalled receiving a phone call from Edward D'Arms of the Ford Foundation. "I was home in bed with the flu, and Ed D'Arms called me to say, 'Dick, we know you asked us for a total of $466,124. Would it be terribly inconvenient, would you mind very much, if we rounded it down to $465,000?'" Flabbergasted but delighted, Dick French said that No, he wouldn't mind at all. Richard F. French, January 26, 1999.

CHAPTER THIRTY-ONE

"WE GOT IT!"

(MARCH 1963)

The Ford grant, to be parceled out over ten years, would enable Noah to fulfill his fondest dreams, to expand and expand, to open up new realms of music and new methods of presenting it. Mac Lowry had in fact encouraged Noah and Dick French to enlarge upon their original ideas. They had accordingly asked for money to double the size of the Wind Ensemble to fourteen players, to pay them for rehearsal and practice sessions, and to revive the Motet Choir. Ford funds could also be used to increase the pay of Concert Ensemble regulars to a range of $8,000 to $10,000, rewarding loyal members and making recruitment easier.

Why then did Noah write to Toni after hearing the news that he was accepting the grant "with a heavy heart and mixed feelings?"[1]

Perhaps the best answer came not from Noah but from Mac Lowry himself. Years later, he noted that the effect of a Ford grant on a deserving recipient was not always or only beneficial.

> [Often], to get [grants], producing artists had to worry about their subscriptions or worry about taking on other activities. And yet the total absolute number of people about [to create or direct art] did not grow in the same proportion. So they were stretched. And some of them were even shrewd enough to say in advance of a grant, 'You're going to stretch me, aren't you?' I'd say, 'Yes, I'm sorry, that's an inevitable consequence of this.'

Lowry reached a melancholy conclusion:

> [These artists] were already working on a twenty-four hour day. How could they work any more?[2]

---

[1]Noah Greenberg-Toni Greenberg, letter, March 11, 1963.
[2]W. McNeil Lowry, in Burns, *op. cit.*, pp. 288-289.

When he said these things, Lowry could have been—and may well have been—thinking of Noah Greenberg.[3]

Noah added in his letter to Toni that he wasn't at all sure about his decision. "I don't know yet—I may still back out by next week."[4] But that same day, March 11, he placed a call to Dick French. "I remember picking up the phone and hearing Noah," Dick said. "He just shouted: 'We got it!'" He remembers nothing despondent or downhearted about Noah's reaction. But he does recall that Noah regarded the Ford grant as a weighty responsibility, one to be taken very seriously.[5]

Noah's standard method of dealing with doubt and hesitancy was to keep rolling onward. Joel Newman, who had stepped aside as librarian-researcher the previous September, said of Noah in this mood, "He was like a locomotive."[6] Back in New York on the night of Sunday, March 17, Noah probably did share with Toni his trepidation about the Ford grant, but he spent little if any time agonizing about it. Nor did he follow up on his hint that he might back out. Within a day or two, he was deep into rehearsals of the Concert Ensemble and the Renaissance Band. The latter was an amalgam of Concert Ensemble instrumentalists and Wind Band members. It had made its concert debut at the Metropolitan Museum's Grace Rainey Rogers Auditorium in April 1962. Putting the two groups together made it possible, as *The New York Times*'s critic observed, to "demonstrate the wide range of sounds that were heard at indoor and outdoor musical gatherings of the time."[7] As well as readying the Concert Ensemble for a March 30 "Y" appearance, Noah was scheduling rehearsals of the Renaissance Band for a concert at Caramoor in late June.

This was not so easy. As Morris Newman observed,

> [Noah] would come back from ... a tour which he'd been eagerly preparing and doing with the regular Pro Musica and suddenly say, 'Oh my God, I haven't even had a rehearsal with the Wind Band for six months. ... What are you doing now?' 'I'm doing a

[3]In the same interview with Joan Burns, Lowry quoted Noah directly on those who patronized the arts to gain status and exercise power. "Noah Greenberg used to say, 'My God! The hangers-on! The parasites!'"
[4]Noah Greenberg-Toni Greenberg, letter, March 11, 1963.
[5]Richard F. French, January 26, 1999.
[6]Joel Newman, April 16, 1997.
[7]Alan Rich, "Pro Musica Plays Dances and Songs," *The New York Times*, April 16, 1962, p.33:4.

show, I'm not available at such and such a time' — and just to get us *together* was a problem because we were all busy.[8]

A day or two after the March 30 concert, a reluctant Noah was once again on an airplane, this time bound for Kuala Lumpur and a four-day symposium on "Cultural Affairs and International Understanding" that, as usual for such events, added nothing to either topic. His sponsor was The American Assembly, a public-policy think tank at Columbia University. Noah should not have made the trip, but Mac Lowry had pressed Noah to go, and he saw no way to refuse.

On April 16, Noah was back in New York. On the 18th, he and Dick French convened a Pro Musica board meeting at which they presented a carefully-worked-out timetable for putting out word of the grant. This called for a press conference on Friday, May 3 and a press release and public announcement the following Monday. Pro Musica itself would be told at a Sunday evening meeting, "to be followed by drinks and buffet supper. Only people currently working with Pro Musica will be invited."[9]

In mid-March, Gordon Myers had told Noah that he would be leaving Pro Musica at the end of the summer. "I was returning to school to earn a doctor's degree in order to get a job teaching on the college level."[10] John Ferrante was also leaving, so "John Ferrante and Gordon Myers will not be invited to meeting as grant does not affect them." But because Gordon's baritone was needed over the summer, a degree of tact was deemed prudent. Accordingly, "Mr. Greenberg will speak to Gordon Myers and invite him and Harriet to supper after the meeting."[11]

Other problems were more substantive. The first Ford check, for a staggering $138,000, was already on its way. It was not to be touched before the beginning of the 1963-1964 season, a month and a half away. The question was what to do with the money beforehand. John Straus of the Macy's Strauses, a friend of Toni's, found a

[8]Morris Newman, November 4, 1998.
[9]*Ibid.* Those invited were the members of the concert ensemble for 1963-1964 (Sheila Schonbrun, Carolyn Backus, Ray DeVoll, Earnest Murphy, Brayton Lewis, LaNoue Davenport, Judith Davidoff, Shelley Gruskin and Paul Maynard) plus the Abbey Singers (Jan DeGaetani, David Dodds, Marvin Hayes and Arthur Burrows), Stuart Gardner (who led the boys' choir), staff members (stage manager Michael Ackerman, librarian-researcher Charles Canfield Brown, secretary Alice Roberts) and members of the Pro Musica board.
[10]Myers, *op. cit.*, p. 102.
[11]Minutes, NYPM board meeting, Apr 18, 1963. NYPM Archives, Box 23, folder iv.

bank, Irving Trust Company, that would accept the funds and insure them in full.

A second issue was the search for new office and rehearsal space. Pro Musica's lease on its ground-floor space at 865 West End Avenue would expire on July 1, 1963.

Pro Musica's library and growing instrument collection were already overflowing their allotted space, and there was no room at 865 for expansion. The board appointed Noah, Arthur Squires, and LaNoue as a committee to canvass the area for new quarters.

The third issue arose from Mac Lowry's reluctance to let Ford be Pro Musica's (or any arts organization's) sole source of support. As the minutes of the board meeting explain,

> [u]nder the terms of the grant, New York Pro Musica must undertake to raise within the ten and one-half year period a minimum of $150,000 from other sources.[12]

So even now money would be troublesome. Noah and Dick French had already started contacting Pro Musica's most loyal private supporters to explain the situation. Lawrence and Ellie Bloedel promptly pledged $2,000 a year for the next ten years, and two of the key members of the "Ladies' Committee," Ursula Corning and Mina Curtiss, $1,000 each. Arthur Squires suggested that Noah "get on phone to raise money."[13] Among those he should contact were the financier and art collector Ben Heller, Standard Oil heiress and arts devotee Rebecca Harkness Kean, Otto Manley, a Mr. F. R. Jeffrey and the stringed-instrument dealer Rembert Wurlitzer.

The urgent quest for new quarters turned up a roomy ground-floor apartment, 1B, at 300 West End Avenue at 74th Street. The building was in the process of being converted from a rental property to a cooperative; one of those involved in the conversion was the singer Harry Belafonte. Noah pronounced the space excellent, and on June 3, 1963, Pro Musica purchased Apartment 1B for $25,000. The maintenance was $416.25 per month.[14]

Noah, Toni, librarian Charles Canfield Brown (a student of Joel Newman's, Brown had succeeded to Joel's Pro Musica job) and stage manager Michael Ackerman spent much of June in moving and overseeing nearly $10,000 worth of carpentry, plumbing, painting and other work on the new quarters. As had been the case with the Rockefeller Foundation grant, some of the musicians felt that Noah

[12]*Ibid.*

[13]*Ibid.*

[14]NYPM Archives, Box 81, folder xiii.

had gone overboard on furnishings, and a few wondered why some of the Ford money couldn't been distributed "to the people who were doing the work"—themselves.

In the middle of the turmoil at 300 West End Avenue, Noah and Toni had to grapple with an entirely different set of pressures. In place of the postponed tour of the Soviet Union, Chris Schang of CAMI had worked with ANTA and the State Department had set up a month-long tour of arts festivals in four other countries. On June 30, Noah led the Renaissance Band in concert at Caramoor, Lucie Rosen's estate in Katonah, in northern Westchester forty miles from the New York. On July 2, the Concert Ensemble made an appearance at Columbia University, performing a program Noah had first worked out in 1956, "The Bible in Early Music." One week later, Noah, Toni, Anne and Jane, with the members of the Concert Ensemble and some members' families,[15] flew from Idlewild Airport in Queens to Amsterdam, one of Noah's favorite cities. A concert at the Hague on July 10 was the first of fifteen Pro Musica would be giving in the Netherlands, Spain, Israel and Yugoslavia.

The tour, like most Pro Musica tours, was both exhilarating and exhausting. Judith Davidoff remembers one "very Noah" episode. On the way into Amsterdam, after a meal that at least in Noah's case included several bumpers of potent Dutch gin, Noah was speeding along even faster than usual. "If we land in a canal," he said waggishly to his already nervous passengers, "roll up the windows. That way we'll float."[16] Noah's colleagues settled for a much tamer boat tour of the city's canals.[17]

After appearances at The Hague, Amsterdam, Middleburg and Otterlo in the Netherlands, Pro Musica traveled to Spain for several concerts at San Lorenzo de El Escorial, the enormous monastery built by Philip II of Spain as "a combination temple, pantheon, study center and meditation refuge"[18] in the hills 30 miles northwest of Madrid. One of the concerts was largely devoted to the *Cantigas de Alfonso el Sabio,* the wonderful thirteenth-century strophic songs in praise of

[15]The concert ensemble personnel on the tour were singers Sheila Schonbrun, Carolyn Backus, Ray DeVoll, Earnest Murphy, Gordon Myers and Brayton Lewis and instrumentalists LaNoue Davenport, Shelley Gruskin, Judith Davidoff and Paul Maynard. In addition, Mrs. Gruskin and Amy (age 4), Judith's husband Sumner Rosen and Edward (age 2), and stage manager Michael Ackerman made the trip. NYPM Archives, Book 36, folder i.

[16]Judith Davidoff, January 29, 1999.

[17]Myers, *op. cit.,* p. 99.

[18]"The Royal Monastery,"homepage,http://banesto.es/banesto.

the Virgin Mary gathered by Alfonso X "the Wise," King of Castile and Leon. It received rave reviews in the local press, as did the "Early Baroque: London, Venice and the Netherlands" program. Afterward, the Librarian of San Lorenzo el Real, Rev. Gregorio de Andres, O.S.A., permitted Noah to handle a superbly illuminated fourteenth-century manuscript (one of two in the library) containing all 414 of the *Cantigas.* Father Gregorio seized the occasion to make a plea for funds to rebind the library's rare music manuscripts. Noah promised to do what he could, and he did later contact possible contributors in New York.[19]

The next stop after El Escorial, San Sebastian, and Santillana del Mar in Spain was a celebrated kibbutz in Israel, Ein Hashofet, about 60 miles north of Tel Aviv. Founded in 1937, Ein Hashofet, "Spring of the Judge," was named for U. S. Supreme Court Justice Louis Brandeis, who helped support a group of the kibbutz's first-generation American settlers. It prided itself—it still does—on being a center of the arts as well as a highly productive enterprise. Pro Musica's "The Bible in Early Music" program was especially well received.

Following a concert in Jerusalem, the group drove north to Haifa on the coastal road. On the way, the Pro Musica caravan stopped at Caesarea, where Noah tested the acoustics of the famed Roman amphitheatre by reciting the Marc Anthony funeral oration from Shakespeare's *Julius Caesar.* "He spoke in a normal voice," Judith Davidoff said, "and from the top you could hear every word."[20]

At the end of July, after a final concert in Israel, (in Tel Aviv), Pro Musica flew to Yugoslavia for three appearances at summer festivals. Two were made in Dubrovnik on the Adriatic and a third in Ohrid in Macedonia. On Tuesday, August 7, most of the Pro Musica party left for the U. S. But Noah, Toni and the girls stayed behind with Judith Davidoff, her husband Sumner Rosen and their two-year old son Edward at a *pensione* in the hills overlooking the city. The children played together in the garden and the grownups enjoyed two blissful weeks of relaxation before the Greenbergs left to drive northward to Trieste and Austria. In July, a letter from Wystan Auden had reached Noah in Israel, telling him that Auden and Chester Kallman would "of course be delighted to see you both on August 26" at the Auden-Kallman summer house in Kirchstetten. As he did for so many visitors, Auden wrote out directions to the

[19]Noah Greenberg-Rev. Gregorio de Andres, O.S.A., letter, April 14, 1964. NYPM Archives, Box 1, folder 8.
[20]Judith Davidoff, January 29, 1999.

Kirchstetten railway station from Vienna and drew a rough map to guide Noah from Route 227 to Kirchstetten village and through an underpass to Number 6 Hinterholz. "Take the cart track to the garage rather than drive up to the front door."[21]

Jane Greenberg, who was four years old at the time, dimly remembers her efforts to climb aboard a large turtle while her father and Auden chatted in the garden.[22] Other details of the visit are likewise uncertain. But Noah had business to conduct in England. So London, not Vienna or another European city, was the last stop on their itinerary.

On Friday, August 30, Noah lunched in London with Sir William McKie, organist and choirmaster of Westminster Abbey, whom he had met while planning the 1960 *Daniel* tour. Noah had a proposition for Sir William. In 1966, the Abbey would be observing its 900th anniversary. Why should not one of the events marking the occasion be a new Pro Musica production of a liturgical drama? Noah and William L. Smoldon, his musicological friend from the early days of the *Daniel* project, had developed one, and in fact its first performances would take place in December in New York.

Unfortunately, Sir William McKie indicated, Westminster Abbey would not be available during the anniversary year. After a brief meeting with Smoldon, Noah flew back to New York. Deadlines were very much on his mind. Anne was in the fourth grade at The Dalton School, and classes at Dalton started on September 9. The next day, Noah was to lead the Motet Choir, the Wind Ensemble and Stuart Gardner's boys' choir in a composite Mass (Josquin, Isaac, Buchner, Verdelot, Schlick). The performance was at the Chapel of the Intercession, and its audience was an important one, members of the International Musicological Society attending the eighth congress of the organization. Even more worrisome, Pro Musica's fall tour was scheduled to begin on October 13.

Noah had less than six weeks in New York to get work started on the new drama production.

For over two years, Noah and Bill Smoldon had been exchanging ideas about a successor production to *Daniel*. Among other sources, they had been considering the Fleury Playbook. A thirteenth-cen-

---

[21] W. H. Auden-Noah Greenberg, letter, July 16, 1963.

[22] Jane Greenberg Ernst, April 30, 1997. Judith Davidoff wonders about this recollection, noting that there was a "good-sized" turtle in the garden of the *pensione* where she and her family stayed with the Greenbergs a few weeks earlier, and that this might have been the turtle Jane was trying to board.

tury manuscript probably compiled at the Abbey of St. Benoît-sur-Loire in north-central France, the playbook contains ten plays. One, *The Representation of Herod* retells the Biblical story (Matt. II:1-20; Luke II:1-18) of King Herod and the three Wise Men, from the annunciation to the shepherds to the Adoration of the Magi in Bethlehem. A second, *The Slaying of the Innocents,* deals with the rage of Herod, the Flight into Egypt, the slaughter of the children and the return of the Holy Family after the death of Herod.

The London music publisher Stainer and Bell had brought out Smoldon's transcription of the Fleury *Representation of Herod.* At the instance of Andrew Porter, Noah had reviewed the edition for the British journal Porter was editing, *The Musical Times.* The writeup had appeared in late 1961. What Noah said makes clear his awakening interest.

> Smoldon's fine introduction will serve as more than helpful encouragement to the imaginative director and the 'acting version' clearly presents the original thirteenth-century material in manageable form. . . .[23]

In January 1962, Smoldon had written to thank Noah for the favorable review, but, reticent perfectionist that he was, had added, "I wasn't at all pleased with that *Herod* edition and I wish I could set about doing it again." He said he preferred another of his transcriptions, *The Son of Gedron.*[24] On January 31, 1962, Noah had gently but firmly put forward his own wishes.

> I am quite surprised to hear that you are not very pleased with your *Herod* edition. . . In fact, I am considering the possibility of preparing a performance of this work. I would very much like to work with your edition and hope that you can supply us with the original Latin underlay."[25]

Over the next eight months, Smoldon and Noah had written back and forth about other dramas. But Noah, once aroused, was not easily diverted. On Sept. 12, 1962, he had reopened the question.

> Two weeks ago I re-studied the Fleury *Herod Play* and I am really taken by it. I have many ideas for its production, and I am now in the process of convincing others of its merits as a stage piece.[26]

[23]Noah Greenberg, typescript copy of review of William L. Smoldon, *Herod, A Medieval Nativity Play,* London. Stainer and Bell. 1960. The bulk of the Greenberg-Smoldon correspondence about *Herod,* along with other *Herod* material, is in NYPM Archives, Box 4, folder 5.

[24]William L. Smoldon-Noah Greenberg, letter, January 5, 1962.

[25]Noah Greenberg-William L. Smoldon, letter, January 31, 1962.

[26]Noah Greenberg-William L. Smoldon, letter, September 12, 1962.

Nine days later, Smoldon, had suddenly broached a new idea. The Fleury Playbook contained a second Herod play, "The Slaughter of the Innocents."

> I have it roughed out. Would you collaborate with me (on a 50/50 basis) to produce an acting version as quickly as possible?"[27]

On October 11, Noah answered, striking while the iron was hot.

> If you are really interested in a future edition of *Herod* . . . I would be interested in seeing your version of "The Slaughter of the Innocents" and perhaps consider collaborating on both.[28]

On December 11, 1962, Noah had let Smoldon know that he was planning to take the *Herod* plays with him "when I leave for a long tour in February."[29] In January 1963, he apologized for not writing sooner. "[D]o understand that I haven't had a moment." He added glumly, "I suppose I will have to resign myself to living without idle moments from now on."[30] But two weeks later, he was singing a much more cheerful tune.

> Just a note to tell you that [your version of] *The Slaying of the Innocents* has arrived and I have spent some time with it. . . . I would like to consider the possibility of doing this work together with the *Herod* play.

Like the master salesman he was, Noah first assumed Smoldon's consent, and then plunged with irresistible enthusiasm into the details of production.

> Back to the *Innocents*. The rubric which refers to the 'lamb' does present problems. I suspect we will have to look through some 12th and 13th century French illuminations to see what they did. I will also consult with an art historian friend of mine . . . Professor Meyer Schapiro of Columbia. I am tempted to say that the nicest thing to do would be to have a live lamb. We are already planning on a sheep dog for the shepherds as well as an ass for Mary (if we do the *Innocents*). This will absolutely mean hiring a zookeeper. It should be great fun.[31]

On April 26, 1963, with the news of the Ford grant echoing in his ears, Noah had written:

---

[27]William L. Smoldon-Noah Greenberg, letter, September 21, 1962.
[28]Noah Greenberg-William Smoldon, letter, October 11, 1962.
[29]Noah Greenberg-William L. Smoldon, letter, December 11, 1962.
[30]Noah Greenberg-William L. Smoldon, letter, January 18, 1963.
[31]Noah Greenberg-William L. Smoldon, letter, January 30, 1964.

I am happy to tell you that the money we have been looking for to produce *Herod* and *Slaying of the Innocents* has been raised. It was very difficult, but we can now plan a production of these two pieces for next December. I would very much like to know if you have any changes to make in either play because I must now make a performing edition based on your transcription. . . . The sooner you get this material to me, the sooner I can go ahead with our plans.

He had offered Smoldon a choice of "a $500 fee for use of the transcriptions and a $25 royalty per performance [or] a $1,000 flat fee with no royalty."[32] On May 5, Smoldon, long since persuaded, had accepted the $500/$25 option.[33]

Combined in a single presentation as *The Play of Herod*, the two Fleury plays thus became the first of the four sacred dramas to be produced under the Ford grant. With Ford money available to cover the costs, Lincoln Kirstein was much less cranky than usual in the role of producer. In fact, Kirstein had brought in his all-star production team. Rouben Ter-Arutunian, the designer of a dozen New York City Ballet productions (including *The Nutcracker*) and many Broadway musicals, was costume and stage designer. Barbara Karinska, City Ballet costumier, was creating the costumes. Once again, Noah and Kirstein had hired Nikos Psacharapoulos as director. In June 1963, Nikos wrote Noah about casting issues. "I will continue my hunt for a Virgin." He was also worried lest the sets become "as fancy and as cute as our original production [*Daniel*]." Noah, unable to resist, wrote back from Spain: "If you are really looking for a virgin, you had better get out of Williamstown."[34]

Casting went smoothly. Noah's "farm system" provided a splendid group of singers to augment the Concert Ensemble regulars. From the Motet Choir came countertenor Thomas Norager, tenors Alva Tripp and Paul Solem, baritones Robert Kuehn and George Papps and bass Rochard Vogt. The Abbey Singers contributed sopranos Jan De Gaetani and Elizabeth Humes, countertenor John Ferrante, tenor David Dodds, baritone Arthur Burrows and bass Marvin Hayes. Only a few singers—Robert Klein, Walter Rhodes, Frank Roberts—were brought in from "outside." Four instrumentalists were needed to serve as "Musicians to the Magi." Three were Concert Ensemble members. LaNoue played a tiny sopranino re-

[32]Noah Greenberg-William L. Smoldon, letter, April 26, 1963.
[33]William L. Smoldon-Noah Greenberg, letter, May 5, 1963.
[34]Nikos Psacharapoulos-Noah Greenberg, letter, June 25, 1963; Noah Greenberg-Nikos Psacharapoulos, letter, July 16, 1963. NYPM Archives, Box 52, folder ii.

corder, Judy Davidoff learned the vielle, a medieval hurdy-gurdy, and Shelley Gruskin mastered the cornemuse, a peasant bagpipe. The fourth instrumentalist was Frederick King, a percussionist, who played the part of the musician to Herod. King, like Marvin Hayes, was black. Noah made no parade of his feelings, but especially after his experience at the University of Mississippi, he quietly sought to add black musicians in his performing groups. The part of a fifth instrumentalist, the "Musician to Mary," was taken by Paul Maynard, who carried and played a bell carillon—Pro Musica's Whitechapel handbells hung on a special frame.

One reason Noah had stopped off to visit Auden the previous August was to ask him to do for *Herod* what he had done for *Daniel*. That is, write a verse narrative that would tie together the stage action, in this case of two separate lays. But on October 11, 1963, with rehearsals already in progress, Auden wrote:

> After making a number of attempts to do a commentary for *Herod*, I have come to the conclusion that it cannot be done, or, at least, that I cannot do it. The incidents have been so frequently versified that anything one writes turns out to be a pastiche of medieval Christmas carols.
>
> All I think you need, frankly, is simply a reading of the Gospel narrative. . . .
>
> I am sure you will believe me when I say that it is not laziness which has made me give up— I should love to have done something—but a conviction that I am not needed.[35]

Noah's reaction to this dismaying development was to call Lincoln Kirstein. Kirstein put forward Robert Lowell as a possibility, and on October 15 Noah wrote to Lowell "at the suggestion of Lincoln Kirstein," sending him a *Herod* script and asking him to write the narrative. "Both Lincoln and I hope that the work will interest you. . . . It would be really wonderful if you could do it."[36] A week went by without answer. On October 23, Pro Musica's devoted secretary Alice Roberts called Noah, on tour in Maine, with word from Kirstein that Lowell too had declined. In the end, Archibald MacLeish wrote a competent but uninspired version.

Somehow, Noah found time to look after Bill Smoldon's interests. Mrs. Robert Woods Bliss of Washington and Mrs. W. Murray Crane of New York were both members of Pro Musica's unofficial "Ladies'

---

[35]Wystan Auden-Noah Greenberg, letter, October 11, 1963.
[36]Noah Greenberg-Robert Lowell, letter, Oct. 15, 1963. NYPM Archives, Box 52, folder ii.

Committee." Both were also board members of the Washington-based Institute of Contemporary Arts, along with such other luminaries as William P. Bundy, Duncan Phillips, and Sir Herbert Read. One or both women probably helped Noah secure an ICA grant to allow an ecstatic Smoldon to make a six-week visit to the U.S., to attend *Herod* rehearsals and performances and to lecture on medieval liturgical drama in Washington, Chicago and New York.

Smoldon arrived on Wednesday, November 20, and took up quarters in the apartment Noah had arranged for him at the Union Theological Seminary on upper Broadway. The next ten days were frantic ones. The assassination of President John F. Kennedy on Friday, November 22, fractured the plans and disrupted the schedules of the whole world, and Pro Musica's plans and schedules were no exception. An appearance at the Library of Congress was canceled, and Renaissance Band members straggled sadly back to New York.

On Monday, November 25, full cast rehearsals of *Herod* began at The Cloisters. These started at five o'clock in the evening, after the building had emptied of visitors, and continued until at least nine o'clock. On Wednesday the 27th, Noah led the Wind Band, Motet Choir and the Abbey Singers in a concert at Hunter College: several works were performed in JFK's memory. On Friday the 29th, the Concert Ensemble played at Vassar College in Poughkeepsie. Noah sped back down the Taconic Parkway to New York in time for a *Herod* rehearsal. Rehearsals went on nightly through December 8. The dress rehearsal was held on the afternoon of Monday, December 9. Performances began that evening, and the last of the eight performances (including two matinées) was given on Saturday the 14th. Noah, drawing on his phenomenal reserves of stamina, was on hand every night.

CHAPTER THIRTY-TWO

$\mathcal{A}$NXIETIES

(FEBRUARY 1964)

$\mathcal{T}$he New York reviews of *Herod* were worshipful. Eric Salzman, invited to a rehearsal, wrote in *The New York Herald-Tribune* the day before the opening performance that Rachel's lament "is an example of the amazing power and subtlety of this apparently simple music."[1] Alan Rich, writing in the same paper two weeks later, expressed himself in even riper terms:

> [A]s the music resounded through the wonderful building at Fort Tryon Park, one felt transported. Not necessarily transported to a specific date some 800 years ago, but transported to that unending realm that is the timelessness of art.[2]

After the final New York performance on December 14, Noah had two weeks in which to relax and enjoy the holiday season. The Greenbergs loved to give parties and they loved to go to parties, and they did plenty of both. At a large Greenberg party, the guests would be the *prominenti*, the leading figures on New York's cultural and intellectual scene. On any given evening *chez* Greenberg, one might find Helen and Elliott Carter, painter John Heliker and Bob La Hoten, Elizabeth Hardwick, Hannah Arendt, Nathalie and Hugo Weisgall, Irving Kristol, Daniel Bell, and Wystan Auden and Chester Kallman. Noah himself would be the greeter and major domo, fetching drinks for each new arrival, cracking jokes, making people feel at home. Toni would typically be sitting on the sidelines, engaged in animated conversation with one or another of the guests.

---

[1] Eric Salzman, "A Medieval Christmas at The Cloisters," *The New York Herald-Tribune,* December 8, 1963, p. 41.

[2] Alan Rich, "Updating the Middle Ages," *The New York Herald-Tribune*, December 29, 1963, p. 27.

The Magi come bringing gifts. Scene from The Play of Herod *at* The Cloisters,
New York City
(Courtesy of the Music Division of The New York Public Library for the Performing Arts
Astor, Lenox, and Tilden Foundations)

There were other, more intimate gatherings as well. Friday night
poker games were a tradition when Noah was in town, and Noah
may well have arranged one on December 20, 1963, the Friday before Christmas. Among the regulars were Noah's old friends Rubin
Baratz and his wife Cherito, Julius Goldstein, and on occasion an
old friend of Noah's, Marie Cooper. Musicians were rather point-
edly not invited. Nine-and-a-half-year-old Anne Greenberg adored
those occasions.

> There was a lot of loud talk and a lot of laughter and excitement.
> They didn't really play for money, it was penny-ante. But I used to
> be allowed to pour people's drinks, especially my Dad's. He taught
> me how to do it. He drank Scotch, maybe Johnnie Walker or maybe
> Chivas. I only remember that it had a red label.[3]

The Christmas tree that always sparked an argument between
Noah and his Aunt Dora was brought home, set up and trimmed.
Claire Brook recalls seeing the Greenbergs' tree for the first time
and looking at it askance. In her experience, Jewish people and especially, God forbid, Socialists simply did not put up Christmas trees.

[3]Anne Greenberg Donovan, June 11, 1997; Rubin Baratz, interview, June 12, 1997.

I asked, 'What's with the tree?' Toni looked a little embarrassed and said, 'Well, it's so nice for the children.'

On New Year's Eve of 1963, Claire and Barry Brook and Toni and Noah celebrated in style. Clad in formal attire, they began with dinner at a fine midtown restaurant and then went on to a party at the home of Lorna and Eric Salzman on Middagh Street in Brooklyn. The composer Edgard Varèse opened the door.

Everybody in music was there. The first person I saw inside was Alan Rich dressed up as Schubert, with tiny little glasses. In the middle of the floor were three beautiful women, paying no attention to anyone else, Cornelia Foss, Amanda Burden, and Ellen Adler. And everybody was kidding Barry and Noah about their tuxedos, pretending that they were waiters.[4]

On Friday, January 3, Noah traveled to Washington, D.C. to lead the Renaissance Band in the concert at the Library of Congress. (This was the new date for the appearance originally scheduled for November 22.) Once again, the reviews were adulatory. Robert Evett blended adulation and shrewd analysis in *The Washington Star:*

One of the best and most important concerts of the season was that offered last night by the New York Pro Musica Renaissance Band. . . .A glance at the program will suggest that it was one of those 16th century smorgasbords of a lot of little pieces sounding very much alike. This is precisely what it was not. Noah Greenberg has a genius for organizing programs so as to achieve the maximum effectiveness from both consistency and variety. Brilliant programming is one of three things which sets the concerts of the New York Pro Musica apart from rival exercises in musical antiquarianism.

A second . . . is verve. His musicology is imaginative. . . . What Mr. Greenberg offers is not a timid reconstruction of what the composers left, but rather a full-blooded interpretation of what they very likely intended. The music never sounds nice-nelly. It is sometimes raucous, blatty, even out of tune, and always exciting.

Third is the element of assurance and authority. When you consider that nobody goes to school to learn how to play the sackbut or the krummhorn, it is amazing—and a tribute to the musicianship of the members of the band—that these young players are so superbly schooled that they can adjust to the quite different requirements of Renaissance instruments.[5]

[4]Claire Brook, August 18, 1998; February 26, 1999.
[5]Robert Evett, *The Washington Star,* Saturday, January 4, 1964,

Almost without pausing to draw breath, Noah and the Renaissance Band returned to New York. The next day, Noah, LaNoue, Shelley, Judith, and Paul boarded a plane to Chicago to join the rest of the *Herod* cast for six performances of the drama at the Rockefeller Chapel of the University of Chicago. It was the beginning of a frantically busy year.

Noah's friend Robert Marsh, music critic of *The Chicago Sun-Times*, loved *Herod*. He called it

> a beautiful synthesis of pageantry and pantomime, set to the purest melodic lines, and illuminated with the sound of bells.

And Marsh held forth on

> the spiritual quality that shone with an intensity that made this medieval liturgical drama as much a religious experience as a theatrical one.[6]

But not all reviews were so favorable. Claudia Cassidy of *The Chicago Tribune*, always on the lookout for a zinger, wrote:

> The trouble with an indelible triumph is that it remains just that—indelible, unequaled, unrivaled. Three years ago New York Pro Musica came to Rockefeller Memorial chapel with a medieval musical play called 'The Play of Daniel,' an ancient, fragile and indestructible work that was enchantment, pure and undefiled. Monday night the group came back to the same vaulted chapel with "The Play of Herod," and it was not like that at all. It was admirable, it was devoted, and often it was beautiful. But it was cool, contrived and remote, and to me its hour and a half without intermission seemed interminable. 'Herod' is really a dead duck..[7]

Noah could not have been too surprised. In November 1960, in the wake of Russell Oberlin's resignation, Cassidy had headlined her review, "Pro Musica Fades." *Herod* was hardly a dead duck, but neither was it a *Daniel*. It was nearly half again as long as *Daniel*, and because it combined two separate plays its action was more diffuse. More to the point, *Daniel* had been a great novelty. The same astonishment and sense of wonder that had greeted the first medieval liturgical drama to be presented in 800 years could not very well have greeted the second.

On January 18 (1964), a week after the last *Herod* performance in Chicago, Noah was leading the Renaissance Band at the "Y" in New

---

[6]Robert Marsh, *Chicago Sun-Times*, Tues. Jan. 7, 1964, p. 30.

[7]Claudia Cassidy, "'Herod' Admirably Done But no Match for Magical 'Play of Daniel,'" *The Chicago Tribune*, Wed. Jan. 8, 1964, Section 2, p. 1:7,8.

York. Then it was off to Syracuse with the Motet Choir and Wind Ensemble for a concert on Tuesday the 21st and from there to Buffalo for a repeat the next day. On February 2, the Concert Ensemble played at New York University. The spring tour began in earnest on February 4. Pro Musica headed north into Massachusetts for three concerts in four days, stopped in New York for a second "Y" appearance, and left town again, this time for five weeks. Noah and his troubadors were at Union College in Schenectady on Wednesday, February 12 and continued westward with stops in Ann Arbor and Albion, Michigan and Valparaiso, Indiana. They then flew to El Paso to begin a long swing through the southwest, California, and the Pacific northwest. But Noah made it only as far as Albuquerque before all the projects and the pressures at last caught up with him.

On this trip, Noah had some writing to do. Accordingly, he had with him his Olivetti Lettera portable. On Washington's Birthday in Albuquerque, this supremely self-confident man rolled a piece of Hotel Alvarado stationery into the little typewriter and poured forth to Toni an astonishing cascade of doubt, anxiety, even despair.

> Please be patient with me—I'm going through something awful and I am not quite sure what it's all about. Could it be just the smoking? Perhaps I should plan to smoke (lightly) to avoid this madness?

But the problem, as Noah knew well, wasn't nicotine.

> What, after all, troubles me? I am terribly anxious about current and future projects: Oxford Herod, Reese article [for the *Festschrift* planned for Gustave Reese, a collection to which all the stars of Medieval and Renaissance scholarship would contribute]. Band replacements, Paul Maynard—who is not going to Russia, the production of Daniel with Herod.

> I am also concerned about my being away from home so much and my relationship to the girls —which bothers me terribly.

Next and most telling:

> I am concerned with your attitude toward my work and my talents. You seem to think I could make it no matter what I did. But I cannot just pick up and leave all this right now. And, of course, I am concerned about our relationship because I don't think you love me enough—or something.

> Maybe I just want to be anxious and create problems where they do not exist. Maybe you love me more than enough but I am just insatiable. All I know is—I'm trouble [*sic*] and cannot relax—even in my sleep.

He tried to pull himself together:

> I cannot wait until this thing [the tour] ends and I get back home.
> Maybe I'll snap out of this nonsense in a day or so. Sweetie, a 1000
> kisses for you and please hug and kiss both Anne and Jane for me.
> Please forgive me for being so damned depressing but it will pass
> and you're the only one I can tell this to.[8]

Noah's sudden attack of *angst* may have had its roots in physical
illness. A week later, on Sunday, March 1, Pro Musica was in Los
Angeles for a concert at U.C.L.A. Noah was being interviewed for a
radio broadcast when he was taken ill and collapsed. A doctor was
called and Noah was taken to the hospital. There, tests showed that
he had been experiencing internal bleeding of unknown origin. The
bleeding stopped and Noah's blood pressure rose to satisfactory levels, but there was no question of his being able to go on with the
tour. Much as he hated to admit it, Noah was not indispensible. He
decided that the tour should continue, under LaNoue's direction,
into northern California, Oregon, and Washington. He himself remained in the hospital for nearly a week, flew back to New York,
and submitted to more tests at a hospital there. On March 10, Pro
Musica's Alice Roberts passed on the news to William L. Smoldon,
back in England.

> Mr. Greenberg returns to New York this evening to recuperate at
> home after nearly a week in a hospital out there . . .[9]

On March 13, Smoldon replied:

> Your letter has just come. I am deeply shocked to hear of Mr.
> Greenberg's illness, and I am writing to him to his home address.
> I am very glad to hear that the doctors think that there is nothing
> serious the matter, but I suppose the fact is that he has been 'burn-
> ing the candle at both ends' as we say. He must surely take things
> just a little easier.[10]

"My condition is not serious now," Noah himself wrote to his
musician friend Milton Katims on March 11, "but I must be extremely
careful."[11] He was much less the invalid in a letter the same day to
LaNoue in Seattle.

[8]Noah Greenberg-Toni Greenberg, letter, February 22, 1964.
[9]Alice Roberts-William L. Smoldon, letter, March 10, 1964. NYPM Archives, Box 4, folder 4.
[10]William L. Smoldon-Alice Roberts, letter, March 13, 1964. NYPM Archives, Box 4, folder 4.
[11]Noah Greenberg-Milton Katims, letter, March 11, 1964. Milton Katims, conductor of the Seattle Symphony Orchestra, was the brother of Herman Katims, a *(cont.)*

I am home safely and a little tired after the plane trip yesterday. The doctor has ordered me to stay in bed and I will undergo a series of tests this coming week to determine what the bleeding point was. Otherwise I feel pretty relaxed and my thoughts keep wandering across the Mississippi . . .[12]

The tests were unrevealing, and Noah rapidly regained both strength and emotional equilibrium. On March 18, he wrote to his contact at California Lutheran College that "I am just now beginning to resume my activities." On the 24th, he was telling Milton Katims:

I am much better now. It looked for a while as though I would need surgery, but as it turns out my ailment can be treated medically. I am happy to say that I have been able to resume my schedule.[13]

What the "ailment" was, Noah did not divulge. (He later identified it as diverticulitis.) Nor, once its symptoms had subsided, did he allow it to slow him down or change his habits. His only concession to the illness was to cancel two lectures scheduled for April.[14] Indeed, Noah simply brushed aside any inner misgivings and in true Noah fashion went on as if nothing had happened.

One of the multiple "activities" Noah resumed was completing the piece of writing he had taken with him on tour. This was a birthday tribute to Noah's friend the musicologist Gustave Reese, to be published in *High Fidelity* magazine. In it, Noah took a look backward at how the music he and Reese loved had begun to find its way from musty manuscripts and archives to the popular ear.

Amusingly enough, it was not the givers of conventional concerts who opened up their programs to the repertory of early music, but the record companies—and, for the most part, not the large record

composer whose work and ideas influenced Noah's mentor Harold Brown. NYPM Archives, Box 37, folder xi.

[12]Noah Greenberg-LaNoue Davenport, letter, March 11, 1964. NYPM Archives, Box 37, folder xi.

[13]Noah Greenberg-Milton Katims, letter, March 24, 1964. NYPM Archives, Box 37, folder xi.

[14]Cancelled lectures included one at Trenton State College, New Jersey, scheduled for April 2. Alice Roberts-Shirley Stagg Batchelor, letter, March 20, 1964: "As Mr. Greenberg's personal physician has urged him to cut down on his exceedingly heavy schedule, we are sorry to inform you that his lecture engagements for this coming spring must be postponed." NYPM Archives, Box 6, folder 16. Another had been scheduled at American University, Washington, D. C. NYPM Archives, Box 6, folder 18. However, Noah evidently did appear as scheduled at Dartmouth College on April 15, the day before a Pro Musica concert at Dartmouth.

companies (who could have easily afforded to do it) but the small
ones, who could not afford to hire the virtuoso ensembles and artists needed to sell recordings of the standard repertory. Given the
LP record and a small operating budget, the small companies were
drawn to the modest (and modestly priced) ensembles of the prac-
titioners of early music, and the partnership was an extraordinar-
ily happy one. Not only is the general public familiar with sonorities and repertory both of which were largely unknown two decades ago, but what began as a curious interest in new music and
timbres has now been broadened and deepended into a cultivated
awareness of musical styles.... Certainly the tyrannical monopoly
of the standard repertory has been seriously weakened."[15]

By Noah's standards, Pro Musica's April schedule, which called
for ten appearances in three weeks, was only moderately demanding. Noah, back in charge, led concerts at Swarthmore, Montclair
(New Jersey) High School, Cornell, Dartmouth, the Taft School (Connecticut), Jordan Hall (Boston). After appearances in Pennsylvania
and Ohio, Noah and the Concert Ensemble drove to Washington,
D.C. For a concert at the Library of Congress on Friday, April 24,
Noah added lutenist James Tyler, a pupil of Joseph Iadone at the
Hartt College of Music, and put on a program of works by Elizabethan composers featuring the lute.

On April 25, Pro Musica returned to New York from Washington
for a major engagement. Lincoln Center for the Performing Arts,
incorporated in 1956, had been a vast construction site for eight years,
and one that devoured money. Originally set at $75 million, Lincoln
Center's price tag had ballooned to $164 million. Mac Lowry of the
Ford Foundation had scorned Lincoln Center as "a big deal that was
really about banking and real estate," not art.[16] Even so, Noah, Dick
French and Chris Schang of CAMI had jumped at the opportunity
to perform there. In September 1962, one of its components, Philharmonic Hall, had been completed. Its well-publicized "Opening
Week" had begun on Sunday September 23. The huge hall was not
the best environment in which to perform or listen to early music,
but Pro Musica had been selected to perform at a 5:30 matinée on
the 26th. Noah had put on a mixed program—Dufay, Des Prez, Isaac,
Cabezon, Weelkes, Morley—to the usual good reviews.

In the spring of 1964, to tie in its programming with the city-wide
World's Fair Festival and the tourist trade it would attract, Lincoln

[15]Noah Greenberg, typescript of article, "A Birthday Greeting to Gustave Reese."
NYPM Archives, Box 6, folder 25.
[16]W. McNeil Lowry, in Burns, *op. cit.*, p. 317.

Noah leads the Renaissance Band. l.rear to front: Paul Maynard, Robert Szabo,
Gilbert Cohen, Arnold Fromme, Robert Montesi; l. center: Martha Bixler (at
regal), LaNoue Davenport; r. center: Donald Plesnicar, Judith Davidoff, Shelly
Gruskin (behind Noah); r. standing: Philip West, Morris Newman,Frederick
King (percussion).
(Courtesy of the Music Division of The New York Public Library for the Performing Arts
Astor, Lenox, and Tilden Foundations)

Center was promoting three weeks of concerts by the cream of the city's musical organizations. The New York Philharmonic and the New York City Opera were two of them, Pro Musica a third. Noah made Pro Musica's three scheduled appearances a demonstration of its musical breadth and versatility. For the April 25 concert, Noah repeated the Elizabethan program presented in Washington the evening before. On May 2, he led the Renaissance Band in sacred and secular works of Renaissance Europe. Two out-of-town engagements then intervened. On Sunday the 3rd, the Concert Ensemble played at Princeton. Wednesday the 6th found Noah in South Bend, Indiana, conducting the Motet Choir in a concert of Renaissance sacred works commemorating the opening of the new library at Notre Dame. On Saturday, May 9, Noah led the same program at Pro Musica's third Lincoln Center concert.

Two days later, Noah was on the move again, taking Toni with him across the Atlantic to Germany. Especially in the three years since the Berlin Wall had gone up, a strong U.S. presence in West Berlin had been seen as a symbol of this country's determination to hold the line against Communist aggression in Europe. For Europeans, this meant a presence on the cultural front as much as—perhaps even more than—a show of military might. Along with many other organizations, the Ford Foundation helped to bolster U.S. involvement in the cultural life of the divided city. Ford had set up an "Artists in Residence" program in Berlin. One of the Ford consultants was the conductor and Bach scholar Karl Haas. In November 1963, at the behest of Joseph Slater, director of Ford's International Affairs Program, Haas had set the wheels in motion for a special symposium in Noah's honor at Berlin's International Institute for Comparative Music Studies. "Let me say from the outset," Haas wrote,

> that, as a musician, I am particularly enchanted with the idea of your coming here, for I have always greatly admired your work and all that you stand for.[17]

The costs of the trip—Noah did not charge a fee—were covered by Ford through the *Deutsche Akademische Austauschdienst*. Toni and Noah left New York on May 11, ate filet mignon aboard Lufthansa Flight 401 and spent ten days in Berlin, staying at the grand luxe Hotel Kempinski on Kurfürstendamm, sightseeing and meeting musicians and music scholars. On the guest list for Noah's May 20 lecture were academic dignitaries, musicologists, museum curators, music publishers, and many composers, among the latter the Americans Roger Sessions, Philip Pires, and Elliott Carter. Noah made a special friend of Alain Daniélou, head of the Institute, later writing to him excitedly about the musical discoveries he made during Pro Musica's Soviet tour.[18]

Back in New York on May 22, with a June tour of music festivals ahead, Noah found himself facing two problems. One was large, one not so large. Both had to be resolved before early fall, when Pro Musica was to set forth on its seven-week tour of Yugoslavia and the Soviet Union. The first was to find a replacement for Paul Maynard.

Paul had unfailingly and brilliantly served Pro Musica since its founding, in ways often hard to measure. Thus, Paul was one of the few players of keyboard continuo accompaniments who could seat themselves at an instrument, read from an unembellished score *at sight*, listen to what the other performers were up to, and improvise

[17]Karl Haas-Noah Greenberg, letter, November 15, 1963. NYPM Archives, Box 27, folder 9.

[18]Correspondence and other materials about this Berlin trip is in NYPM Archives, Box 27, folder 9.

a right-hand part that was both harmonically correct and musically elegant. This is no small task in a slow movement. In a fast one, it is a strenuous test of the fingers, the eye, and the imagination. It can turn an uninspired performance into an exciting one.

Paul Maynard could do more. In early music, much of the detail of instrumentation and expression is left to the performers. Rehearsals therefore involve a good deal of experimentation. It is often necessary to try different combinations of instruments, differing tempos and rhythms, different modes of expression. Always interested in questions of musical strategy, when something wasn't working Paul would say, "Noah, let's try it this way," and sketch out a new possibility at the keyboard. And Paul would uncomplainingly put aside keyboard virtuosity for the portative organ, the psaltery or even the bell carillon—whatever served the needs of the music.

Paul himself may have helped Noah find a successor. Edward Smith, twenty-nine in 1964, was born in Michigan and grew up in southern Wisconsin. He had graduated from the music conservatory at Lawrence College in Appleton in 1957 and had spent a year in Italy studying composition with Luigi Dallapiccola on a Fulbright Fellowship. In 1960, Smith entered Paul's alma mater, the Yale School of Music, as a student of harpsichordist Ralph Kirkpatrick. He had received his Master's degree in 1963 and had gone out to Illinois to teach. Paul knew Kirkpatrick well and may have learned of Smith from him. Like Paul, Ed Smith was an accomplished continuo player with a keen interest in performance practice. He would stay with Pro Musica for four concert seasons.

Noah had the reputation of reacting with anger or sullen indifference whenever anyone left Pro Musica. Gordon Myers declares that after he had sung with Pro Musica for the last time, in Dubrovnik in 1963, all he got when he tried to thank Noah for "six years of wonderful and exciting performances" was a "limp handshake" and silence.[19] But with Paul Maynard, nothing remotely like this occurred. On the contrary, Noah pushed his friends in music hard to find Paul work appropriate to his talent. Through Joel Newman, Noah had met the teacher and music theorist Saul Novack, who in 1964 was chair of the Music Department at Queens College. There was nothing timid about Noah's approach to Novack on Paul's behalf.

> He called me and got me on the phone and said, 'Now listen, Saul! Paul Maynard is getting tired of touring and being away from his family. Is there anything you can do for him?'[20]

[19]Myers, op. cit., p. 102.
[20]Saul Novack, April 14, 1997. Barry Brook was also on the Queens College (cont.)

As it happened, there was something. With help from Noah's old friend Barry Brook, Novak did it. They secured Paul Maynard a tenured position at Queens College, where he taught harpsichord and organ and led the college's Collegium Musicum until his death in 1998.

The other problem with which Noah had to contend was a polite but determined rebellion on the part of the three women members of the Concert Ensemble.[21] The subject: dress, and, more specifically, the formal concert dresses they wore onstage. Pro Musica had evidently been paying only part of the cost of the dresses and none of the cost of alteration, repair, and drycleaning. With an extended tour in Eastern Europe in prospect, the question of what clothing to wear and how best to take care of it was a serious matter. Arthur Squires's friend Beatrice Farwell had joined the Pro Musica board. At a board meeting on June 4, she commented, perhaps a shade patronizingly, on the mixture of dress issues.

> Miss Farwell reported that she had met with Sheila Schonbrun to discuss new dresses for the female members of the Concert Ensemble. Speaking for the three girls, Sheila told Miss Farwell that:
>
> a) They think that Pro Musica should provide their dresses and the cleaning of them on the grounds that they are uniforms and cannot be used for any other purposes.
>
> b) They would like two sets of dresses for Russian Tour, namely the dresses they have now and new ones. There would then be no cleaning on tour. They said they never have any cleaning on tour, even in this country.
>
> c) Sheila complained about Martha Gould's dress. She recommended the designer Diana Blair who would do them for $150 each plus cost of goods.
>
> d) They would prefer velvet or velveteen because they can hang it up in shower and steam it, dark colors, simpler designs—less dragging on the floor, etc.
>
> e) They would like a set of rules . . . as to when they are to get new dresses based on how much the dresses are used rather than periods of time.

---

faculty. Noah may have sounded him out about employment for Paul before contacting Novack.

[21]The three were gambist Judith Davidoff, soprano Sheila Schonbrun, now married to LaNoue Davenport, and soprano Elizabeth Humes, a Hartford native and Skidmore College and Hartt College of Music graduate who had replaced Carolyn Backus at the beginning of the 1963-1964 season.

f) Finally, Sheila said that if there is any disagreement, the girls would like to meet with the Board and plead their cause.[22]

The board (probably unprepared for a serious discussion of the issue) took no action one way or the other. New dresses were forthcoming in 1965, but to the best of Judith Davidoff's recollection the "girls" went off to Russia in September with only one concert dress apiece.[23]

---

[22]Minutes, NYPM board meeting, June 4, 1964. NYPM Archives, Box 23, folder 4.

[23]Judith Davidoff, January 22, 1999. The males on the tour wore tails for their concerts. Judith remembers that "the only Russian most of the men learned" was the Russian phrase that meant "heavy starch," used each time they gave their stiff-shirt dickeys to the hotel laundries.

CHAPTER THIRTY-THREE

⊂ℳoscow to Tblisi

(OCTOBER 1964)

"⊂ℋnnie is growing up. This was the first time within memory that she was so upset by my leaving." So Noah wrote on September 24, 1964 aboard a TWA jetliner headed for London.

> Janie sort of looked on at her [sister's] tears with surprise. It was truly painful to walk out quickly. I must write to the children constantly even though the Russian mails will be slow.[1]

Three weeks before, the Greenbergs had been vacationing on Shelter Island, its tranquil twelve square miles tucked between the north and south forks of Long Island in Peconic Bay. There had been swimming and boating and fishing and quiet evenings in the house Noah had rented for the month on Sandpiper Lane. Noah also found time in late August or early September to go with Anne to a movie she, like thousands of other New York kids, was dying to see. The Beatles' first film, *A Hard Day's Night,* had premiered in New York on Tuesday, August 11 and was playing at local theaters on the Long Island mainland. For a Dalton School fifth-grader, getting to it was an urgent matter, well worth a ferry ride.

> I have always remembered going on the ferry to the cinema . . . and a wonderful ride home [afterward] laughing and talking about the film and my [D]ad likening it to the Marx Brothers genre. I was thrilled, as he was a big Marx Brothers fan.[2]

Noah had needed a rest, and August had supplied one. The day after Labor Day, however, the family was back in New York. The

---

[1]Noah Greenberg, private journal of tour to Yugoslavia and the U.S.S.R., September-November 1964. (Hereafter, "Russian journal.") Entries will be identified by month and day.

[2]Anne Greenberg Donovan, e-mail message, March 3, 1999.

day after that, September 8th, Noah had begun rehearsing in earnest for the Russian tour.

Now, sixteen days later, Noah was alone on the London flight. He had a stop to make before flying eastward, via Yugoslavia, to the Soviet Union. In the air, he began the journal that he'd promised himself to keep faithfully throughout the tour. "TWA and its movies," he grumbled prosaically, "make it totally impossible for one to get any sleep." But he did manage to doze for two hours before arriving in London at 7:20 in the morning.[3] Almost immediately, he changed planes and flew on to Amsterdam, where he was a guest at an Amsterdam Concertgebouw concert conducted by Bernard Haitink. Noah enjoyed the concert and the festivities that followed it, but the evening was an inessential pleasure, a tribute to his status in the broader world of music beyond early music.

The next day, he flew via Zurich to Zagreb, met the company and continued to Belgrade where he could stretch out and gain some "much needed sleep."[4]

Pro Musica gave five concerts in Yugoslavia and flew to Vienna early on Saturday, October 3, to catch an Aeroflot flight to Moscow. The next day, Pro Musica was given the standard treatment for fairly important visitors to Cold War Moscow: a bus tour—the Kremlin, Gorky Street, the University— then a Bolshoi Swan Lake at the Palace of Congresses. Noah led the first rehearsal in Russia on Monday morning and the first concert, at the Moscow Conservatory, that evening. Sheila, Elizabeth Humes and Earnest Murphy all had colds, which added to the pressure.

After the concert, Noah wrote worriedly:

> Company is very edgy! I have never seen them like this. I'm sure they'll be back to normal after a few days. All were unusually nervous for the first concert but performances were almost all first rate.

His chief concern throughout the entire tour was audience response.

> The audience (full house) was a bit cool at first; I thought they were an audience of older people. Unfortunately very few youngsters. It seems to me such an audience comes to our concerts with many pre-conceived notions about music in general and performance in particular. Ours, after all, is a new departure . . .

---

[3]Russian journal, September 24.
[4]Russian journal, September 26.

Noah later learned that Pro Musica had been billed in the tour cities simply as an "American Orchestra." Audiences, accordingly, expected symphonic music and were mystified by much of what they were hearing. (Having been told for decades that racism was universal in the U.S., they were also wide-eyed at the presence of Fred King.) In Moscow and everywhere else, however,

> [t]he singing—especially the slow pieces, *Draw a Sweet Night* of Wilbye, *The Willow Song*—won their hearts. . . . They loved the Ward *Weep Forth Your Tears.* Oh yes, *It Was a Lover and His Lass* had to be repeated!

The first night, Noah led two encores,

> but [we] could have gone on and on. About 14 curtain calls, lots of stamping of feet, shouting and marked applause. Very moving— even if they probably do this with all performers.[5]

At the concert the next evening (Tuesday, October 6), "the audience was again cool to begin with and very excited by intermission." During the intermission, the virtuoso violinist David Oistrakh and other Soviet musical luminaries came backstage to greet the visitor. Toni, newly arrived in Moscow, reached the Conservatory in time to be seated in Oistrakh's box for the last part of the concert. Toni had traveled with Sumner Rosen, Janet Gruskin and several other Pro Musica spouses. She would stay in Moscow to sightsee over the weekend (Sumner Rosen also stayed behind) and rejoin the tour in Tblisi. Noah was delighted to see her, but noted that "she looked exhausted and overexcited."[6] Overcome by jet lag, Toni slept until 1:30 the following day.

"Great problems," Noah wrote on Wednesday the 7th.

> Ray [DeVoll] has lost his voice and he is really indispensible to the Flemish-Burgundian program tonight. We rehearsed the entire program without him and had to make certain changes. I dropped the Dufay *Ave Regina* and the Josquin *Parfons Regrets.*

But even though Ray was so ill that he had to stay in the hotel, the final concert in Moscow "went extremely well. The band played its best and the singers sang admirably. It's a great company."[7]

On Thursday the 8th, an open day, Noah and Toni toured the Kremlin art collections. They were accompanied by Andrei Volkonsky, a composer who was also—according to Noah—"the only

[5]Russian journal, October 5.
[6]Russian journal, October 6.
[7]Russian journal, October 7.

Pro Musica in Moscow's Red Square, 1964.
(Courtesy of the Music Division of The New York Public Library for the Performing Arts
Astor, Lenox, and Tilden Foundations)

harpsichordist in Moscow (perhaps the USSR)." Noah and Charles Brown had brought with them sets of Pro Musica recordings and multiple copies each of books on music and related topics, to be presented as gifts.[8] In addition, Pro Musica brought a few copies each of hardcover books on music history by Gustave Reese, Manfred Bukofzer and Denis Arnold, plus sets of Pro Musica records, and some recorders. Volkonsky's hunger for access to scholarly works on early music inspired them to give Volkonsky "a complete set of our recordings and as much music and music history books as we could spare." (Despite Volkonsky's covetous glances, Noah could not spare Pro Musica's harpsichord.) In return, Volkonsky gave Noah a seventeenth-century *Book of Hours*.

For Noah, the real excitement began on Sunday, October 11.[9] Pro Musica returned to Moscow, then boarded a jet for the flight to Tblisi. The occasion triggered an outburst of Noah's ebullience.

> We saw all of the Ukraine and then the snow capped Caucasian Mountains. Glorious sight! Tblisi feels like the Southwest USA at first. I was greeted by the director of the Philharmonic — a handsome, big, vigorous looking Georgian wearing the Georgian version of a ten gallon hat. We were also greeted by a glorious sunset, heavy wind, clear skies and a crescent *moon*.[10]

Like so many American travelers to Georgia, Noah fell in love with the region and its peoples. His journal suddenly blossoms with description. He writes lyrically of townscapes ("[t]he streets are crowded, clean, and Mediterranean in feeling"); markets ("persimmons, pomegranates, peaches, grapes, apples, pears, variety of greens, beautiful tomatoes, cauliflower, eggplant, green beans, dried beans, pickled greens, live chickens, dried fish, various meats, sausages. Each stall was a sight"); of food and drink ("a tremendous feast, beautifully prepared and tasty. Lots of fresh vegetables, skewered meat and broiled tomatoes").[11]

---

[8]The books were mostly paperbacks. The list is an interesting survey of what was available in paperback format on music history and medieval and Renaissance aesthetics and musical performance practice: *The Pelican History of Music*, Vols. I,II; Anthony Baines, *Musical Instruments Through the Ages*; Thurston Dart, *The Interpretation of Music*; Charles Homer Haskins, *The Renaissance of the 12th Century*; Erwin Panofsky, *Studies in Iconology*; Ferdinand Schevill, *Medieval and Renaissance Florence*; Paul Oskar Kristeller, *Renaissance Thought*; Johann Huizinga, *The Waning of the Middle Ages*; Wylie Sypher, *The Four Stages of Renaissance Style*; Basil Willey, *The Seventeenth-Century Background*.

[9]Russian journal, October 8.

[10]Russian journal, October 11.

[11]Russian journal, October 11, October 12, October 20.

Georgian folk music utterly enchanted him.

> I have heard about this music but this was a revelation. 3 and 4
> part polyphony, some of it sounding like the XIV C. Italian caccie,
> some like Perotin, some like English early medieval music—oth-
> ers like Spanish XII C. polyphony. . . . The vocal pieces . . . were for
> tenors and basses. Solo, duo, trio and choir—up to 40 men. Fabu-
> lous ensemble, virtuoso ornamentation. . . I came away enthralled
> —a new area of remarkable music.[12]

Noah would bring back tapes of this music to the United States
and play them again and again for friends and musical colleagues.
The conducting also fascinated him. At an afternoon concert at the
Tblisi Conservatory, the leader of a sextet of males voices

> was the youngest of all—about 20—who comes from a long line of
> village singers. He had perfect command of his group and uses
> his eyes, eyebrows, chin, and head, never hands. The entrances,
> cut-offs, pitch, dynamic changes, tempi, were all perfect. It made
> a profound impression on the whole [Pro Musica] company, espe-
> cially the singers.[13]

For the first of the three Tblisi concerts, the Elizabethan program,
the house was only two-thirds full, the organs kept going out of
tune and the audience never stopped talking. The second concert
was a different story. There was still talking, but "the house was
jammed—the boxes at double capacity." The galleries were filled
with the young people Noah loved to have in Pro Musica audiences.
By now, most of the singers were nursing colds, coughs and sore
throats, but "still, it was a fine concert."[14]

The afternoon of the final concert in Tblisi (Wednesday, October
14), Noah somehow picked up rumors that Nikita Krushchev had
been deposed. There was no visible sign of change and no public
unrest, but he decided not to tell the company for fear of alarming
people. The following morning found Pro Musica in the ancient
Georgian capital city of Mtskheta. At an eleventh-century church
built over an even older (sixth-century) church, they heard still more
Georgian singing.

> Some members of the congregation have a special prayer and hymn
> —and this was the truest and most unsophisticated polyphony one
> could hear in the Middle East. It was 3-part and it sounded like
> Stravinsky.

[12]Russian journal, October 12.
[13]Russian journal, October 13
[14]*Ibid.*

Paul Khutchma, a musicologist at the Conservatory,[15] told Noah
later that day that Krushchev's "retirement" would be announced
the next morning. Again Noah said nothing to the company. Instead, everyone rested to be in good form by evening for a formal
farewell dinner. The dinner itself was delightful. It "went on and
on, a parade of fine dishes—innumerable toasts—all with fine Georgian wine." But there were "strange tensions at work on both sides.

> [T]he high points were the toast to the visiting Russian cultural
> dignitary, the singing of "Swanee River" (!) by Khutchma—and
> everybody's joining him—and the reprise—a speech by Robert
> [Montesi?] on The Movement [the anti-Vietnam War movement]
> and "We Shall Overcome"—everybody locking hands and rock-
> ing mournfully.

Brayton Lewis then stood up to sing "Water Boy," but introduced
it in a way that "had the officialdom hysterical. It reinforced the
prop[aganda] about us—which they don't believe!!" Noah sat there
shaking his head, but reported that he never said a word to Brayton
about the matter. The after-dinner entertainment ended with songs
by a group of Georgian folk singers.

> Marvelous!!! Superb!!! They rode down to town with us in the
> bus singing all the way. That was a little corny but still great! Lots
> of kisses. In fact, I had to kiss all the Georgian folk singers, Kutchma,
> etc.

Noah concluded joyously, "It was grand."[16]

---

[15]Khutchma, a scholar of Georgian folk polyphony, was the source of the tapes of
that Noah brought back with him to the U.S.
[16]Russian journal, October 15.

CHAPTER THIRTY-FOUR

*T*BLISI TO LENINGRAD

(NOVEMBER 1964)

*E*arly on Friday, October 16, Pro Musica boarded an ancient two-engine plane for the 100-mile hop from Tblisi to Yerevan, the capital of Soviet Armenia. Beforehand, Noah told the company that Krushchev had been peacefully removed from office. "There was no alarm. (The blessings of being apolitical!)"[1] But Noah and Toni wondered uneasily about the reaction at home, about what China might do, and about the political capital that Republican presidential candidate Barry Goldwater might make of the situation. The only immediate effect on Pro Musica was that Yula and Marina, the Goskonzert representatives and interpreters, "upset about the changes in Moscow," no longer mixed at table with the Americans and forgot to tell them that the students and faculty at the Yerevan Conservatory had planned a reception for them. As a result, Pro Musica, to Noah's embarrassment, failed to appear.

The colds and sore throats plaguing the singers kept Noah busy rearranging programs, but the concerts in Armenia went smoothly enough. One highlight of the three-day stay was a drive to Lake Sevan in the north of the tiny republic, an afternoon of boating and a "sumptuous feast" at a modern hotel overlooking the lake.

> The *great* treat was a performance by three musicians—2 dudenci [duduc: a reed woodwind similar to a shawm] and a drum. The solo [duduc] player—Gasparayan—was a great artist. Finally we heard true, unadulterated Armenian folk music, and it was very special. Gasparayan. a young, handsome man (about 33) also played a 'sopranino' fipple flute, with a rare brilliance that makes our best western recorder players seems like amateurs. . . .[2]

[1]Russian journal, October 16.
[2]Russian journal, October 19.

Noah also noted with pleasure a tour of the Matandaran, a library housing an internationally famous collection of Armenian illuminated manuscripts. Again there was "unashamed" farewell kissing as Pro Musica left Yerevan by plane for Baku.

The hotel in Baku was "a horror," but the food in the restaurant was delicious and at the end of dinner on the evening they arrived, the Mayor of Baku arrived in person to apologize for the poor accomodations. There were full houses for both concerts in Baku, and standees for the second. The evening of the second concert (Wednesday, October 21), Toni remained at the hotel to pack and rest. Noah brooded in his journal about her imminent departure.

> How sad that she leaves tomorrow. It will not be as easy without her. The thought of spending tomorrow night alone here is depressing. But I am glad she is getting back to the children. I have *never* missed them as much as now and think about them constantly.

The next day was even worse.

> We . . . had lunch and were off to the airport to send Toni to Moscow. I had such mixed feelings about her leaving. The children need her desperately, but so do I! I cannot wait for the girls to grow up so that we can be together always.[3]

The next stop on the tour (on Saturday, October 24) was Piatigorsk, a spa resort in the hills. Noah, LaNoue, and Fred King wandered from the hotel by themselves to have a look at the Operetta Theatre where they were to play. They found themselves in animated conversation with a friendly group of actors from the repertory company. "What a delight not to be chaperoned!" The Russians wanted to know if Americans were "interested in peace and friendship, [and] did Goldwater the fascist have a chance to win, and were really joyful and reassured by our answers." Asked if he was married, Noah pulled out pictures of Anne, Jane, and Toni. He also showed them a picture of his father in front of the Shrub Oak house.

> [T]hey wanted to know if he was in business. When I told them he was a retired shoeworker, they were delighted and bowled over.

One of the actors grew so excited that he took off his wristwatch and stuck it in Noah's pocket, saying in broken English, "For your girls." Noah tried to hand it back, but the man refused, saying it was "a gift from the heart."[4]

---

[3]Russian journal, October 21 and October 22.
[4]Russian journal, October 24.

Sheila was so hoarse that evening that Pro Musica had to perform without her. Noah cobbled together a program—mixed Flemish and Baroque—and the audience, sometimes inattentive, did applaud and ask for many curtain calls.

The next morning (Sunday, October 25), Noah and two companions, Ron Roseman and Judith Martin (the Wind Band's alto shawm and tenor shawm players) traveled by cab the few miles to Kislovodsk. The others would join them there later.

> If Piatogorsk is beautiful, Kislovodsk is ravishing. Completely sheltered by mountains, it has 320 sunny days a year!

The trio had been invited to lunch by a musician Noah had met in Piatogorsk. Their host, identified in the journal only as V., was an oboist with the local symphony orchestra. V. had met American oboists Henry Schuman and Philip West the year before, when both were on tour with Newell Jenkins's Clarion Concerts. Schuman had sent V. new reeds for his instrument and these, plus some pointers, had made V. "ten times as good" as he had been.[5] "I cannot do justice to the warmth of V. and his wife," Noah wrote later.

> The wonderful shashlik, tomoto salad, sproten, radishes with greens and sour cream. The lamb had been marinated and then roasted on sword skewers over a wood fire.

The meal was the least of what tugged at Noah.

> But the circumstances there. It would take many pages. Their 2 children (13 and 11—girl and boy.) Their great hospitality and ability to rise above the situation. The bitterness mixed with love. Indescribable!

An equally dramatic encounter took place during the intermission of the evening's concert.

> An Itzaak Kornman came backstage. [He] spoke a beautiful Yiddish, an extremely alert man. Great music lover terribly hungry for 'new' music. . . . His talk I couldn't begin to put down, but it was a recital of life and circumstances of a 70-year-old Jewish engineer on a pension. . . . The tragedy of the war, the loss of two sons who were officers of the Red Army. Heartbreaking! Revealing! I understand the Jewish situation in a new light. Gave him a Monteverdi record and I nearly burst into tears (as he did) when we said goodbye.[6]

---

[5]Philip West, March 11, 2000. In fact, according to West, he, Schuman, and a number of others put together a purse and bought a good oboe, which they sent to V. via friends in another touring orchestra.

[6]Russian journal, October 25.

The trip to the next city, Yalta, ended in a breathtakingly beautiful drive from the airport to the Black Sea resort, "drenched in sunlight under [a] clear blue sky." But it left the company—and Noah — "extremely exhausted." That night (Tuesday, October 27), Noah awoke to discover bleeding that he feared might be a recurrence of his diverticulitis. Within an hour, the bleeding stopped and his stark fear gave way to relief.

> But during that hour I was trying to figure out how the company would perform without me and how I would get to London or N.Y. as quickly as possible.

The next morning, Noah blamed the attack on the unaccustomed exercise in Kislovodsk the day before. "The mountain walk really took it out of me."[7]

Two days later, Noah and Judith Davidoff attended a reading by actor Ilya Grigorich of some tales by Sholom Aleichem. They had been told on good authority that Grigorich would read in Yiddish as well as Russian, but only after Noah asked did Grigorich oblige with "*London, vos brennst du?* in a beautiful Russian *stetl* Yiddish." Noah and Judith went backstage after the performance to thank him. "He was very apologetic about not doing more, but it was a Russian evening." Had he known in advance, he added, he would have given the important American visitors a private reading.

Noah spoke Yiddish to a few of his local contacts who he was sure would understand him, but people, he found, were wary.

> Rifkin [a violinist], I feel, was *vergoyished*, but Block [director of the symphony orchestra] concealed [his knowledge of Yiddish] and avoided me during our entire stay.

"*Vergoyished*," a wonderful Yiddish word, means (more or less) "turned into a non-Jew." But in fact Noah was wrong about Rifkin. Rifkin wasn't *vergoyished* so much as fearful. After the final concert in Yalta, the violinist waited for him in the street. After an outpouring of praise of the music, there came

> something in terribly fractured Yiddish about relatives (uncles, sons) in L[os]. A[ngeles]., whom he's lost touch with but if we can contact them to say he is 'free and healthy.' He left us one block from the hotel.[8]

Noah had come down with a cold, and by the time Pro Musica reached Kiev (on Friday, October 30), his energy level was low. He

[7]Russian journal, October 26.
[8]Russian journal, October 29.

toured the city the morning after the first concert, taking note of Kiev's postwar recovery. But "feeling progressively worse," he spent the afternoon "holed up" in his hotel room with a book.

After the second Kiev concert, at Brayton's suggestion, Pro Musica held a Hallowe'en party in Noah's suite. Judith Davidoff laughed at the memory.

> We all made costumes out of whatever we had, which wasn't much. Brayton made a hat out of his sink stopper.[9]

"It was just what we needed," Noah wrote. "We had cookies, wine and vodka—and sang to all hours. It was really great fun, and everyone relaxed."

The third concert went even better than the second. After a tumultuous ovation, Noah had to go back onstage and stammer out his few Russian words of thanks and farewell.[10]

Because the Kiev airport was fogged in, Pro Musica had to endure a ghastly thirteen-hour train journey to the next stop, Minsk, arriving at two in the morning. Noah declined de luxe accomodations and shared his compartment with cornettist Bob Montesi, bass sackbut player Robert Szabo and the ANTA representative, Gertrude Macy.

> We started with vodka and a dice game shortly after departure and it continued for 13 hours until our arrival in Minsk. . . . I came out eight rubles ahead.

On Wednesday, November 4, Pro Musica performed at six in the evening, then returned at nine to hear David Oistrakh perform the Brahms Violin Concerto with the Minsk Philharmonic. Noah, in true Harold Brown fashion, rated Oistrakh's Brahms as "very, very well played . . . but so schmaltzy and old-fashioned." Oistrakh, however, was a "sweet man." What especially interested him about the Oistrakh concert was the nature of the audience.

> I have not seen these [intelligent-looking, well dressed] people on the streets and in the shops. . . . Odd! They really look like another breed and most attractive.

Evidently Noah did not realize that, whatever Pro Musica's audience, David Oistrakh's was the Soviet *nomenklatura*.

After the concert on November 5, an encounter with a Latvian variety singer named Goldie curdled the atmosphere. Goldie spoke

---

[9]Judith Davidoff, January 29, 1999.
[10]Russian journal, October 31, November 1.

perfect English and claimed to have one brother in Israel and another in Norwalk, Connecticut. He later joined Noah, Chuck Brown and Fred King at dinner afterward.

> His statements made one realize how attractive the Soviet position was to European artists. The security, the clear-cut direction, etc. Readymade for hacks, death for really creative artists.

Noah was outraged when Goldie started in "objecting to music that has no melody because it does not appeal to people—and that's what music is for." Noah's comment, recklesssly voiced aloud, was that Stalin's absolutist position on music seemed not to have changed much under his successors. "Thoroughly sickening discussion," Noah observed, "and convinced me never to talk to this type of person about the artist again."[11]

The next evening (Thursday, November 6), Pro Musica left Minsk and that night arrived in Leningrad (called now as in Czarist days St. Petersburg). Noah's relief was palpable. "What a magnificent town after what we had seen," he wrote.

> Leningrad . . . has a marvelous air about it. Its architectural style is so winning. Its buildings, canals and squares. The *turn* of the canals and streets are a joy. I supposed this is typical weather, very cold and snowy: one must really bundle up to go out, but the air is so refreshing. Perhaps I'm so delighted after living in all those provincial cities that the smell and feel of a big city excites me. I cannot wait to get to the Hermitage . . . I will probably spend every free moment there.[12]

The company was quartered at the splendid old Hotel Europa.

> We had dinner in a private dining room overlooking the main one. The band was very up-to-date and at times the entire floor below was twisting or doing the conga. Everyone was having a big Western time and really enjoying it.

On November 7, Noah turned down tickets to the military parade. He tried to make his way to The Hermitage, but parts of the Nevsky Prospekt were cordoned off and The Hermitage itself was closed. On the way back to the hotel, a group of Leningrad teenagers regaled Noah and Arthur Burrows with stories about Krushchev's downfall, gleefully insisting that he was now behind bars. Noah was rightly skeptical.

---

[11]Russian journal, November 4, November 5.
[12]Russian journal, November 6, November 7.

That afternoon, tenor Ray DeVoll and countertenor Earnest Murphy threw "a delightful party for the company in their suite, which is nicer than mine."

Waiting for Noah at the U. S. Consulate were letters from Toni, Alice Roberts, and Dick French. One from Toni, written from London two weeks earlier, brought Noah up to date on Toni's adventures in Moscow and London on the way home. The second, only a week old, was typewritten and filled with family news, instruction and wifely admonition.

> Dick [French] was at the airport with the girls. They were wonderful to see and I was very grateful to Dick. (He had picked them up at Dalton right after lunch and had a hysterical two hours with them.) . . . I was very happy to get back. Mostly because of Annie and Janie of course, but also simply being home. Is this another sign of middle age? [Toni was 37.] Not really because I enjoyed the trip also. I guess I'm just too well-adjusted for words!

Toni went on to tell Noah what she had bought at the Moscow airport and what *he* was to buy on his way home. (Caviar at $1.22 a jar, painted wooden boxes and "something—a book or cufflinks or anything you choose"—for Toni's Uncle Jack Perlow.)

Toni next turned her attention to diet, Anne's and Noah's.

> I was very upset to find that Annie had put on more weight again and I am determined to do something about it. . . . It will take a long time and be difficult but I think we *MUST* do this for her and I hope that you will stick with it too. It's a question also of common sense: if you simply don't buy delicious fresh rye bread, it won't be there to eat. Right?

In brisk, sensible fashion Toni covered bits of Pro Musica business. She closed with "Much love, many kisses to last two weeks," then added a piece of big news in ink at the top of the page: "Annie shook hands with [President Lyndon B.] Johnson outside of Jackie Kennedy's house."[13]

"The letters from Toni today were real balm," Noah wrote in his journal on November 7. "I am so anxious to get back to her and the children." In an odd passionate echo of Toni's own letter, he added:

> God! I love them *so*! Perhaps it's middle age—or am I well adjusted? Or do I just plain love them? I think I do![14]

---

[13]Toni Greenberg-Noah Greenberg, letter dated "Sunday morning," written on October 24, 1964; letter, October 30, 1964.

[14]Russian journal, November 7.

CHAPTER THIRTY-FIVE

$\mathcal{A}$ HOTEL ROOM IN RIO

(JULY 1965)

$\mathcal{P}$ro Musica, its members thoroughly exhausted, arrived in New York on Thursday, November 14 (1964). Toni had returned two weeks earlier, and since then she had been complaining to Chris Schang of CAMI—"gently," she assured Noah—about the dearth of publicity on the Soviet tour. Apart from one item in *Musical America* and a brief story in *The New York Times*, the event had gone unremarked by the American press. Schang, Toni wrote, had shrugged.

> He said that very little could be done from here; it's not all that newsworthy any more. He also felt that stories should originate from Russia and seemed to think that this was Gertrude Macy's responsibility.[1]

Noah, tired as he was, wasted no time in trying to remedy the situation. He called Barry Brook at Queens College. Brook, chairman of the New York chapter of the American Musicological Society, arranged for Noah to be the guest speaker at a chapter meeting to be held on November 21, a week after his return. The topic was "New York Pro Musica in the Soviet Union." As a rule, attendance at a chapter meeting would have been no larger than 20 or 30, including graduate students, but for this occasion Noah supplied a 72-person guest list of his own.

The list is doubly revealing. First, it testifies to Noah's shrewd sense of public relations. Noah lumped his invitees in three groups. The first included board members, musicians and people interested in music—e.g., Israel Horowitz of Decca, Dr. William Kolodney of

---

[1]Toni Greenberg-Noah Greenberg, letter, Oct. 30, 1964. Gertrude Macy, who had accompanied the tour for of the State Department, had little interest in music.

th "Y"—who had been doing business with Pro Musica for years. The second was made up of private contributors to Pro Musica, the Bloedels, Lincoln Kirstein, and James Merrill among them (plus those like Richard Rodgers who Noah hoped would become contributors). The third group consisted of decision-makers at large public and private foundations. W. McNeil Lowry and Edward F. D'Arms of Ford were naturally included, as were Donald L. Engle of the Martha Baird Rockefeller Foundation and Chadbourne Gilpatric of the Rockefeller Brothers Fund. There were also lesser lights like John Thompson of the Farfield Foundation, Sol Markoff of the New York Foundation, Milton Rose of the Whitney Foundation and Mrs. May E. McFarland of the Doris Duke Foundation.[2]

Noah's list also speaks eloquently of the breadth and depth of his acquaintanceship. It is a sure indicator—if one is needed—of success and standing. Noah himself had come to be one of those fortunate folk who "knew everybody" and was known in turn, a bit of an icon in his own right, and in any case a acknowledged member of New York City's cultural community.

The lecture invitation was thus a thank-you for past support and an implicit appeal for support in the future. It was also a call for a certain sort of publicity. Only four journalists were invited, and of the four only one, Alan Rich, worked for a daily newspaper. A speech to a group of musicologists was hardly hot news. The dailies would not be interested. But Noah saw the occasion as an opportunity to attract the attention of "serious" writers on cultural affairs like Rich, Owen Anderson of *Music Journal,* and Martin Mayer.[3]

The text of Noah's address has not survived, but it is easy to identify the themes on which he would have touched. One would have been the lack of advance publicity in the Soviet Union and the corresponding bafflement on the part of Soviet audiences. Another, related to the first, would have been the dearth of scholarly knowledge of early music. Noah would have named the few Soviet musicians he had met who displayed interest in Renaissance and Baroque music. He would have spoken of the Georgian folk polyphony that had caught his fancy. And he would surely have regaled his audience with anecdotes of delayed flights, agonizing train journeys,

---

[2] NYPM Archives, Box 6, folder 14.
[3] Martin Praeger Mayer, author of widely-read books on business topics (*Madison Avenue, U.S.A., The Lawyers, The Bankers*), had been an aficionado of Pro Musica since attending a rehearsal of the Salamone Rossi program in 1953. He had written about Pro Musica in Dr. Max Ascoli's magazine *The Reporter,* had reviewed its records for *Esquire,* and had even prepared a Pro Musica fundraising brochure.

spectacular scenery, wonderful meals, and audiences tepid at first but wildly cheering by the end of the program.

What he would not have voiced, in all likelihood, was political opinion. Denouncing Stalinist politics was an exercise for a different, younger Noah. This one was all music. Except on the issue of black civil rights, the political animal was asleep.

As usual, Noah's schedule had him feverishly busy, but at least most of Pro Musica's pre-Christmas engagements were in New York. The Concert Ensemble played Burgundian and Flemish works at the Harvard Club on Wednesday, December 2, an engagement arranged by Harvard alumnus Dick French. On December 4th, the combined Concert Ensemble and Wind Band appeared at the Library of Congress in Washington, performing the Early Baroque program they had taken to the Soviet Union. The concert was broadcast live over public radio station WGMS. On the 5th, the company was back in New York, playing the Early Baroque program at the Grace Rainey Rogers Auditorium. On Wednesday, December 9, Pro Musica gave the first of the season's four performances of *Herod* at St. George's Church. The first of five performances of *Daniel* took place on Monday, December 28. In between, the Concert Ensemble played the Burgundian-Flemish program on two successive evenings at The Cloisters (December 17 and 18) and on the night of the 19th at a People's Symphony Concert at Washington Irving High School. That left Noah nine free days at the end of the month for rest, relaxation, poker, party-going, and party-giving.

Guests at Greenberg parties were expected to provide, and did provide, their own entertainment. Rubin Baratz remembered a party at the Greenbergs', almost certainly in December 1964, at which Wystan Auden, Dwight Macdonald, and the art critic Harold Rosenberg were all present. Rosenberg's new book, *The Anxious Object*, about Abstract Expressionism and that uncertain novelty called Pop Art, was still making news and provoking argument. "I thought it was amusing," Baratz said. "Each of [the three] gathered a little crowd around him, each one well separated from the others, so that he could hold court uninterrupted."[4]

It may have been at this same party that Noah cornered Lincoln Kirstein to put before him once again the idea of producing a Pro Musica presentation of John Skelton's early sixteenth-century morality play *Magnyfycence*. Noah described his latest effort in a letter

[4]Rubin Baratz, June 11, 1997.

to Yolanda and Walter Davis, the latter a professor of English, whom he had met at Notre Dame in May 1964.

> On the strength of the success of *Herod* and *Daniel*, even when they run back to back, I have reopened the question of M[*agnificence*]. I waited until I got Kirstein in a drunken state and then twisted his arm. In fact, all I said was, 'When are you going to have the guts to let me do it?' And he said, 'That's a great idea.' Whether we can actually accomplish it for next year, I don't know.

As Noah well knew, Kirstein's interest could readily flag.

In the same letter, Noah apologized for not having written sooner. His excuse was a beleaguered man's plaint.

> I know it is terribly disgusting of me not to have written to you before this. My time is simply not my own any more. I dream of the day when I can tell all my work to go to hell and I can act like a totally irresponsible person for about a month, but my schedule doesn't allow that. . . .[5]

The hectic pace of that schedule continued into 1965. After a New Year's Day *Daniel* performance in New York, Noah took one day off and traveled to Washington on Sunday, January 3, to set up for two performances each of *Daniel* and *Herod* at Washington Cathedral. After the second *Daniel*, Noah was interviewed by Meryle Secrest, then an obscure cultural-affairs reporter for *The Washington Post*, now well known for her biographies of Leonard Bernstein, Frank Lloyd Wright, and Stephen Sondheim.

> Greenberg is still mildly surprised at the excitement which he aroused by what began as a rather erudite interest in music that the world at large had regarded with indifference, if indeed its existence was known at all.

But Noah, with years of interviews under his belt, knew exactly what he wanted to tell the public.

> 'The plays have been known about since the mid-19th century but nothing was done about it because people just didn't take to the style. Why now? I suppose in our great search for roots and tradition, as we approach Doomsday,' and he smiled wryly, 'we have found that man's expression at all times is fascinating and sometimes very beautiful.'

This theme is one Noah had been elaborating in his lectures, sometimes lightly, sometimes seriously, over several years. In a 1962 talk on Renaissance music at Union Theological Seminary, he said:

[5]Noah Greenberg-Yolanda and (Professor) Walter Davis, letter, January 11, 1965. NYPM Archives, Box 54, folder vii.

Thanks to our 'cultural explosion,' the LP, a search for 'roots'—
whatever—audiences everywhere are interested in Baroque, Renaissance and Medieval music."[6]

A few weeks later, on the occasion of the 400th anniversary of the
Geneva Psalter, he had struck a graver note.

In this period of rapid changes [and] phenomenal scientific
achievment, accompanied by the ever-present threat of mass de-
struction, many of us need the support that only 'roots' can give.
Partly as an escape (who can deny it) but primarily to reinforce
our belief in Man and the good he can accomplish.[7]

For us insecure moderns, Noah is saying, a hunt for cultural
"roots" in the art of the distant past is a valid way to escape the
frightening present and at the same time reaffirm lasting human
virtue. It is an interesting generalization for someone not much given
to generalizing, one very much in the main stream of modernist
thought. It is certainly the closest that Noah the plain-spoken prag-
matist ever came to a philosophic explanation of the appeal of early
music.

In the Secrest interview, Noah was much too shrewd to linger on
such abstractions. He moved quickly on to a simpler formulation.

'[The plays] are very much like the stained glass windows, if you
know how to read them,' Greenberg said, 'they tell in a very simple,
straightforward way, a Biblical story. . . .There is no malarkey and
no larding; it's all very condensed. A modern composer, given
this story, would run it for four or five hours. Yet here is the essence of drama, once you accept it in the framework in which it is
written. It runs the gamut of human emotion, from the humorous
to the tragic.'[8]

On Saturday, January 9, the day of the final *Herod* performance,
Noah lectured on liturgical drama at Dumbarton Oaks under the
auspices of the Institute of Contemporary Arts. Back in New York,
it was business as usual. That is, there were long daily rehearsals
for a Concert Ensemble appearance at the "Y" on January 16 and a
repeat performance at Colgate on January 28. There was a lecture at

[6]Noah Greenberg, typescript of notes for lecture, "Early and mid-Renaissance Music," Union Theological Seminary, Tuesday, June 19, 1962. NYPM Archives, Box 6,
folder 11.

[7]Noah Greenberg, typed draft of lecture, "Music of the Reformation Period," delivered at Calvin College, Grand Rapids Michigan, Thursday, August 23, 1962. NYPM
Archives, Box 6, folder 19.

[8]Meryle Secrest, "Director's Consuming Interest in Medieval Music Finds Acclaim,"
The Washington Post, January 6, 1965.

the Yale School of Music in New Haven, followed by a Pro Musica concert at Sprague Hall. There was a Renaissance Band concert at the "Y" on February 20. Always, there were letters to answer and requests to consider. Some of the latter were zany. On January 29, for example, Abe Polsky, a theatrical producer, wrote to Noah to engage Pro Musica as "a band of wandering minstrels" in a musical comedy to be based—the idea is mind-boggling—on Niccolò Machievelli's novel *Mandragora*. In case Pro Musica could not appear, Polsky added thoughtfully, perhaps "you might be able to assist in the training of a few select musicians." Noah politely declined.[9]

On February 25, Noah presided over a board meeting. The minutes indicate the extent to which Noah, in part by his own choice, was immersed in detail. Thus, Toni reported the death of John Turner, a fan who had helped Pro Musica with much-needed cash contributions in the early years. Turner had left Pro Musica $2,500 in his will, and Noah wanted the May 1 concert at the "Y" to be dedicated to Turner's memory. Noah also wanted to deal with some vexing aspects of the out-of-town drama presentations. In particular, "the manger [in *Herod*] is murder to move—it was built by union builders and has to be moved by union movers." Also, the costumes needed refurbishing. *Daniel* and *Herod* had both made money in Washington: in fact, well over $6,500. If Noah wanted a new manger and new costumes, the dollars were there. But Noah told the board that he would dip into the drama profit only with reluctance. He would rather spend the money on new repertoire and raise extra money for scenery and costumes.

Most important, Noah wanted to create a new Pro Musica post, that of administrative director. For years, he and Toni between them, with the help of Pro Musica's succession of secretaries, had been carrying the burden of organizing the tours, making the travel arrangements and dealing with CAMI, the State Department, the various unions and local presenters. They could do this no longer. Apart from being exhausting, it was an utter waste of Noah's talents as program builder and musical director. Noah, moreover, had a candidate for the new job, a thirty-seven-year-old Yale Drama School graduate named George Mallonee. It was Noah's idea to start Mallonee as stage manager—a kind of glorified "band boy"— so that he would learn Pro Musica's ways from the bottom up. He

[9]Abe Polsky-Noah Greenberg, letter, January 29, 1965; Noah Greenberg-Abe Polsky, letter, February 19, 1965. NYPM Archives, Box 37, folder xii.

would then be put in charge of the drama program and the tours. When Dick French chimed in, saying that he could no longer continue as Pro Musica's president unless Mallonee or someone like him were hired, the board was convinced. Noah was authorized to hire Mallonee at a salary of $500 a month.[10]

On February 26, Noah was back in Washington leading the Burgundy and Flanders program at the Library of Congress. On the 27th, he repeated the program at the Sanders Theater in Boston. These were the first two stops on a swing through the midwest, the south, New England and Canada that called for 29 concerts in 36 days.

Since February 1, Martin Luther King and his colleagues had been leading voter-registration marches in Selma, Alabama. Mass arrests and threats were the norm, but the marching continued. On February 3, Malcolm X, back from Paris and London, lectured at Tuskegee on "racial imagery in international relations:" three thousand students "squeezed into the aisles and window casements of Warren Logan Hall" to hear him. Eighteen days later, vengeful agents of Black Muslim leader Elijah Mohammed gunned Malcolm down. Hope for unification of the two wings of the civil-rights movement flickered and died. And on March 7, Alabama state troopers and a gaggle of racists threw themselves on the marchers as they crossed the Alabama River on the Edmund Pettus bridge, smashing them with clubs, bullwhips and even, according to eyewitness accounts, rubber hoses wrapped with barbed wire.[11]

"The news from Selma is ghastly," Noah wrote to Toni on March 8, en route to Greenville, South Carolina, "and the thing will get worse unless the Gov't. steps in this week."[12] (Not until August, when President Johnson signed the Voting Rights Act of 1965 into law, did Federal power put a stop to the violence.) Noah had reason enough to be jittery about the state of affairs in the Deep South, although nothing on earth was going to keep him from delivering his motley squad of Jews, gay men, former and not-so-former radicals —LaNoue and Sheila, married in late June 1964, lived in a kind of commune in Stony Point where the use of controlled substances was not unknow—and other threats to the southern social order, to wher-

[10]Minutes, New York Pro Musica board meeting, February 25, 1965. NYPM Archives, Box 23, folder iv.
[11]Taylor Branch, *Pillar of Fire*, p. 577; Tim Weiner, "Congressman and His Colleagues Re-enact March," *The New York Times*, Monday, March 8, 1999, p. A12:1.
[12]Noah Greenberg-Toni Greenberg, letter, March 8, 1965.

ever CAMI had booked it. The tour included stops at two black institutions, Tuskegee Institute itself, just 70 miles from Selma, and Fisk College in Atlanta. Noah's purpose in going to Greenville was to give a concert, arranged in January, for the benefit of the National Association for the Advancement of Colored People. He had worried at the time of the booking that, McAlister Auditorium, where the concert was to be held, might be off-limits to black people. In fact, Herbert Hill, NAACP Labor Secretary, wrote to the president of the Greenville chapter that

> Mr. Greenberg want[s] to be certain that the concert will be opened to colored persons and that seating will be on a non-segregated basis as the contract provides.[13]

It was. The benefit was a success—so much so that Noah later wrote a cautiously optimistic tribute to A. J. Whittenburg, the chapter president:

> The work that you and your friends have done in Greenville has borne wonderful fruit. I know it's not all 'sugar and spice,' as you so aptly put it, but one can actually see daylight ahead.[14]

The spring tour came to a quiet close on April 3 at East High School in Waynesboro, Pennsylvania. Only two concerts for live audiences were planned for April and May. But several "non-live" projects were pending. Decca had scheduled a recording session for the Renaissance Band in April, and a second session for the Concert Ensemble in May. Pro Musica was to tape three performances for National Educational Television's "World of Music" program. The first, an all-Josquin program, was due to air on Wednesday, April 21. The second and third, each featuring the Renaissance Band, would be shown on the 26th and 27th of May. Another more elaborate television appearance came next. NET had agreed to pay Pro Musica $18,500 for the right to tape *The Play of Daniel* at The Cloisters and show it no more than three times. The taping would take place in late June, but intensive rehearsing would be needed. Finally, Noah had to prepare the Concert Ensemble in a number of new works.

The first three weeks of June were largely given over to the NET *Daniel*. As a later account pointed out, "The Cloisters provided the perfect setting for the presentation of the play," the more so because a taped production was not confined to one location hall as the origi-

[13]Herbert Hill, Labor Secretary, NAACP-A. J. Whittenburg, letter, January 25, 2965. NYPM Archives, Box 39, folder 1.
[14]Noah Greenberg-A. J. Whittenburg, letter, April 20, 1965. NYPM Archives, Box 39, folder 1.

nal live production had been, but could make use of the whole complex of Romanesque halls and cloisters.

> But in taping the play there was one formidable problem. The building is open to the public six days a week, which meant that the shooting would have to be done around the clock on the one day it is closed—Monday. There would be little time for a succession of takes, little time for at first not succeeding, and trying again.

This meant weeks of rehearsal, during which

> every movement of the players and the many cameras was . . . plotted on maps and models of the six galleries where the play would be performed.

Production started at six o'clock on the evening of Sunday, June 20. It was a mess, with rehearsing, costume fitting and stage setting going on during the setup for taping.

> Hundreds of lights, miles of thick black cable, cameras, booms, and dollies were somehow installed in their proper places that evening.

At 6:30 a.m. on Monday, George Mallonee, clipboard in hand, shouted instructions to the cast and taping began. The production people had divided *Daniel* into more than 30 separate scenes, and the camera work went on hour after hour. The usual retakes were needed,

> some . . . because of a boom shadow, or because Belshazzar didn't die convincingly, or because a singer's lip motion was not 'in sync' with the recorded music. Crews and cumbersome equipment had to move quickly from cloister to cloister; while one scene was being taped another was set up. Airplanes droned overhead at just the wrong moment. At 3:00 A.M., the two sleepy lions napping in the Romanesque Hall were wakened, to pounce upon Daniel when he was thrown into their den.[15]

That was the last scene. At 3:30 a.m., Noah and the cast dragged themselves homeward, leaving cleanup to George Mallonee and the production crew. By 10 a.m., when The Cloisters opened to the public, not a trace of the twenty-one-hour effort remained behind.

An indication of Noah's standing, and also of the pressures to which he was subject, comes up in a latter dated July 2 (1965) to the President of the United States. In it, Noah *declines* a Presidential invitation to the White House Conference on Education to be held

---

[15]"Televising the Play of Daniel," in *Metropolitan Museum Bulletin*, December 1965, pp. 159-164. NYPM Archives, Box 54, folder xix.

later that month. Despite his interest in education and his aware-
ness that it is a grave breach of etiquette to turn down the President,
Noah had no choice.[16] On Tuesday, July 6, Noah and the 10 members of the Concert Ensemble boarded a jet for the 12-hour flight to
Rio de Janeiro, the first stop on a month-long tour of South America.
Accompanying them were George Mallonee, a Miss Nassif of the
State Department's Cultural Affairs Division, Chris Schang of CAMI
and his wife Jane, Sheila's and LaNoue's children, Dori, Mark, and
Stefan and Judith's and Sumner's son Edward, now four and a seasoned traveler. Like the three earlier foreign tours, this one was
under ANTA-State Department sponsorship. But unlike those tours,
where established agents and presenters could help smooth Pro
Musica's path, this one turned into something between a comedy of
misadventures and a genuine nightmare.

Things started to go awry almost at once. The weather in
Rio was humid, rainy and miserable. After a sleepless plane journey and a sleepless night in the hotel, Noah had to be affable at a
midday press conference on July 7 and then go on to rehearse a difficult program—"Florentine Medieval and Renaissance Music Honoring the 700th Birthday of Dante"—with barely an hour and a half
to go before the concert. Only a thousand people showed up in a
house, the *Teatro Municipal*, that could seat 2,200. The concert itself
went remarkably well. Afterward, Chris and Jane Schang insisted
that he go out with them for a late dinner. Noah was exhausted but
agreeable,

> but after a terrible fight with the cab driver because meter was too
> high, we got to all eating places too late for food—we ended up in
> a vulgar night club where I had a drink and then excused myself
> after about 15 minutes. . . . He [Chris] can't seem to make things
> <u>work</u> right half the time.[17]

He was even less pleased with the Schangs when Chris Schang
came backstage during the second of Pro Musica's two Rio concerts
to tell Noah "the program was not right. Too sad, too sophisticated,
the audience didn't get it." Noah bit his tongue and told Schang to
wait, and at the end of a "wonderful" program there were a dozen
curtain-calls and a standing ovation. The Schangs later invited Noah
to join them for dinner the evening before they were to return to the
U.S., only to cancel the date "because something else had come up."
Once again Noah, who needed the Schangs and CAMI, said noth-

[16]NYPM Archives, Box 6, folder 4.
[17]Noah Greenberg-Toni Greenberg, letter, July 8, 1965.

ing to Chris, but to Toni he wrote: "That Chris (and his wife too) is such a smuck [sic]. . . . How gauche can you get?"[18]

Much more serious trouble arose in Såo Paulo. On his return to New York, Chris Schang was supposed to bring Toni checks that Oscar Alcazar, CAMI's sub-agent for South America had written to Noah for Pro Musica's fees and expenses over the first two weeks of the tour. But in Såo Paolo, the Brazilian impresario, Dante Viggiani, paid Miss Nassif $5,000 in American dollars for these same fees. The awful thought occurred to Noah that without the $5,000 Señor Alcazar might not, and probably did not, have enough cash in his account to cover his checks. Because of Brazilian currency controls, getting U.S. dollars out of Brazil and into Señor Alcazar's New York bank account was a problem. It had to be done — and was done — in Rio de Janeiro, not Såo Paulo.[19] But only an eleventh-hour phone call to Toni stopped her from depositing the Alcazar checks too soon and having them bounce.

Back in Rio for this transaction, Noah discovered that the Embassy had received two cables. One bore the news that it was impossible to hire a hall in Santiago, Chile. The other indicated that Ecuador was in the throes of a heat wave, and as a result Pro Musica's appearance in Quito had had to be canceled. "Well, there goes the 3rd week," Noah wrote philosophically.

In the same letter, he veered away from logistics to register his reaction to a book.

> I've just finished Henry Roth's Call It Sleep. Wonderful but frightening novel. It meant so much to me. I so identified with David [the half-crazed hero], though God knows I didn't have a nightmare of a childhood. The book is almost too terrible, because it makes you realize what a dungheap the slums were and what a miracle that good people came out of them.[20]

One can imagine Noah, alone in his hotel room in Rio or Buenos Aires, late at night after a concert; too much adrenalin in his system to let him sleep; revisiting scenes that he thought he had left far behind; wondering by what freak of fortune he had managed to escape from *there* and find his way to *here*.

---

[18]Noah Greenberg-Toni Greenberg, letter, July 10, 1965.

[19]In the event, Miss Nassif took the $5,000 to the U.S. Embassy, which deposited it in its own account, wrote a check for $5,000 to Oscar Alcazar and sent it via diplomatic pouch to Washington, whence it made its way to New York.

[20]Noah Greenberg-Toni Greenberg, letter, July 13, 1965.

CHAPTER THIRTY-SIX

$\mathcal{T}$WO DEATHS

(JANUARY 1966)

$\mathcal{T}$he high point of the South American adventure came in cold, rainy Buenos Aires. That there could be a high point at all seemed unlikely. An appearance at the cavernous but acoustically superb *Teatro Colón* loomed ahead. Even though the concert at the beautiful *Museo Nacional de Arte Decorativo* had drawn "the chic-est audience you ever saw" and an enthusiastic press, Noah was uneasy. And lonesome. "I want to go home," he wrote, comically echoing Anne's homesick letters from her first sleep-away summer camp. "I want you & Jane & Shelter Is."[1]

Two nights later, things were different.

> It was quite an evening. We had no time to warm up on stage because the opera finished after 9 and we started at 10!!! Can you imagine the mess that followed the opera? We had no time to try out this big, splendid (magnificent) house that seats 3500 and for us had 3000.

> Well — we gave the concert and it's a tough program. They were polite to begin with and then started getting carried away. At the end they were shouting — that 3000-person shout — almost animal sound but my! — it's exciting. 4 encores and at least 18 curtain calls![2]

After that however, things slid steadily downhill. Back at the hotel at an ungodly two in the morning, the company had to be awake at eight for the flight to the next tour city, Montevideo. They made it to the airport on time, only to find that their flight was delayed. Six and a half hours later, the flight was cancelled, and Pro Musica had

---

[1]Noah Greenberg-Toni Greenberg, letter, July 16, 1965.
[2]Noah Greenberg-Toni Greenberg, letter, July 18, 1965.

to return in frustration to the hotel. (Fortunately, they had kept their hotel rooms.)

> Everyone was exhausted and started getting snippy with [Miss] Nassif—who started to cry—and finally said, "I quit!"

Noah, veteran of a thousand shipboard and airport delays, took the situation calmly. But when LaNoue started carrying on about refunds for the unused portions of his children's tickets, Noah's annoyance flared. Before the tour began, he had made LaNoue Assistant Director and given him responsibility for overseeing Pro Musica's instrumental rehearsals. But now he snapped, "Under his direction the ensemble would disintegrate at the first crisis." He ended his account of events on a note of exasperation: "What the hell I am doing here, I don't know! I want to come home!"[3]

Four days later, Pro Musica did reach Montevideo, only to learn that the Irving Trust Company in New York, having at last received five thousand U. S. dollars on account, had instructed its correspondent bank in Buenos Aires to issue a check to Pro Musica in Argentine pesos at the official rate. Accepting this arrangement would have cut Pro Musica's fee in half. In contrast, Noah had nothing but praise for the USIS and U.S. Embassy staff members. "They always make sure all arrangements are in order (hotels, transportation of instruments, artists, etc.). Without them we would really be in a fix here."[4]

After Montevideo came Lima, and mail from home finally caught up with the tour. Noah was pleased that Jane liked her day camp and firm on not allowing Anne to come home early from *her* camp. As for Pro Musica, the company was more or less relaxed, but a certain amount of bickering was still going on, especially between Miss Nassif and George Mallonee. Still, "somehow they manage to keep working together, which they have to." Best of all, because appearances in Guatamala and Panama had been cancelled, stops in Bogotà and Mexico City were all that remained. In less than a week, Noah would be home. "It can't come soon enough for me."[5]

A day or two after Noah's return to New York, he, Toni, and Jane were on their way to Shelter Island. A certain number of people Noah and Toni knew, it developed, had already discovered the low-key pleasures of the place. Harold Schonberg, music critic for *The*

[3]Noah Greenberg-Toni Greenberg, letter, July 19, 1965.
[4]Noah Greenberg-Toni Greenberg, letter, July 23, 1965.
[5]Noah Greenberg-Toni Greenberg, letter, July 26, 1965.

Noah on Shelter Island,
September 1965
(Courtesy Greenberg family)

New York Times, owned a home there. Earnest Murphy's companion Fred Conklin had family ties to Shelter Island that went back to the eighteenth century. Martin Mayer and his wife vacationed there. And Lucy and Joe Dames, Noah's friends from his Workers Party and seafaring days, were also Shelter Islanders.

The photograph (see above) taken on the Saturday of Labor Day weekend (September 4, 1965) expresses to perfection what Noah sought and found on Shelter Island. A tanned, relaxed Noah stands in the grass of a sizeable field. He is barefoot but wearing a sweater: it is, after all, the last weekend of the season. In Noah's left hand is a fishing-rod taller than he is. From his right dangles an impressive string of fish.

The smile on his face says that for days on end his thoughts have been on nothing more profound than boating, swimming and sunshine. Pro Musica is out there somewhere, but for a day or two more it will be on the far side of the horizon.

*   *   *

Since 1951, the Berlin Festival had by its own official account been "a cultural showcase of the West at the zenith of the Cold War." The account hastily adds that the Festival was "not a tool to widen the gap but rather to build a bridge between East and West, between North and South." Perhaps, but in its early years the Festival was designed to dandle Western-style freedom and vigor in music, film, and dance before the envious eyes of the Ossies (East Germans) and their neighbors further to the East. "Music," moreover, "has always lain at the heart of the *Berliner Festwochen*': there is no top-ranked orchestra in the world that has not played in the *Festwochen* . . ."[6]

Pro Musica's turn to perform there came in October (1965). A Festival appearance had been a natural outcome of Noah's November 1963 visit to Berlin, and in every respect it was a huge success. The logistics were handled with flawless efficiency, and the concerts, three in all, were joyously received. There was time, too, for other musical interests. On the morning of Monday, October 11, Noah and some of the company paid a visit to Alain Danièlou's International Institute for Comparative Music Studies, where they listened first to Tibetan sacred music from Danièlou's collection and then to "delightful" African pygmy songs. ("I wish Annie could have heard [them].")

That afternoon, the curatorial staff of the Berlin Conservatory's instrument collection, one of the world's finest, opened the collection, normally closed on Mondays, to Pro Musica. Judith, LaNoue, Shelley, and Ed Smith were permitted to play some of the instruments. Judith tried various viols and a violone, the latter being the direct ancestor of the double bass. Noah, the high school double bass player, was much taken with the violone. Said Judith: "It had six strings [the double bass has four or five]. It had a D-D setting which Noah was very eager to have me add to my kit."[7]

The concert that evening, the second of the three, was held in a "period" auditorium,

> the Eichelgaleria of the enormous Charlottenburg Palace. It is tiny, narrow, and candlelit, so it was hot & smokey by the 2nd half. The place was jammed and the audience very responsive. We had to do many encores, as we did the night before, and *then* the audience wouldn't leave.

Noah had the energy for a post-concert drink with the visiting American composer Gunther Schuller, ("Very bright man, I think"). But he wrote the next morning that

---

[6]"Wir über uns/About us," Web site, Berliner Festspiele, http://www.berlinerfestspiele.de/ueberuns/aboutus.html#fest-wochen, p. 1.
[7]Judith Davidoff, February 2, 1999. The "D-D setting" gave the violone a range from the D almost two octaves below middle C to the D just above middle C. This is considerably greater than the range of the string bass. Noah was conscious that a violone would add great force to a continuo part, especially in larger-scale works.

I'm taking it easy today because the last 3 [days] have been very hard. The concerts, Germany, the language problem, etc. — it's quite wearing.[8]

Pro Musica flew back to New York on October 13, but Noah lingered in Europe for several more days, visiting Zurich and Rome in search of engagements for a 1966 State Department-sponsored European tour. Warsaw, he had been told, was already a likely possibility.

Noah was in New York by October 20. That day, he brought the Pro Musica board up to date about the South American tour (badly organized but a smash hit nonetheless) and the Berlin Festival visit. At his prompting, the board voted a pay raise to Concert Ensemble artists and a fee increase to LaNoue for his work as Assistant Director. Also, Noah had devised a strategy to ease the pressure of the ceaseless touring. This was to break up the tours with workshops, each lasting several days to a week. Sponsored by a college music department, a workshop could feature master classes by Concert Ensemble members, a lecture by Noah himself, a student concert, and one or more concerts by Pro Musica. The fee would of course be much larger than the fee for a single appearance, and Pro Musica would enjoy the luxury of remaining in one spot for a respectable length of time. As he told the board, Noah had scheduled 1966 workshops at Stanford in April and at Oakland University in June-July. He also reminded board members of the party to be held at The Cloisters after the concert (The Florentine program) on December 2.

During this brief stay in New York, Noah turned his persuasive powers on Marvin Hayes. Brayton Lewis, it seemed, was thinking of retiring and accepting a teaching job in Lima, Peru where he had friends on the faculty of the university. Brayton broached the possibility to Noah, and Noah lost no time in inviting Hayes, a superb musician, to join the Concert Ensemble as its bass. But Hayes's wife, a psychologist, had been offered a very good job on the West Coast and Brayton thought twice about retiring. In the end, the Hayeses moved west and Brayton remained with Pro Musica.[9]

Noah conducted the Florentine program at the "Y" on Saturday, October 23. Then, as if he were boarding a people mover at an airport, with Toni, the girls and New York receding slowly as they waved their goodbyes, he was off on the Concert Ensemble's fall

[8]Noah Greenberg-Toni Greenberg, letter, October 12, 1965.
[9]Earnest Murphy, March 10, 1999. After retiring from Pro Musica in 1967, Brayton Lewis did move to Lima, Peru, living there until his death in 1998.

tour, repeating the Florentine program at Dartmouth and Skidmore Colleges and the Library of Congress. After a jog north to Princeton on November 1, the tour took Pro Musica south to Durham, Williamsburg, and Sweet Briar, then into Indiana, Illinois, and Michigan before circling homeward via Ohio, Pennsylvania, and upstate New York.

In Durham, Noah found time to write to his gifted young cousin Michael Davidson, who had given up the piano in favor of the cello and was now playing with the New Orleans Philharmonic under Werner Torkanowsky.

> [On tour] I have time to relax a bit — writing, reading, studying. You will have to learn how to do this if you tour at all. . . .It is a lucky thing that you are working with an exciting conductor. Alas —this is not always so! He has a fine reputation and should help make your work there exciting.

He added some family news.

> Toni & the girls are fine and although I've just left I miss them already. It is sometimes very difficult to leave. Annie is doing fairly well on the 'cello & Janie wants to study the piano—she says. Perhaps will start soon.[10]

The Saturday after Thanksgiving, Noah led the Concert Ensemble in the Spanish-Colonial Spain program at the "Y."

Because he knew he would be in New York in December, he felt free to accept an intriguing invitation. Allan Kaprow, an abstract painter and art historian, had become well known for fathering the works on the borderline between art and theater known as "Happenings." Kaprow, on the faculty of SUNY Stony Brook and keenly interested in art education, was dismayed by the sharp cuts in New York educational budgets for "extras" like music and art. As energetic and creative as Noah himself, Kaprow wanted to sell the incoming administration of Mayor-elect John V. Lindsay and the Board of Education on his plan to bring professional artists into the city's public schools. He knew he needed the support of New York's creative community; and to gain such support he set about organizing a December 15th luncheon conference at Stony Brook on his proposal.

On Kaprow's blue-ribbon list were John Cage, Merce Cunningham, the artists Helen Frankenthaler and Robert Motherwell (at the time, Frankenthaler's husband), George Segal, and Michael

---

[10]Noah Greenberg-Michael Davidson, letter, November 3, 1965.

Kirby. These were all personal friends. In addition, Kaprow invited
Howard Conant, the head of the Department of Art Education at
NYU, art educator Jerome J. Hausman, and John B. Hightower,
Nelson Rockefeller's director of the New York State Council on the
Arts. It is not clear who mentioned Noah's name to Kaprow—it
may have been Frankenthaler—but Noah accepted with alacrity.[11]

On December 10, Noah led the Concert Ensemble in another appearance at the Harvard Club and found himself in hot—or perhaps only lukewarm—water. Barry Brook had arranged the appearance in connection with the thirtieth anniversary of the New York
chapter of the American Musicological Society. All seemed to go
well, until Dick's superior at the Union Theological Seminary, where
he was teaching, received an irate letter from Denis Stevens, then
teaching at Columbia,[12] with copies directed to AMS. board members. Stevens claimed that Pro Musica's appearance had been engi-
neered by Noah's AMS cronies Dick French, Barry Brook, and
Gustave Reese in an effort to shut out other groups, especially his
own, the Accademia Monteverdiana. Stevens further claimed that
AMS should have given him special consideration because he would
have performed without fee, whereas Pro Musica had insisted on
being paid. Noah, who had known Stevens for years, was furious.
He worried that Stevens's letter might damage Dick French's career. But Barry Brook and others assured him that Stevens was simply jealous of his success and that Dick would come to no harm.

Noah's cousin Rema recalled that another unfortunate event, the
death of her grandfather—Uncle Moniek's father—occurred in December. Rema, now married to Harvey Sessler, remembered that at
the funeral Noah and her husband were standing together at the
back of the chapel. The canned eulogy, she said, set Noah's teeth on
edge.

> My poppa [grandfather] was a wonderful man but the rabbi didn't
> know him from Adam. And Noah said to Harvey, 'When I die, I
> don't want one word said. And I want an Orthodox funeral and a
> pine box.'[13]

On December 11, Noah led the Concert Ensemble in the Spanish-
Colonial Spain program at a Peoples Symphony concert at Wash-

[11]Noah Greenberg-Allan Kaprow, letter, November 29, 1965. NYPM Archives, Box
7, folder 6.
[12]Stevens had written music criticism at Oxford and in India, produced programs
of Renaissance and Baroque music for the BBC and directed a madrigal group, the
Ambrosian Singers.
[13]Rema Sessler, March 1, 1997.

ington Irving High School. With Anne and Jane home from school for the holiday break, there was time to enjoy life, to watch the *Play of Daniel* on television on Christmas Eve, and to take a deep breath before the annual performances of *Daniel* began on Tuesday, December 28.

Meanwhile, a very different type of theatrical performance had settled in for a long run in New York. The first act, indeed, had opened on July 27, when Noah was in Lima, Peru. The central figure, if not exactly the protagonist, was Michael Joseph Quill, the 60-year-old head of the Transport Workers Union representing some 8,000 New York City subway workers. On that July day, Mike Quill announced that he had decided on the terms of a new contract with the New York City Transit Authority. The current contract was due to expire at midnight on December 31 (1965). If the NYCTA found the new terms unacceptable, Quill said, his people would have no alternative except to strike.

After this ominous beginning, the action slowed to a standstill until Friday, November 5, three days after the New York City mayoralty election. That day, Quill dropped his demands on the desk of Mayor-elect Lindsay. The specifics made the city's politicians and businessmen tremble. Quill wanted an across-the-board 30 percent salary increase for TWU members. He would accept only a two-year contract, which meant that all too soon he would be back at the bargaining table with more demands. If these requirementws were not met, Quill would call a strike. He did say that the strike, instead of beginning at midnight on New Year's Eve, would be delayed until five in the morning of New Year's Day, to allow revelers to make their way home.

On December 7, Mayor Wagner stepped in. Lame duck though he was, he persuaded the TWU and the Transit Authority to meet with him, and by December 9 he was reporting "progress": Quill in fact agreed to postpone the December 15 strike deadline. But over Christmas, the negotiations stalled and afterward broke down entirely. On December 27, the TWU voted to strike. On New Year's Eve, the Transit Authority secured a Condon-Wadlin injunction. Mike Quill publicly tore up the papers and jeered at Mayor Lindsay—he always mockingly mispronounced the name as "Lindley"— as "a babe in the woods." At five in the morning on New Year's Day, the subways stopped running.

Noah and Toni had sidestepped the problem. On New Year's Eve afternoon—a Friday—they had left Jane and Anne in New York and driven out to Shelter Island. There they and another couple, Hildreth and Aaron Kritzer, spent the evening with Lucy and Joe Dames. The Greenbergs were especially elated: they had just put down a deposit of several thousand dollars on a Shelter Island house that they wanted to make their permanent summer home. The Kritzers shared their excitement. They had just bought a house themselves in East Hampton. The talk was of summer holidays and contentment, with the radical years left far behind.

The Greenbergs were back in town on Saturday, before the effects of the strike began to tell, but thereafter they, along with millions of others, bore the full weight of it. For the next thirteen days, New Yorkers truly suffered. By January 4, half of the city's working people were unable to reach their jobs. By the 7th, morning traffic jams were lasting six and a half hours. In Manhattan, people—office workers, executives, old people, small children, everybody—mostly walked. The school buses were running, so that Anne and Jane were able to get across town to Dalton. And Noah was one of the lucky ones. It was only about a twenty-minute walk down West End Avenue from 865 to Pro Musica's offices..

Arthur Squires too was covering ground afoot on West End Avenue. "Well, I must have seen [Noah] on the 4th or 5th," he said.

I was walking to midtown on some kind of an errand. . . . It must have been in connection with my [engineering] consulting. . . . I bet you I had a report under my arm that I was going to get Xerox'd to mail off to a client, but whatever. I stopped by Pro Musica. I knew that [Noah] was preparing and picking the music for a big concert of Machaut. . . . Noah saw me and sort of grabbed me, as Noah would . . . 'Ya gotta hear this song I just discovered for Liz [Humes] to sing in the Machaut concert, it's just right for her, it's so great.' So he sat down [at the piano] and started banging away and singing, and I was a little impatient. I'm afraid that it didn't register. Under other circumstances I might have been more receptive, more sensitive to what he was trying to convey, but then I dashed off . . .[14]

He was always sorry that he had been in such a hurry.

Noah had the evening free on Friday, January 7, and he and Toni went out to dinner and a movie with Claire and Barry Brook. The movie was *Darling*, the funny, cynical British hit film that won Julie Christie an Academy Award for her portrayal of a model who sleeps

[14]Arthur M. Squires, December 5, 1997.

her way to the top of the London fashion world, marries into Italian nobility, and becomes a *principessa*. The film delighted all four moviegoers. "Afterward," Claire Brook recalled,

> we went to our separate apartments and called each other up. I forget who was talking to whom, but we were all on the phone together. And afterward I said to Barry, 'Did you hear the way Noah was breathing?' It was stentorian, he was laboring.[15]

But then, as Russell Oberlin said, "Noah would huff and puff cutting meatloaf. Of course, some of that was just, 'Oh look, this is going to be so delicious.'"[16]

The Concert Ensemble was to appear in Brooklyn the evening of January 8. With the strike still on, Noah had booked two rental sedans from his favorite agency, Avis ("We Try Harder") for the trip from Manhattan. LaNoue would drive one car, Noah the other. Since he had the use of a car all day, Noah said, why not make the most of it? He and Toni could drive downtown to Greenwich Village and eat a civilized Saturday lunch at one of their favorite restaurants, Sea Fare. As Toni later told friends and family, they had arrived at the restaurant, ordered lunch, and were eating when Noah began moving his left arm restlessly. "I must have hurt it conducting, it's really killing me, I need to exercise it." If he wanted to swing his arm around, Toni told him, he should "do it in the men's room" and not disturb the other diners. Noah left the table and stepped into the men's room. When he failed to emerge after fifteen or twenty minutes, Toni grew worried and asked the waiter to check. The waiter found Noah half-conscious on the floor. He had suffered a heart attack.

Toni called Noah's doctor, Paul Essermann, an ambulance was summoned, and Noah was taken to University Hospital and admitted to the Coronary Care Unit. While Toni waited anxiously, Noah was given the first of a series of tests to determine the nature of the attack and the degree of damage to the heart. While this was happening, Toni, practical and controlled on the surface, began making the necessary phone calls. She called Earnest Murphy at his home on East 94th Street, told him the news, and asked him to come by the hospital to pick up the keys to the rental car, still parked in the Village. She then called home. Jane was there with the maid, but Anne was at the movies with a friend. The idea had been that

[15]Claire Brook, February 9, 1995.
[16]Russell Oberlin, January 28, 1997.

at the end of the film Anne would call the apartment and Noah, with the rental car at his disposal, would pick up the two girls and drive them home. These arrangements, obviously, would have to be changed. Toni, or perhaps Earnie Murphy, called LaNoue. The Brooklyn concert would have to go on as scheduled, and LaNoue would direct.

Earnie arrived at the hospital to collect the car keys. "I saw Noah," he said, "he was conscious, he could talk."[17] Earnie stayed only a moment, then left to fetch the car.

Anne remembers that when she and her friend made their way to the street after the movie, it was cold and rainy.

> I did call home, and somebody, I don't remember who, told me to come home right away: 'Take a cab.' I said, 'I don't have the money for a cab.' The person at home said, 'Take a cab and somebody will meet you downstairs with the money." I knew something was wrong but I didn't know what. I was scared.[18]

The hours dragged by at the hospital, but by nightfall the first battery of tests had been given and Noah was resting comfortably. The Concert Ensemble had made it to Brooklyn. Judith Davidoff remembers the evening well.

> Sam Levinson [the comedian], for some reason the m.c., made a tasteless remark about Noah, who was in the hospital . . . We went to a party afterward. Toni called the host to give him an update. She said Noah was much better and she had been told to go home and rest. Everybody was very relieved and we relaxed and enjoyed the party.[19]

Toni arrived at home to find Anne waiting up for her. Toni was upset, of course, but very much in command of herself.

> She said that one good thing that could come of all this was that Dad would have to stop travelling so much and spend more time at home in New York.[20]

Mother and daughter talked for quite a while and went off to bed somewhat easier in mind. Then, in the small hours—around four in the morning, according to Arthur Squires, but probably somewhat earlier—came the shattering phone call. Undetected and perhaps not detectable at the time, an aneurism had formed in Noah's aorta.

---

[17]Earnest Murphy, March 10, 1999.

[18]Anne Greenberg Donovan, June 11, 1997.

[19]Judith Davidoff, February 13, 1999.

[20]Anne Greenberg Donovan, June 11, 1997.

A tiny tear in the inner wall of this critical artery had allowed blood to leak into the void between the inner and outer walls. With each beat of Noah's heart, more blood pushed into the void. A bulge formed. It grew and grew until it suddenly cut off the flow of blood to body and brain. Death was virtually instantaneous. As Arthur later told the story, "[Noah] was in intensive care, the nurse heard a gasp and the vital signs had stopped."[21] Noah was just three months shy of his 47th birthday.

Dry-eyed, Toni began to let the world know. "Toni called me about five in the morning in Shrub Oak," said Noah's cousin Rema. "I just remember wondering what I could do. I think I just paced around for two hours." On Rema's mind was the terrible responsibility of telling Noah's mother, in frail health for years because of her own heart, that her only child had died.

> I called her doctor. He said, 'Go into her medicine chest and get her nitroglycerine and shove it under her tongue and tell her.' So I did that.

Lillie Greenberg turned to stone.

> No emotion, just shock and stone. And she went to her closet. I asked her, 'What are you doing?' And she said, 'I'm getting my clothes for the funeral tomorrow.' I said, 'Don't do that, come with me, let's be together.'

Rema succeeded in persuading Noah's parents to walk with her to her house. But a worse horror lay ahead.

> I started calling all the relatives and they gathered there. And probably about two o'clock in the afternoon [Lillie] seemed to be impatient. And I said, 'Where are you going?' 'I'm going to get my clothes.' Well, this time her husband walked with her. And they walked down—we have a flagstone path. She walked down, and she dropped dead. With her two sisters in the house.[22]

The day of a death is a hundred hours long. At some point on the Sunday of Noah's death, Claire Brook came to see Toni.

> She was standing by the window looking out. And she said, 'Look what he did to me.' He had no will. Not a penny of insurance. She had two small children. At 46, who thinks of dying?[23]

Toni's bitterness and anger were understandable: they are stock reactions to an unforeseen premature death. They were shared, too,

---

[21]Arthur M. Squires, December 5, 1997.
[22]Rema Sessler, March 1, 1997.
[23]Claire Brook, February 9, 1995.

by Anne and Jane. "Absolutely," Jane confirmed. "It was, 'How *dare* this man die on us like this?'"[24] More pathetic was Anne's question to her mother on the day of Noah's funeral: "Can I stop playing the cello now?"[25]

Noah may have repeated to Toni what he had said a few weeks earlier to Harvey Sessler, that when he died he wanted an Orthodox Jewish funeral, a pine box and, above all, no meaningless eulogy. Equally, Toni herself may have decided on these as the appropriate last rites. She and Noah were thoroughly secularized Jews, agnostic if not atheistic. But Toni loved her family, and her family was rigorously Orthodox. Its members, well-to-do as they were, would have frowned on anything other than an austere Orthodox funeral for a son-in-law, and burial as prescribed within 24 hours of death.

Accordingly, and to the dismay of many of those who filed into Riverside Chapel at 11:45 on the morning of January 10, there was no music. None. Nor were there comforting words spoken by any of the dozens of loving and articulate friends who could have offered comfort. Instead, there was a brief service in Hebrew followed by the *Kaddish*. That was all. For some, it was a bleak occasion. But a stunned and grieving Joel Newman carried away with him an unforgettable image of what it is to mourn.

> On that awful day at Riverside Funeral Parlor I slid into a seat and a few moments later this great burly form comes and sits right in front of me, with all the creases in his face. Auden. And he never stopped crying.[26]

[24]Jane Greenberg, April 29, 1997.
[25]Anne Greenberg Donovan, February 19, 1997.
[26]Joel Newman, April 16, 1997, March 2, 1999.

CHAPTER THIRTY-SEVEN

$\mathcal{A}$FTERMATH

(1966-1974)

$\mathcal{A}$ccording to her daughter Jane, Toni became "deeply depressed and spent weeks in bed" after Noah's funeral, seeing few people and nursing her shock and anger. A child's sense of time is vague, and Toni may well have taken to her bed for some days or even a week. About her anger, there is no shred of doubt. Said Jane, "My mother would tell me what a lousy father my Dad had been, meaning that he was always away and when he was home he was always working."[1] But ten days after the funeral, Toni was taking an active part in Pro Musica affairs, in particular in the search for Noah's successor. With Paul Maynard as her lieutenant, she was also beginning to plan the event into which she would pour her energy for months to come, a memorial concert for Noah. To make sure that the concert was a perfect occasion, she decided not to hold it in the spring, when schedules would be crowded and other commitments would interfere, but to delay it until fall.

Virtually every singer and instrumentalist ever connected with Pro Musica took part in the concert, held on October 16. Paul Maynard conducted. Bernie Krainis came back to play, and so did Paul Ehrlich and Joe Iadone. Russell, Charles, and Betty sang, and Arthur Squires, Jean Hakes, and Bethany with them. A highlight was the Heinrich Isaac *Quis dabet capiti meo aquam* sung by the male voices. This, subtitled *Lament on the Death of Lorenzo de Medici*, was the work Pro Musica had sung the year before in Washington in memory of John F. Kennedy. Irving Lowens spoke briefly.

> Noah was a wonderful person, very real, very warm, very complicated, and those who knew him loved him. He was both rough

---

[1]Jane Greenberg, March 3, 1997.

and gentle, both selfish and selfless. He had small patience with fakes and fourflushers; he had endless patience with those who were genuine and humble. He was no esthete, but a man of graces, and strength, and wit, and even though his world was music, he was widely concerned about the non-musical troubles of the world and with attempts to make the world a better place . . ."

Strangely, given the many gay men and women who loved Noah and whom Noah loved, Lowens also felt the need to remark in his first draft that Noah "was anything but a pansy." And even after dropping that, he said of Noah in the talk itself that he was "thoroughly masculine."[2]

After the memorial concert, Toni at 40 began, slowly and painfully, to pick up the pieces of her life. At first, money was a problem. A proud person, Toni sought no help from her prosperous family: to have done so would have been to admit failure. She stayed on as board member and treasurer (later president) of Pro Musica, but also held a number of paid jobs.

Toni's life changed when her uncle, Jacob Perlow, died in the 1980s. As well as being her "Uncle Jack's" heir, she was an executor of his large estate and the person charged with overseeing his many philanthropic bequests. She became known as a shrewd but generous donor, and her interest in Jewish affairs led to memberships on the boards of the Hebrew University and YIVO. After a brief and unhappy stay on the Upper East Side of New York in the mid-1970s, Toni moved to the White House at 262 Central Park West. She lived there for the rest of her life.

For Anne and Jane Greenberg, "It was very bad for three or four years after my father died." Anne rebelled against Toni's tart-tongued parental discipline and rigid ideas of proper behavior. The Dalton School Anne found both "good and bad. I was always Noah Greenberg's daughter, and that wasn't good." What she meant, she explained, was that Dalton made much of her when her father was alive—Dalton always does welcome the children of New York celebrities—but turned chillier after Noah died.[3] What Dalton failed to do for Anne was instill in her any desire to go to college. Soon after her graduation in 1973, Anne left New York (and her mother's watchful eye) and went to live in London. She has lived there—with frequent return visits to this country —ever since.

---

[2]Irving Lowens, typescript draft of address in memory of Noah Greenberg, delivered at Hunter College on October 16, 1966. NYPM Archives, Box 7, folder 12.
[3]Anne Greenberg Donovan, February 19, 1997.

Having abandoned the cello, Anne never took up another musical instrument. But she loves music, and she is pleased that her two sons (she was married in 1975 to Londoner Ian Donovan) are "into" it professionally, one as a drummer, one as a guitarist.

Jane Greenberg stayed at Dalton through 1971. Because she was unhappy in the city, Toni agreed to consider a boarding school, and among the schools on her list was the Buxton School in Noah's old stamping-ground of Williamstown, Massachusetts. Jane fell in love with Buxton—she is now a trustee—and after Buxton with Skidmore College in Saratoga Springs, New York. Since graduating from Skidmore, she has lived and raised her children in Saratoga Springs. She divorced her husband, George Ernst, in 1998, abd narrued Paul Cameron in June 2000.. Neither Jane nor her two sons are musicians.

The Greenberg daughters had long been reconciled with their mother when Toni learned, in 1988, that she was afflicted with cancer. She immediately took steps to control the remainder of her life, encouraging Anne and Jane to buy homes and making certain that her own affairs were in order. One of the details that especially concerned her in the weeks before her death led her to call Claire Brook with a request. "At my funeral, I would like Barry to speak. And I'd like him to talk about Noah." Anne and Jane were with her in New York at the time of her death, on December 2, 1990. They saw to it that, as she wished, she was buried near her mother Pauline and her adored father Max in the Orthodox section of Beth David Cemetery in Brooklyn, the same cemetery in which Noah had been buried 24 years before.

Barry Brook did speak at the service, and afterward Anne and Jane came up to him to thank him for "putting their father to rest."

Within a year of Lillie Greenberg's death, Noah's father Harry remarried a woman "who played cards, who crocheted, who did all the things [Lillie] would never have dreamed of doing."[4] Harry Greenberg died in 1978.

*   *   *

In his obituary for Noah, the *Herald-Tribune*'s Eric Salzman took pains to note that "[t]he New York Pro Musica is expected to continue its activities." In fact, Pro Musica outlived Noah by eight years. For several of those years, it continued to operate successfully and perform with distinction. John Reeves White, a fine keyboard player from Indiana University, led the organization through March 1970.

[4]Rema Sessler, March 1, 1997.

After White's departure, Paul Maynard returned as interim director and was succeeded in May 1972 by George Houle, who had started the early music program at Stanford University. All three men were dedicated musicians, but the climate in which they had to operate was changing. Other groups were vigorously contesting Pro Musica's virtual monopoly over the early music repertoire. The sound of early instruments was no longer novel. Pro Musica itself gradually lost many of its seasoned members, and replacements of equal talent were not easy to find.

During 1973, it became clear that Pro Musica had run out of steam. It had also run out of money. The bulk of the Ford grant had been received and spent. By the end of the year, George Houle had learned that being a jack-of-all-trades practical musician was very different than being a professor of music in a university setting. Houle, in anticipation of the International Petrarch Convocation to be held in New York in May 1974, had prepared a program of madrigal settings of Petrarch's verse. On January 9, 1974, the eighth anniversary of Noah Greenberg's death, Dick French released a statement that the Petrarch concert would be Pro Musica's last public appearance.

On March 6, 1974, the State University of New York at Purchase acquired Pro Musica's music library for its appraisal price of $45,000, payable in three installments.[5]

Pro Musica had already sold off its Flentropp chamber organ and its Rutkowsky & Robinette harpsichord to an organist-choirmaster in Minnesota and its Renaissance organ and sackbuts (Renaissance trombones) to SUNY Purchase. On May 13, 1974, three days before Pro Musica's farewell appearance at a private concert at the Morgan Library, Toni, on behalf of Pro Musica, sold the remainder of the instrument collection to N.Y.U. The price for the 70 instruments was $39,000.[6]

One more matter remained open, the disposition of the stage sets and costumes for *Daniel*, *Herod*, and the two dramas produced after Noah's death, *The Resurrection Play of Tours* and an early opera *La Dafne*. In October 1974, Toni sent the costumes to the Costume Collection of the Theatre Development Fund. Pro Musica would still own the costumes, but they could be rented by the Collection at below-market rates to non-profit theatrical organizations.[7] That left

[5]Madeleine Cosman-Toni Greenberg, letter, March 8, 1974. NYPM Archives, Box 22, folder 5.
[6]NYPM Archives, Box 22, folder 3.
[7]NYPM Archives, Box 22, folder 2.

the sets. In April 1975 a rescuer appeared. James Parks Morton, the culture-loving Dean of the Cathedral Church of St. John the Divine, accepted the sets on behalf of the Cathedral.

*   *   *

The influence of Noah Greenberg on musical repertoire has been pervasive and profound. In the summer of 1964, Noah wrote to a high school student:

> I do not know whether you are preparing yourself for a musical career, but if you are, I urge you to study the great works of the medieval and Renaissance times. I assure you that my explorations are only a beginning in a much unexplored field.[8]

In the last few years of Noah's life, rival early-music performing groups were already springing up. After his death, in Earnest Murphy's wry phrase, "Wherever we went, little Pro Musicas sprouted on every campus."[9] There are scores of little Pro Musica *collegia* today, tooting, strumming, and singing with gusto the music of the Middle Ages, the Renaissance, and the Baroque. Noah would have reveled in the freedom with which today's early musicians root around in the vast pre-classical repertoire. It is true, as Michael Steinberg wrote, that

> Noah . . . never became so infatuated with what he was doing as to believe that anything at all was worth reviving as long as it was old enough and neglected enough. Pro Musica's repertory was huge, not only because Noah was endlessly curious, but because he hated the way the 'standard repertory' concept had paralyzed program-making in 18th- and 19th-century music, and he was determined not to let Josquin's 'Missa pange lingua' turn into the Renaissance counterpart of the Brahms First. . . .[10]

Nevertheless, Noah would have savored such examples of music he never lived to hear as David Munrow's performances of Machaut, Borlet, Binchois, and Dufay and William Christie's brilliant readings of French Baroque opera. They and many others have turned over new pages of a book that Noah was the first to open.

---

[8]Noah Greenberg-Michael Zimmerman, letter, July 21, 1964. NYPM Archives, Box 39, folder i. Zimmerman was president of the Triad Music Club of Highland Park (Illinois) High School. He had come backstage after a Pro Musica performance at Ravinia to make Noah an honorary member of the club.

[9]Earnest Murphy, March 10, 1999.

[10]Michael Steinberg, "Of Noah Greenberg," undated clipping from *The Boston Post*. NYPM Archives, Box 46, folder i.

Noah was also the first to bring the bracing timbres of krummhorn and shawm, regal and bell carillon to modern audiences. He would have applauded the refinements that time and research have contributed to instrument-building and performance. In the many university programs of instruction in early instruments, he would have seen the fulfillment of his idea of the Wind Band. And who can deny that, beginning with Russell Oberlin, Noah's never-ending search for and employment of countertenors set a trend and brought the male alto voice into the musical mainstream?

Controversy over the instrumentation of early music still smoulders and occasionally bursts into flame. It must be underscored that Noah Greenberg was leery of fanciful instrumentation. He spoke disparagingly of Thomas Binkley's heavily Arabized arrangements of French and Spanish medieval works. A report of an "over-orchestrated" performance of *Daniel* directed by René Clemencic in Vienna disturbed him. The jazzy rhythms and hotsy-totsy percussion of some current renderings of medieval dances—one advocate of this style called it "the Big Band sound of the middle ages!"—like the flashier contemporary manifestations of Gregorian chant, might have made Noah laugh. But he never would have tolerated them in his own work, and neither do today's serious performers of early music.

Sadly but inescapably, a third of a century after Noah's death, memories of his and Pro Musica actual performances have faded. Of Pro Musica's approach, Alan Rich could write:

> Noah, his singers, and his instrumentalists stormed into the archives with flags flying. The music they began to play and record was not violated or trashed or jazzed up for modern ears; it was simply performed with awareness that it, too, had once been part of a vital, ongoing culture.[11]

But few people really remember what it was like to be present at the "Y" or The Cloisters, at Ravinia or Jordan Hall. So today's musicians, concertgoers, and critics have to take Pro Musica's marvelous performance tradition on trust.

If the many Pro Musica recordings were reissued, they would demonstrate—amply and conclusively—how good Pro Musica's artists were. The records would bring home what conservatory graduates with strong techniques and years of experience in the

[11]Alan Rich, "Noah's Work Has Been Done," *New York Magazine*, Vol.7, No. 5; February 4, 1974, p. 62.

hurly-burly world of practical music can make of the Medieval, Renaissance, and Baroque repertoire. They would also prove, again
beyond cavil, the central truth of Noah Greenberg's "overriding
philosophy, that vitality and expressiveness did not just enter the
art of music in modern times."[12]

Noah, who lived his many lives so boldly and died so soon, scoffed
at the idea of a hereafter in which good deeds were rewarded and
bad deeds punished. The "here and now" was what mattered.

If making music was a good deed, fine. If not, also fine. Either
way, Noah had wanted nothing more than to spend his time on earth
making music.

---

[12]*Ibid.*

$\mathcal{A}$CKNOWLEDGMENTS

$\mathcal{I}$n the introduction, I wrote of the need to explore the several worlds of which Noah Greenberg was citizen. Many people have helped me do the exploring. Richard French, Anne Greenberg Donovan, and her sister, Jane Greenberg Cameron, are first among them. Their enormous contributions were noted in detail in the introduction. It is a pleasure to thank them again here.

Noah's cousins Rema Sessler and Michael Davidson were also of inestimable help. I am grateful to both for information and anecdote about Greenberg and Davidson family history, politics, and culture. Also large is the debt I owe to Edith Schor, Noah's first wife. Edith is no worshipper of Noah Greenberg, who caused her much unhappiness. But she willingly and without rancor chronicled their twelve years together. Edith has also permitted me to choose from a large group of photographs.

Noah's comrades from his Trotskyist years have led me patiently and with kindness through their personal histories as well as through the tangles of left-wing ideological debate. Jane Greenberg Cameron gave me the name of the first member of this group I met, Jesse Simons. Jesse has proved to be a shrewd guide to events throughout most of Noah's adult life. In addition, Jesse has permitted me to make use of his unpublished essay, "Remembering Noah Greenberg."

Through Jesse, I met Rickie Flanders. I am very grateful for Rickie's vivid descriptions of life in the shipyards of San Pedro. Equally valuable have been her lucid expositions of the postwar travails of the American left, of its loss of faith, and of its drift away from socialism toward social democracy and neoconservatism.

I thank Lucy Dames very much indeed for her recollections of Noah's musical mentor Harold Brown, and also for the opportunity to read through Brown's Four Little Preludes for piano and view several of his wartime letters to Noah. Lucy also put me in touch with her first husband, Edward Riesenfeld, a singer in his younger days, who shared Noah's interest in English vocal music.

The late Albert Glotzer, a veteran socialist functionary, spoke with me at length about Max Shachtman and his associates, Martin Abern and James P. Cannon, in the American Trotskyist movement. Sadly, Al Glotzer died as this book was nearing completion. I wish he could have lived to read it. Both Rickie Flanders and Jesse Simons directed me to Phyllis and Julius Jacobson, Herman Benson, and the late Carl Rachlin.

Clara Meyerson Hancox's memories made Noah the Bronx teenager come alive. She introduced me to Rubin Baratz, whose own memories added to the portrait. Israel Kugler was another rich source of Workers Party lore. His first cousin, Israel Horowitz has been a major source of information and anecdote about Pro Musica on disk.

From the beginning, several of the first-generation members of Pro Musica have gone far out of their way to lend help and support. No one who knows Russell Oberlin will be surprised that this sage and scrupulous artist somehow managed to convey an enormous amount of information about Noah, Pro Musica, music, his colleagues, and himself without uttering a single unfavorable word about anyone.

Russell urged me to contact Bernard Krainis. Brilliant recorder-player, cofounder with Noah of Pro Musica, Bernard was quick to share his flavorful recollections and and his indispensible knowledge of the evolving early music scene. His death in August 2000 spread grief among many. I take comfort in the thought that he had read with approval those pages of this book in which he appears.Bernard also passed me on to another key member of the early Pro Musica, Betty Wilson Long. Arthur Squires, for many years president of Pro Musica, was as informative on Noah's musicianship and on the art of singing as on the tiny organization's often shaky finances.

Other Pro Musica singers who were similarly forthcoming and generous were Ruth Daigon, Bethany Beardslee, Jean Hakes, and Sheila Schonbrun. Gordon Myers not only regaled me with tales of his performances and Noah's behavior, he allowed me to quote freely from his riotous autobiography I Sing -- Therefore I Am. Robert White explained in detail what it was like to sing for Noah as successor to

Russell Oberlin. Earnest Murphy became not only a Pro Musica singer but a mainstay of the Greenberg family after Noah's death.

The cellist and composer Seymour Barab was Noah's friend. For the sake of friendship, he became one of Pro Musica's first instrumentalists. I am also grateful to Seymour for information about Noah's first ventures into recording. Sonya Monosoff added her own description of being transformed—temporarily—from outstanding violinist to reluctant performer on the treble viol.

Herman Chessid contributed stories of playing the harpsichord in Pro Musica recording sessions. Another distinguished harpsichordist, Albert Fuller, spoke to me of the power of *The Play of Daniel.*

LaNoue Davenport followed Bernard Krainis as Pro Musica's player of recorders, and rapidly took on much broader responsibilities, in time becoming Pro Musica's associate director. LaNoue's mellow restrospective heightened my understanding of how dearly this little band of musicians loved their work, their director and, despite the inevitable tensions, one another. He is another who did not live to judge the end result of his help.

Morris Newman's rollicking account of the formation of Pro Musica's Wind Ensemble was a delight to hear and is an important piece of Pro Musica history. I am also greatly indebted to Judith Davidoff for her accounts of happenings, musical and non-musical, during the last years of Noah's life.

The piano virtuoso Eugene Istomin began by offering me his reminiscences of Noah, went on to explain Harold Brown's importance in Noah's and his own musical development, and ended by giving me, best of all, his friendship. Nancy Brown, Harold Brown's second wife and widow, spoke with me about her late husband's temperament and confidence in his musicianship. She also very kindly granted permission to print excerpts from Harold's correspondence with Noah.

Joel Newman became my expert on a key aspect of Noah's musicianship, his ingenuity at devising Pro Musica's programs. He has also lent his expertise on many other Pro Musica matters, from its instrument collection to Noah's recruitment strategies.

Father Rembert G. Weakland, O.S.B., made the transcription that was the basis of Pro Musica's *The Play of Daniel.* The Most Reverend Rembert G. Weakland, O.S.B., Archbishop of Milwaukee, spoke with me at length about *Daniel* and granted permission to make use of his correspondence with Noah for this book. The youthful

Benedictine monk and the archbishop are the same remarkable music-loving man, and I, like so many others in all departments of life, am deeply grateful to him.

Convention decrees that an author express special gratitude to his editor. Claire Brook's enthusiasm, encyclopedic knowledge of the musical scene, and editorial finesse have been a steady source of aid and comfort in a world mostly devoid of real editors. But more needs saying as well. Claire and her late husband, the musicologist Barry S. Brook, were close friends of Toni and Noah Greenberg. Claire has thus been source as well as editor. But she has only offered, never imposed, her views and insights on her author. Barry Brook's kindness to others in his field was (and is) legendary. His kindness to me during the sadly short time we were friends, I shall never forget.

*   *   *

It is both obligation and pleasure to thank as well: Elizabeth Aaron (of the Mannes College of Music); Avel Austin; Margaret Rabi and Dr. C. Christian Beels; Daniel Bell; Elliott Carter; Edward Cramer; Stanley Engelstein; Peter Flanders; William W. Frayer, M.D.; Julius Goldstein; Diane Hubbard; Jeanie M. James (Archivist, The Metropolitan Museum of Art); Irving Kristol; Robert Levenstein; Marian Daigon Levine; Patricia Livingston; Hildy Limondjian; Robert Long; Suzanne Lubell; Joseph Mazur; Carl S. Miller; Robert Montesi; Barbara Mueser; the late Saul Novack; Joel Meltz Ockenheim; Shirley Perle; I. Mike Pincus; Sig Rosen; Carl Schachter; Blanche Saia; Jeanne Wacker; Ronald A. Wilford; Birgitta Lieberson-Wolfe.

It goes without saying—or should—that while these people have contributed time, effort, their memories and more, in no way are they responsible for the mistakes of fact or errors in judgment of the author. These shortcomings are mine alone.

*   *   *

Something more than mere thanks is owed to a number of libraries and institutions for help beyond the call. Foremost among them is the Rare Books and Manuscripts section, Music Division, The New York Public Library for the Performing Arts at Lincoln Center. Its current head, John Shepard, succeeded Suzanne Sommer Thiemann when Ms. Thiemann became chief of the Music Division in place of Jean Bowman. All three were of inestimable help in guiding me to and through the 106 boxes of Pro Musica archives and in suggesting other avenues of research. Never have John Shepard and his colleagues missed a beat, even during the months when the library was uprooted from its Lincoln Center home and set down in temporary quarters on West Forty-third Street. Special thanks go also to Suki Thiemann for telling me of the days when she, a graduate student in musicology, held a day job as Noah Greenberg's secretary at the Pro Musica offices.

The Tamiment Institute/Ben Josephson Library at the Bobst Library, New York University. For access to the American Committee for Cultural Freedom archives at Tamiment, I am grateful to Daniel Bell, their custodian. Dr. Debra E. Bernhardt, Head of Collections of the Robert F. Wagner Labor Archives, dug deep into the archives to find a copy of Noah Greenberg's LP record of I.L.G.W.U. labor songs and made available a cassette tape of this rarity.

The Manuscripts and Archives Division of the Sterling Memorial Library, Yale University. My thanks to Christine Weideman for help in seeking material in the Dwight Macdonald Papers.

The Music Division of the Library of Congress, where Robin Rausch and director Wayne Shirley searched (in vain) for letters and performance information on the original production of *The Play of Daniel*, supposedly at the Library.

The Dance Collection, New York Public Library for the Performing Arts at Lincoln Center, and to Karen Nickerson, archivist in charge of organizing the Lincoln Kirstein Papers.

The YM-YWHA of New York, the "92nd Street Y," and Stephen Siegel, Librarian/Archivist, for a small marvel of research in compiling a detailed list of Pro Musica "Y" performances, programs, audience counts, and box-office figures and for documenting Dr. William Kolodney's remarkable career.

The Folger Shakespeare Library, Washington, D.C., and to Richard Kuhta, Librarian.

The San Pedro (California) Historical Society, and Arthur A. Almeida, President and Anne Hansford, Archivist, for supplying wonderful maps, photographs, and detailed descriptions of San Pedro's labor history and World War II shipbuilding.

Special Collections, Teachers College Library, Columbia University, and David Mint, Librarian, and Betty Winnick, Associate.The Berkshire Athenaeum, Pittsfield, Massachusetts, and Madeline Kelly, Reference Librarian. James Monroe High School, Bronx, New York, and Edward Ost, Librarian, and Tom Porton, Alumni/ae Coordinator and Senior Advisor. The Office of Alumni Affairs and Development, Columbia College, and Ms. Joan Rose.

* * *

BIBLIOGRAPHY

BOOKS

Ball, George W. *The Past Has Another Pattern: Memoirs.* New York. W. W. Norton & Company. 1982.

Barrett, William *The Truants: Adventures Among the Intellectuals.* Garden City NY. Anchor Press/Doubleday. 1982.

Bell, Daniel *The End of Ideology.* Glencoe, IL. Free Press. 1960.

Beevor, Antony and Cooper, Artemis *Paris After the Liberation: 1944-1949.* New York. Doubleday [division of Bantam Doubleday Dell Publishing Group, Inc.] 1994.

Bloom, Alexander *Prodigal Sons: The New York Intellectuals & Their World.* New York. Oxford University Press. 1986.

Branch, Taylor *Pillar of Fire: America in the King Years 1963-65.* New York. Simon & Schuster. 1998.

Broyard, Anatole *Kafka Was the Rage.* New York. Carol Southern Books [an imprint of Crown Publishers]. 1993.

Burns, Joan Simpson *The Awkward Embrace: The Creative Artist and the Institution in America.* New York. Alfred A. Knopf. 1975.

Carse, Robert *There Go the Ships.* New York. William Morrow and Company. 1942.

_____ *Lifeline: The Ships and Men of Our Merchant Marine at War.* New York. William Morrow and Company. 1943.

_____ *A Cold Corner of Hell: the Story of the Murmansk Convoys.* Garden City, N.Y. Doubleday. 1969.

Clarke, Gerald *Capote: A Biography.* New York. Simon and Schuster. 1988

Cohen, Joel, and Snitzer, Herb *Reprise: the Extraordinary Revival of Early Music.* Boston. Little, Brown. 1985.

Coleman, Peter *The Liberal Conspiracy.* New York. The Free Press, a Division of Macmillan Inc. 1989.

Copland [Aaron]/Perlis [Vivien] *Copland: 1900 Through 1942.* New York. St. Martin's/Marek. 1989.

_____ *Copland Since 1943.* New York.St. Martin's Press. 1989.

Davies, Norman *Heart of Europe: A Short History of Poland.* Oxford U.K. Oxford University Press. 1984.

Douglas, John Scott, and Salz, Albert *He's in the Merchant Marine Now.* New York. R. M. McBride & Company. 1943.

Engel, Lehman [ed.] *Three Centuries of Choral Music: Renaissance to Baroque.* New York. H. Flammer.1939-68.

Fiedler, Leslie, *An End to Innocence.* Boston. Beacon Press. 1955.

Howe, Irving, *A Margin of Hope: An Intellectual Autobiography.* San Diego. Harcourt Brace Jovanovich. 1982.

Hubbard, Frank, *Three Centuries of Harpsichord Building.* Cambridge. Harvard University Press. 1965.

Kierstein, Lincoln *Mosaic: Memoirs.* New York. Farrar, Straus & Giroux. 1994.

Kirk, H. L. *Pablo Casals, A Biography.* New York. Holt, Rinehart and Winston. 1974.

Kraus, Henry *In The City Was A Garden.* New York. Renaissance Press. 1951.

Macdonald, Dwight *The Ford Foundation: the Men and the Millions.* New York. Reynal. 1956.

Mackenzie, Colin *Sailors of Fortune.* New York. E. P. Dutton & Co., Inc. 1944.

Martin, George *The Damrosch Dynasty: America's First Family of Music.* Boston. Houghton Mifflin Company. 1983.

McCarthy, Mary *Intellectual Memoirs: New York, 1936-1938.* New York. Harcourt Brace Jovanovich. 1992.

Mendelson, Edward [ed.] *The Complete Works of W.H. Auden: Libretti, 1939-1973.* Princeton. Princeton University Press. 1993.

_____[ed.] *As I walked out one evening: songs, ballads, lullabies, limericks and other light verse* by W. H. Auden; selected by Edward Mendelson. London. Faber & Faber. 1995.

Menefee, Selden *Assignment U.S.A.* New York. Reynal & Hitchcock, Inc. 1943.

Merrill, James I. The Seraglio. New York. Alfred A. Knopf. 1957.

_____*A Different Person: A Memoir.* New York. Alfred Knopf. 1993.

Miller, Charles H. *Auden: An American Friendship.* New York. Paragon House. 1983.

Myers, [James] Gordon *I Sing, Therefore, I am.* Mt. Morris, New York. Leyerle Publications. 1998.

Nicholas, Lynn H. *The Rape of Europa: the Fate of Europe's Treasures in the Third Reich and the Second World War.* New York. Vintage Books [a division of Random House]. 1995.

O'Brian, Patrick *Post Captain.* New York. W. W. Norton & Co. 1990.

Phillips, Cabell *The 1940s: Decade of Triumph and Trouble.* [Vol.2 of *The New York Times Chronicle of American Life.*] New York. Macmillan Publishing Co. Inc. 1975.

Plimpton, George *Truman Capote: in Which Various Friends,Enemies, Acquaintances, and Detractors Recall His Turbulent Career.* New York. Nan A. Talese/Doubleday. 1997.

Podhoretz, Norman *Making It.* New York. Random House. 1967.

_____ *Breaking Ranks: A Political Memoi*r. New York. Harper & Row. 1979.

Read, Oliver and Welch, Walter L. *From Tin Foil to Stereo:Evolution of the Phonograph.* Indianapolis, Indiana. Howard W. Sams & Co., Inc. 1976.

Reisenberg, Jr., Felix *Sea War: The Story of the U.S. Merchant Marine in World War II.* New York. Rinehart & Co. 1956.

Rivers, Larry   *What Did I Do?* New York. HarperCollins Publishers. 1992.

Rosenberg, Harold *The Tradition of the New.* New York. Grove Press. 1961.

Roth, Henry *Call It Sleep.* New York. Avon Books. 1964. [c1935].

Sawyer, L. A. and Mitchell, W. H. *The Liberty Ships: The History of the 'Emergency' Type Cargo Ships Constructed in the United States During World War II.* Cambridge MD. Cornell Maritime Press, Inc. 1970.

Sayre, Nora *Previous Convictions.* New Brunswick NJ. Rutgers University Press. 1995.

Simon, Kate *Bronx Primitive: Portraits in a Childhood.* New York. The Viking Press. 1985.

_____ *A Wider World: Portraits in an Adolescence.* New York. Harper & Row. 1986.

Smoldon, William L. *The Music of the Medieval Church.* [Cynthia Bourgeault, ed.] London. Oxford University Press. 1980.

Ultan, Lloyd, and Hermalyn, Gary *The Bronx in the Innocent Years, 1890-1925.* New York. Harper & Row. 1985.

Wald, Alan M. *The New York Intellectuals: The Rise and Decline of the Anti-Stalinist Left from the 1930s to the 1980s.* Chapel Hill NC and London. The North Carolina University Press. 1987.

White, Theodore H. *In Search of History: a Personal Adventure.* New York. Warner Books, Inc. 1979.

Wrezin, Michael *A Rebel in Defense of Tradition: Dwight Macdonald.* New York. Basic Books. 1994.

Zamoyski, Adam T*he Polish Way: a thousand-year history of the Poles and their culture.* London. John Murray. 1987.

ARTICLES

Cyrus, Cynthia J. "'Music': Introduction to Medieval Music," in *On Line Reference Book for Medieval Studies.* 1997. Blair School of Music. Vanderbilt University.

Glotzer, Albert and Marguerite "Max Shachtman — A Political/Biographical Essay," *Bulletin of the Tamiment Institute*/Ben Josephson Library, 50: April 1983.

Jenkins, Nicholas "The Great Impresario," *The New Yorker*, April 13, 1998.

Macdonald, Dwight "The Slave of Hebrew," *The New Yorker*, November 28, 1959.

Rich, Alan "Noah's Work Has Been Done," in *New York Magazine*, January 25, 1974.

Shargel, Bella Round "Leftist Summer Colonies of Northern Westchester County, New York," in *American Jewish History*, IX, summer, 1994.

LIBRARY ARCHIVAL COLLECTIONS

New York Pro Musica, Archives, 1952-1980

> 106 boxes, ca.1,200 folders in eight series [uncatalogued]. Correspondence (holographs, typescript, business files, contracts, programs, press releases, photographs, schedules, and clippings, constituting the office files of the New York Pro Musica during its active years. Special Collections, Music Division, The New York Public Library for the Performing Arts at Lincoln Center.

The Max Shachtman Papers

> Unpublished manuscripts, correspondence, notes, and internal bulletins of Max Shachtman (1904-1972), socialist, Trotskyist and founder of the Workers Party (1940-1950). The Archives of the Tamiment Institute/Ben Josephson Library, New York University Libraries.

American Committee for Cultural Freedom Archives

> 17 boxes. Held at the Tamiment Institute/Ben Josephson Library, New York University Libraries. Access restricted.

Dwight Macdonald Papers

> 1865-1984 (inclusive), 1920-1978 (bulk), 84 linear ft. (198 boxes). Unpublished finding aid in repository. Arranged in eight series: I. Correspondence. II. Research and Writing. III. Teaching and Lectures. IV. Trotskyist Movement. V. Politics Magazine. VI. Miscellany. VII. 1984 July Addition. VIII. 1985 November Addition. Manuscripts & Archives Collection, Sterling Memorial Library, Yale University, New Haven CT.

William Kolodney Dissertation

> "History of the Educational Department of the YM-YWHA: A Report of a Type C Project." New York. Dr. Kolodney's unpublished dissertation for the degree of Ed. D., Advanced School of Education, Teachers College, Columbia University. 1950.

PRIVATE COLLECTIONS OF PAPERS, INTERVIEWS

As of November 2000, the following people have allowed me access to and use of material from their collections of papers, letters, photographs and Greenberg memorabilia: Rubin Baratz; Lucy Dames; Anne Greenberg Donovan; Jane Greenberg Cameron; Clara Hancox; Robert Levenstein; Joel Newman; I. Meyer Pincus; Edith Schor; Jesse Simons, the Most Reverend Rembert G. Weakland, O.S.B. All, and some 60 other individuals, have also been interviewed.

DISCOGRAPHY

$\mathcal{U}$nder Noah Greenberg, the New York Pro Musica made 28 LP recordings. The first seven, all monaural, were issued by Esoteric Records, New York NY, from May 1953 through January 1955. In 1954, Greenberg signed a three-record contract with Columbia Records, New York NY. In 1957, Pro Musica began recording exclusively for Decca (U.S.). Greenberg led Pro Musica in 14 of the 16 Pro Musica Decca LPs released before his death in January 1966. (The fifteenth was a mixture of works directed by Greenberg and those conducted by his successor, John Reeves White. The sixteenth was a Paul Maynard recording of solo keyboard works.) The relationship with Decca continued after Greenberg's death, with eight more recordings made and released, the final release being issued in August 1969.

In 1954 and 1955, single recordings were released by Counterpoint (a successor to Esoteric) and by Period Records. In 1968, Horizon magazine released a Pro Musica LP as a special promotional item. This contains some re-released and some newly-recorded material. Within weeks after Greenberg's death, all seven Esoteric recordings were re-released as a "memorial album" by Everest Records, Los Angeles CA. The release led Pro Musica to sue the company to recover royalties: the suit was settled in 1968.

The final New York Pro Musica recording, made in 1973, the year before it disbanded, was conducted by George Houle.

Only three Pro Musica recordings are currently available, as re-releases in CD format.

Esoteric / Counterpoint Recordings, New York NY

Esoteric ES 515 [LP, mono]
George Frederick Handel: *Music for Ancient Instruments and Soprano Voice*   Rec. 1953

Esoteric ES 516 [LP, mono]
Adriano Banchieri: *Festino - A Renaissance Madrigal Entertainment to be sung on the evening of Fat Thursday before Supper*
                                                   Rel. May 1953

Esoteric ES 519 [LP, mono]
John Blow, *Ode on the Death of Mr. Henry Purcell* / Henry Purcell, Instrumental & Vocal Selections.   Rel. May 1953

Esoteric ES 520 [LP, mono]
Thomas Morley: *Elizabethan Madrigals, Canzonets and Ballets*
                                             Rel. September 1953

Esoteric ES 521 [LP, mono]
English Medieval Christmas Carols   Rel. October 1953

Esoteric ESJ-6 [LP, mono, 25cm]
An Elizabethan songbag for young people
                                             Rel. September 1954

Esoteric ES 535 [LP, mono]
Henry Purcell: *Songs*   Rel. January 1955

Counterpoint CPT 540 [LP, mono]
Children's Songs of Shakespeare's time   Rec. 1953

Everest Records, Los Angeles CA

Everest 6145 / SDBR 3145 [LPx7, mono / stereo: re-release of Esoteric LPs]
Noah Greenberg conducting the New York Pro Musica - *An Anthology of Their Greatest Works*
                                    Rec.: [1952/56], rel. [after 1966]

Period Records, New York NY

Period PL 597 [LP, mono]
Anthology of Renaissance Music
Rec. November 1953; Rel. 1954

Columbia Records / Odyssey Records, New York NY

Columbia ML 5051 [LP, mono]
Evening of Elizabethan Verse and Its Music   Rec. 1954

Columbia ML 5159 [LP, mono]
Vocal Music of Claudio Monteverdi   Rec. 1954

Columbia ML 5204 [LP, mono]
The Music of Salamone Rossi, Hebreo of Mantua   Rec. 1954

Odyssey "Legendary Performances" 32 16 0087 [LP, mono: re-release of ML5159]
Vocal Music of Claudio Monteverdi
Rec. 1954; Rel. 1968 or prior

Decca (US) Recordings / Horizon

Decca "Gold Label Series" DL 9400 [LP, mono/stereo]
Music of the Medieval Court and Countryside
Rec. August 1957; Rel. October 1957

Decca "Gold Label Series" DL 9402 / DL 7 9402 [LP, mono/stereo]
The Play of Daniel
Rec. January, February 1958 ; Rel. August 1958

Decca "Gold Label Series" DL 9404 / DL 7 9404 [LP, mono/stereo]
Sacred Music of Thomas Tallis
Rec. 1958 [?]; Rel. February 1959

Decca "Gold Label Series" DL 9406 / DL 7 9406 [LP, mono/ stereo]
Elizabethan and Jacobean Ayres, Madrigals & Dances
                                        Rec. 1959 [?]; Rel. August 1959

Decca "Gold Label Series" DL 9409 / DL 7 9409 [LP, mono/ stereo]
Spanish Music of the Renaissance   Rec. 1960 [?]; Rel. April 1960

Decca "Gold Label Series" DL 9410 / DL 7 9410 [LP, mono/ stereo]
Josquin Des Préz: Missa *Pange Lingua*, motets and instrumental
pieces   Rec. January, February 1960; Rel. January 1961

Decca "Gold Label Series" DL 9412 / DL 7 9412 [LP, mono/ stereo]
*Music of the Early German Baroque: Heinrich Schütz & Melchior
Franck*   Rec. November 1960; Rel. May 1961

Decca "Gold Label Series" DL 9413 / DL 7 9413 [LP, mono/ stereo]
Heinrich Isaaac: *Music for the Court of Lorenzo the Magnificent/*
Jacob Obrecht: Missa *Fortuna desperata*
                                      Rec. February 1961; Rel. August 1961

Decca "Gold Label Series" DL 9415 / DL 7 9415 [LP, mono/ stereo]
*Instrumental music from the Courts of Queen Elizabeth and King
James*   Rec. March 1961; Rel. Feb. 1962

Decca "Gold Label Series" DL 9416 / DL 7 9416 [LP, mono/ stereo]
Spanish medieval music   Rec. January 1962; Rel. August 1962

Decca "Gold Label Series" DL 9418 / DL 7 9418 [LP, mono/ stereo]
Medieval English Carols and Italian Dances
                                      Rec. April 1962; Rel. October 1962

Decca "Gold Label Series" DL 9419 / DL 7 9419 [LP, mono/ stereo]
Renaissance Festival Music - Flemish Dances and Venetian Music
                                            Rec. May 1962; Rel. January 1963

Decca "Gold Label Series" DL 9420 / DL 7 9420 [LP, mono/ stereo]
Ludwig Senfl: Composer to the Court and Chapel of Emperor Maximilian V   Rec. May 1963; Rel. January 1964

Decca "Gold Label Series" DL 9421 / DL 7 9421 [LP, mono/ stereo]
It was a lover and his lass: Music of Shakespeare's time
                                            Rec. September 1963; Rel. April 1964

Decca "Gold Label Series" DL 9424 / DL 7 9424 [LP, mono/ stereo]
Renaissance Bands   Rec. April 1965; Rel. October 1965

Decca DXA 187 / DXSA 7 187 [LP, mono/stereo]
The Play of Herod   Rec. January 1964; Rel. September 1964

Decca "Gold Label Series" DL 9425 / DL 7 9425 [LP, mono / stereo]
Early Baroque Music of Italy
                                            Rec. May 1965; Released January 1966

Decca LPs recorded and released after Noah Greenberg's death

Decca "Gold Label Series" DL 9428 / DL 7 9428 [LP, mono/ stereo]
Florentine Music   Rec. May, June 1967; Rel. January 1968

Decca "Gold Label Series" DL 7 9431 [LP, stereo]
Ah Sweet Lady: The Romance of Medieval France
                                            Rec. March 1967; Rel. October 1967

Decca "Gold Label Series" DL 7 9434 [LP, stereo]
The Kynge's Musicke
Rec. January, April, May 1968; Rel. September 1968

Decca "Gold Label Series" DL 7 9435 [LP, stereo]
Petrucci: First Printer of Music
Rec. April, May 1968; Rel. February 1969

Decca "Gold Label Series" DL 7 9436 [LP, stereo]
Music of the Spanish Theater in the Golden Age
Rec. January 1969; Rel. August 1969

Decca "Gold Label Series" DL 10040 / DL 7 10040 [LP, mono / stereo]
William Byrd - Keyboard Music
Rec. 1961 {?]; Rel. November 1961

Decca "Gold Label Series" DL 7 9438 [LP, stereo]
Medieval Roots [A selection of re-released works from earlier
Decca LPs, some directed by Noah Greenberg, others by John
Reeves White]   Rel. [?]

Decca DI 7 9174 [LP, stereo]
Side A: "Anne of a Thousand Days," soundtrack from the film;
Side B: "Music of the Tudor Court;" re-released selections from
DL9415, DL9434   Rel. March 1970

Horizon DL 34541 [LP, stereo]
Music for a medieval day
Rec. April 1968 [some works prior]; Rel. June 1968

Musical Heritage Society, New York NY

Musical Heritage Society MHS 1953/4 [LP, mono / stereo]
Marco da Gagliano: *La Dafne*   *Rec. 1973; Rel. 1974 [?]*

Re-releases

Rykodisc TCD1056 [CD]
English Medieval Christmas Carols
Re-release of Esoteric ES 521

MCAD2 10102 [CDx2]
The Play of Daniel - The Play of Herod

Rec.: 1958 / 1964
Re-release of Decca DL 7 9402

Millennium Classics UMD 80 565 [CD]
Praetorius - Susato: *Renaissance Dances*
Re-release of Decca DL 7 9424 and 7 9419
Rel. 1999

I am grateful to Israel Horowitz, former director of A & R for Decca (U.S.) Classical and the supervisor of Pro Musica's Decca recordings, for information about the recording and release dates of items in the Decca series, and for other information about the recordings.

Further discographic details are available at the excellent Internet Pro Musica discography set up and currently maintained by Pierre F. Roberge:

http://www.medieval.org/emfaq/performers/nypm.html

I am also grateful to M. Roberge for permission to draw on his work.

Index

Rossi, Salamone
  recordings of, 244
  The Songs of Solomon, 154
Roth, Henry, *Call It Sleep*, 372
Rothko, Mark, 8
Rottenberg, Marcus, 241
Rovere, Richard, 143
Royaumont, 298
RTF (Radiodiffusion-Telévision-Fran-
  çaise), 298
Rubin Artists Management, 218
Rubin, David W. 260
Ruff, Willie, 6n
Rukeyser, Muriel, 168
Rundquist, George, 96
Russian Revolution, 15
Ryan, Mrs. John Barry, 309
Saia, Blanche, 43-44, 46
Saint Joan (Shaw), 223
Sainte-Chapelle, 291
Salle Gaveau, Paris, 295, 296
Salzman, Eric, 337, 388
Samuel, Harold, 32
San Lorenzo de El Escorial, 327
San Pedro, CA, 60
San Remo (tavern), 8
Sandberg, Carl, 149
Santa Trinità, 297
Saratoga Springs, N.Y., 388
Scarlatti, Domenico, 5
Schachter, Carl, 212
Schang, Chris, Jr. , 261, 269, 302, 342,
  362, 371-372,
Schang, Fred, 261, 269
Schapiro, Meyer, 3, 236, 238, 275, 331
Schevill, Ferdinand, 352n
Schlesinger, Arthur, Jr., 143
Schmidinger, Paul, 215
Schnabel, Artur, 58
Schneider, Alexander (Sasha), 100-104,
  176
Schoenberg, Arnold, 9
Schola Cantorum Basiliensis, 154n
Schonberg, Harold C., 171, 364-375
Schonbrun, Sheila, 305, 308, 312, 325n,
  327n, 346-347 *see also* Jones, Sheila
School of American Ballet, The, 2, 174
Schor, Edith, 44, 46, 48-50, 52,65, 142,
  143
    errand for Haganah (1945), 80
Schubert, Franz, 22
  Ave Maria, 153
Schuller, Gunther, 376
Schuman, Henry, 357

Schütz, Heinrich, 39, 190
  Kleine geistliche Konzerte, 306
  Musicalische Exequien, 134
Schuyler, George, 143
Schwartz, Delmore, 7
Schwarz, Frederick A.O., 318
Schweitzer, Albert, 101
Scott, Rev. Marshall, 96
*Scriptorum de musica medii aevi nova
  series* (Coussemaker), 228
Searle, Dr. Robert, 96
Secrest, Meryle interviews Greenberg,
  365-366
Segal, George, 378
Segovia, Anrzees, 245
Seidman, Fanny, 59
Senfl, Ludwig, 305
Serkin, Rudolf, 101
Sermisy, Claudin de, 109, 211
Sessions, Roger, 9, 344
Sessler, Harvey, 379
Sessler, Rema Davidson, 15, 23, 107,
  130, 278, 379, 384
Seyden, Jeanette and Alfred, 58
Shachtman, Max, 40, 46, 48, 53, 86-87
    and Trotskyism,40
    Communist Party expulsion, 41
    Workers' Party, 48
Shakespeare Festival (1957), 238
Shelter Island, 348, 373, 374
Shrub Oak Park, 18, 278
Sien, Jerold, 240
Silent Night, 153
Silone, Ignazio, 143
Simon, Kate, 22, 32
Simons, Jesse, 10, 27, 42, 45, 533, 55, 57-
  58, 69, 72, 109, 110, 145, 181, 313
    and classical music, 51
    as I.L.G.W.U. officer, 110
    marriage to Rickie Kimmel, 50
Simons, Rickie, *see* Flanders, Rickie
Singer, Isaac Bashevis, 16
Siscoe, Frank (State Department), 319
Skelton, John, *Magnyfycence*, 274, 364,
  365
Skidmore College, 388
Slater, Joseph, 344
Slaying of the Innocents, The 330, 331 *see
  also Play of Herod, The*
Smith, Edward. 345
Smith, Gerald L.K. 68
Smith, Willie "The Lion," 6n
Smoldon, William L., 219n, 228, 231-33,
  236, 237, 251, , 300, 329, 330, 334, 340

Wright, Leverett (CAMI), 319
Wurlitzer, Rembert, 326
Yale Drama School, 235
Yale School of Music, 81, 140
Yerevan Conservatory, 355
Yiddish, 14, 16, 17, 122
YM-YWHA (Young Men's and Young
   Women's Hebrew Association; the
   92nd Street "Y") 8, 149,199, 180, 187
   concerts (1958-1959), 254, 266
   concerts (1962-1963), 311

YM-YWHA
   concerts (1964-1965), 338-339
Yonah Schimmel's knishes, 204
Young Audiences, Inc., 308
Zalsow, Milton, 28, 42, 48
Zefiro torna (Monteverdi) 216, 226
Zemachson, Arnold, 23-24, 25
   compositional style of, 24
Zemachson, Simon, 23
Zorina, Vera (Birgitta Lieberson-
   Wolfe), 175, 176, 211, 245

14